URBAN LEGENDS

In memory of Bill Scott
Poet, Folklorist, and Storyteller (1923–2005)

URBAN LEGENDS

A COLLECTION OF INTERNATIONAL TALL TALES AND TERRORS

EDITED BY
GILLIAN BENNETT AND PAUL SMITH

GREENWOOD PRESS
Westport, Connecticut • London

Library of Congress Cataloging-in-Publication Data

Urban legends : a collection of international tall tales and terrors / edited by Gillian Bennett and Paul Smith.

    p. cm.
    Includes bibliographical references and index.
    ISBN 0–313–33952–X (alk. paper)
    1. Urban folklore.   2. Tall tales.   3. Horror tales.   I. Bennett, Gillian.   II. Smith, Paul, 1947 Mar. 6–
    GR78.U72   2007
    398.2–dc22   2006038685

British Library Cataloguing in Publication Data is available.

Library of Congress Catalog Card Number: 2006038685
ISBN–13: 978–0–313–33952–3
ISBN–10: 0–313–33952–X

First published in 2007

Greenwood Press, 88 Post Road West, Westport, CT 06881
An imprint of Greenwood Publishing Group, Inc.
www.greenwood.com

Printed in the United States of America

The paper used in this book complies with the Permanent Paper Standard issued by the National Information Standards Organization (Z39.48–1984).

10 9 8 7 6 5 4 3 2 1

R0429869954

Copyright Acknowledgments

The authors and the publisher gratefully acknowledge permission for use of the following material:

Excerpts from Paul Homes, "Mystery Child Murders Spread Fear in Kabul." Yahoo! News (December 8, 2001).

Excerpts from "Beatle Spokesman Calls Rumor of McCartney's Death Rubbish." *New York Times* (October 22, 1969). Copyright © 1969 by the New York Times Co. Reprinted with permission.

Excerpts reprinted from the *Journal of Emergency Medicine*, Vol. 4: 411–414, Slay, R. "The Exploding Toilet and Other Emergency Room Folklore." © 1986 Elsevier, Inc.

Excerpts from © *Performance and Practice: Oral Narrative Traditions among Teenagers in Britain and Ireland*, Michael Wilson, 1997. Ashgate Publishing Limited.

Excerpts from Daniel Cohen, *The Headless Roommate and Other Tales of Terror*. New York: M. Evans and Company, 1980.

Excerpts form Bill Ellis, *Aliens, Ghosts, and Cults: Legends We Live*. Jackson: University Press of Mississippi, 2003. Chapter 6 "The Frackville Angel" (Ellis 2003, 107). Reproduce by permission of University Press of Mississippi.

Excerpts from Reimund Kvideland and Henning Sehmsdorf, eds., "Jesus as Hitchhiker," in *Scandinavian Folk Belief and Legend*. Minneapolis University of Minnesota Press, 1998, pp. 385–386.

Excerpts from Alan Dundes, "Bloody Mary in the Mirror: A Ritual Reflection of Pre-Pubescent Anxiety." *Western Folklore 57* (1998): 119–35. Reprinted in Alan Dundes, *Bloody Mary in the Mirror*. Jackson, MS: University Press of Mississippi, 2002, pp. 76–94 (Dundes 2002, 83). Reproduced by permission of University Press of Mississippi.

Excerpts from "Parents Kill Their Own Son, " page 136, From Richard M. Dorson, "Polish Tales from Joe Woods," *Western Folklore* 8 (1949): 131–45.

Excerpts from "Penguin Story Is a Fishy Tale." Megan Tench–*The Boston Globe*. Copyright © 2005 Globe Newspaper Company, Inc.

Excerpts from Bill Scott, *Pelicans and Chihuahuas and Other Urban Legends*. St Lucia: University of Queensland Press, 1996. Courtesy of University of Queensland Press.

Excerpts from Dionizjusz Czubala, "Aids and Aggression: Polish Legends About HIV-Infected People." *FOAFtale News* 23 (September 1991): 1–5 (Czubala 1991, 3).

Excerpts from Bennett Cerf, *Laughing Stock*. New York: Grosset and Dunlap, 1945. Story pp., 131–132.

Excerpts from Alexander Woollcott, "The Man in the Middle." Courtesy of *The New Yorker*/Conde Nast Publications, Inc.

Excerpts from *Gene Perret and Linda Perret, Gene Perret's Funny Business: Speaker's Treasure of Business Humor for All Occasions*. Englewood Cliffs, NJ. Prentice Hall, 1990.

Excerpts from Dionizjusz Czubala, "The 'Black Volga': Child Abduction Urban Legends in Poland and Russia." *FOAFtale News* 21 (February 1991): 1–3 (Czubala, 1991), 1.

Excerpts from Linda Dégh and Andrew Vázsonyi, "The Crack on the Red Goblet or Truth and Modern Legend." *Folklore in the Modern World*. Ed. Richard M. Dorson. *World Anthropology Series*. The Hague and Paris: Mouton, 1978, pp. 253–272.

COPYRIGHT ACKNOWLEDGMENTS

Excerpts from "Baby! What an Earful!" from *The Mirror* [London]. October 19, 1988, pp. 30. Courtesy of Trinity Mirror Group.

Excerpts from Simon Bronner, *Piled Higher and Deeper*. Berkeley Folklore Archives, 1974, 1990. Reprinted with permission of Simon Bronner.

Every reasonable effort has been made to trace the owners of copyright materials in this book, but in some instances this has proven impossible. The author and publisher will be glad to receive information leading to more complete acknowledgments in subsequent printings of the book and in the meantime extend their apologies for any omissions.

CONTENTS

CONTENTS

ACKNOWLEDGMENTS

Our sincere thanks goes to the many people who have helped us gather this compilation together. To our friends and colleagues Sandy Hobbs and Jan Brunvand for help with film and literature references, to Sandy Hobbs again for proofreading, to Michael J. Preston for library research and support, to Brian Chapman for allowing access to his personal archives, to Ervin Beck for allowing as access to field-work recordings, and to Andrew Bennett for reading and checking early drafts. We would also like to thank Jed Baker for cross-checking online material; Amada Power, Karen Patterson, Brent Slade, Chris-Anne Stumpf, and again Jed Baker, for checking material for Appendix Eileen Collins for formatting bibliographies; and Inter-Library Loans staff at Memorial University of Newfoundland for finding material for us.

Last, but not least, as always thanks to our partners, Andrew Bennett and Martha Griffiths, for patience and support.

INTRODUCTION

Welcome to the world of urban legends.
The stories you are about to read are very diverse. They include tales of:

- The teenagers who, after speeding away from Lovers' Lane, found the bloodied hook from a maniac's false hand on the handle of their car door;
- The woman whose house was robbed when she returned to a department store to claim a stolen purse;
- The boy who was castrated in the toilet of a downtown store;
- The car that was sold at a ridiculously low price by a vengeful wife;
- The man who blew himself up when he threw a cigarette butt down the toilet;
- The woman who sprayed herself with glitter mistaking it for feminine deodorant;
- The garden gnome who went on vacation to Disney Land.

You've possibly heard a number of these stories, or something like them, and you may be saying to yourself, "Oh I was told that story, but didn't it happen to someone in New York, or was it Paris?" This is not surprising, for these tales are to be found in most parts of the world and are told in many languages.

Urban legends are told by all types of persons regardless of age, sex, or occupation. They surface all the time in our everyday conversations and are told in much the same way we would tell a joke, or a "good story," or report exciting or disturbing local events. Alongside these informal oral means of communication, e-mail and the Internet have become major ways for people to enjoy the stories as the use of computers has grown over the past ten years, both in the workplace and at home. The main difference, perhaps the only difference, is that now people can tell their stories to dozens, if not hundreds, of people at the same time at the push of a key. So nowadays the process by which a story travels round the world is speeded up.

The list of themes covered by urban legends is almost endless. Although the common tendency is to associate the term with sensational, gory stories, there are almost as many comic urban legends. So stories about murder, violence, revenge, contaminated food and drink, sharp practice, and accidents with technology are balanced by tales of absurd events, embarrassing situations (especially sexual ones), pleasant surprises, ironic turns of fate, and practical jokes.

Though urban legends are regarded as a modern phenomenon, it would be erroneous to think that they have no ancestors in traditional narratives. Many modern tales can be traced back for decades, if not centuries. The story of "The Murdered Son," for example, goes back at least to the beginning of the seventeenth century, and the "Blood Libel Legend" to the Middle Ages. Indeed, many of the stories are modern only in the sense that they have been recently told and are clothed in modern dress. There will always be a relentless updating of older stories through the inclusion of relevant topical ideas, images, and issues. Nevertheless, traditional though they are and bizarre though their content often is, urban legends are not "fairy tales." They are not stories of fabulous beasts, enchanted forests, witches and magicians, ghosts and fairies, set in a fantasy world. These stories are set in our own world, and in places we can recognize or even visit, and they have emerged from events and ideas found in our social world and in our interaction with others.

So, how we can tell whether a tale is, or is not, an urban legend? The answer is that we can't always do this, but clues can be found in the content and in the way the story is told. Here are some guidelines:

Outrageous Content in an Everyday Setting: Urban legends describe extraordinary events—happenings that are startling in some way, bizarre, absurd, frightful, gross, or horrifying. But these extraordinary things are supposed to happen to ordinary people in the here and now and seem to have relevance to the lives of ordinary people. This makes them more than merely "good stories" (though they nearly always *are* good stories); it makes them important and discussable as well as entertaining.

Anonymous Origins: Urban legends do not appear to have authors, although claims of authorship do sometimes occur and, just occasionally, a possible origin is found.

Multiplicity: Multiple examples of any one legend will be circulating at any one time and place, and no two examples of the supposedly same story will be exactly alike (unless they have been forwarded unaltered via e-mail).

Time Frame: Even though they may have been told for several hundred years or have roots in historical fact, urban legends are set in the "here and now" and they always claim to be new.

Structure: Urban legends are often shaped along the lines of detective stories or jokes. The story line does not always give us a view of the action "off stage," or tell us the whole story until the very last minute. Consequently, the final sentences of an urban legend, like a good "whodunnit," often wrap up the story and explain all, or like a joke end with a humorous punch line or an absurd outcome.

The "FOAF" Element: These stories are seldom, if ever, told as first-person experiences; it is not even very common for storytellers to say they had it first-hand from somebody else. Usually they claim that it happened to "this girl" or "this man," or to somebody at least two removes from themselves—"my friend's cousin's girlfriend" or a "friend of a friend" (the "FOAF"). In one sense they are claiming some connection to the characters in the story; in another sense they are putting some distance between themselves and the events. So, though the "FOAF" element authenticates the story by making it personal, it also distances the narrators a little from the events so they are less accountable for the truth of the tale. This distancing may not necessarily be intentional, however, but simply the way the narrator first heard the story.

Truth: It is almost impossible to be absolutely certain whether the events described in an urban legend ever took place, and most attempts to track the origin of a legend have failed.

Belief: If we accept a legend, it is because we trust the source of the information. This applies, of course, to most things we are told by friends or the news media. Legends are no different in this respect. If a story sounds likely, fits our view of the world, reflects the way we think the world works, and comes from a trusted source, it is easy to believe it. For this, and other reasons, some form of statement about belief, either positive or negative, appears to be a common feature of urban legends. Tellers of urban legends may say, "I know it's weird, but it really happened," and hearers may respond, "I don't believe it!" Similarly, among the information given on most urban legend websites is the creator's assessment of whether the story is "true" or "false."

Function: Not everyone tells urban legends for the same reason. Some people are bringers of news, others are providers of entertainment. A single tale may carry a number of messages depending on the teller. In general, urban legends provide an opportunity for individuals to explore and discuss with others some contemporary issue from their chosen viewpoint or to share a "good story."

Perhaps not surprisingly, the short, concise format of urban legends, coupled with their air of plausibility and startling plots, makes them liable to be spread by other means than word of mouth or other forms of personal communication. They are particularly attractive to journalists, writers, and filmmakers. Since the 1900s urban legends have been spread through the news media, firstly through newspapers and magazines, then later via radio and television. They have also become part of the entertainment industry and are often to be found in films made for the big screen, as well as on television where they have provided the basis for such series as *Mythbusters*, *Supernatural*, and episodes of the *X-Files*. Urban legends have also regularly been incorporated into short stories and novels, and may also be presented as jokes, rumors and gossip, and in settings ranging from after-dinner speeches to church sermons. Some urban legends, particularly those of a more gruesome nature, are also told at storytelling sessions such as slumber parties and campfires, where teens and children compete to frighten one another.

* * *

Research on urban legends has been undertaken by scholars in such divergent disciplines as parapsychology, social psychology, anthropology, history, business management, sociology, communication studies, English language, English literature, and Native American studies. However, it is folklorists who have been the most persistent and enthusiastic researchers.

Folklorists began getting interested in the subject in the years following World War II. In many cases this was because of the large number of rumors and stories they had heard while serving with the armed forces; in others it was as a result of postwar employment initiatives such as the Works Progress Administration (WPA) which sent out researchers to collect examples of local culture and folklore. In Europe the years 1940 to 1960 saw huge efforts being put into the collection of traditional culture and verbal art (epics, folktales, and legends). Researchers began discovering what they saw as a "new" story-form alongside the traditional legends they were supposed to be collecting. At first these new stories were rejected as "not folklore," but a number of scholars were wise enough to see they were just as "traditional," though in a different way. Owing to the vigor with which these stories were championed by such scholars as American folklorist Linda Dégh, gradually the concept of "urban" legend (or "modern legend" or "modern folktale," as they were first called) began to get established and to be thought worthy of study.

The first conference on the subject was called in 1969 by American folklorist Wayland D. Hand. Among those who contributed were Richard M. Dorson (one of the first scholars to describe urban legends and include examples in his books), Alan Dundes (who championed the psycho-analytical approach to legends), Linda Dégh (one of the most influential legend scholars of her generation), and Jan Harold Brunvand (whose name later became synonymous with urban legend collection). The proceedings of this conference were later published (see Hand 1971).

It was not till the 1980s, though, that urban legends became the focus for annual meetings of folklorists. In 1982, the first of a series of continuing annual conferences solely devoted to this topic was held at the Centre for English Cultural Tradition and Language at the University of Sheffield, England. Between 1984 and 1990 the proceedings of these meetings were published in the "Perspectives on Contemporary Legend" series (see Bennett and Smith 1988, 1989, 1990; Bennett, Smith, and Widdowson 1987; Smith 1984). In 1988 the International Society for Contemporary Legend Research (ISCLR) was inaugurated. ISCLR now publishes the journal *Contemporary Legend* and the newsletter *FOAFtale News*.

* * *

This book is arranged in nine thematically related chapters, each with approximately fifteen sections. Each section ends with a brief bibliography and a note which refers readers to related stories. The Appendix and Further Reading Section are both designed as guides to resources for those who wish to do further reading or research.

The stories in the collection, and the information about them, have been compiled from our own files, from the files of friends and colleagues, from newspapers and magazines both in print and online, from folklore books and journals, compilations of jokes and stories, and from correspondence. The choice of which stories to include, however, reflects our own approaches to urban legend and the information about them reflects our own interests. Unlike many other collectors and commentators, we do not here try (except in rare cases) to interpret the legends in any way or to give any social or psychological explanations for their popularity. What interests us here is not what the stories "mean," but how they have been told, by whom, and in what form, when and where. Neither do we attempt (except in rare cases) to tell readers whether the stories are "true" or "false." Unlike many urban legend books and websites, this volume is not designed as a "rumor-buster." This is because, we do not see untruth as a defining criterion of urban legends; rather, we think that one of the things that help to define a legend is *uncertainty* about whether it is true (the "If it's true, it's important, but *is* it true?" principle). This approach also leads us away from including a lot of material which nowadays is found in legend compilations and on urban legend websites. We do not associate urban legends with "credos," "myths," or the sort of misinformation that used to be called "popular fallacies." So readers will not find here an item such as "Rats are systematically bred in South African sewers, made into fur coats, and exported to the USA as mink, ermine, and seal" (Dickson and Goulden 1983, 42). There is another reason for excluding this sort of material, and that is that we believe legends are *stories* of some sort. If we had come across an item that began, "My friend's mother bought a beautiful fur coat in Harrods, London," and ended, "It was fur from sewer rats. Isn't that dreadful?" we might have included it. Such an item would be more than a statement of belief; it would be a story. It would have a beginning, a middle, and an end (though not necessarily in that order), it would be fixed in a specific place (though different versions might locate it in different places), and it would have a cast of characters (though these, too, might change from telling to telling).

We believe that stories are valuable and exciting things regardless of their truth value. The process of urban legend creation and evolution is never ending and ever changing. Old tales resurface in new forms and new tales constantly await to be discovered. The world around us is altering all the time, but fear and laughter will always be with us, and will lead us to continue to swap our stories of the weird, the wonderful, the absurd, and the terrifying.

FURTHER READING

Bennett, Gillian, and Paul Smith, eds. *Monsters With Iron Teeth: Perspectives on Contemporary Legend III*. Sheffield: Sheffield Academic Press for the International Society for Contemporary Legend Research in association with CECTAL, 1988.

———, eds. *A Nest of Vipers: Perspectives on Contemporary Legend V*. Sheffield: Sheffield Academic Press for the International Society for Contemporary Legend Research in association with CECTAL, 1990.

———, eds. *The Questing Beast: Perspectives on Contemporary Legend IV*. Sheffield: Sheffield Academic Press for the International Society for Contemporary Legend Research in association with CECTAL, 1989.

Bennett, Gillian, Paul Smith, and J. D. A. Widdowson, eds. *Perspectives on Contemporary Legend II*. Sheffield: Sheffield Academic Press for the Centre for English Cultural Tradition and Language, 1987.

Dickson, Paul, and Joseph C. Goulden. *There Are Alligators in Our Sewers and Other American Credos: A Collection of Bunk, Nonsense, and Fables We Believe.* New York: Delacorte, 1983.

Hand, Wayland D., ed. *American Folk Legend: A Symposium.* Berkeley, CA: University of California Press, 1971.

Smith, Paul, ed. *Perspectives on Contemporary Legend: Proceedings of the Conference on Contemporary Legend,* Sheffield, July 1982. CECTAL Conference Papers Series, 4. Sheffield: CECTAL, 1984.

CITY LIFE

When scholars and researchers first began discussing the "new" legends, it was assumed that the stories were modern phenomena, either because they depended on modern inventions such as automobiles, or because the storytellers were sophisticated young city dwellers not the rural peasants folklorists were used to collecting legends from. As information about the "new" legendry began to accumulate, it was realized that the newness was illusory and that most of the stories were parallels or descendants of much older narratives.

More, perhaps, than the stories elsewhere in the book, many of the legends in this chapter create the same impression of "newness." They depend on the paraphernalia of modern living from car insurance to garden gnomes, or on urban constructions such as subways and shopping malls; alternatively, they may be the products of recent political circumstances such as the threat of terrorism, or anxieties about the intrusion of the "wild" world into the suburbs. However, research is already establishing that some of these legends are rooted in traditional themes and tales ("The Double Theft" is one example, as are fears of being kidnapped into the sex trade). Others spread through modern communication networks so rapidly that they became "traditional" in a very short time ("The Grateful Terrorist" and "The Dying Child's Wish").

For other stories of city life see: Drugged Children; Killer Clowns

ALLIGATORS IN THE SEWERS

When anybody thinks of an urban legend, in all probability this is the one they think of. The story is very simple: supposedly people buy baby alligators or crocodiles as pets and when they grow too big they flush them down the toilet, so now there is a whole colony of crocs or gators living below the streets of New York or other cities. Very often these creatures are said to be very large, albino, and/or blind.

Such allegations were repeatedly made during the twentieth century. One of the people who took a particular interest in these stories was "Fortean" writer Loren Coleman. (Charles Fort collected accounts of weird happenings and used them to bolster his argument that the world was a good deal more mysterious than modern science allowed, full of creatures not recognized by modern zoology and forces not recognized by modern physics.) Coleman points out that alligators and other crocodilians are one of the most frequently mentioned animals in "Fortean" events. Among other events that Coleman mentions are alligators falling from the sky in South Carolina; alligators, caimans, and crocodilians being found in cotton bins in Texas, in water ditches in Illinois, and in basements in Kansas; and alligators being caught alive at Brooklyn Museum subway station (Coleman 1983, 66). Appendix II of Coleman's *Mysterious America* (1983) is a list of eighty-four similar cases reported between 1843 and 1983, and his 1974 essay, "Erratic Crocodilians," contains a four-page checklist of media reports of mystery alligators/crocodiles/caimans (seventy from the United States, eight from elsewhere). The latter is preceded by an introductory commentary suggesting that the sightings may be of known, but rare, creatures such as giant salamanders (Coleman 1974).

The first account which Coleman found from the United States came from the *Charleston Evening Post* (August 11, 1843) and tells how a crocodilian fell to earth during a thunderstorm. However, the first time it was claimed that crocodiles or alligators had been found in a city's sewers was 1935. This account is also the only authenticated event. The story was covered in the *New York Times* of February 10, 1935, and told how two young men shoveling snow saw an alligator churning about in an icy manhole (Coleman 1983, 67–69).

Stories about alligators in sewers are not, however, confined to the United States. Among many other things that Paris (France) is famed for is its huge underground network of sewer tunnels, to which many legends are attached. One of these is the belief that crocodiles and alligators live and breed there. From 1990 to 1996, the British folklore magazine *Dear Mr Thoms* and its successor, *Letters to Ambrose Merton*, followed the legend of the Paris crocs in contemporary newspaper accounts.

The first of these items was contributed in 1990 when French folklorist Véronique Campion-Vincent sent in two accounts from the newspaper *France-Soir* (March 1984). The reports said that sewer workers had suddenly found themselves face-to-face with a young crocodile "à l'allure noble et fière" (of noble and proud appearance). Firemen and sewer workers were sent to rescue it, but it put up a good deal of resistance. It was not the first time sewer workers had encountered a crocodile, *France-Soir* reported; they had seen several during the course of a few months, "No doubt after they had been carelessly abandoned by their masters." Since the place they were found was just below the Quai de la Mergisseries, which is renowned for shops selling animals, the implication was that the animals had escaped from some shop owner there ("Update: Crocodiles"). In 1995, Sandy Hobbs noted another Paris crocodile-sighting reported by *France-Soir* in June of that year entitled "Cache-Cache Croco" (hide-and-seek croc). In this incident, gendarmes, firemen, soldiers, a vet, and the river police were all called to the scene and tried, unsuccessfully, to lure it out with bait (Hobbs 1995). In a later note, Véronique Campion-Vincent reported that the first crocodile had eventually been rescued from the sewers and was now alive and well at the aquarium in Vannes, Britanny ("The Crocodile from Paris Again").

This legend shows up as the plot of the 1980 film "Alligator," in novels such as Alan Sharp's *Night Moves* (1975) and the 1975 film of the same name; and in Thomas Pynchon's novel V (1963). It also features in many collections of "credos" and "popular fallacies" such as Dickson and Goulden's *There Are Alligators in Our Sewers* (1983).

Example

Geronimo stopped and told Profane how it was. Did he remember the baby alligators? Last year, or maybe the year before kids all over New York bought these little alligators for pets. Macy's was selling them for fifty cents, every child, it seemed, had to have one. But soon the children grew bored with them. Some set them loose on the streets, but most flushed them down the toilets. And these had grown and reproduced, had fed off rats and sewage, so that they now moved big, blind, albino, all over the sewer system. Down there, God knew how many there were. Some had turned cannibal because in their neighborhood the rats had all been eaten, or had fled in terror. (Pynchon 1963, 42–43)

FURTHER READING

Coleman, Loren. "Erratic Crocodilians and Other Things." *Info Journal* 3.4, Whole No. 12 (1974): 12–18.

———. "Alligators-in-the-Sewers: A Journalistic Origin." *Journal of American Folklore* 92 (1979): 335–338.

———. *Mysterious America*. London: Faber and Faber, 1983. See pp. 60–70 and Appendix II.

———. "Alligators in the Sewers." In *Contemporary Legend: A Reader*. Compiled by Gillian Bennett and Paul Smith. New York: Garland, 1996, pp. 154–166.

"The Crocodile from Paris Again." *Letters to Ambrose Merton* 6 (June 1996): 25.

Dickson, Paul, and Joseph C. Goulden. *There Are Alligators in Our Sewers and Other American Credos: A Collection of Bunk, Nonsense, and Fables We Believe*. New York: Delacorte, 1983.

Hobbs, Sandy. "Another French Crocodile." *Letters to Ambrose Merton* 3 (August 1995): 7.

Pynchon, Thomas. *V*. London: Vintage, 1963.

"Update: Crocodiles." *Dear Mr Thoms* 25 (April 1992): 21–22.

See: The March of the Sewer Rats

BACKWARD BUILDINGS AND OTHER ARCHITECTURAL ERRORS

This is the story of an eminent architect or civil engineer who makes an embarrassing mistake. The theme is expressed in innumerable local legends about public buildings being built back to front, or freeways adding to the traffic chaos they were meant to ease, or university libraries being built on soft ground so the building sinks under the weight of books.

Example

At SUNY at Stony Brook students look to the "bridge to nowhere ... " Built in 1970, the bridge leads from the second floor of the union building to the north wall of the library where it stops in a dead end. According to legend, the bridge was supposed to go into the library but the library was built backwards. Why, "there are skylights in there that point the wrong way," students say.... (Bronner 1990, 148)

FURTHER READING

Bronner, Simon J. *Piled Higher and Deeper: The Folklore of Campus Life*. Little Rock, AR: August House, 1990. See pp. 144–148.

Brunvand, Jan Harold. *Encyclopedia of Urban Legends*. New York: Norton, 2001. See pp. 15–16, 29–30, 384–386.

Mikkelson, Barbara. "That Sinking Feeling." http://www.snopes.com/college/halls/sinking.asp

THE CHANDELIER

This humorous story has been around since the 1950s, maybe longer. Gillian Bennett's husband heard it in the late 1950s whilst part of a student delegation to Russia, but as far as we know its first appearance in print was as a true story about the visit of the 1972 Canadian ice-hockey team to Moscow. The story then was that, owing to his fears that his hotel room might be bugged, Phil Esposito, one of the team members, had destroyed a priceless chandelier. It had happened like this: whilst searching his room for hidden microphones, he found what he thought was an electronic listening device under his bed, and unscrewed it; the "listening device" was actually the metal plate holding up the chandelier in the room below.

The story appears in Phil Esposito and Peter Golenbock's memoir, *Thunder and Lightning* (2003, 110), but Esposito denies responsibility and points the finger of suspicion at two Air Canada pilots. The story appears with the pilots as the culprits in a 2002 newspaper article about the Canadian team's 1972 Moscow tour. Among many other rumors and anecdotes, the journalist recalls that one team member was supposed to have thrown an expensive mirror into the street and that two Air Canada pilots had unscrewed a "suspicious-looking plate under the rug at Hotel Intourist, unwittingly plunging a $3,000 chandelier to the ballroom floor below" (Feschuk 2002).

The story has also been told about Dr Joseph Luns, Secretary General of NATO, 1971–1983. It is said that, before his first visit to Moscow, he was warned about the dangers of electronic eavesdropping and advised to inspect his room for hidden microphones. On reaching the hotel, he began a careful search but could find nothing. Then he noticed a bulge under the carpet and when he lifted the carpet up, he saw a wire running toward the center of the room. He snipped the wire clean through and, "as he rose in triumph, there was the sound of an appalling crash from the room below as the chandelier fell from the ceiling" (Brann c. 1980, 146).

However, more recently the story has been updated by switching the scene to the United States and featuring those old urban legend standbys, a honeymoon couple. In the Reader's Digest *Laughter, The Best Medicine*, for example, a pair of honeymooners at the "Watergate Hotel," Washington, DC, are afraid of being overheard, so they search the room for bugging devices. The story proceeds as usual except that the chandelier falls on the unfortunate couple in the room below (*Laughter, The Best Medicine*, 148).

Gillian Bennett heard the story in the mid-1980s as told by a secretary in the English Language Department at the University of Sheffield (UK). This is how she told it:

Example

I heard this story. I thought it was true, but very funny. There was this couple who went to Moscow. They enjoyed their stay but were quite nervous about security and things like that.

Well, they got it into their heads that their hotel room was bugged, so one night they set about searching their room for a hidden microphone. They looked in the cupboards and behind the pictures—everywhere! They didn't find anything, but they were still suspicious. So they moved the bed, and they saw a little bump in the carpet. "Ah-Hah! Here's a hidden microphone!" So they rolled back the carpet and, sure enough, there was a sort of knob-thing, like a screw. So they thought that if they unscrewed this little knob they would be able to take the bug out and make their room secure. So they set to work. They twisted and twisted this screw until it came out....

... And a huge chandelier fell to the ground in the ballroom below! They'd unscrewed the thing that held it up! (Bennett Collection)

FURTHER READING

Brann, Christian. *Pass the Port Again*. Revised ed. Cirencester, UK: C. Brann, c. 1980.

Brunvand, Jan Harold. *Encyclopedia of Urban Legends*. New York: Norton, 2001. See pp. 48–49.

Esposito, Phil, and Peter Golenbock. *Thunder and Lightning. A Hockey Memoir*. Toronto: McClelland and Stewart, 2003.

Feschuk, Dave. "Behind the Curtain." *National Post* [Canada] (September 21, 2002). http://www.nationalpost.com/utilities/story.html?id={A0ECCD52-E1F7-410B-BB67-CBEE2748D55F

Laughter, The Best Medicine. Montreal, London and Sydney: The Reader's Digest, 1998.

THE COLANDER LIE DETECTOR

In the 1990s this amusing story, also known as "The Home-Made Lie-Detector," routinely circulated on the Internet and was sent in to folklore magazines on numerous occasions. It featured in publications as different as the *Wall Street Journal* and *Playboy* and was mentioned in Ann Landers' column on January 4, 1998. It has been part of oral folklore since the 1960s and its earliest appearance in print seems to have been in the *Philadelphia Inquirer* of June 22, 1977.

The story still appears in the international press from time to time. The latest sighting being an article in the *Sydney Morning Herald* of August 19, 2004. The anonymous author refers to it as "an old and no doubt apocryphal story" about a group of detectives who connect their suspect up to an ordinary office photocopier, which duly gives its verdict. The article then goes on to allege that British troops conducting counterinsurgency operations in Aden in the 1960s "reputedly" tied terror suspects up to an old IBM mainframe computer, explaining that radiation from their lie detector would drain away their manhood unless they told the truth. The word "reputedly" tells it all—the author wants to sound authoritative but knows he is dealing with folklore ("How the Truth Comes Out").

There is an unusual Canadian variant which is told as a (true) personal experience in Peter MacDonald's *From the Cop Shop: Hilarious Tales from Our Men and Women of the Badge* (1996, 179). Here a policeman investigating a series of burglaries stops a drunken man in a car and tells him he had better confess because he has a mobile lie detector in his pocket. He then pulls out his breathalyzer, which, of course, registers "Fail" when the suspect answers.

The most common variant of the lie detector story attaches itself to the Radnor police, as in our example below.

Example

In Radnor, Pennsylvania, the police may have violated the rights of a suspect by attaching a metal colander to his head and connecting the colander to the office copier with metal wires. A message reading "He's lying" was placed in the copying machine.

Each time the interrogators got an answer they didn't trust, they pushed the copy button—and out would come the message. Convinced the jury-rigged polygraph was accurate, the suspect confessed.

When the Police Department in Radnor was contacted to verify this published report, Detective Murphy laughed and said, "Nothing like that ever happens." ("Defying Belief")

FURTHER READING

"Defying Belief." *Glimpse* (Publication of the International Society for General Semantics) 38 (December 1986). Reprinted in *Dear Mr Thoms* 34 (May 1994): 19.

"How the Truth Comes Out." *Sydney Morning Herald* (August 19, 2004). http://www. smh.com.au/articles/2004/08/19/1092889266542.html?oneclick=true

MacDonald, Peter V. *From the Cop Shop: Hilarious Tales from Our Men and Women of the Badge.* Toronto: Stoddart, 1996.

Mikkelson, Barbara. "Next Case on the Court Colander." http://www.snopes.com/legal/colander.htm

See: Radar Traps and Speed Cameras

THE DISAPPEARING ROOM

Sometimes called "The Foreign Hotel" or "The Vanishing Lady," this story was first noted in the 1930s by New York columnist Alexander Woollcott, who had a good eye for an urban legend. Woollcott said he had first heard it some years earlier and that it had come from the archives of the French secret police. At first, he says, he believed the story, but then he discovered a virtually identical tale in a 1913 novel *The End of her Honeymoon* by Mrs Belloc Lowndes. Later he found an even earlier account in a British newspaper dated 1911, and then an acquaintance told him that the story had been printed in the *Detroit Free Press* in 1889 "to fill a vacant column in the next morning's issue" (Woollcott 1934, 65). So we can assume that the story was perhaps in the region of 50 years old by the time Woollcott first noticed it. A recent appearance was in the British newspaper *The Guardian*, where it was updated to present-day concerns about a possible epidemic of bird flu by being told as a cautionary tale about the unscrupulousness of the French tourist trade (Hyde 2006).

The story has been the subject of, or an interlude in, several other literary works including *She Who Was Helena Cass* (Lawrence Rising, 1920), Ernest Hemmingway's *The Torrents of Spring* (1938), Ralph Strauss's "The Room on the Fourth Floor" (1947); and it is included as "Maybe You Will Remember" in Alvin Schwartz's *Scary Stories 3* (1991). It has lived on in several film plots. In an article of August 2006, Sandy Hobbs analyzed ten films that utilize the theme, including Alfred Hitchcock's "The Lady Vanishes" (1938), Otto Preminger's "Bunny Lake is Missing" (1965), and Anthony Darnborough and Terence Fisher's "So Long at the Fair" (1951). According to Hobbs, US films based on, or using, the story include "The Midnight Warning" (1932), "Dangerous Crossing" (1953), "Flightplan" (2005), and the TV film "Into Thin Air" (1955). There are also two early German films "Unheimliche Geschichten" (1913) and "Verwehte Spuren" (1938).

Throughout all these many versions from news, literature, and films the essential plot stays pretty constant. However, some of the details vary. Though the main character remains for the most part a young woman, the person who vanishes may be, not a mother, but a friend, a lover, a brother, a husband, or a child. The scene may be set, as in Woollcott's version, in a hotel or it may be a train or a plane. The disease that is being covered up may be cholera as well as plague; and in some versions the disappearance is due to a kidnap ("The Lady Vanishes," "Bunny Lake is Missing"), a hijack ("Flightplan"), or a conspiracy ("Dangerous Crossing"); in these latter versions, which also lack the hotel setting, it is only a person who disappears not a person and the room she was in.

Example

This is how it is described in Ernest Baughman's Type and Motif-Index of the Folktales of England and North America. *(Baughman's description is based on a story he had read in* Colliers *magazine in January 1949).*

A woman and her daughter take a room in a Paris hotel. The mother becomes ill. The physician sends the daughter to a remote part of the city for a special medicine. When she returns to the hotel, she is unable to find her mother. Moreover, she finds that the room which she thinks they have taken is unfamiliar, that it has obviously been redecorated and refurnished in her absence. The manager and the staff profess never to have seen her before, and the names of her mother and herself are not on the register. In some variants she never does find the explanation for the situation; in others it is explained that the mother is discovered to have bubonic plague and that this means is used to prevent panic and also loss of business to the hotel. (Baughman 1966, motif Z552*)

FURTHER READING

Barnes, Daniel R., and Paul Smith. "The Contemporary Legend in Literature—Towards an Annotated Check-List, Part 2." *Contemporary Legend* 2 (1992): 167–179. See pp. 172–179.

Baughman, E. M. *Type and Motif-Index of the Folktales of England and North America.* The Hague: Mouton, 1966.

Briggs, K. M., and R. L. Tongue. *Folktales of England.* London: Routledge and Kegan Paul, 1965. See pp. 98–99.

Hobbs, Sandy. "Disappearance and Denial: A New Look at a Legend Motif on the Screen." *FOAFtale News* 65 (August 2006): 1–6.

Hyde, Marina. Untitled column in *The Guardian* Manchester and [London] (March 14, 2006).

Schwartz, Alvin. *Scary Stories 3: More Tales to Chill Your Bones.* New York: Harper Collins, 1991. See pp. 102–105.

Woollcott, Alexander. *While Rome Burns.* Harmondsworth: Penguin, 1934. See pp. 60–65.

THE DOUBLE THEFT

This story of theft-upon-theft has been reported for at least 30 years in Europe, Canada, Australia, Great Britain, and Ireland. It is a close relative of the "Theatre Tickets" legend which also often features two thefts, but here the first theft is of a purse from the restroom of a prestigious downtown department store. The first theft leads immediately to a second, more serious theft, and may have been the motive for the original one.

Though it has all the appearance of modernity, "The Double Theft" is a traditional story. Australian folklorist Bill Scott points out that there is an Islamic fable called "The Sheep and the Purse" that uses the same basic plot. A shepherd has a sheep stolen from him. While searching for it he meets a man near a well; this man is the thief, though the shepherd does not know this. The thief says he has dropped a purse full of silver down the well, and asks the shepherd to dive into the well and retrieve it for him. His reward will be half the silver in the purse. So the shepherd strips off and dives into the well. When he resurfaces, the thief has gone and so have the shepherd's clothes (Scott 1985, 237–238, citing Idries Shah, *The Way of the Sufi*).

Example

A woman customer . . . goes to the lavatory in the ladies cloakroom [at Harrods in London], and puts her handbag on the floor beside her. The lavatory partitions are of the sort which leave a gap between wall and floor, and a hand comes through this gap and whips her bag away. Before she can emerge the thief has escaped, but she reports her loss to the shop manager. She returns home. A few hours later her phone rings: "This is Harrods; a bag has been found which may be yours; please come to the manager's office to identify it." But when she reaches the store there is no bag there, and none of the staff have phoned her. Returning home, she sees her own bunch of keys in the lock, and finds the flat burgled and all her jewellery gone. (Buchan 1981, 6)

FURTHER READING

Barnes, Daniel R. "Interpreting Urban Legends." *Arv* 40 (1986): 67–78. Reprinted in *Contemporary Legend: A Reader*. Compiled by Gillian Bennett and Paul Smith. New York: Garland, 1996, pp. 1–16.

Buchan, David. "The Modern Legend." In *Language, Culture and Tradition: Papers on Language and Folklore Presented at the Annual Conference of the British Sociological Association, April 1978*. Ed. A. E. Green and J. D. A. Widdowson. CECTAL Conference Papers. Leeds and Sheffield: The Institute of Dialect and Folklife Studies/The Centre for English Cultural Tradition and Language, 1981, pp. 1–15.

de Vos, Gail. *Tales, Rumors, and Gossip: Exploring Contemporary Folk Literature in Grades 7–12*. Westport, CT: Libraries Unlimited, 1996. See pp. 174–175.

Scott, W. N. *The Long and the Short and the Tall: A Collection of Australian Yarns*. Sydney: Western Plains Publishers, 1985.

Smith, Paul. *The Book of Nastier Legends*. London: Routledge and Kegan Paul, 1986. See pp. 56–57.

See: The Theatre Tickets; Unexpected Returns

THE DYING CHILD'S WISH

The background to this legend is another traditional belief—the idea that anyone who collects a certain number of useless objects such as ring-pulls or used stamps can "redeem" them in aid of some good cause. Several such rumors claimed that anyone collecting *x* number of stamps or ring-pulls or cigarette packets (or some similar thing) could contribute to a good cause—perhaps by buying a sick person a kidney dialysis machine or funding a vital surgical operation. The majority of these rumors have been unfounded.

One particular set of stories told of a child whose aim was to collect the largest number of cards of some sort (business cards, for example, or "Get Well" cards). One early example was the case of "Little Buddy," which surfaced in Scotland in the early 1980s. A Citizen's Band (CB) radio enthusiast took a call from a boy with the code name "Little Buddy" who was collecting "call cards," cards circulating among CB enthusiasts that verified the number of countries contacted by the CB operator. A campaign was organized to help Little Buddy achieve his aim, and cards started to arrive from all over the world. Even then-president of the United States, Ronald Regan, contributed to the appeal. However, suspicions soon began to be raised that there was no such person as Little Buddy, and in 1988 the Post Office tried to put a stop to the appeal. Despite their efforts, appeals kept on being made.

Then the legend began to mutate; now Little Buddy was supposed to be a young boy dying of cancer and appealing for postcards to be sent to him so he could get into *The Guinness Book of Records*. As late as 1988 the stamp collectors newsletter was carrying a request saying that: "An 8-year-old boy is dying of cancer and wants to be in *The Guinness Book of Records*." While this was still going on, similar appeals were being made for "Paul," and "David," or "Colin" aged seven and "expected to die before Christmas." There was no evidence that any of these children existed.

The best-known actual appeal was launched by the family of Craig Shergold of Carshalton, Surrey (UK) in September 1989. The aim was that Craig would collect in the region of 1,266,000 "Get Well" cards and so be listed in the *Guinness Book of Records*. Within two months the goal had been reached and the appeal was closed. However, notice of the appeal had spread far and fast and was unstoppable. Chain letters were being sent out, and prominent people, including the then British Prime Minister Margaret Thatcher, were publicly supporting the appeal. Again, though, the story was changing; now Craig was supposed to be collecting business cards, not "Get Well" cards.

The Ann Landers column in *The Sacramento Bee* (June 21, 1991) called the continuing appeal "a scam," and emphasized that the Shergold family had not asked for business cards to be sent and that while "they appreciate the kindness of the American people," it was turning into a nightmare they would like to stop.

But nothing and nobody seemed to be able to stop it. In October 1991 a statewide conference of California educators heard an announcement about a little boy called Craig Shergold who lived in Southern California and wanted to break the record for receiving the most "Get Well" cards. By the spring of 1992, Craigs were popping up all over America.

Example

Britain is being swept again by one of those bouts of manic benevolence in which thousands of people are collecting "get-well" cards for "Colin, aged 7," who is expected to die from cancer before Christmas and wants to get into the *Guinness Book of Records as the* owner of the world's biggest collection of get-well cards. [...]

Churches in Yorkshire have been praying for Colin and collecting cards for him. A leaflet circulating in the county asks for each card to be addressed to Colin and to include the sender's name and address—"otherwise the cards do not qualify."

Colin's address is not given, nor is the address of his home or the hospital in which he is supposed to be a patient. In the manner of chain letters someone is named at the end of the leaflet as the person nominated to collect the cards.

In the end, the collector of the cards sends them on to someone else, who sends them on to someone else, who sends them—then all inquiries reach a dead end, leaving someone holding hundreds of cards and with no idea of where to send them. (Parkin c. 1981)

FURTHER READING

Brunvand, Jan Harold. *Too Good to Be True: The Colossal Book of Urban Legends*. New York: Norton, 1999. See pp. 461–465.

Guigné, Anna Elizabeth. "The 'Dying Child's Wish' Complex: The Case of the Craig Shergold Appeal." *Contemporary Legend* new series 1 (1998): 116–133.

"Miracle in the Mail: Little Craig Shergold's Recovery Was in the Cards." *People Weekly* (June 10, 1991): 63, 66.

Parkin, Michael. "Cards Galore for the Invalid Who Never Was." *The Guardian* (c. 1981). Clipping in *Dear Mr Thoms* 7 (June 1988): 11.

See: New Lamps for Old: Redemption Rumors

THE FALSE CONFESSION

This modern legend of deception, sometimes known as "The Note on the Windshield," seems to have been first noticed in the summer of 1963 in a Herb Caen column of the *San Francisco Examiner*. Then in the fall, Caen reported a variant he had read in the [London] *Daily Mirror* (Brunvand 1989, 118–119). Caen wrote about the story again in 1971; and, according to Jan Brunvand, it appeared in the *Mirror* newspaper again in 1973—this time as a Reg Smythe "Andy Capp" cartoon (Brunvand 1999, 331). We have not seen this cartoon but Andy was drawn as a stereotypical politically incorrect working-class Northerner and "The False Confession" is just the sort of mean-spirited trick that Andy would pull.

The story must have been in pretty wide circulation about that time because it also appears in one of Bennett Cerf's many collections of humorous stories (Cerf 1970, 363). Our example, which comes from Ireland, also probably dates from this period as it relates to the Gay Byrne Show (Byrne 1972). During the 1970s Brunvand was also collecting many versions from correspondents throughout the United States (California, Alaska, New England). He heard the story again in Pittsburg in 1983 and his father-in-law told him a version from Buffalo (New York State) in the late 1990s.

Since that time the legend of "The False Confession" has featured in numerous story compilations, including Daniel Cohen's *The Beheaded Freshman* (1993, 42–43), and David Holt and Bill Mooney's *Spiders in the Hairdo* (1999, 44).

Example

A woman rang the Gay Byrne Show and said that she had seen a man crash into a parked car with nobody inside. He jumped out of his car and scribbled a note, which he left on the windscreen wiper. When the woman whose car had been dented returned to it, she read the note. It said, "There's a woman across the street who saw me crashing into your car. She probably thinks I'm writing down my name and phone number for you to contact re damages, but I'm not. Ha ha!" (Dillon-Malone 1996, 73)

FURTHER READING

Brunvand, Jan Harold. *Curses! Broiled Again! The Hottest Urban Legends Going.* New York: Norton, 1989.

———. *Too Good to Be True: The Colossal Book of Urban Legends.* New York: Norton, 1999.

Byrne, Gay. *To Whom it Concerns: Ten Years of the Late Show.* Dublin: Gill and Macmillan, 1972.

Cerf, Bennett. *The Sound of Laughter.* New York: Doubleday, 1970.

Cohen, Daniel. *The Beheaded Freshman and Other Nasty Rumors.* New York: Avon Books, 1993.

Dillon-Malone, Aubrey. *The Guinness Book of Humorous Irish Anecdotes.* Enfield, UK: Guinness Publishing, 1996.

Holt, David, and Bill Mooney. *Spiders in the Hairdo.* Little Rock, AR: August House, 1999.

FLOORED

The story in our example below about an old lady who laid grass on her living-room floor to save the trouble of taking the dog out for a walk was told by a British politician. It was one of his favorite examples of the weird way people behave. He heard it twice (told as true by local government housing officials), first in Oldham in the 1960s, then in Stockport in the 1970s (industrial towns in north-west England). A similar story was reported from the south London borough of Croydon. Folklorist Steve Roud overheard his boss and another colleague talking in the public library where he works. His boss was recounting events he said had happened in the 1960s. Like the story from the north of England, this tale was designed to show how ignorant (and, it is implied, undeserving) people could be. His story was that firefighters constantly had to be called out to apartment blocks where asylum seekers were being housed: this was because the migrants didn't know what electric cookers were and kept on lighting fires on the living-room floors to prepare their meals (Roud 1992). Roud's item was followed up by a note from Scottish folklorist Sandy Hobbs who reported that he had had a query from a former student who was a social worker: she wanted to know whether it could be true, as a colleague alleged, that a poverty-stricken client had laid tarmac on the living-room floor to save the expense of carpet (Hobbs 1992).

These stories may be compared with accounts from 1970s Sweden about recent immigrants from Yugoslavia, Greece, and/or Turkey allegedly laying soil on their floors in order to keep chickens or grow potatoes, Finnish immigrants allegedly ripping up wooden floors and laying down sand so they don't have to take their children to the playground, and gypsies allegedly breaking up the floors to grow potatoes or lighting fires in the living room rather than using the kitchen (Klintberg 1989). More recently (June 2003) a story circulated on the Internet that people visiting a Native American reserve noticed holes sawed through the house walls just over the bathtub. This had been done, it was said, so that their horses could reach inside to drink from the tub. Allegedly the residents were so lazy they couldn't be bothered to go outside to water their horses ("The Hole Truth").

Example

The local council had built some new homes for rent, what in the UK is called "social housing." The design was a new one; they called them "cottage flats" because the buildings looked like an ordinary 2-storey cottage but in fact consisted of two independent apartments, one on the ground floor and one on the floor above. Anyway, the homes had not long been occupied for the first time before the downstairs tenants in one of the new cottage flats reported that the ceiling was damp. The housing officer went round and diagnosed the problem as condensation caused by inadequate ventilation. So he explained that they would redecorate the ceiling but the tenants must be sure to open windows regularly to let some air in. OK so far, but sure enough a few months later the tenants were back complaining of damp. This went on for some time, the housing officer getting more and more exasperated, the tenants more and more upset, until the old lady in the upper apartment fell ill and died.

When the housing officer entered the old lady's flat he found that she had laid turf on the floor to save the trouble of going out to walk the dog (Bennett Collection).

FURTHER READING

Hobbs, Sandy. "A Social Worker's Tale." *Dear Mr Thoms* 25 (April 1992): 29.
"The Hole Truth." urban-legends@yahoogroups.com (accessed on June 28, 2003).
Klintberg, Bengt af. "Legends Today." *Nordic Folklore: Recent Studies*. Ed. Reimund Kvideland and Henning K. Sehmsdorf in collaboration with Elizabeth Simpson. Bloomington and Indianapolis, IN: Indiana University Press, 1989, pp. 70–89. See pp. 74–75.
Roud, Steve. "In My Library." *Dear Mr Thoms* 24 (January 1992): 11–13. See pp. 11–12.

THE GRATEFUL TERRORIST

Within a month of the tragic events of 9/11 the Internet was full of legends and rumors about terrorism; about 60 percent of those from America, and Canada were stories about foreknowledge. The most common of these told the story of a woman (it was usually a woman) who, in return for some small kindness or courtesy, was warned not to go near the Twin Towers on September, 11 or to stay away from the Baltimore Tunnel, or not to go to any shopping malls on Halloween, or not to drink Coca Cola (or in some versions Pepsi) after a certain date (Mikkelson). Another popular legend told how a woman's Arab boyfriend suddenly disappeared leaving her a note saying he wouldn't be able to see her again, but as a parting gift he was warning her not to take a plane journey on September 11 and not to shop at any malls on October 31 (Fine and Khawaja 2005).

Stories like this were widely circulated in Australia and the United Kingdom too, by word of mouth, e-mail, and newspapers. Members of the London-based Folklore Society sent several examples, mainly newspaper cuttings from national newspapers, to the society's newsletter. A man of "Arab appearance" was said to have warned a woman in London's prestigious department store, Harrods, not to travel on the tube that evening; an "old Arab guy" supposedly warned a friendly woman to stay out of Central London that weekend. An Australian correspondent sent in a story about "an Islamic guy" who warned a woman who'd returned a wallet he'd dropped to stay out of Melbourne for the next three weeks, and stay away from Sydney altogether ("Terrorist Myths").

Literally thousands of stories like this were reported and gave rise to scares such as that which hit the south London borough of Croydon at the end of December 2005. The town was awash with rumors that it was about to be hit by a terrorist attack, following stories that a Good Samaritan returning a dropped wallet to the person who lost it had been told not to go into the Whitgift shopping center because some kind of bombing or attack would happen. The result was that the shopping center was partially evacuated after a man was spotted carrying a smoking box. What had really happened was that a security guard was delivering a cash box fitted with a smoke device that activated if the box had not arrived at its proper destination within a certain time (Austin 2005).

Even before that, though, the stories had become so commonplace that parodies began to be passed round. For example, a woman was said to be warned to stay away from the English town of Luton, "What? she asked, "Is it going to be attacked?" "No," said the man, "It's just such an awful place." In a similar parody reported in both the United Kingdom and Australia, a woman is warned not to go to a certain restaurant; "Why?" she says, "Is there going to be an attack?" "No," says the guy, "I went there last night and the dessert selection is extremely limited" (Sircar 2002).

Example

A story said to be jamming the switchboards at police stations throughout the UK is about a dark-haired man who is queuing at a gas station (or McDonald's or a supermarket or a post office—wherever) in Blackpool (or Slough or Preston or

Llandudno) and finds he is short of money to pay by a few pence. The person gives him a few coins to help out. The man is surprised and very grateful. "Thank you so much," he says, "and stay out of Birmingham (or Manchester, or Sheffield, or Chester) at the weekend."

Some versions say witnesses go to the police, and successfully identify the man as a terror suspect.

In Cheshire, where several people reported the incident to the police at second hand, the press initially suspected that someone was deliberately going round queues and whispering warnings; but police could not find anyone who had experienced it personally, and "after investigation are treating it as nothing more than an urban myth." ("Terrorist Myths")

FURTHER READING

Austin, Ian. "It's my cash box not a bomb!" icCroydon (December 30, 2005). http://iccroydon.icnetwork.co.uk/news/headlines/tm_objectid=16530374%26method=full%26siteid=53340-name_page.html

Fine, Gary Alan, and Irfan Khawaja. "Celebrating Arabs and Grateful Terrorists: Rumor and the Politics of Plausibility." In *Rumor Mills: The Social Impact of Rumor and Legend*. Ed. Gary Alan Fine, Véronique Campion-Vincent, and Chip Heath. New Brunswick, NJ: Aldine Transaction, 2005, pp. 189–205.

Mikkelson, Barbara. "Not the Real Thing." http://www.snopes.com/rumors/cocacola.htm

Sircar, Sanjay. "Terrorist Myths." *FLS News* 38 (November 2002): 8–10.

"Terrorist Myths." *FLS News* 36 (February 2002): 5–6.

THE MALL ABDUCTOR

This story, which has circulated since the mid-1990s, is related to the classic story of "The Hairy-Handed Hitchhiker" but seems to be a distinct legend. It is always difficult to establish a clear history of an urban legend, but, as far as we can tell from reports in folklore magazines, this story began in late 1995 or early 1996 in the United Kingdom. Such an incident was reported by a secretary at the Department of English Language and Linguistics at Sheffield University (UK) as something that had really happened in December 1996 at a local college. In March 1997 the Sheffield story was printed in *Letters to Ambrose Merton* (Wiltshire 1997).

By 1998 it had crossed the Atlantic. It was reported as a considerable scare in Columbus, Ohio, in 1998 (Hathaway and Doyle 1999), and it was in "hot circulation" in a Saskatchewan (Canada) town in mid-March 1999 (PH 1999). The same story was reported from Scotland in 1999, and the following year from Manchester (England) and Sydney (Australia). It was widespread in Sydney again in 2000, and in Scotland the same year. In 2001 it was circulating once more in Canada in the form of an e-mailed warning. Another e-mailed warning circulated in 2004 about attempted abductions from Walmart stores, and a similar message, entitled "A New Form of Kidnapping," was spread via e-mail in the spring and summer of 2006.

The basic plot stays the same in all versions. A respectable-seeming man carrying a briefcase tries to trick a woman into letting him get in her car at a shopping mall or department store; she becomes suspicious and refuses. Later, ropes or duct tape and a weapon of some sort are found in the man's briefcase. The details of the would-be abductor's trick vary from telling to telling. Maybe he tells her he has chased off some hooligans who have been trying to open her car door and now is late for his train and needs a ride to the station; maybe she discovers she has a flat tire and the stranger helps her to fix it, but now needs a ride to the other side of the mall to recover his own car; maybe the man reports that somebody has reversed into her car and he has reported the accident, but now he is late and needs a ride—and so on. In each case, the man puts his briefcase into the back seat of the car, so when the woman becomes suspicious and drives off without him, the contents of the briefcase prove the man's criminal intentions.

Our example comes from Cheshire (UK). A friend sent the story in a letter to Paul Smith in June–July 1996 and it was printed in the December 1996 issue of *FOAFtale News*. Note the complicated and lengthy chain of friends-of-friends involved in its transmission. The ending of the tale (which we have not printed) tells how our friend tried to check on the veracity of the story by calling the store and the police. Eventually he was able to establish that no such incident had been reported to the local police station. In these ways, this is a perfect example of urban legend telling.

Example

My daughter was told, by a colleague at the school where she works, that a friend of this colleague had told her the following story, which had been told to this friend by a further informant—a four-step sequence.

A woman shopping in our local Sainsbury's [supermarket] returned to the car-park (quite large and regularly frequented) to find a man standing by her car. The man was well dressed and personable, carrying a briefcase. He reported that four boys had been interfering with the doors of her car, and that there had been some damage. He had chased them off and followed them across the car park, but they had escaped.

The woman found some damage to the locks, but opened up the car and found it drivable. The man then told her that as a result of chasing off the boys, he had missed his train, and would be glad of a lift [ride]. The woman agreed, but suggested that he put his briefcase in the car and "back her out" [that is, stand behind the car and give her directions to help her reverse the car out of the slot in the car park GB]. This he did, but she drove straight off and went to the police station and told her tale.

The police were initially sceptical, but were asked to open the briefcase. Inside were two knives, a coil of rope, and a large stick. (Froome 1996)

FURTHER READING

Froome, Derek. "Would-be Assailant Frustrated." *FOAFtale News* 40/41 (December 1996): 19.

Hathaway, Rosemary, and Larry Doyle. "Terror (?) at Tuttle Mall, Columbus, Ohio, USA." *FOAFtale News* 44 (May 1999): 2–4.

PH [Philip Hiscock]. Footnote to Hathaway and Doyle *FOAFtale News* 44 (May 1999): 2–4.

Wiltshire, Robin. "The Case in the Car." *Letters to Ambrose Merton* 9 (March 1997): 7–8.

See: The Hairy-Handed Hitchhiker; Mall Slashers

MALL SLASHERS

Also called "Ankle Slashers," or "The Slasher under the Car," this legend has been widespread in the United States since 1978. Since that date there have been about two dozen rumor scares in at least twenty different states, the stories often surfacing during the winter holiday period. It is said that thieves and/or rapists hide under cars parked at shopping malls, and slash at the victim's Achilles tendon with a knife or tire iron in order to immobilize them. Sometimes the motive is said to be rape, and sometimes, especially around Christmas time, the motive is theft. The story has been collected from places as far apart as Washington, DC, and Phoenix, Arizona. When challenged to show an authoritative report of these incidents, the rumormongers tend to say that the police are engaging in a cover-up to avoid bad publicity (Brunvand 2001, 388–389).

In 1992 *Fortean Times* writer, Bob Rickard, reported that panic had spread in two Illinois towns in October of the previous year because of these rumors. Fears about the "mall slasher" were so acute that the police department set up a helpline; in the first week they received 600 calls. Despite police assurances that there was no substance to the rumors, department store managers were warning their customers to be alert (Rickard 1992).

However, by then the story had already started to mutate. During panics in Tacoma, WA, in 1989, and Chicago in 1991, it had been said that the "mall slashers" were committing their crimes as part of an initiation ritual ("Mall Slashers in Chicago"). Then in 1993 there was a report from Carnegie Mellon University, Pittsburg, PA, that students throughout the city believed that, as part of their initiation, gang members had to go to the Ross Park Mall, hide under a car, and slash the driver's ankles; the victim would reach out to grab his/her ankles, and the gang member would then slice off the driver's fingers ("Ankle Slashers at the Mall").

After 1993 most tellings of the "Mall Slasher" legend gave gang initiations as the motive for the ankle slashing, and the scene began to shift from shopping malls to gas station forecourts. Thus the legend began to merge with the "Lights Out" story. Tales of "Mall Slashers" continue to be told at the present day.

Example

BE ALERT AT GAS STATIONS
It has become a ritual of gang members to take one body part from women as an initiation into gangs. The rule is that it has to be in a well-lit area and at a gas station, so be careful. They tend to lay under the car and slash the female's ankles when she goes to get in her car, causing her to fall and then they cut off a body part and roll and run. (extract from an e-mailed warning 1999)

FURTHER READING

"Ankle Slashers at the Mall." *FOAFtale News* 29 (March 1993): 11.
Brunvand, Jan Harold. *The Baby Train*. New York: Norton, 1993. See pp. 134–138.
———. *Encyclopedia of Urban Legends*. New York: Norton, 2001.

"Mall Slashers in Chicago." *FOAFtale News* 24 (December 1991): 11
Rickard, Bob. "The Mall Slasher." In "Social Panics." *Fortean Times* 61 (1992): 38.

See: The Assailant in the Back Seat; Lights Out!

THE MAN IN THE MIDDLE

In its original form this ironic story was repeatedly told to journalists in New York during the 1930s and 1940s. The scene was the New York subway, and the characters were a girl returning late at night alone and three desperate-looking fellow travelers sitting together opposite her. The girl is particularly frightened by the man in the middle who is staring fixedly at her face, or at the expensive watch she is wearing. The story ends in one of two ways: either the girl jumps up and slaps the man's face, whereupon he slumps forward dead; or another traveler enters the compartment and persuades her to leave, then tells her the man in the middle is dead.

This story was not new in the 1930s, however, as a correspondent told journalist Alexander Woollcott, who had featured it in his column in *The New Yorker* in 1930. The correspondent said that the story had been published in a magazine *The Bookman* in 1902. The scene in that version was a horse-drawn bus traveling down Fifth Avenue, and the story went that two men got on, dragging a third between them. An observant woman noticed what nobody else had seen—the third man had his throat slit from ear to ear.

There are many other ways to tell this story. In some versions, usually called "The Dead Drunk on the Subway," the dead man is assumed to be only drunk. For example, in 1949 a slightly different version was contributed to a folklore magazine by an Associated Press feature writer. In this version two men get in a subway train supporting a man who looks dead drunk. They get off, leaving him alone. The train goes around a curve, the man slides to the floor, "dead as a herring . . . drilled neatly through the head . . ." (Lowry 1949).

There are also two English versions from the 1960s and 1970s. In a story collected in the cities of Manchester, Nottingham, Bradford, and Newcastle in the early 1960s, a girl gets into a train and finds a seat in a crowded compartment. At the next stop all the passengers alight except the man facing her. She leans forward to ask him what time the train gets in, but he doesn't answer. She asks him again; still no answer. So she touches him on the shoulder to get his attention. At this point, he topples forward—dead (McKelvie 1963, 348).

There is also a strange story from the 1970s which mixes "The Man in the Middle" with "The Stolen Corpse" to give a story about a poor Neapolitan family working in the north of Italy whose grandfather dies. The family can't afford the cost of a coffin so they dress him in his Sunday best and take him with them on the train, propping him up between them. For some reason they have to get out at a station and, leaving it a bit late to reboard the train, have to scramble in wherever they can. When they eventually find their way back to their former seats, grandpa has disappeared. Eventually the other passengers confess—when the train left the station it started with such a jolt that a suitcase fell off the luggage rack on to the old man's head and "killed" him. In a panic they had pushed him off the train (Dale 1978, 46–47).

A recent reappearance of this story was in 2003 when it was sent to the Snopes website by an e-mail correspondent. This version is virtually identical to that heard by Alexander Woollcott in New York in 1930, except that the dead person is a woman not a man and there is no suspicion that she was drunk (Mikkelson). Rather tamer versions today feature a girl who thinks she is being stared at and slaps a man only to find he is blind, and a story about an Iranian riot started by a man who accused another of leering at his wife (it turned out the man was cross-eyed) ("Riot Erupts After Grocer Arrested for 'Flirting'"). Also there are comparable stories about a group of friends who go for an all-night drinking session on the evening before one of them is getting married. The bridegroom-to-be gets so drunk he passes out, but, nothing daunted, his friends drag him from bar to bar and prop him up in a corner in each one. At the end of the night, they drag him home and put him to bed. In the morning he is found dead—in fact, he had died about halfway through the mammoth drinking binge. It was a dead man that they had propped up in the corner of bar after bar (forwarded to forteana&yahoogroups.com July 31, 2002).

Example

I wonder if readers can throw any light on a gruesome story which I have just been told (April 2005) and which I am sure must be an urban myth. As usual this is said to have happened to a friend of a friend and seems to be going the rounds among female university students. The story goes that a young woman was sitting in a railway carriage and noticed three other girls sitting together at the far end. They were the only people in the carriage. The lone girl noticed that the middle girl of the threesome continually stared at her, and she felt intimidated. The train ticket collector then arrived, looked at the lone girl's ticket, and told her it was invalid and she must leave the train. He followed her off the train and then told her that her ticket was fine but he had had to make up a ruse to get her off since the two girls who had been sitting either side of the "staring" girl had strangled her and that was why she had such a fixed expression. This just cannot be true. The student daughter of a friend of mine told this to her father and believed it to be true, saying it happened to a friend of a friend of hers, whom she herself did not know. (Rowe 2005)

FURTHER READING

Dale, Rodney. *The Tumour in the Whale: An Hilarious Collection of Apocryphal Anecdotes*. London: W. H. Allen, Universal Books, 1978.
Lowry, Cynthia. "Folktales." *Western Folklore* 8 (1949): 174–75.
McKelvie, D. *Some Aspects of Oral, Social and Material Tradition in an Urban Industrial Area*. Leeds: Unpublished PhD Thesis, 1963, pp. 320–361.
Mikkelson, Barbara. "Dead Man Rocking." http://www.snopes.com/horrors/gruesome/subway.asp
"Riot Erupts After Grocer Arrested for 'Flirting'" *Tehran (Reuters)* July 31, 2000.
Rowe, Tina. "The Staring Girl." *FLS News* 47 (November 2005): 6.
Woollcott, Alexander. "The Man in the Middle." "Shouts and Murmurs" column. *The New Yorker* (February 22, 1930): 18.

THE MARCH OF THE SEWER RATS

Among many urban tales about rats (junkie rats, cat-killing rats, rats mistaken for dogs, rats in fast food, and so on) there is a hoary old favorite based on the belief that all the rats in a city's sewers move home from time to time en masse. This story has been current in British cities since at least the beginning of the twentieth century. The rats are said to move out from the sewers in a formation led by a King Rat, or a large white rat, or a blind rat.

The account below was told to Gillian Bennett by a 60-year-old woman in 1982, as true, and located in Manchester a large commercial city in northwest England.

Example

Oh! My father-in-law saw that! Ooh, yes! No doubt about that! When he was quite young. In Manchester! He was working quite late at the office, which he very often did, especially when he was younger, and he heard these stories, you know, of it happening. And it was a sort of damp, foggy November night and the King Rat, yes, DID lead them.

You know how these big offices used to have these great big steps? And he got onto sort of the third step, and got into the doorway, and he said, "They do! They move from one part of the town to the other part of the town, and there's a King Rat and he leads them." Oh! he was absolutely petrified! It is the biggest rat of the whole shebang.

But he said he couldn't start counting them. They just MOVED! Oh, yes! It was no story. He saw this! I don't know when. It'd be going back to before or just after the First World War. I should think round about that time. That's when he saw them. Oh, I think so. (Bennett Collection)

FURTHER READING

McKelvie, D. *Some Aspects of Oral, Social and Material Tradition in an Urban Industrial Area.* Leeds: Unpublished PhD Thesis, 1963. See p. 348.

See: Alligators in the Sewers

THE MUTILATED SHOPPER

This is one of the several gruesome tales of city life that are located at shopping malls, in restrooms, or department store fitting rooms. For example, legends of abductions for sex slavery are regularly set in this environment, as are stories about the malicious castration of small boys. Similarly, during an organ theft panic in Italy, women were said to be kidnapped from fitting rooms and taken to underground rooms equipped for transplant surgery.

In the story of "The Mutilated Shopper" a woman goes into the fitting room of a downtown department store, or a dress shop in a mall, to try a dress on. She doesn't come out, and eventually the worried husband, who has been waiting for her, alerts the staff. They enter the fitting room and see the woman covered with blood. Her rings are missing, and so is the finger she wore them on. The peak popularity of this story was in the mid-1970s to early 1980s.

Example

A lady and a man were shopping in Sears. And she said to her husband, "I am going to go into the dressing room to try this on" and he said that he would meet her in the car. So, she was in there and it got to be like 9.30, closing time, and she hadn't come out. So he got worried and he went back into the store. He found two security guards and he told them his wife was in there. They told him no one was in there. They checked around the store and they found her in the dressing room. And she was on the floor and someone apparently cut off her finger, her wedding finger, and took her diamonds and she was lying on this floor. And they took her to the hospital. (Wachs 1990, 144)

FURTHER READING

Brunvand, Jan Harold. *Encyclopedia of Urban Legends*. New York: Norton, 2001. See p. 103.

Wachs, Eleanor. "The Mutilated Shopper at the Mall: A Legend of Urban Violence." In *A Nest of Vipers: Perspectives on Contemporary Legend V*. Ed. Gillian Bennett and Paul Smith. Sheffield: Sheffield Academic Press for the International Society for Contemporary Legend Research in association with CECTAL, 1990, pp. 143–160.

See: The Castrated Boy; Stolen Body Parts 5 (Kidney Thefts); White Slavers

THE NATIVITY PLAY

There are several variants of this humorous tale. The story below was heard in Sheffield (UK) in the 1980s. In other versions Joseph knocks on the inn door and asks, "Is there any room in the inn?" The innkeeper replies, "Sure, we've got lots of room. Come in!" Tales also circulate about other nativity plays performed by small children: in one the child playing Mary forgets her lines. When the shepherds ask what the baby will be called, the child answers, "Julia!"

Example

During rehearsals for the school nativity play the little boy who was playing the part of Joseph kept persistently arriving late and, more to the point, never seemed to know his part. Eventually, as things were not going well, three days before the dress rehearsal the teacher organising the play switched the boy playing the innkeeper, a minor role, with Joseph. The lad playing the innkeeper was, of course, delighted but the other child was very disgruntled.

The dress rehearsal came and all went very well except that the boy who had initially played Joseph tended to be rather sulky in his new part as innkeeper. All boded well for the first performance the next evening and, in due course, the parents and members of staff were assembled to watch the culmination of weeks of effort and hard work.

In the main the play started well and things were flowing very smoothly. Even the new innkeeper looked cheerful for a change. Mary and Joseph strolled up to the door of the inn and Joseph asked if there was a room for the night. Yes, said the innkeeper, he could find a room for Mary but, as far as he was concerned, Joseph could piss off. (Smith 1983, 83)

FURTHER READING

Smith, Paul. *The Book of Nasty Legends*. London: Routledge and Kegan Paul, 1983.

RADAR TRAPS AND SPEED CAMERAS

Over the past few years numerous legends have circulated about roadside speed cameras and radar traps. The earliest of these dates from the time the technology was new, which coincidentally was the same time technologies such as microwave ovens were being introduced. In the 1980s a story was circulating in the north of England about a couple who were driving along a country road and spotted a microwave oven abandoned on the side of the road. They quickly reversed the car, jumped out, and put the microwave into the back of the car. A mile or two further on they were stopped by the police who arrested them for having stolen police equipment. They had mistaken a roadside speed trap for a microwave oven.

A more elaborate version of the story later circulated in the press. Here, the female driver was charged with speeding in a built-up area though her speedometer had never registered more than the regulation 30 mph. The evidence was in the back of her car. The speed detector she had stolen from the roadside thinking it was a microwave oven, was registering her speed as 60mph. The explanation was that the speed trap had been designed to be stationary, so it had added the 30mph the driver had first passed it at to the 30 mph it was now traveling at to arrive at the conclusion that the driver had passed through a built-up area at twice the permitted speed (Smith 1992, 47).

Other recent rumors and legends about drivers and speed traps include stories about Dutch motor cyclists who repeatedly zoom past speed cameras at night to use up all the film, "boy racers" who believe that if you drive past a speed camera fast enough the camera will not be able to recognize the car, a truck driver who deliberately backed his vehicle into a speed camera, and one who tried to blow one up (Clement 2003).

Example

This one [appeared] after the recent installation of speed cameras by the police in Brisbane. (These recently cost me $80 for exceeding the speed limit by 4kph!). A man driving home notices the camera flash as he drives by. He is convinced that he is legal, so after thinking about it when he arrives home and sure the camera is faulty, hops back into his car and drives past the camera at well below the limit. To his angry delight the camera again flashes, so he does it again after driving round the block. To his sorrow three tickets arrive in the mail later; one for exceeding the limit by 6kph and the other two for driving without a seatbelt (an offence here)! He had been so upset he had forgotten to belt up . . . New technology certainly breeds new legends. (Bill Scott, personal communication)

FURTHER READING

Clement, Barrie. "News Flash: Speed Cameras Are Making Our Roads Safer." *The Independent* [UK] (February 12, 2003). http://news.independent.co.uk/uk/transport/story.jsp?story=377585

Smith, Paul. "'Read All About It! Elvis Eaten by Drug-Crazed Giant Alligators': Contemporary Legend and the Popular Press." *Contemporary Legend* 2 (1992): 41–70.

See: The Microwaved Pet

ROAMING GNOMES

This story was very popular in Australia and the United Kingdom in the 1980s. The events, supposing they had really happened, were a practical joke and gave rise to copycat practical jokes and stories among people who were familiar with the legend. There was a rash of gnome-stealing and gnome-swapping; and, on occasion, people left gnomes on friends' doorsteps with a message tied round the neck saying "There's no gnome like your own gnome" (a pun on the proverb, "There's no home like your own home"). Australian folklorist Bill Scott reported that a "host" of gnomes went missing at the same time and were later discovered grouped in a semicircle in a clearing in the bush "holding a meeting" (personal communication).

Stories about Roaming Gnomes appeared in the mass media from about 1986 onward. One was featured in the United Kingdom men's magazine *Mayfair* in August 1986; here the gnome wrote to say that he was having a wonderful time in China where the "people [are] much more my size." An Australian TV channel reported on a family whose gnome had "gone walkabout." In March 1987 a letter to the Australian *Kalgoorlie Miner* announced the formation of the GLO, the Gnome Liberation Organization, and three days later a letter was printed from "Major Dennis Bloodknock Rtd" on behalf of a rival group, the Society for the Liberty of Gnomes ("Major Bloodknock" was one of the characters in the 1960s British cult comedy series, "The Goon Show") (Hults 1988, 90–92). The "Roaming Gnome" legend was used in the film "Amélie" (2001); Amélie sends her father's gnome traveling with an air-hostess friend of hers, and the father receives postcards until the gnome arrives back home.

Few or no gnomes seem to have roamed from home in the United States, but maybe there were some Roaming Flamingos. A correspondent told Jan Brunvand that her ornamental flamingos went missing from her front lawn. Round about Christmas she began getting postcards from her flamingos postmarked from all over the southern part of the country. They told her they didn't like the cold so had flown south for the winter. They returned in the spring. Similarly, it was reported in *FOAFtale News* in 1994 that a man from Athens, Georgia, had a pink plastic flamingo stolen by Halloween pranksters. Soon after, he received a postcard signed by "Phil, the Flamingo," and soon had a collection of fifteen letters from the bird. These included photographs of a "family reunion" in Florida, and news from the Grand Canyon, Mount Rushmore, Old Faithful and the Warner Brothers studio in Hollywood (where Phil said he hoped they'd notice his talent and charisma). On December 6 Phil quietly returned to his home in Athens with a travel bag taped to his neck containing a small bar of soap, crackers and instant soup, a pen, and a bag of birdseed ("Flying Flamingos").

Not to be outdone by gnomes or flamingos, a rabbit garden ornament, which disappeared from its home in New York, sent photographs to his owners showing him in Reno, Nevada, and the Virgin Islands, at an airport, in a bus station, and building sand castles on a beach. One day he returned home and was found propped against the windshield of the family car ("Who Framed Roving Rabbit?"). Larger garden ornaments also went missing in order to take a vacation, including an almost life-sized fiberglass statue of the founder of Kentucky Fried Chicken, and a 7-foot-high stuffed grizzly bear who said he had been to Disneyland and had attended the Olympics in Seoul (Brunvand 1989, 308–310).

Example

Some people over in Sydney had a gnome by their garden pond, one of those with a little fishing rod. Then one day, it was gone. But a week later they got a postcard from the Gold Coast. It said, "Having a great holiday. Lots of good fishing here. Missing you. Love from your gnome." Then suddenly one day it was back beside the garden pond, wearing sunglasses, carrying a little suitcase, and well tanned with a good layer of brown shoe polish. (Bill Scott, personal communication)

FURTHER READING

Brunvand, Jan Harold. *Curses! Broiled Again! The Hottest Urban Legends Going.* New York: Norton, 1989. See pp. 305–310.
"Flying Flamingos." *FOAFtale News* 32 (February): 8.
Hults, David S. "Roaming Gnomes." *Australian Folklore* 2 (1988): 87–92.
"The Strange Saga of Norman Gnome." *Dear Mr Thoms* 26 (June 1992): 20.
"Who Framed Roving Rabbit?" *Dear Mr Thoms* 14 (January 1990): 10.

THE SEVERED FINGERS

This story of an abortive attempt to break open the trunk of a car was popular in Europe during the 1950s and 1960s. Several versions were collected in northern cities of the United Kingdom in the late 1950s when the people who try to break into the car were often said to be antisocial "Teddy Boys." The story was also known in Scandinavia at about the same time (Kvideland and Sehmsdorf 1988, 391–392), and during the 1980s it became popular in Ireland (Ní Dhuibhne 1983, 57). In each case the would-be attackers are foiled and lose one or more of their fingers.

By 1975 a version of the tale had already surfaced in Australia. The brother of Australian folklorist Bill Scott told him a story about a young man who took his girlfriend to a drive-in movie in his Volkswagen (VW "Beetle") car. In this story the young man is parked next to a car full of louts who are drinking heavily. When he remonstrates with the louts they jump out of their car and try to lift the VW off its wheels. However, by then the young man has engaged the gears and taken the brake off. The car bounds forward, and the louts are forced to drop it. The young man escapes, but the louts lose their fingers (Scott 1981, 368).

The popularity of the story is probably due to the fact that the victim gets his revenge on his attackers without getting himself involved—it's "poetic justice." The basic plot differs very little from telling to telling, the only real point of difference being that, in some, the attackers get their fingers accidentally amputated in the trunk of the car when it falls or is slammed shut, in others the fingers are cut off because the attackers do not know that the car they are vandalizing is a rear-engine model (like the "Beetle"). All the stories are very localized, the storytellers asserting that the events happened at a well-known local road junction.

Related legends about members of motorcycle gangs who threaten motorists with chains and whose amputated fingers are later found still attached to the chain circulated in Germany and Scandinavia (Klintberg 1989, 78–79). The nearest American equivalent seems to be a story reported in the Los Angeles Times (August 20, 1989). This is a tragicomic multiple-episode story about a man who tries to find how much fuel he has left by sticking his finger in the gas tank. The flap is spring-loaded and it shuts with a snap, trapping his finger. A passing truck driver stops and offers to help by going to the gas station for some fuel while the man goes on trying to free himself. However, the "helpful" guy just makes off with the trapped man's wallet. The trapped man flags down a police patrol car with his free hand. For twenty minutes the police work away with a coat hanger to try to free the man, but finally give up and call the fire department. While all this is going on in the glare of flashing lights from patrol car and fire truck, a car pulls up behind with a drunken driver behind the wheel. When the highway patrolmen ask if he needs help, the car driver replies, "No, I'm just stopping for the traffic lights" (via e-mail from Brian Chapman).

Gillian Bennett's father told her the story below in Manchester (UK) in the early 1980s.

Example

Did you heard the one about fingers being caught in the boot [trunk] of a car? It was at the traffic lights at Victoria Avenue and Rochdale Road. These were people who knew the person who told me.

They were stopped at the lights and a gang of yobs crossed the road and started to attack the car, rock it about you know, and try to turn it over. They had their fingers under the boot and were trying to open it. Anyway, the chap, the driver, managed to open his door, ran round, and banged the boot shut like that (!), and drove off as soon as the lights changed.

When he got home, he went round the back to get his luggage out and he found four fingers stuck in the boot.

They rang round the hospitals to see if anyone had been admitted with four amputated fingers! (Bennett Collection)

FURTHER READING

de Vos, Gail. *Tales, Rumors, and Gossip: Exploring Contemporary Folk Literature in Grades 7-12*. Westport, CT: Libraries Unlimited, 1996. See p. 117.

Dhuibhne, Eílís Ní. "Dublin Modern Legends: An Intermediate Type List and Examples." *Béaloideas* 51 (1983): 55–70.

Klintberg, Bengt af. "Legends Today." In *Nordic Folklore: Recent Studies*. Ed. Reimund Kvideland and Henning K. Sehmsdorf in collaboration with Elizabeth Simpson. Bloomington and Indianapolis, IN: Indiana University Press, 1989, pp. 70–89.

Kvideland, Reimund, and Henning Sehmsdorf, eds. *Scandinavian Folk Belief and Legend*. Minneapolis, MN: University of Minnesota Press, 1988.

Mikkelson, Barbara. "Severed Fingers." http://www.snopes.com/horrors/gruesome/severed.htm

Scott, Bill. *Complete Book of Australian Folklore*. Sydney: Lansdowne, 1981.

See: The Choking Doberman; The Hook

SIT!

Sometimes called "The Elevator Incident," this popular legend has been widespread since at least the mid-1970s and is still told today. At heart it is a story about the humiliating consequences of racial stereotyping. Two people are involved—a black celebrity, and a nervous woman. The location is Las Vegas, Atlantic City, or New York; the events are usually said to occur in an elevator. A typical story is that the lady, a naive stranger to the city, is in the elevator when a black man gets in with a big dog: the woman is sure she will be attacked, so when the man gives the dog a command, the lady obeys. The misunderstood command is either just "Sit!" or "Sit, Lady!" or "Sit, Whitey!" ("Lady" or "Whitey" being the name of the dog), and the lady promptly sits down. Alternatively, the man may already be in the lift (with or without a dog).

He tells the woman to "Hit the floor" (meaning, press the button for the floor she wants); terrified, the woman drops to the floor.

The story has been told about a number of black celebrities including Eddie Murphy, Reggie Jackson, Lionel Ritchie, Magic Johnson, O. J. Simpson, Jesse Jackson, and Michael Jackson. As told about Eddie Murphy, the story ends with Murphy sending a lavish floral bouquet to the lady's room with a note, "Thank you for the best laugh I've had in years." Murphy denies that this incident occurred.

A recent sighting of this version of the story was on the Internet in 1997, but there are earlier stories dating from the 1960s and 1970s, which utilize the same basic plot. In these variants the unattractive quality that leads to humiliation is not racial stereotyping but naivety and undue deference. The best known of these legends is set in the British Houses of Parliament. One story is that a group of foreign tourists were being shown round the House of Commons on the day of the State Opening of Parliament, and were quite overwhelmed by the pomp and ceremony. The tourists heard the Speaker of the House of Commons, who was clad in his rather grand official attire, call out to attract the attention of a friend who happened to be passing, "Neil!" So they dropped to their knees where they were, and knelt. In the 1970s the story became attached to a Tory grandee, Lord Hailsham, who served in successive Conservative administrations in both the House of Commons, where he was known as Mr Quintin Hogg and in the House of Lords, where he was known as Lord Hailsham after he inherited his father's title. He was never the Speaker of the House of Commons, but he served in the House of Lords as Lord Chancellor (1970–1974 and 1979–1987). His strange name, the change in the way he should be addressed, and the fact that at one time or another during his career he had sat in both Houses of Parliament seems to have caused some confusion for some storytellers and commentators. As a result a whole new legend series has grown up about a character called "Sir Quentin Hoff," who was Speaker of the House of Commons, and rejoiced in the unlikely (and imaginary) title of "Keeper of the Woolsack" (Dickson and Goulden 1993, 154; de Vos 1996, 215).

Examples

1. Do you know the South African story—is this folklore?—of the South African woman who went to the States on holiday. She was terrified of all black people as she felt they would realise she was South African and would penalise her for this. Well, she was staying at the Sheraton in New York city, when she had to get into a lift with a black man and his dog. As soon as the lift closed, the

black man said "Down, Lady!" and the poor woman, nearly wetting herself with anxiety, sank down on the floor. The man started to laugh and said, "I was talking to my dog. Her name is Lady." The woman burst into tears and got out at her stop. The black man happened to be Lionel Ritchie, and the next day the woman went to pay her bill prior to leaving for S.A. when she found the bill paid by Ritchie. (Hind 1990)

2. The awesome majesty of the Palace of Westminster has been known to stir the soul of the most ripped-off tourist, but never more so than in the dank and dreary November of 1979.

Lord Hailsham, the Lord Chancellor himself, was strolling across the lobby of the House of Commons when he saw Neil Marten, a Tory MP and long-standing friend. Hailsham, ever attentive to such details, recalled that it was Marten's birthday and gave an imperious wave to his friend, as he called out: "Neil!"

A troupe of camera-clad tourists crashed to their knees as one. (Hardy 1987, 45)

FURTHER READING

Cerf, Bennett. *Laugh Day: A New Treasury of over 1000 Humorous Stories and Anecdotes* New York: F. Watts, c. 1965. See p. 420.

de Vos, Gail. *Tales, Rumors, and Gossip: Exploring Contemporary Folk Literature in Grades 7-12*. Westport, CT: Libraries Unlimited, 1996.

Dickson, Paul, and Joseph C. Goulden. *Myth Informed*. New York: Perigree Books, 1993.

Hardy, David. *What A Mistake!* Secaucus, NJ: Castle, 1987.

Hind, Cynthia. "South Africans in Elevators." *FOAFtale News* 20 (December 1990): 10–11.

SMILEY GANGS

In February 1989, schools in south London were swept by a major panic caused by a rumor that gangs of football hooligans (said to be supporters of Chelsea Football Club) were touring local schools. They caught children and demanded to know which football team they supported. If the answer was not Chelsea they cut each side of the child's mouth with a razor, knife, or bit of broken glass, then hit the child in the stomach so he/she opened his/her mouth to scream and widened the wound into a grotesque smile. The rumor, known as "the Chelsea Smilers," spread very rapidly, as did the resultant panic, sweeping through a large number of south London boroughs and spreading eastwards into the neighboring county of Kent (Roud 1989).

"Smiley Gang" fears were not new in Britain. In the 1950s a very similar story about a smile cut with a razor was told in Newcastle-upon-Tyne (northeast England) about a gang from Glasgow (Scotland), and in 1971/1972 there was some panic in Liverpool (northwest England) after rumors spread about a "Green Jackets" gang who carved noughts and crosses on their victims' faces.

Recently (2002–2003), similar stories about "Smiley Gangs" have circulated in Belgium, France, and the Netherlands. Here it is ethnic gangs rather than football gangs who are said to be terrorizing people, and the victims are supposed to be women rather than children. Initially the rumors were spread by word of mouth, and then by the newspapers, radio, and TV, e-mailed chain-letters, weblogs, and on Internet message boards (Burger 2004).

Example

During the autumn of 2003, the Netherlands was shaken by a minor rumor panic by the story of the Smiley Gang. This ethnic gang was said to corner women and force them to choose between "a rape or a smile." The ones that opted for the smile received a razor-slash across the face which left a hideous smiley-shaped scar. (Burger 2004)

FURTHER READING

Burger, Peter. "From FOAFtale to Media Legend: The Case of the Smiley Gang." Abstract of paper presented at the *22nd Annual Perspectives on Contemporary Legend Conference*, July 21–24, 2004. Printed in *FOAFtale News* 59 (August 2004): 3.

Roud, Steve. "Chelsea Smilers: A Preliminary Report on a Gang Violence Rumour." *FOAFtale News* 15 (September 1989): 1–2.

See: Lights Out!; Mall Slashers

THE THEATRE TICKETS

This tale of theft and deception has been around for at least 30 years and has been recorded in the United States, United Kingdom, Netherlands, Germany, Sweden, Norway, Finland, Spain, Italy, and Australia. It is a close relative of "The Double Theft," and may have precursors in legends about the clever

British con woman, Mary Carleton (d. 1673). The Mary Carleton story lacks the first theft, but tells how Mary took a lodging in London, and conned the other residents into trusting her, then invited them all to go with her to a play she had tickets for. While they were all absent, her maid, on her instructions, burgled the house and took goods worth £200 (a huge amount in those days). Mary gave her companions the slip after the play, rejoined her maid, and they were never heard of again (Shojaie Kawan 2005, 144–146).

One of the first appearances noted by folklorists in the twentieth century was a letter in the Scottish *Sunday Post* (May 19, 1985) warning other readers about a current scam. As a hairdresser, the correspondent wrote, "I hear many stories. A recent one should put the public on their guard . . ." (Stupart 1985). There follows the legend of "The Theatre Tickets."

In "The Theatre Tickets" stories, a car battery, a barbecue grill, or a car is stolen or "borrowed" or damaged while it is standing outside the victim's home. The owner is then lured away from home by a note which offers an apology and free tickets to a classy event—an opera, a symphony concert, a ballet, a top sports event, or a meal at a famous restaurant. In both cases, of course, the victim is robbed a second time by the same thief.

The "Theater Tickets" legend is quoted in a very influential sociology textbook, Erving Goffman's *Frame Analysis* (1975). Goffman took his example from a newspaper report in the Philadelphia *Evening Bulletin* of January 25, 1972. Our example below tells the story as recounted by Goffman:

Example

True tale, new racket gimmick, or one of those strange stories that pops up every now and then and makes the rounds? Goes like this:

A Northeast resident found his car stolen one morning. Two days later, it was returned, with a note on the front seat saying: "Sorry, car had to be taken for an emergency . . . leaving two tickets for a sports event to make up for the inconvenience."

The car owner was delighted, took his wife to the sports event with the free ducats, returned to find their home completely ransacked. (Goffman 1975, 468)

FURTHER READING

Barnes, Daniel R. "Interpreting Urban Legends." ARV 40 (1986): 67–78.

de Vos, Gail. *Tales, Rumors, and Gossip: Exploring Contemporary Folk Literature in Grades 7–12.* Westport, CT: Libraries Unlimited, 1996. See pp. 176–177.

Goffman, Erving. *Frame Analysis*. Harmondsworth, UK: Penguin, 1975.

Shojaie Kawan, Christine. "Legend and Life: Examples from the Biographies of 'Ā'ishah Bint Abī Bakr, Mary Carleton, and Friedrich Salomo Krauss." *Folklore* 116 (2005): 140–154.

Stupart, Gordon. "Warning." Letter in The Scottish *Sunday Post* (May 19, 1985). Clipping reproduced in *Forum: Newsletter of the British Folk Studies Forum* 1 (1985): 19.

See: The Double Theft; Unexpected Returns

UNEXPECTED RETURNS

These are stories where somebody unexpectedly returning to home or car uncovers a crime.

In 1988 the magazine My *Weekly* carried a supposedly true story about a couple who were going on holiday. When they arrived at the airport, they found they had come without some vital document and had to return home. When they got home, they found their cabdriver robbing their house.

At much the same time, tales and rumors were circulating in Scotland by word of mouth about a woman who left her car in the car park of a downtown store. For some reason she had to return a minute or two later, only to find her car was gone. The car-park attendant explained that a flustered man had approached him and said that his daughter had been taken suddenly ill. The man said that his own car wouldn't start, so he was borrowing another of a similar make to get her to hospital; as soon as his mission was accomplished he would return the car. The woman was incensed and ran off to find a policeman. When she returned with the policeman, her car was back where she had left it.

This is not the end of the story. In some versions, the policeman asks her to check her car to make sure that everything is in order. She does this, and finds that her four new tires have been changed for four very used ones. The car-park attendant is charged with running a tire racket. In other versions there are two policemen, an old one and a young one. The old one advises her that, since no harm has been done, she should drop the complaint; the young one asks her to check her car. Again, the tire switch is discovered. The older policeman and the car-park attendant are both charged with theft (Bowman and Hobbs 1990).

Example

My daughter-in-law's friends were going on holiday and took a taxi to the airport. At the check-in, they discovered they'd left their flight tickets at home. There was nothing for it but to go back for them, so the husband took a taxi home. Arriving at his house, he was puzzled to see another taxi parked outside. The house door was open, and they caught their earlier taxi-driver robbing the house. He already had the TV, video, and several other items in his taxi. The police were called and the thief detained. But what if the people hadn't forgotten their tickets? (Bowman and Hobbs 1990)

FURTHER READING

Bowman, Marion and Sandy Hobbs. "Unexpected Returns." *FOAFtale News* 18 (June 1990): 11.

See: The Double Theft; The Theatre Tickets

URBAN JUNGLE BEASTIES

Since at least the 1930s folklorists and "Forteans" (followers of Charles Fort who believed that science was under-documenting the planet's natural phenomena) have noted accounts about pumas, lions, leopards, panthers, various big cats, and "mystery beasts" appearing well outside their natural habitat. Scientists have dismissed such sightings in a variety of ways—they say that the animals were escapees from zoos and menageries, or the witness was mistaken, or the animal was actually an ordinary cat which distance and/or bad light had made to seem unnaturally large, and so on. But the witnesses have been adamant that what they saw was real, clearly visible, and absolutely out of the ordinary.

On August 10, 1982, for example, a Secret Service officer saw a mysterious feline "about half the size of a full-grown lion" loping along Madison Avenue N.W. in Washington, DC, and disappearing behind the Iranian embassy. At the end of May 1984, a huge black panther was seen prowling the streets of Manchester, Michigan, and a few days later one was spied on Long Island, New York, near exit 70 of the expressway. In July of the same year an African lion was sighted in a suburb of Cleveland, Ohio; the following month at least five people saw a black panther near the Fisher Body Plant in Flint, Michigan; and in December of that year people in a suburb of Cincinnati, Ohio, spotted what was variously described as a "mountain lion," or a "roaring lion," or a "Bengal tiger." In February 1985 a 37-year-old man was sitting in a van in Fort Worth, Texas, when he heard a roar. "It was a lion," he said, "and he was big, and he was mad about something" (Coleman 1985, 63–65). Other reports from the United States include accounts of a "lion hunt" in Erie County, Pennsylvania, in June 1993 ("Lion hunt called off"). A later Pennsylvania "mystery cat" scare was monitored by folklorist Bill Ellis. He describes how a woman from Yeadon, Pennsylvania went to her back door to let her Rottweiler dog out, and saw an animal as large as a Great Dane but certainly not a dog (the Rottweiler was scared of it). By the end of the day ten other Yeadon residents had called the police claiming to have seen the animal or heard it growling. At first the reports were dismissed by the police but then a police officer saw an animal he positively identified as a puma sitting on a mound of dirt and wearing a choker chain round its neck. It ran off "doing an easy thirty," and a major hunt was set in motion. By the time the press took up the story, the animal was being called a "cougar," and was said to be "as elusive . . . as a sighting of dear dead Elvis himself" (Ellis 1995, 10).

In Australia, folklorist Bill Scott collected ten "mystery cat" reports from eyewitnesses. In one account, a "tough farmer" and his neighbors saw "a big black panther" near their homes in Eastern Australia; in another, the daughter of a former National Park ranger ran indoors saying she'd seen a big black cat outside the window and the former ranger measured the footprints it had left (each one 4 inches long); in yet another story, an old man remembered having seen "a beast" in the 1930s that sent shivers down his spine (see our example); finally, in 1979 a mountain lion was spotted in Kangaroo Valley and in 1981 a black panther was twice reported as on the loose there. A mountain lion was also reported in 1987 in the Dromana area (Scott 1996, 27–33).

In France during the 1980s there were numerous sightings of big cats and other wild beasts. In the Drôme region, for instance, there were several sightings of a wild beast: at Réauville in December 1988 hunters, firemen, and gendarmes all turned out to hunt a big cat which a 14-year-old boy reported having seen when he was out walking his dog; in a village near Suze-la-Rousse a sports teacher spotted something like a lynx when he was out jogging; and in January 1989 a cabdriver reported that at about 7 o'clock one evening he had seen an animal cross the road in the light from his high beam. It was quite unlike anything known in the local forests; it was about 1.8 meters long, grey on top and white underneath, and it had a long, thin tail. In all, there were about twenty such accounts from France in the 1980s: these included a lion at Noth,

Creuse district (1982); panthers at Pornic, Loire-Atlantique (1982) and Le Touquet, Pas-de-Calais (1986); according to one report, this one was supposed to be feeding off rabbits and small children (Kirkup 1989, 3). Then a puma or a lion was spotted at Var (in 1983, 1987, and 1988). (Campion-Vincent and Renard 1992, 154–157).

In the United Kingdom, there have been persistent reports about the "Surrey Puma" (since 1963), the "Beast of Brassknocker Hill" (since 1979), the "Beast of Bodmin" (since 1992), the "Beast of Sydenham" (2005), the "Exmoor Beast," and the "Durham Puma" ("Family of pumas at large"). An article in the quality Sunday newspaper *The Observer* in 1992 suggested that: "[I]t is believed that exotic cats may have been terrifying British peasants for centuries. One school of thought suggests there may be a native British cat yet to be identified." The author went on to list eighteen regions from Scotland in the north of the United Kingdom to Cornwall in southwest England where big cats were supposedly seen from 1988 to the date of writing. These included a "huge animal with a long flowing tail" (Sussex 1989), a "lynx-like cat" (seen from a train in Hampshire 1985), a "fen tiger" (Cambridge 1990) and, from the Isle of Wight off the south coast of England "reports going back to 1940" (Young 1992, 16).

Example

I'm looking down from the old gate and there was a beast about so high [gesturing]. It was no dog, it was a cat. It was sort of motley brown, dark brown and light brown. It had a round face with white on the front and sides and two ears pricked up and a very long tail. I tell you I could feel shivers down my back. I had no rifle. I had nothing. Anyhow, it just turned round and went away down the brush. I don't know if it was a tiger or a leopard or what it might have been but there was this bloody great thing and, honest to God, I'd seen staghounds and greyhounds and this was as big as any of those. About two foot high at the shoulder but more gut than a greyhound dog, a more flappy gut. And a great big tail.... They reckon it was all bullshit, but I was there. (Scott 1996, 29–30)

FURTHER READING

Campion-Vincent, Véronique, and Jean-Bruno Renard. *Légendes urbaines: Rumeurs d'aujourd'hui*. Paris: Payot, 1992.

Coleman, Loren. *Curious Encounters: Phantom Trains, Spooky Spots, and Other Mysterious Wonders*. Boston, MA: Faber and Faber, 1985.

Ellis, Bill. "Another Pennsylvania Mystery Cat." *FOAFtale News* 36 (January 1995): 9–10.

"Family of Pumas at Large …" *The Northern Echo* [Durham, UK] (May 8, 1992): 6. Reprinted in *Dear Mr Thoms* 30 (April 1993): 23–14.

Kirkup, James "Truth Stranger than Legend: Contemporary Legends in Europe and the Orient." *FOAFtale News* 15 (1989): 2–4.

"Lion Hunt Called Off." *The Hazleton Standard Speaker* (June 3, 1993). Reprinted in *Dear Mr Thoms* 31 (July 1993): 19.

Scott, Bill. *Pelicans and Chihuahuas and Other Urban Legends*. St Lucia, Queensland: University of Queensland Press, 1996.

Sieveking, Paul. "A Field Guide to the Mystery Beasts of the British Isles." *The Independent* [London] (March 26, 2005): 24–25.

Young, Susan. "Are Big Cats on the Prowl in Britain?" *The Observer* [London] (June 14, 1992): 5.

See: Alligators in the Sewers; The March of the Sewer Rats

WHITE SLAVERS

The selling of women and girls for the sex trade has been a real threat in the past. It is estimated, for example, that at any one time in the region of 400 persons earned a living by procuring girls for the trade in Victorian London. They would advertise for "beautiful young girls between twelve and fifteen suitable for adoption"; homeless and jobless girls would reply to these advertisements and be sold into brothels around the world (Rush 1980, 64–67).

The illegal sex trade continues to the present day, but the urban legend "take" on it differs from the reality. In reality it is now mostly impoverished girls from Eastern Europe, the Gulf States, the Philippines, and Indonesia who are entrapped into prostitution abroad by offers of employment in the West. In urban legends, however, the position is reversed. Girls from the United States, Australia, and affluent Western European countries are said to be sold into sex slavery in the East. In the legends, the means of trapping the victims has, of course, to change with the changed circumstances, so it is claimed that girls are abducted from the street, or from restrooms in malls, or fitting rooms in department stores.

The story may be told, for instance, of a little girl who goes to use a restroom while her mother waits outside. Too much time passes, the mother gets worried, and alerts store security. They enter the restroom and find that the girl has had her hair cut and dyed, and is dressed in boy's clothes. She is found just in time; in a few more minutes a "little boy" would have left the restroom and been sold into sex slavery abroad (Langlois 1987, 116).

Legends circulating in Belgium in the 1960s dispensed with the restroom setting and told of girls drugged with sedative-laden needles hidden in gloves sold in high street shops. A helpful store assistant would offer to take the suddenly sick girl to a private room for a rest, but it would all be a trick. Once in the private room the girl would be doomed: she would quickly be sold into the "White Slave" trade (Top 1990, 275). Similar tales had circulated in the United States in the 1920s and 1930s. Again, the women were supposed to be injected with sedatives in a dress shop, or beauty parlor, or theater, and then spirited away into slavery abroad (Brunvand 2001, 478–479).

A common story circulating in Europe during 1940–1960 (perhaps earlier) took an identical form to legends circulating in post–World War II Berlin (Germany) concerning the alleged trade in human flesh. Briefly, in this story a young girl is enticed to a house to deliver a letter. In stories adapted to concerns about white slavers, the letter contains just one word, "Satisfied?" (for the contents of the Berlin letter, see the first example in our discussion of "Urban Cannibals and Human Sausage Factories," see p. 275). The house is raided, the girl is discovered just in the nick of time as the abductors prepare to dope her with tranquillizers; five other girls are found, drugged, and bound, ready to be shipped out for the white slave trade (Barlay 1968, 63–64).

In some countries, especially France where stories of white slavers were circulated widely in the 1960s, they were associated with the garment trade and took on an anti-Semitic cast (Morin 1971; Kapferer 1990). Other "White Slave" rumors born out of prejudice and suspicion include stories told among white people in India in the 1960s about Anglo-Indian girls approached in the street by men purporting to be able to get them jobs as dancers in cabaret shows: the girls signed a contract and found themselves shipped to South America for the sex trade (Sircar 2001, 18); stories also proliferated about women chloroformed on Mexican beaches then sold into sex slavery ("White Slavers in Mexico").

The example below was told to Gillian Bennett in Manchester (UK) in 1982 by a 72-year-old woman who remembered it as a rumor from the 1920s.

Example

Now this about women being made unconscious . . . Now, this would be going back about sixty years—yes, I'll be seventy-two next month. Well, when I was just a schoolgirl, there used to be these tales going around (I think possibly it was done to scare us, to stop us taking unnecessary risks). We were told that people came up to you in the street, you know, and talked to you, asked you directions or something, and then suddenly put a needle in your arm. And that was you, you see, you were in the white slave trade. Oh, we used to hear that regularly. (Bennett Collection)

FURTHER READING

Barlay, Stephen. "The Not-So-Tender Trap." *Penthouse* 3.4 (1968): 63–66.

Brunvand, Jan Harold. *Encyclopedia of Urban Legends*. New York: Norton, 2001.

Kapferer, Jean-Noël. *Rumors: Uses, Interpretations, and Images*. New Brunswick, NJ: Transaction Publications, 1990. See pp. 113–121 and 232–233.

Langlois, Janet. "Urban Legends and the Faces of Detroit." In *Michigan Folklife Reader*. Ed. Kurt C. Dewhurst and Yvonne R. Lockwood. East Lansing, MI: Michigan State University Press, 1987, pp. 107–120.

Morin, Edgar, with the collaboration of Bernard Paillard, Evelyne Burguière, Claude Capulier, Suzanne de Lusignan, and Julia Vérone. *The Rumour in Orléans: Jews Accused of White Slaving: A Modern Myth*. (Trans. Peter Green). London: Anthony Blond, 1971.

Odean, Kathleen. "Slavers in Minnesota: A Psychological Reading of the Legend." *Midwestern Journal of Language and Folklore* 11 (1985): 20–30.

Rush, Florence. *The Best Kept Secret: Sexual Abuse of Children*. Englewood Cliffs, NJ: Prentice Hall, 1980.

Sircar, Sanjay. "Urban Legends from India." *Letters to Ambrose Merton* 25 (Spring 2001): 1–22.

Top, Stefaan. "Modern Legends in the Belgian Oral Tradition: A Report." *Fabula* 31(3/4) (1990): 272–278.

"White Slavers in Mexico." *FOAFtale News* 12 (February 1989): 1.

See: The Castrated Boy; Mall Slashers; The Mutilated Shopper; Urban Cannibals and Human Sausage Factories

HORROR

Horror is the heartland of urban legend. This chapter contains some of the best-known and best-loved stories, the ones that have been used and reused in film and literature and that folklorists have studied most often. Some of them—"The Hairy-Handed Hitchhiker" and "The Hook," for example—are classics. Others—such as "The Cadaver Arm" and "Little Alf's Stamp Collection"—have been around for some considerable time, but are less familiar. Yet others—"Aren't You Glad You Didn't Switch on the Light?" and "Lights Out!"—have only recently emerged or are still emerging. What they have in common is a more than usually outrageous plot concerning more than usually innocent characters. They contain clichéd elements of horror, and conclude in horrific surprises. Violence, blood, mutilation, madness—they're all here, fortunately in unbelievable forms.

Enjoy!

For other tales of horror see: The Blood Libel Legend; The Body in the Bed; The Cadaver Arm; The Cadaver Relative; The Corpse in the Cask; The Hair Curler Revenge; The Mall Abductor; Mall Slashers; "Mary Whales I Believe in You"; The Murdered Son; The Poisoned Dress; Stolen Body Parts; The Superglue Revenge

"AREN'T YOU GLAD YOU DIDN'T SWITCH ON THE LIGHT?"

This story is a development and amalgam of two older student horror stories, "The Doggie Lick" and "The Roommate's Death." In "Aren't you glad you didn't switch on the light?" the psychological situation is the same—a girl is unaware until too late that a killer is on the loose, a companion is dead, and she herself has been in great danger. The social setting is very often the deserted dorm as in "The Roommate's Death," and the climactic ending is an ironic gloating message written on a mirror as in "The Doggie Lick."

A version collected on the Internet in 1997 tells how a girl student was studying late and went back to her room to get some notes she needed. So as not to disturb her roommate she didn't switch the light on, but crept quietly to her desk and took out the papers. When she eventually returned to her room, she found a message on the mirror "Aren't you glad you didn't switch on the light?" The roommate has met a horrific end and lies mangled in the corner.

Our example was collected on the campus of University of Northern Colorado in the fall of 1999.

Example

Hannah: Tanya once told me about this murder that happened at some school her friend went to in Colorado.

Joanne: Not UNC I hope.

Kara: For real.

Hannah: No, not UNC. Anyway, I don't remember exactly how it goes, but I'll try. So like, there's this girl who goes out to some party one night, but her roommate didn't feel like going out. Well, later that night the girl had to get something from her dorm room. She didn't want to wake her roommate so she found it in the dark. The next morning when she came home there were police all around and when she went into her room she found her roommate murdered. Then when she looked in the mirror she saw written in blood, "Aren't you glad you didn't turn on the light?"

Kara: Isn't that in the movie *Urban Legend*?

Hannah: I never saw it.

Joanne: Me neither.

Kara: Wouldn't that freak you out? (Tucker 2005, 91. *Source*: A paper submitted to Professor Rosemary Hathaway by Katy Nellsch and Heather Tinnin)

FURTHER READING

Emery, David. "Aren't you glad you didn't switch on the light?" http://urbanlegend.about.com/library/bllight.htm

Tucker, Elizabeth. *Campus Legends: A Handbook.* Westport, CT: Greenwood Press, 2005.

See: The Doggie Lick; The Roommate's Death

THE ASSAILANT IN THE BACK SEAT

This is not a single legend but a group of related stories sometimes called "The Thug/Killer/Maniac in the Back Seat" that have been circulating in English-speaking countries and Western Europe since the early 1960s.

In its oldest and simplest form it is a story of a motoring nightmare. A woman driver parks her car or is tricked into stopping on the highway, and, unknown to her, a dangerous psychopath gets in through one of the rear doors and crouches down on the back seat where she cannot see him. He reveals his presence only when she has driven for some time and cannot easily stop. The first of our two examples takes this form and was collected from a 20-year-old girl in Stockport (UK) in 1982. Mostly the assailant is not identified, but in one Canadian variant from the 1980s it is supposed to be the Devil himself in the back seat (Rosenberg 1980). More recently the "maniac" is said to be a gang member, about to complete a ritual of rape, kidnapping, or mutilation (Leong 2005).

In alternative versions that have become increasingly popular, the maniac does not reveal his presence but stays hidden in, or sometimes under, the car while he prepares to attack. There are several ways to tell this variant of the story. Sometimes it is said that the driver—usually a girl—is rescued by a quick-thinking pump attendant who has seen the attacker creep into the car. Sometimes the story blends with the "Lights Out!" legend. In this version the girl is scared by another car or a truck, driving threateningly close and blinding her with its high beam. These versions have an ironic twist—the story ends with the terrified girl discovering that the driver who is apparently threatening her is actually trying to rescue her. The real assailant is hiding in the back of the car. The discovery is sometimes brought about when the girl pulls into a gas station and the car or truck pulls in after her to warn her. In other versions she drives all the way home with the driver/trucker following. When she gets home her husband or boyfriend goes to grab him but he points to the maniac in the back seat and together they overpower him. Our second example, which was told by teens in southwest England in the early 1990s, takes this form.

"The Assailant in the Back Seat" provides the initial scare in the film "Urban Legend," and has turned up in "Nightmares" (1983), "Mr Wrong" (1984), and "Suspicions" (1995). It is a favorite with compilers of scary stories (see, for example, Schwartz 1981, 66–68), and it featured in the pilot episode of the popular TV series "Supernatural."

Examples

1. I heard that one about a criminal hiding in a car. Well, that was in, you know the car park in Stockport? There was a man— Well, she didn't see the man at first, he must have been lying down on the floor in the back.

   She got in the car and started it up, then she looked in the mirror and she saw this man behind her, and he had a great big—what do you call it? A great big CLEAVER—that's what he had, and he was sat right behind her!

   She tried to jump out, but she couldn't 'cos of the traffic. And she had to drive on, and she had this THING looking at her in the back. As soon as she had a chance she just DIVED out of the car, and the police got him. That was in STOCKPORT! (Bennett Collection)

2. There's this lady and she's coming home from work quite late and she's on the motorway and there's this little dog and it's in agony, like it's broken its leg or something. So she's pulled over and she's helped it and it's all right again and it starts walking again.

   And she went on in her car. And there's this car right up behind her, really behind her car and the lights are all right on her and she's really scared and this car is following her and it's followed her right up to her house. She got out of her car and ran into her house and she's really scared. And there's a knock at the door, so she opens the door and there's this man and he goes, "I was following you because there was this man who got into your car when you were helping the dog."

   He'd got into the back of the car. (Wilson 1997, 226)

FURTHER READING

Brunvand, Jan Harold. *Encyclopedia of Urban Legends*. New York: Norton, 2001. See pp. 229–230.

Cord, Xenia E. "Further Notes on 'the Assailant in the Back Seat'." *Indiana Folklore* 2.2 (1969): 47–54.

Drake, Carlos. "The Killer in the Back Seat." *Indiana Folklore* 1.1 (1968): 107–109.

"The Killer in the Back Seat." *FOAFtale News* 31 (November 1993): 6.

Leong, Melissa. "Hoax E-mail Makes Toronto Women Fearful: Women's Advocate Forwards Claim of Gang Kidnappings." *National Post* [Toronto] (December 2, 2005), http://www.canada.com/nationalpost/story.html?id=f7953b37-f7a3-4b5f-b014-294dda868ad0-&k=96855

Rosenberg, Neil V. "The Devil in the Back Seat." *Bulletin of the Folklore Studies Association of Canada/Bulletin de l'Association Canadienne pour les Études de Folklore* 4.3 and 4 (1980): 13–19.

Schwartz, Alvin. *Scary Stories to Tell in the Dark Collected from American Folklore*. New York: Lippincott, 1981.

Wilson, Michael. *Performance and Practice: Oral Narrative Traditions among Teenagers in Britain and Ireland*. Aldershot, UK: Ashgate, 1997.

See: Lights Out!; Mall Slashers; The Hairy-Handed Hitchhiker

THE BABY ROAST

Grisly tales of babies being cooked by drugged, drunk, or crazy babysitters have been known since at least the 1940s in America and elsewhere. These, or very similar legends (often called "The Hippie Babysitter"), have been reported from places as far apart as Argentina (Langer 1952), Canada (Fowke 1976, 265), and Micronesia (Mitchell 1973, 187–189). Sometimes they are reported as traditional tales, sometimes as legend or news. Such stories also regularly turn up in popular collection of gross or scary stories (example, Busby 1998, 8–17; Cohen 1983, 33–37). "The Baby Roast" was used as an episode in the 1992 movie "Candyman," in "No Deposit, No Return" ["Hilary's Blues"] (1972), and "Preheat to 425" (2006).

A historical case, apparently a real happening, was reported by British medical historian Roy Porter who had found the account in a 1748 issue of *The Gentleman's Magazine*. It tells how after a christening at Beddington in Surrey the nurse was so drunk that after she had undressed the baby, instead of putting it in its crib, she put it behind the fire. She had been so befuddled with drink that she had mistaken the baby for a log (Porter 1982, 35).

Example

A young couple leave their new baby in the care of a teenage babysitter. When they call up to check that everything's OK, the babysitter says, "Everything's great and I've just put the turkey in the oven for you." They can't understand this, because they're vegetarians! They puzzle and puzzle and eventually decide they'd better leave early and go home to see what's up. They look in the oven, and there's the baby trussed up like a turkey and cooked to a crisp. There's some LSD on the table and the babysitter's on the floor stoned out of her mind (Bennett Collection)

FURTHER READING

Brunvand, Jan Harold. "The Baby-Roast Story as a 'New American Urban Legend'" In *The Study of American Folklore*. 3rd ed. New York: Norton, 1986. See pp. 476–501.

Busby, Cylin. *The Chicken-Fried Rat: Stories Too Gross to Be True*. New York: Harper Trophy, 1998.

Cohen, Daniel. *Southern Fried Rat and Other Gruesome Tales*. New York: M. Evans, 1983.

Fowke, Edith, ed. *Folklore of Canada: Tall Tales, Songs, Stories, Rhymes, Legends, and Jokes from Every Corner of Canada*. Toronto: McClelland and Stewart, 1976.

Langer, Marie. "Le 'mythe de l'enfant roti'." *Revue française de psychanalyse* 16 (1952): 509–517.

Mitchell, Roger E. "Micronesian Folktales." *Asian Folklore Studies* 32 (1973).

Porter, Roy. *English Society in the Eighteenth Century*. Harmondsworth, UK: Pelican, 1982.

See: The Corpse in the Cask; Grandma's Ashes; The Microwaved Pet

THE BABYSITTER AND THE MAN UPSTAIRS

One of the most widespread and popular urban legends, this story has been known since at least the 1960s. It has been told orally, it has appeared in print and online, it has been a favorite in popular compilations of scary stories (Schwartz 1981, 61–71; Young and Dockery Young 1993, 27–30). "The Babysitter and the Man Upstairs" appears in several movies, including "Foster's Release" (1971), "When a Stranger Calls" (1979; 2006), "The Sitter" (1977), "Adventures in Babysitting" (1987), and "The Babysitter" (1995); it also provides an incident in the classic horror film "Urban Legend" (1998) (see the Appendix).

The basic plot is like our first example below, which was collected in Scotland in 1980, but there are countless variants. In some, the police get the girl out of the house before the gruesome murders are found; in some the children are found hanging from the ceiling with their faces chopped off; and in one the baby has been decapitated and the babysitter's hair turns white overnight. In some versions the phone calls are hoaxes perpetrated by one of the children, and in a new twist, a story from 1999 has the child hoaxer kill the babysitter when he is discovered (Jole 1999, 5). There is also a well-known comic version; the anonymous caller does not mention the children, he just says "Bits and pieces" and when the babysitter goes upstairs she finds the children in bits and pieces (Wilson 1997, 224–225).

In storytelling sessions a basic plot can get influenced by film versions and other people's stories. This is what seems to have happened in our second example below, which was part of an oral storytelling session by students at the University of Leicester (UK) in the early 1980s. It is interesting to know, too, that the students said that when they first heard this story, the boys went over to the girls' dorm and started scratching on the windows whispering "Have you checked the children?" (Bennett 1989).

A story about a babysitter and a clown statue started surfacing on the Internet in 2004 which may be a variant on the standard legend. Here the babysitter wants to watch satellite TV but the only TV with satellite service is in the bedroom, so she rings the children's parents to ask permission to use the bedroom, and also, she adds, is it OK to throw a blanket over the clown statue because it's giving her the heebie-jeebies. The parents panic and tell her to call the police as they don't have a clown statue. The "Clown" turns out to be an intruder, and the implication is that he has been biding his time to attack either the children or the babysitter.

Examples

1. There was a babysitter who was looking after three children one night. During the course of the evening she heard strange noises outside so she locked the doors of the house. Shortly after that she had a phone call from a man telling her she should go upstairs to see how the children were. She ignored the phone call and continued watching the television. A short while later the phone rang again and the same voice repeated the message to go upstairs and check the children. She decided to phone the police and they said they would intercept any calls should he phone again. Sure enough the phone rang a third time and the voice insisted that she went upstairs. A minute or two later the police rang telling her to get out of the house as quickly as possible. The girl ran out of the

house screaming. When the police arrived they discovered the three children with their throats cut. The police had traced the phone call to the extension in the upstairs bedroom where the man had lurked, killing one of the children before each phone call. The girl, unknowingly, by locking the doors had locked herself in the house with the killer. (Buchan 1981, 11–12)

2.

Narrator 1. This girl's babysitting, right? And she's sort of downstairs. Put the kids to bed safely and keeps on getting phone calls. Yeah, and somebody saying, "Have you checked the children?" you see ... Anyway, she went upstairs to check, didn't she? And the kids were dead, weren't they?

Narrator 2. And she went down the stairs and the man was there, wasn't he? Yeah.

Narrator 1. And it ended up with the man chasing her to the front door, and she'd bolted it all when the phone calls started coming through to make sure she was safe inside and she just—

Narrator 3. —thinks, "I'll put all these bolts and things." OOOOHH!!—

Narrator 2. —and she just gets out in time, doesn't she?

Narrator 3. Yeah, and she runs into a bloke in front of her. So you think that's the bloke, you know, that's coming to GET her, but it's—

Narrator 2. The police, isn't it?

Narrator 1. That guy is looked after, right? They put him in jail and many years later when she's a mother, there are little children of hers, she gets the same sort of situation. "Have you checked the children?" She's been out, she's been out and she comes in, "Have you checked the children?" and she opens the wardrobe and her husband's dead in the wardrobe. (Bennett Collection)

FURTHER READING

Bennett, Gillian. "Playful Chaos: Anatomy of a Storytelling Session." In *The Questing Beast: Perspectives on Contemporary Legend IV*. Ed. Gillian Bennett and Paul Smith. Sheffield: Sheffield Academic Press for the International Society for Contemporary Legend Research in association with CECTAL, 1989, pp. 193–212.

Buchan, David. "The Modern Legend." In *Language, Culture and Tradition: Papers on Language and Folklore Presented at the Annual Conference of the British Sociological Association, April 1978*. Ed. A. E. Green and J. D. A. Widdowson. CECTAL Conference Papers. Leeds and Sheffield: The Institute of Dialect and Folklife Studies/The Centre for English Cultural Tradition and Language, 1981, pp. 1–15.

Ed. [Keith Cunningham]. "The Upstairs Murderer Rationalized." *Southwest Folklore* 3.1 (1979): 1–2.

Jole, Douglas. "Some Legend Variants." *FOAFtale News* 44 (November 1999): 5–6.

Preston, Cathy Lynn. "Babysitting and the Man Upstairs: Negotiating the 'Politics of Everyday Fear'." *Contemporary Legend* new series 2 (1999): 109–136.

Samuelson, Sue. "'The Man Upstairs': An Analysis of a Babysitting Legend." *Mid-America Folklore* 12.3 (1984): 1–10.

Schwartz, Alvin. *Scary Stories to Tell in the Dark Collected from American Folklore*. New York: Lippincott, 1981.

Wilson, Michael. *Performance and Practice: Oral Narrative Traditions among Teenagers in Britain and Ireland*. Aldershot, UK: Ashgate, 1997.

Young, Richard and Judy Dockery Young. *The Scary Story Reader*. Little Rock, AR: August House, 1993.

See: The Doggie-Lick

THE BATMAN RAPE

This is one of a pair of stories that can be told in two ways—either as a tale of a comic accident (see "Batman Frolics") or as a horror story about rape.

The horror story version, which we call "The Batman Rape," was told in a flurry of intense interest at Columbia University New York in the 1980s at the same time as the comic version was spreading rapidly elsewhere. It formed part of a set of "crime victim" narratives in which the victims were said to have been subjected to rape, muggings, and other violent assaults. The story obviously had homophobic overtones and a racist dimension too, since the rapist in the Batman costume was usually said to be an African-American.

Stephen Winnick, who has written about this story, sees it as one of several on the subject of homosexual rape and/or the deceptions of women. He connects it to stories in Gershon Legman's *No Laughing Matter: The Rationale of the Dirty Joke* (1975, 154), to a betrayal story in the Welsh mythological cycle *The Mabinogion*, and to Clytemnestra's betrayal of Agamemnon in the Greek classics.

Example

A few years ago, a gruesome narrative was in wide circulation among the undergraduates at Columbia University in New York City. According to the tale, a male first year undergraduate is picked up at a neighborhood bar by a woman and accompanies her home. As they are about to enter her apartment, she tells him that she enjoys "kinky sex." He is naive and doesn't really understand what she means until he sees her bedroom, which is full of whips, chains, and other sado-masochistic paraphernalia. He allows himself to be undressed and chained, naked and upside-down, to her bed-frame. At that point, the woman opens the closet, and an enormous black man in a Batman suit jumps out and rapes the helpless student. (Winnick 1992, 1)

FURTHER READING

Winnick, Stephen. "Batman in the Closet: A New York Legend." *Contemporary Legend* 2 (1992): 1–21.

See: Batman Frolics

THE BOYFRIEND'S DEATH

This classic campus horror story has been popular since at least the 1960s and is known throughout Europe, Canada, and the United States. It is a favorite with compilers of scary stories (see, for example, Cohen 1980, 88–93; Schwartz 1981, 61–67), and it still appears in the press or on the Internet as a news item (Moran 2003). It has featured in the popular TV series "Supernatural," and it is thematically related to horror films such as "He Knows You're Alone" (1980), "I Know What You Did Last Summer" (1997), "Urban Legend" (1998), and "Lovers' Lane" (1999). In "Campfire Tales," an anthology film of 1997, a couple are attacked by werewolves and the man is disemboweled; in other respects the tale mirrors the events and details of "The Boyfriend's Death."

In Arizona the story merges with a local legend about "Thump-Thump," a "black and blurry ghost-like thing" that thumps on the roof of parked cars (Ed. 1981). Versions from Sweden often begin by saying that a local girl had a pen pal from Germany, England, or Turkey who suddenly stopped writing. Then sometime later the Swedish girl got a letter from a mutual friend saying that the German/English/Turkish girl had been confined to an institution totally mad (the reason for her insanity is the usual "Boyfriend's Death" story). There is also at least one version where the roles are reversed: the boyfriend stays in the car while the girl goes to seek help and is later found hanging from a tree (Jole 1999, 6).

Elsewhere the legend picks up local characteristics drawn from the scenery or buildings of the area. For example, British folklorist Michael Wilson, collected ten versions of the story from young teenagers in Devon, many of them connected either to the local high-security prison or to local folklore about the "Exmoor Beast" (see "Urban Jungle Beasties" p. 38).

Example

I heard this one off one of my mates in the primary school.

There's just been a newsflash that some madman had escaped from the Dartmoor prison and so everyone was told to lock their windows and doors and everything.

There was a couple driving along in the car and they stopped at a petrol station 'cos they needed some oil, and it was about twelve o'clock at night and—'cos they'd heard the newsflash—the husband said, "Right lock all the windows and doors and when I come back I'll give three knocks and then you can let me in, like that."

So he went away and she waited five minutes, ten minutes, and about an hour later she started getting really worried.

Then she heard three knocks coming on the roof. So she was just about to open the door and the knocks carried on, the knocks didn't stop and she was getting really scared. She saw a dent of like two feet on the roof and the police pulled up and they said, they told her to get out of the car and come quietly and don't look back. So she went along, she looked back and there was a madman from Dartmoor prison, on the roof with an axe in one hand and the bloke's hair in the other, his head as well, banging it up and down on the roof. (Wilson 1997, 205)

FURTHER READING

Barnes, Daniel R. "Interpreting Urban Legends." *Arv* 40 (1986): 67–78. Reprinted in *Contemporary Legend: A Reader*. Compiled by Gillian Bennett and Paul Smith. New York: Garland, 1996, pp. 1–16.

Cohen, Daniel. *The Headless Roommate and Other Tales of Terror*. New York: M. Evans and Company, 1980.

de Vos, Gail. *Tales, Rumors, and Gossip: Exploring Contemporary Folk Literature in Grades 7–12*. Westport, CT: Libraries Unlimited, 1996. See pp. 298–312.

Ed. [Keith Cunningham] "'Mr. Hook' Meets 'Thump-Thump'" *Southwest Folklore* 5.4 (1981): 52–58.

Jole, Douglas. "Some Legend Variants." *FOAFtale News* 44 (November 1999): 5–6.

Moran, Chris. "Monster Legend is Alive and Well in South County: Tale of Hairy Proctor Valley Beast Has Persisted for Years." *Union-Tribune* [San Diego, CA] (August 24, 2003), http://www.signonsandiego.com/news/metro/20030824-9999_1m24monster.html

Schwartz, Alvin. *Scary Stories to Tell in the Dark Collected from American Folklore*. New York: Lippincott, 1981.

Wilson, Michael. *Performance and Practice: Oral Narrative Traditions Among Teenagers in Britain and Ireland*. Aldershot, UK, UK: Ashgate, 1997.

See: The Assailant in the Back Seat; The Hairy-Handed Hitchhiker; The Hook

THE CADAVER ARM

This classic medical students' legend has been round since at least 1945 when Ernest Baughman noted its appearance at Indiana University (Baughman 1945). In the same year, story compiler Bennett Cerf also told the tale in *The Saturday Review of Literature* (Cerf 1959). Since that time it has been told all over the English-speaking world. The legend is about a group of medical students who are having their first experience of the dissecting room. They steal a body part and use it to play a trick on somebody else—with horrific results. There are several variants.

In one version, the students take an arm, put a quarter between its fingers, and offer it to a tollbooth attendant as they exit the campus. He dies of shock. In another version, they take a hand or a foot, and tie it to the doorknob or light switch in a fellow student's room, or put it in his/her bed; the victim is later found dead with the hand clutching his/her throat, or white-haired, stark mad, and nibbling on the stolen body part (Bronner 1990, 159–162).

In folktale indexes, the story is usually classified as one of several types where the victim dies of fright as the result of a heartless practical joke. A large number of this story-type feature fraternity/sorority initiation rites. And this is the third way to tell the legend of "The Cadaver Arm." Richard M. Dorson, for example, has a tale in which a sorority pledge is blindfolded and told to shake hands with a pickled hand that the initiates have "borrowed" from a university laboratory (Dorson 1959, 259). It is possible that this is the older form of the story since Jan Brunvand's *Encyclopedia of Urban Legends* notes that a Spanish novel of 1928, *The Tree of Knowledge*, has an incident where a student offers another person a cadaver hand to shake (Brunvand 2001, 447).

Of course, as an element of a horror story rather than the whole of one, there are much older examples. For example, in John Webster's Jacobean shocker, *The Duchess of Malfi*, first staged in 1612, the imprisoned Duchess is tortured this way by one of her mad and wicked brothers. The scene is played in the dark. The brother pretends he has brought her husband to her and offers a hand for her to kiss: "Here's a hand to which you have vowed much love," he says and proffers a dead man's hand. Upon touching it, the Duchess shrieks and calls for lights. When the lights are turned on, she and the audience realize that she has been attempting to kiss the hand of a corpse (Act 4, scene 1).

During the 1960s and 1970s, the most frequently collected variant was the "roommate-going-mad" story. Versions from this period can be found in the work of American folklorists Daniel R. Barnes, Simon Bronner, and Alan Dundes, and in Canadian folklorist Edith Fowke's collection of Canadian folklore (Fowke 1976, 265–266). The story has also been collected from Australia and the United Kingdom (see, for example, Dale 1978, 76–78; Scott 1996, 151; Smith 1986, 79–80).

Example

The most common variation of "The Cadaver Arm"... often involves a novice medical student or student nurse who doesn't quite cut it. In most versions the student is also given antisocial characteristics; he or she is an arrogant snob, a loner, a grind, a braggart, or a snoop. From Berkeley, for example, comes this account: "This is a new med student. He went out on a date and got back late and his roommate and a bunch of the fellas decided to play a trick on him. This guy was really struggling and he was a new student, and the pressure of it all. And they didn't like him very well—he was kind of a study type—he worked late in the lab and he was really trying and he was kind of a teacher's pet kind of creature, not a very strong character. And they put the hand of one of the cadavers that they had worked on that day in his bed. And they're all waiting for some huge noise or something and nothing really happens. So they go in, and they find him and he's sitting in the closet chewing on the hand and his hair's all white." (Bronner 1990, 159)

FURTHER READING

Barnes, Daniel R. "Some Functional Horror Stories on the Kansas University Campus." *Southern Folklore Quarterly* 30 (1966): 305–312.

Baughman, Ernest W. "The Cadaver Arm." *Hoosier Folklore Bulletin* 4.2 (1945): 30–32.

Bronner, Simon J. *Piled Higher and Deeper: The Folklore of Campus Life*. Little Rock, AR: August House, 1990. See pp. 159–162.

Brunvand, Jan Harold. *The Baby Train*. New York: Norton, 1993. See pp. 315–317.

———. *Encyclopedia of Urban Legends*. New York: Norton, 2001.

Cerf, Bennett. "Trade Winds." *Saturday Review of Literature* 24 (March 1945): 16–17. Reprinted in *Bennett Cerf's Bumper Crop of Anecdotes and Stories, Mostly Humorous, About the Famous and Near-Famous*. 2 vols. New York: Garden City Books, 1959. See vol. 2, p. 316.

Dale, Rodney. *The Tumour in the Whale: An Hilarious Collection of Apocryphal Anecdotes*. London: W. H. Allen: Universal Books, 1978.

Dorson, Richard M. *Modern Folklore*. American Folklore. Chicago: University of Chicago Press, 1959.

Dundes, Alan. "On the Psychology of Legend." *American Folk Legend: A Symposium*. Ed. Wayland D. Hand. Berkeley, CA: University of California Press, 1971, pp. 21–36. See esp. pp. 31–32.

Fowke, Edith, ed. *Folklore of Canada: Tall Tales, Songs, Stories, Rhymes, Legends, and Jokes from Every Corner of Canada*. Toronto: McClelland and Stewart, 1976.

Scott, Bill. *Pelicans and Chihuahuas and Other Urban Legends*. St Lucia, Queensland: University of Queensland Press, 1996.

Smith, Paul. *The Book of Nastier Legends*. London: Routledge and Kegan Paul, 1986.

See: The Cadaver Relative; Death from Fear

THE CASTRATED BOY

This is one of several gruesome tales that are located at shopping malls. Here, the story is that the boy is attacked in the men's restroom of a department store while the mother waits outside. When the boy fails to return, a male staff member is sent into the restroom and finds him lying in a pool of blood, mutilated, and sometimes dying. If the reason for this mutilation is given—and that is not always the case—"gangs" are supposed to be doing this as part of an initiation ritual, or "cults" are sacrificing him as part of a religious ceremony.

Folklorists who have collected and studied this legend have often seen it either in Freudian terms (see Carroll 1987), or as part of the infamous "Blood Libel Legend" (see Ridley 1967), or as a racist rumor (Langlois 1987). The victim is nearly always said to be a white child (often blond) between 4 and 10 years old. Occasionally he is supposed to have been attacked in a public park, or in downtown public toilets, or the restroom of a shopping mall. The legend has been particularly prevalent in the United States and United Kingdom, and peaked in popularity from the 1960s to the 1980s. The example below was reported from Barnsley, Yorkshire (UK) in 1984.

Example

One day a ten-year-old boy went shopping with his mother. He needed to go to the toilet so his mother let him go to a public toilet in the shopping precinct. When he did not come back, she began to get worried. A policeman was passing by, so she stopped him and she explained what had happened. The officer went over to the toilet block to look for the boy, and found him lying in a pool of blood in one of the cubicles, with a crowd around him. He was still alive but was in a highly critical condition. According to an eye witness, the poor boy had been castrated by an ethnic gang. (Smith Collection)

FURTHER READING

Brunvand, Jan Harold. *The Mexican Pet: More "New" Urban Legends and Some Old Favorites.* New York: Norton, 1986. See pp. 151–156.

Carroll, Michael P. "'The Castrated Boy': Another Contribution to the Psychoanalytic Study of Urban Legends." *Folklore* 98 (1987): 216–225.

Langlois, Janet. "Urban Legends and the Faces of Detroit." *Michigan Folklife Reader.* Ed. Kurt C. Dewhurst and Yvonne R. Lockwood. East Lansing, MI: Michigan State University Press, 1987, pp. 107–120.

Ridley, Florence H. "A Tale Told Too Often." *Western Folklore* 26 (1967): 153–156.

See: Mall Slashers; The Mutilated Shopper; White Slavers

THE DOGGIE-LICK

This story, which is sometimes called "Humans Can Lick Hands Too," has been told in America, Canada, and Europe for ghoulish thrills since at least the 1980s and it has remained popular ever since. It tells of an intruder under a girl's bed, first imitating her pet dog by licking her hand, then killing the dog and leaving a chilling message on the wall or the bathroom mirror. Some versions, like those collected by folklorist Simon Bronner, include the spooky phone calls detail common in stories such as "The Babysitter and the Man Upstairs" (Bronner 1988, 150–152).

Two interesting new versions turned up at the beginning of the twenty-first century. One is simply a more elaborated version of the original story. The girl already knows there is a murderer at large because she has read about it in the newspaper. So, when she goes to bed she takes Rover the dog with her. She instructs Rover to lick her hand once if the murderer is on the street, to lick twice if he is on the lawn, three times if he is in the house, and four times if he is in the room. The dog licks, once, twice, three times, but she ignores him, rolls over, and goes back to sleep. Only when Rover licks her hand four times does she get up and switch the light on. There is no sign of the murderer, but she finds the dog stabbed in the chest and hanging from the showerhead. And there is a message for her written in the dog's blood, "People can lick too!"

The second version, which is sent by e-mail, proceeds in the conventional way. The girl is alone and, as her parents instructed, has locked all the windows (except one she can't fasten properly) and barred all the doors. She takes the dog upstairs with her and, every time she is disturbed in the night, she reaches down and the dog licks her hand reassuringly. The story ends in the usual way, but then suddenly turns into a chain letter:

> Now it is time for you to lock all the windows and doors. This letter is the only chain letter that is true. This did happen many years ago, and the man who killed the dog was never caught. If you delete this letter you will suffer the same fate as the girl in the story did, years after the dog was killed. She was raped and killed in the same town and same house as the dog. Do not dismiss this letter, because if you do, a horrible thing will become of you, everyone will soon know your name. But only because it will be the headline of your local newspaper for a long time. It will read "Small Town Murderer On The Loose!" You can not chance your luck on a chain letter so serious as this. Give up your chance to send this letter to 23 people and you will be giving up your chance to live. You were warned. I hope that I will not see any murder stories in the papers anytime soon. And now I bid you a good day. And one more thing . . . you only have 23 minutes. . . . Sorry.

In the 1980s English folklorist Michael Wilson collected seven versions of the "Doggie Lick" story from teenagers in southwest England, several of them located on Dartmoor, a wild and forbidding area where a notorious prison is located. They all end with a punch line: in two of them this is "Guess who licked your hand last night?"; in three it is "Humans [or Men] can lick too"; in one it is "The devil can lick too" (Wilson 1997, 209–213).

One of the English teenagers' stories, however, is told as a comic story: the main body of the narrative is full of the typical atmospheric effects of horror stories but ends, amid laughter, with the absurd anticlimax "and there was a man there that was licking her hand." This treatment of the theme connects the legend to older tales told as humorous anecdotes. For example, in a Russian story a husband returning home late one evening gets into bed with his wife and, hearing something scratching under the bed, puts his hand down to the dog and asks, "Is that you, Jack?" The wife's lover, who is hiding under the bed, replies, "Yes, it's me" and licks his hand (E. A. Warner, personal communication). This treatment of the theme is echoed in a cartoon from the 1950s that shows an adulterous couple in bed, the dog snoozing quietly at the foot of the bed, and the husband under the bed licking the lover's hand; the caption is "Fido likes you, doesn't he?"

An early version of this tale comes from sixteenth-century London. The seducer is in bed with the beautiful wife and the husband is hiding under the bed in a fit of cowardice brought on by hearing the seducer say he has killed three men. When the husband gets restless and starts fidgeting, the seducer asks the wife what's under the bed. She replies that it is a little pet sheep. To authenticate this lie the husband says "Baaa" (Zall 1963, 130–131).

Example

There was a lady who lives in a little cottage up on the top of a hill and about half past nine she goes up to bed and every night, when she goes to bed, she hangs her hand over the bed and the dog would lick her hand to sleep.

So she goes to bed, she puts her hand down and she goes to sleep.

She wakes up in the morning and the dog is just all splattered around the room. There's blood all up the walls, his head's on the end of the bed and his legs are hanging off, and the wall it's got in blood, "Guess who licked your hand last night?" (Wilson 1997, 210)

FURTHER READING

Bronner, Simon J. *American Children's Folklore*. Little Rock, AR: August House, 1988.

Fowke, Edith, ed. *Folklore of Canada: Tall Tales, Songs, Stories, Rhymes, Legends, and Jokes from Every Corner of Canada*. Toronto: McClelland and Stewart, 1976. See p. 266.

Smith, Paul. *The Book of Nasty Legends*. London: Routledge and Kegan Paul, 1983.

Wilson, Michael. *Performance and Practice: Oral Narrative Traditions among Teenagers in Britain and Ireland*. Aldershot.: Ashgate, 1997.

Zall, P. M., ed. *One Hundred Merry Tales*. Lincoln.: University of Nebraska Press, 1963.

See: AIDS Aggressors (Mirrors); "Aren't You Glad You Didn't Turn on the Light?"; The Choking Doberman

THE HAIRY-HANDED HITCHHIKER

This classic modern horror story about a motorist who finds that the "old lady" he/she has kindly given a ride to is actually a murderer in disguise has been reported from South Africa, Silesia, Germany, Holland, and France. It appeared in the advice column of an Australian newspaper in 1987 ("Still Horrified Brisbane"), and it was well enough known in the 1930s to feature in journalist Alexander Woollcott's column in *The New Yorker* (Woollcott 1933).

The 1980s probably saw the peak of interest in this story, no more so than in the United Kingdom, where the would-be assailant was usually identified as "The Yorkshire Ripper," a serial killer who was being urgently pursued by the police. Gillian Bennett first heard the story at this time from a friend who had heard it from a colleague at a Tameside (UK) hospital. The friend reported that he had told his colleague that it sounded like a folktale to him. The colleague, however, was puzzled and insisted that he had missed the point, "It was HIM . . . don't you SEE?" she asserted.

It was at this time, too, that the strangest variant of the legend was told. It seems to be a melding of the "Hairy-Handed Hitchhiker" story with stories of the party-going ghost variety of "The Vanishing Hitchhiker" legend and perhaps with "The Devil at the Disco." The story went that, while a group of girls were at a disco in a town near the border of Yorkshire and the neighboring county, they met a nice young girl who was there on her own. At the end of the evening, she was offered a ride home with the others. One by one the girls arrived home and were dropped off, leaving just the driver and the girl they had met at the disco. As they drove along alone, the driver noticed that the other girl had hairy hands. Panic set in. The driver deliberately stalled the car, got the other girl to get out and push, then drove off fast. A small axe was later found in the car where the "girl" had been sitting (Buchan 1981, 9).

With few exceptions, modern versions all concentrate on the discovery of a weapon and a coil of rope in the basket "the old lady" is carrying, which confirm the driver's suspicions that the "old lady" is actually an axe-murderer or a homicidal maniac. However, older versions of the story (told in the days of the horse-and-cart) often feature a male driver, and the motive for the "old lady's" disguise is highway robbery. Another difference is that, often as not, it is not the "old lady's" hands that are the giveaway but the beard or stubbly chin hidden under a bonnet or shawl. In a version from Michigan, recorded by folklorist Richard M. Dorson, for example, a man driving a horse and buggy through a swamp sees an old lady by the road and offers her a ride. She is using a walking stick, wearing an old-fashioned bonnet, and carrying a little basket. During the journey the horse is frightened and rears up, almost tipping the old lady out; her bonnet slips back to reveal a stubbly chin. The buggy-driver lets his own hat fall off, and asks "Grandma" to get down and pick it up for him. He drives off without her, and when he gets home finds two pistols and $800 in cash in her basket (Dorson 1956, 97–100).

German folklorist and urban legend collector Rolf Wilhelm Brednich quotes an account in a German newspaper of 1896 which tells of the adventure of a wine merchant from northern France on a business trip to Belgium. He is carrying a good deal of money when an old lady totters up and asks for a ride. The story ends when the businessman sees her hairy hands and pulls off the old lady's hood to reveal "the bearded face of a strong man." Later he discovers a revolver, a dagger, and a hammer in her basket (quoted in Schmidt 2000, 2). A similar English version comes from an even earlier date. It tells how a named Derbyshire man encounters an old lady late one night and offers her a ride in his cart. He soon spots her masculine-looking hands, drops his glove, and asks her to get down from the cart to pick it up for him. He whips up his horse and speeds off without her, certain he has just escaped the clutches of a highway robber. The man named as the hero of this tale was a real person who died in 1884, so that fixes the date of his story to the mid-century (Perkins 1982, 42–43).

Returning to our own day and age, versions circulated on the Internet in 2003 which take the story away from these sorts of mundane explanations and give it an almost supernatural feel. In these stories the girl driver finds the old lady in the back of her car in the mall and calls the security guard. He ejects the old lady from the car, and takes her home. The girl continues on her way. Under some newspapers on the back seat she finds a hammer, an axe, and a spade, which she throws into the street. After that she always makes sure her car doors are locked, but one day she comes back to her car and sees the old lady sitting there as before—"I've come for my things, Dearie," says the old lady with a sinister smile. This creepy ending, which suggests that the old woman was not only dangerous but otherworldly, combines the usual plot with a detail common in children's scary stories; that is, the dead person who returns for stolen property.

The first story below was one of four told-for-true in or near Yorkshire (UK) in the early 1980s; the second is a humorous one told by a group of students in the English midlands a few years later, when "The Yorkshire Ripper" scare had died down.

Examples

1. I tell you what I was told. I thought it was absolutely dreadful. It was a rumor that was going about, and I was told. Some time ago . . . I'm trying to remember the details . . . Some woman had parked her car in Kendal's [department store] car park and when she went back to the car she found a funny old lady sitting in the car. Have you heard this? And she pleaded and begged for a ride. She said she had to get somewhere and she wanted a ride, and this person gave her a ride.

   And then, when they were sitting in the car, she noticed that the hands weren't a woman's hands. It was a MAN dressed up as an old lady. So this person was very clever, and she realized that it wasn't a real old lady so she stopped the car and made some excuse to get the old lady out of the car somehow or other. You know, tricked them into getting out of the car, slammed the door, and drove off.

   But it wasn't an old lady, it was a man. We were told the police were looking for this person. (Bennett Collection)

2.

   Student 1. Well, there's this woman and she's picked up this guy. Well, she doesn't know he's a guy, He thinks she is a little old lady, and he's got her in the car. And it's really raining hard and they're in the middle of a wood. The old lady's holding a handbag and the woman notices she's got really hairy hands. She realizes something weird is going on! GRRR! So she pretends she's burst a tire and puts the car into a skid, and gets her to get out and have a look.

   Student 2. The little old lady?

   Student 1. Yeah, the little old lady. It's a "him" really, you see!

   Student 2. I know, but how can she say, "OK, you little old lady. You've got to change the bloody wheel!"

   Student 1. Well it's a guy, so please—You're ruining it!

   Student 2. It's not feasible!

   Student 1. Anyway, she goes burning off, and afterwards she finds a rope and an axe in the old lady's handbag. (Bennett Collection)

FURTHER READING

Barnes, Daniel R. "Interpreting Urban Legends." *Arv* 40 (1986): 67–78. Reprinted in *Contemporary Legend: A Reader.* Compiled by Gillian Bennett and Paul Smith. New York: Garland, 1996, pp. 1–16.

Buchan, David. "The Modern Legend." *Language, Culture and Tradition: Papers on Language and Folklore Presented at the Annual Conference of the British Sociological Association, April 1978.* Ed. A. E. Green and J. D. A. Widdowson. CECTAL Conference Papers. Leeds and Sheffield: The Institute of Dialect and Folklife Studies/The Centre for English Cultural Tradition and Language, 1981, pp. 1–15. See p. 9.

Dorson, Richard M. *Negro Folktales in Michigan.* Cambridge, MA: Harvard University Press, 1956.

Perkins, Elizabeth M. *A Tree in the Valley.* Bognor Regis, UK: New Horizon, 1982.

Schmidt, Sigrid "The Hairy-Handed Hitchhiker and His Relatives in South Africa." *FOAFtale News* 47 (October 2000): 1–3.

Seelhorst, Mary. "'The Assailant in Disguise': Old and New Functions of Urban Legends about Women Alone in Danger." *North Carolina Folklore Journal* 34 (1987): 29–37.

"Still Horrified Brisbane." Letter to Christine Cameron's "What's Your Problem?" column. *The Courier Mail* [Brisbane, Australia] (July 14, 1987): 20.

Woollcott, Alexander. "Story-Teller's Holiday," "Shouts and Murmurs" column. *The New Yorker* (April 15, 1933): 26.

See: The Assailant in the Back Seat; The Boyfriend's Death

THE HOOK

This urban legend classic has been reported since at least the 1950s and is known throughout the English-speaking world and in many parts of Europe too. It has been told at scout camps, summer camps, and slumber parties; and by students everywhere. As well as being told orally, it has appeared in a large number of popular compilations of legends and horrors (see, for example, Schwartz 1981, 61–63), and in films, including "Meatballs" (1979), "Candyman" (1992), "I Know What You Did Last Summer" (1997), "Urban Legend" (1998), and "Lovers' Lane" (1999). It has been a major influence on "slasher" movies, and has featured in "anthology films" such as "Campfire Tales" (1991; 1997).

Example

There was this young couple and they were parked in a wood . . . in the back seat, you know?

They had the radio on playing smoochy music and suddenly the broadcast was interrupted by a warning about a maniac. He was on the loose. He had escaped from the local lunatic asylum and everybody was being warned to be careful. You'd know it was him 'cos he had a hook for a hand and was very dangerous.

Well, the asylum was near to this wood so the girl freaked out and said she wasn't staying any longer and he'd got to take her home. Well, she was screaming and crying (she was scared, you know), and he was swearing and cussing 'cos he was so disappointed.

So, anyway, in the end he just slammed the car into gear and roared off. Screeched to a stop outside the girl's home, jumped out still in a temper, shouting about how silly she was, and how she'd spoiled it all, etc. And there was a hook hanging off the door handle! (Bennett Collection)

FURTHER READING

Barnes, Daniel R. "Some Functional Horror Stories on the Kansas University Campus." *Southern Folklore Quarterly* 30 (1966): 305–312.

Ellis, Bill. "'The Hook' Reconsidered: Problems in Classifying and Interpreting Adolescent Horror Legends." *Folklore* 105 (1994): 61–75.

Schwartz, Alvin. *Scary Stories to Tell in the Dark Collected from American Folklore*. New York: Lippincott, 1981.

Tucker, Elizabeth. *Campus Legends: A Handbook*. Westport, CT: Greenwood Press, 2005. See pp. 87–88.

See: The Boyfriend's Death; The Hairy-Handed Hitchhiker

LIGHTS OUT!

The story of the "Lights Out" gang initiation ritual spread throughout the United States by word of mouth, photocopy, fax, e-mail, and media accounts during the summer and fall of 1993. It warned that a mysterious and vicious gang initiated new members by making them drive round at night with their lights either off or on high beam. When other motorists flashed their headlights in warning or protest, they became the target for the ritual; the initiate was then supposed to follow that driver home and murder him or her. A "Blood Initiation" weekend was supposed to occur during 25/26 September when the "well-known Bloods Gang" took in new members.

The rumor seems to have started in Memphis, then rapidly spread to Chicago, Boston, Harrisburg, Irvine, Pittsburgh, and Wichita. In Pittsburgh, the authorities reacted by alerting 5,000 employees of the city's schools. The rumor struck particularly hard in Massachusetts, Illinois, Michigan, New York State, California, and Texas. No incidents were reported over the weekend, of course, but that didn't stop the story quickly spreading to Central America where it caused panic in Mexico and Guatemala.

The panic died down for a time, then was revived. This time, the story was quickly debunked, but nevertheless it spread rapidly, and was reported in the press in Ottawa (Canada), also in San Diego, Santa Fe, Milwaukee, Pittsburg, and other parts of the United States between 1998 and 1999.

The story continues to be told on the Internet and via e-mail messages warning of initiation rituals of the "Blood Gang" or a "Blood Initiation Weekend." It has spread to the United Kingdom, where it takes the form of a hoax e-mail supposedly from the London Ambulance Service, which has been forced to issue a formal denial.

Example

Beware!!
There is a new Gang initiation!!
This new initiation of murder is brought about by Gang Members driving around at night with their car lights off. When You flash your car lights to signal them that their lights are out, the Gang Members take it literally as "LIGHTS OUT," so they follow you to your destination and kill you! That's their initiation.
Two families have already fallen victim to this initiation ritual. Be aware and inform your families and friends.
Do not flash your car lights for anyone!!

Barbara Mikkelson, whose discussion on the Snopes website is probably the most informative, suggests that the legend is likely to be an update of a 1980s scare about Hell's Angels, riding about dazzling car drivers with their high beam and committing murder, again as part of an initiation ritual.

This story is basic to the 1998 horror film "Urban Legend." Some familiarity with this story is also important for understanding modern variants of "The Assailant in the Back Seat."

The example is a flyer circulating in Chicago in early September 1993, and reproduced in *FOAFtale News* 31.

FURTHER READING

"Lights Out Gang Initiation." "Just In" column. *FOAFtale News* 31 (November 1993): 5–6.

Mikkelson, Barbara. "Lights Out!" http://www.snopes.com/horrors/madmen/lightsout. asp

See: The Assailant in the Back Seat; Mall Slashers

LITTLE ALF'S STAMP COLLECTION

This classic wartime atrocity story, sometimes referred to as "The Message under the Stamp," circulated in Germany and the United Kingdom during the First World War, and was widely believed to be true. Though the story was absolutely without foundation, it has provided the model for atrocity claims in subsequent conflicts. Over time, many rumors about horrendous mutilations have circulated, but this one—which seems to have been first reported in 1917 in the respected British newspaper *The Guardian*—took off and came to symbolize the brutality of war. Briefly the story line is that a family receives a letter from a relative in an enemy prisoner of war camp. He says he is OK and is being treated quite well; then, in a "PS," he asks them to steam off the stamp for Little Alf's stamp collection. There is no Little Alf in the family, and nobody has a stamp collection, but they steam off the stamp anyway. Hidden under the stamp they find a message about a horrifying mutilation, "They have torn out my tongue."

The story was revived in November 1942 during World War II, and took America by storm. It was first heard in Chicago, then rapidly spread to New York and New England. It was picked up by Gallup Poll interviewers in Illinois, New Mexico, Wisconsin, San Francisco, Ohio, Oregon, Idaho, Montana, Alaska, and Washington. It was circulated so widely in Nashville, Tennessee that the local newspaper went to considerable lengths to try to trace it. It even offered a reward of $1,000 for the original letter. No one came forward to claim the reward.

The story of "Little Alf's Stamp Collection" has been used many times in war to exemplify the barbarity of the opposing forces both as an army and as a people, though of course the nationality of the perpetrators of this horror changes according to which side the narrator is on. A more recent appearance of this legend is as a cartoon in *The Big Book of Urban Legends*. Called "The message under the stamp," it shows the arrival of a letter from Saigon written by an American soldier during the Vietnam war—again with the same shocking message hidden under the stamp (Fleming and Boyd 1994, 76).

However, the legend seems to have originated much earlier than any of these conflicts. David Jacobson, who did a great deal of research on it for his postwar book on rumor (1948), traced it to the American Civil War. "In those early days," he says, "Little Alf was no more than a Confederate lad, a prisoner in a northern prison camp, who wrote to his mama in the South" (Jacobson 1948, 293). He says it also circulated during the Franco-Prussian War of 1870–1871.

The mutilation varies very little from account to account: tearing out tongues is the clear favorite, followed by gouging out eyes. Accusations about the amputation of limbs, especially hands and feet, are sometimes mentioned in these stories, and certainly appear in many other claims of wartime atrocities both in the past and in recent times. Chapter 8 of Jacobson's *The Affairs of Dame Rumor* gives an authoritative and deeply disturbing description of wartime legends about fearful mutilations and other atrocities. The example below is taken from this book.

Example

[In 1918] a clergyman was seated in a local restaurant. Opposite him at the table a stranger recited the rumor with all the drama and dogma of a religious fanatic,

"This friend of mine's boy," the stranger at first confided, "is in a Boche prison camp. He sends a letter home and tells how things are all right with him and all that. It seems he likes everything, even the stamp on his letter. That stamp, he tells his ma, is a rare one and she ought to soak it off for little Alf's stamp collection.

"Now," the stranger revealed, "they ain't got no little Alf in the whole family. But my friend does what their boy says. They steam off that stamp."

The stranger's eyes glistened. His lips became thin and taut and he said, "Underneath the stamp they find a message that the boy couldn't put in his letter."

The man seemed completely overcome by the emotional impact of his own story. His voice had become shrill and every word was emphasized as though he wanted everyone within earshot to keep it in his mind forever. "It says," he went on, "they have torn out my tongue." (Jacobson 1948, 287–288)

FURTHER READING

Fleming, Robert Loren, and Robert F. Boyd Jr. *The Big Book of Urban Legends*. New York: Paradox Press, 1994.

Jacobson, David J. *The Affairs of Dame Rumor*. New York: Rinehart and Company, 1948.

THE ROOMMATE'S DEATH

This classic legend has been a campus favorite in Europe, Canada, and America since at least the 1950s. It is one of the most collected and most studied horror stories among folklorists. It is equally popular with compilers of scary stories (for example, Schwartz 1984, 49; Young and Dockery Young 1993, 39–41), and a version appears in the film "Urban Legend" (1999). It has also made an appearance in the popular TV series "Supernatural."

The story usually features girl students who for some reason have stayed on in their dorm after the other girls have returned to their families. The staple features of the story are the knocking on the door, the scratching and gasping in the hallway, the bloody fingers, and the dead roommate. Other embellishments may be a maniac with an axe, a message written in blood, or the survivor going mad and/or having her hair turn white overnight. The story can be told for gruesome thrills or become the focus of jokes and hoaxes, as folklorist Sylvia Grider demonstrates in an essay which describes an outbreak of storytelling about a "Hatchet Man" in an Indiana University freshman dorm (Grider 1980).

A British folklorist has found a short story written in 1925 featuring this legend, or something very similar. A man is dared to stay alone all night without a light in a haunted house. His friends leave him a scary story to read. After he has read it he accidentally extinguishes his candle and he is left in total darkness. When his friends enter the room disguised as ghosts to scare him he shoots them in terror. The story he has been left to read is about two sisters who have been left alone in a house in London. They hear a noise downstairs and one of them goes to investigate, locking the other one in the bedroom. She hears footsteps approaching, the door is unlocked and the footsteps approach the bed. She reaches down and touches the fur on the bottom of her sister's robe, then faints in horror. In the morning their father finds that terror and shock has turned one daughter into a white-haired madwoman. The other one has had her head half sawn off by a homicidal lunatic lurking downstairs. Then, clad in her blood-stained robe, she has dragged herself upstairs to try to warn her sister (Shearman 1989, 8–9).

The story below was told on Western Kentucky University campus in the mid-1960s.

Example

During the semester break, all but two of the girls in the dormitory went home. It was a cold, windy night and the girls, alone in the large dormitory, were afraid to leave each other.

During the night, they heard numerous dragging sounds and became even more jumpy. After talking for some time, one of the girls decided to stop being foolish and go to her room on the floor below the one in which she was staying, to get some books. She told her friend not to unlock the door until she heard three knocks.

Her friend, waiting in the room, became worried after almost an hour had passed. Later, she heard a scratching sound at the door and became terrified as it persisted. Afraid to move, she sat huddled in a corner until she finally fell asleep. Waking early the next morning, she went to the door to unlock it, planning to go after her friend.

She opened the door to see her friend lying dead in a pool of blood and several bloody scratch marks on the door. (Tucker 2005, 88)

FURTHER READING

Barnes, Daniel R. "Some Functional Horror Stories on the Kansas University Campus." *Southern Folklore Quarterly* 30 (1966): 305–312. See p. 307.

Bronner, Simon J. *Piled Higher and Deeper: The Folklore of Campus Life.* Little Rock: August House, 1990. See pp. 170–172.

Conrad, JoAnne. "Stranger Danger: Defending Innocence, Denying Responsibility." *Contemporary Legend* new series 1 (1998): 97–115.

Grider, Sylvia. "The Hatchet Man." In *Indiana Folklore: A Reader.* Ed. Linda Dégh. Bloomington, IL: Indiana University Press, 1980. 147–178.

Maynard, Lara. "Locked Doors: Bearer-Centred Interpretation of 'The Roommate's Death' and Other Contemporary Legends." *Contemporary Legend* new series 1 (1998): 97–115.

Schwartz, Alvin. *More Scary Stories to Tell in the Dark.* New York: Harper and Row, 1984.

Shearman, A. M. "Some Continuities in Literary Survival and Folk Memory." *Motif* 9(1) (1989): 8–10.

Tucker, Elizabeth. *Campus Legends: A Handbook.* Westport, CT: Greenwood Press, 2005. See pp. 88–93.

Young, Richard and Judy Dockery Young. *The Scary Story Reader.* Little Rock.: August House, 1993.

See: The Babysitter and the Man Upstairs; The Boyfriend's Death; The Doggie-Lick

3

ACCIDENTS, FATE, AND CHANCE

The stories in this chapter share many themes and story elements. Most are comical, though often the comedy is of a pretty crude or cruel variety. Accidents and actions which in other legends are taken seriously (deaths, dirt, bodily harm, revenge, cruel turns of fate, sexual misunderstandings, and social embarrassments) are here made a joke of. Men get glued to the toilet, or have the toilet explode when they sit on it, and girls find themselves catapulted down ski slopes with their panties round their ankles. Respectable ladies are betrayed into theft, jealous husbands are betrayed into vandalism, and tricksters find the tables turned on them. Men who cheat at sex find themselves cheated of an inheritance, and suicides escape with their own lives but unintentionally take someone else's. The world depicted in these legends is as remorseless as it is surprising and funny.

There are other stories that similarly involve bizarre and cruel twists of fate, but what distinguishes the stories in this chapter is that they are, in a sense, consequence-less. There is no moral drawn from the events, and no "what-happened-next" element. The story has no other point than its absurdity, and it ends when the absurdity is played out to the end.

For other stories about accidents, fate, and chance see: Bunny Bounces Back; The Cat and the Salmon; The Chandelier; Dead Again; The Failed Suicide; The Fatal Cleaning Lady; The Loaded Dog; The Murdered Son; The Seemingly Dead Revive

ACCIDENTS GALORE

This is really a group of related legends rather than one specific type. The thing they have in common is that they consist of a whole string of episodes, each one being a ridiculous accident. The story often ends with the paramedics who have attended the accident laughing so much that they drop the victim off the stretcher. The best, and longest, of this sort of story was printed in a folk song club magazine in the 1970s (Winship 1978). It tells how a couple are in bed when the wife hears noises downstairs and sends her husband down to investigate. He is wearing only "a well-ventilated pair of pyjama trousers." The dog goes with him and, while the man is bending over, the dog pokes his cold nose through the opening in the pyjamas. The husband shoots forward through a plate glass door and cuts his forehead. The wife sends for an ambulance. With the husband safe in hospital, she starts cleaning up the blood from the doorframe. She does this job with an alcohol-based cleaning fluid and a swab of cotton wool, then flushes the cotton wool down the toilet. The husband comes home, and—as is his custom—retires to the bathroom and sits on the toilet to have a consoling smoke. When he has finished the cigarette, he drops the butt down the toilet, the toilet explodes, and he is once again catapulted forward, bursting the stitches in his head. The paramedics come back again and start loading him onto a stretcher. When he tells them what has happened, they laugh so much they drop the stretcher. He falls heavily on the floor and breaks his leg. Other examples proliferate.

One of the most popular variants features a man and his motorbike. It was printed in the September 1991 issue of the *Motorcyclist* magazine, though the editor commented that he had seen at least half a dozen versions of the legend in the last 30 years. In this story a biker is cleaning his machine on the patio. When he starts it up to see how it is running, he loses control and it crashes through a plate glass patio window. He has several cuts and bruises, so his wife calls the paramedics, and starts cleaning up the mess he's made. She mops up the gasoline with toilet paper which she dumps in the toilet. The tale then continues like the story above.

Jan Brunvand, who collected this legend from a colleague, found an earlier version from 1984 in the same biker magazine. In that version the man broke his TV set while trying to move his bike into the living room out of the rain. This version carried the headline, "Not that old story!" (Brunvand 1993, 116). The motorbike variant obviously crossed the Atlantic because our example below was clipped from a British newspaper in 1992 and reprinted in a folklore magazine.

Example

A gent buys a new BMW 750cc motorbike and invites his friends round to admire it, over drinks. Things get a little cheerful and he is challenged to ride it INTO the house. He does so; loses control on the hall carpet and crashes into the kitchen wall, breaking his leg. An ambulance is called. His wife mops up the petrol [gas], which she swills down the lavatory. The biker returns, limping in plaster. He goes to the loo, smoking, blows himself up. The same ambulance crew arrives again. What on earth has happened now? They are told—and promptly drop the stretcher breaking his other leg. ("Stop Press")

FURTHER READING

Brunvand, Jan Harold. "A Blast Heard Around the World." *Contemporary Legend* 3 (1993): 103–119.

"Stop Press." *Dear Mr Thoms* 24 (January 1992): 27.

Train, John (Compiler and Annotator). *True Remarkable Occurrences*. New York: Clarkson N. Potter Ltd., 1978. See pp. 14–15 and 59.

Winship, Eddie. "Casual Jottings on the Modern Folk Tale." *Sandy Bell's Broadsheet* 6.3 (1978): 3–4.

See: Ding, Dong, Dinner Bell; The Exploding Toilet; The Mole Hill and the Jaguar; The Nude Bachelor; The Ski Run

THE DOUBLE WHAMMY

An ironic tale of mistakes and misfortune was widely told in Australia in the 1990s about a car accident and a cat. It seemed to be related to a story Jan Brunvand called the "Body on the Car" which circulated in the United States in the 1980s, and to a story which British writers Phil Healey and Rick Glanvill called the "Green Goddess Cat."

The American story is the simplest. It tells of a drunken motorist who rolls home in the small hours. Still hung-over, he stumbles to the garage and is just about to pull away from the house when his wife runs out shouting that he has forgotten his packed lunch. When she sees the car, the wife stops dead in her tracks and starts screaming. Embedded in the grille of the car is the lifeless body of an 8-year-old girl (Brunvand 2001, 40–41).

The "Green Goddess Cat" is supposedly a true story that also goes back to the 1980s, or maybe even to the 1960s, and closely resembles "Dead Again" legends. A cat is stuck in a tree, the distressed owner calls the fire brigade to rescue it, which they do. Off they drive—straight over the cat which has leapt out of its owner's arms into the path of the fire truck (Healey and Glanvill 1992, 92–93; Rees 1994, 35–36).

The Australian story combines these elements in a single story full of black humor. A motorist (not drunk) is driving home from work when he runs over some animal. A compassionate sort of man, he jumps out of the car to see what damage has been done. He sees a cat lying in the road. It looks OK, but knowing how hard he hit it, and thinking it must have terrible internal injuries, he puts it out of its misery by wringing its neck (or in some versions, by hitting it with a shovel). The story now develops in two different ways. In one version a woman comes shrieking out of a nearby house abusing him and accusing him of wantonly killing her cat. He is too shocked to argue so he just walks round the front of the car and prepares to drive off. Then he sees the mangled body of a cat embedded in his radiator grille and realizes he has now killed two cats. Other versions omit the confrontation with the woman; the driver just drives home rather shaken. When he gets home his wife comes out to greet him and starts screaming. She has seen a cat's broken body jammed against the car hood. Then the police arrive—the cat's owner has seen him kill her perfectly healthy cat and has called the emergency services.

Example

A man driving home from work . . . hits a cat crossing the road. Concerned, he pulls up and finds a cat lying in the gutter apparently unconscious. He kills it quickly so it won't suffer, then drives home. When he gets there his wife points out that there is a dead cat wedged behind the front bumper, and at that moment the police arrive to arrest him for killing a cat that has been harmlessly sleeping in the gutter. The horrified owner had watched and taken down his registration number. (Scott 1996, 84)

FURTHER READING

Brunvand, Jan Harold. *Encyclopedia of Urban Legends*. New York: Norton, 2001.

Healey, Phil, and Rick Glanvill. *Urban Myths*. London: Virgin, 1992.

Rees, Nigel. *The Guinness Book of Humorous Anecdotes*. Enfield, UK: Guinness Publishing, 1994.

Scott, Bill. *Pelicans and Chihuahuas and Other Urban Legends*. St Lucia, Queensland: University of Queensland Press, 1996.

See: Bunny Bounces Back; The Cat and the Salmon; Dead Again

THE DOUGH BULLET

Sometimes called "The Biscuit Bullet" or "The Brain Drain," this humorous story was very popular and widespread in all media, written and oral, between about 1994 and 2000. The story went that a woman was discovered sitting in her car in a state of severe shock. Her head was in her hands and what looked like brain tissue was oozing out between her fingers. She was convinced she had been shot in the head. What had really happened was that the woman had been shopping and had bought a can of Pillsbury dough; the can had exploded in the heat of the car and the dough had hit the back of her head with some force. When she put her hands to her head to find out what had hit her, she felt the dough and concluded that it was her brains bursting out of a gunshot wound.

Folklorist Jan Brunvand began collecting this story in 1995 when people in the Midwest were experiencing an unusually hot summer (Brunvand 1995), and (as often happens with "new" urban legends) a correspondent promptly wrote back to say that he was responsible for the legend as he had witnessed the original events and had told everybody about it ("The Biscuit Bullet Legend: Is it my Fault?").

The story continued to be forwarded to magazines like *FOAFtale News* and websites such as SNOPES until 1999. By then, other "witnesses" had claimèd that these were real events, though none of these accounts were authenticated. The legend was, for example, presented as a true story in the *Orlando Sentinel* in May 1996, in the *Fresno Bee* in 1996, and the *Knoxville News-Sentinel* in April 1998; it was also taken up by the Associated Press and run as a true "dumb blonde" story in early 1999 (Mikkelson).

Example

A lady named Linda went to Arkansas last week to visit her in-laws, and while there, went to a store. She parked next to a car with a woman sitting in it, her eyes closed and hands behind her head, apparently sleeping. When Linda came out a while later, she again saw the woman, her hands still behind her head but with her eyes open. The woman looked very strange, so Linda tapped on the window and said, "Are you okay?"

The woman answered, "I've been shot in the head, and I am holding my brains in."

Linda didn't know what to do, so she ran into the store, where store officials called the paramedics. They had to break into the car because the door was locked. When they got in, they found that the woman had bread dough on the back of her head and in her hands.

A Pillsbury biscuit canister had exploded, apparently from the heat in the car, making a loud explosion like that of a gunshot, and hit her in the head. When she reached back to find what it was, she felt the dough and thought it was her brains. She passed out from fright at first, then attempted to hold her brains in. ("Biscuit Bullet Text")

FURTHER READING

"The Biscuit Bullet Legend: Is it my Fault?" *FOAFtale News* 39 (June 1996): 8.

"Biscuit Bullet Text." *FOAFtale News* 42 (May 1997): 4. Reprint of an e-mail sent to Jane Gadsby, Memorial University of Newfoundland, April 1997.

Brunvand, Jan Harold. "'Biscuit Bullet' Stories Wanted." *FOAFtale News* 38 (December 1995): 6.

Mikkelson, Barbara. "The Biscuit Bullet." http://www.snopes.com/crime/safety/biscuit.htm.

THE EXPLODING TOILET

This very popular legend is a perennial favorite with the press and oral storytellers alike. The title is self-explanatory. The basic story does not change much from telling to telling, though the reasons for the toilet exploding vary; in some versions it is hairspray that causes the explosion, in others it is insecticide, in others kerosene or gasoline, and in others it is stain remover. Of course, there is always some unfortunate person (usually a man) sitting on the toilet when it explodes, and it is usually his wife who has flushed some sort of inflammable substance down the pan. Like tales of "Accidents Galore," modern versions of "The Exploding Toilet" often end with the paramedics laughing so much that they drop the victim and cause further injuries.

Both Jan Brunvand and Paul Smith have made studies of one of the best-known exploding toilet tales (Brunvand 1993; Smith 1992). This began its life as a "true" story published in the *Jerusalem Post* (Israel) in August 1988. The story was titled "Battle with cockroach ended in hospital," and told how "an encounter with a cockroach last Thursday" in Tel Aviv "resulted in burns, two broken ribs and a broken pelvis for a Givatayim resident" (Rotem quoted in Smith 1992, 45). Supposedly, a Tel Aviv woman had found a cockroach in the living room, threw it in the toilet, and sprayed insecticide on it. Unaware of what had been going on, her husband went to the toilet and threw his cigarette butt into the bowl. The toilet exploded, burning him. The paramedics were called and began carrying him down the stairs. When they heard how the accident had happened, they couldn't stop laughing, and dropped the stretcher. That is when he got the broken ribs and pelvis.

The story was taken up by Reuters press agency and widely circulated round the world. However, many journalists recognized it as an urban legend and printed rebuttals. The South African *Sunday Times*, for example, printed an article titled "Some stories never die—they just go round and round." Picking up on the "paramedics drop stretcher" ending, the article announced that that element of the story was at least 20 years old and had originally been told about a plumber from Budapest whose injuries had been caused by his wife giving him "a playful squeeze" and startling him (compare "Ding, Dong, Dinner Bell" below). "Very funny—in whatever guise," the report ends, "but don't believe a word of it" (quoted in Smith 1992, 48).

So it was that the *Jerusalem Post* had to print a retraction giving a history of their story, and Reuters took up the retraction. In consequence newspapers worldwide began to carry exposés. However, the story continued to run. As late as October 1988, the *Weekly World News* printed the story and even named the victim: "Imagine his surprise," the story began, "when mild-mannered Saul Frankel sat down on the potty, dropped a lit cigarette butt in the bowl—and the toilet exploded in flames" (quoted in Smith 1992, 57–58).

Since then the story has remained a perennial favorite turning up in a variety of media (see Dundes and Pagter 1991, 396 for a cartoon version with accompanying text). It has also become a staple element in medics' storytelling. In a 1986 article, "The Exploding Toilet and Other Emergency Room Folklore," Robert Slay comments that most of the "emergency room myths" he knows will customarily begin with somebody saying, "I'll tell you the most bizarre patient story you've ever heard, and I know it's true, because I heard it from the interns who took care of the victim" (Slay 1986, 411). Slay's version of "The Exploding Toilet" (which forms our example below) was told to him by two nurses who had heard it from a friend-of-a-friend. He says he had heard the story recounted in emergency rooms from Boston to Los Angeles.

However, like many other urban legends, this story is not entirely new. Jan Brunvand has found earlier versions from rural America. One correspondent, for example, wrote to him relating what he called a "very ancient farm story" about Grandpa dropping his pipe down the toilet hole in the outhouse and letting off such an explosion that Grandma remarks that it's a good thing he hadn't let *that* off in the house. Another rural story, he says, was attached to a named local character and was one of a series of tales and anecdotes about this man. The story was that his wife once cleaned paintbrushes with turpentine and got rid of it in the outhouse when she had finished. The man dropped his cigar butt down the hole, setting off an enormous explosion. At which, the man remarked, "It must have been something I ate." Variants with this punchline seem to have been well known in the 1920s and 1930s (Brunvand 1993, 110–112).

Example

One Sunday morning, Dad sought his solitude in the bathroom with the Sunday papers. As with many other Dads nationwide, he was merely trying to avail himself of one of the few pleasures afforded to a middle-aged family man . . . Unbeknown to the soon-to-be-victim was the fact that his wife had just left the bathroom after getting ready for church.

Before leaving the bathroom, Mom had sprayed her hair with an aerosol hairspray. Since there just a small amount of spray left in the can, Mom wisely decided to spray the last little bit into the toilet, so the kids would not get at it. As Dad settled on the commode in blissful solitude, he extinguished his half-smoked cigarette by dropping it between his legs into the bowl. By all accounts, there was a terrific explosion that blew Dad completely off the toilet and inflicted some rather nasty burns on his vulnerable anatomy. Mom and the family burst into the bathroom and broke Dad's arm with the door.

When the paramedics arrived, they were laughing so hard that they dropped the burned and broken breadwinner, further injuring him. (Slay 1986, 412–413)

FURTHER READING

Brunvand, Jan Harold. "A Blast Heard Around the World." *Contemporary Legend* 3 (1993): 103–119.

Dundes, Alan, and Carl R. Pagter. *Never Try to Teach a Pig to Sing: Still More Urban Folklore from the Paperwork Empire*. Detroit, MI: Wayne State University Press, 1991.

Rotem, Michael. "Battle with Cockroach Ended in Hospital." *The Jerusalem Post* (August 25, 1988): 12.

Slay, Robert D. "The Exploding Toilet and Other Emergency Room Folklore." *Journal of Emergency Medicine* 4 (1986): 411–414.

Smith, Paul. "'Read All About It! Elvis Eaten by Drug-Crazed Giant Alligators': Contemporary Legend and the Popular Press." *Contemporary Legend* 2 (1992): 41–70.

See: Accidents Galore; Ding, Dong, Dinner Bell; Framed; Glued to the Loo

THE FIVE-POUND NOTE/THE UNINTENTIONAL THIEF

This story of unjust suspicion has been around in Europe, Australia, New Zealand, and North America since at least 1855, when an article entitled "A Lady's Memory" appeared in the *London Times* on the May 18 repeating a story first heard in the *Sheffield Times*. In this story a very respectable lady thinks she has been robbed of her pocket-book containing "three crown pieces" and accuses three young men who had the misfortune to be standing near her. The young men are searched by the police without the pocket book being found. It has, of course, been lying all the time at home on top of a chest of drawers. Half a century later, in 1912, British folklorist Katharine M. Briggs heard a similar story from a friend in Scotland. Later the story was reported as fact in the Indianapolis *Sunday Star*, March 3, 1946 (headnote to Briggs and Tongue 1965, 101), and in the (London) *Observer* (Hobbs 1978, 77). Folklorists have been collecting it in the United Kingdom, United States, Australia, New Zealand, Germany, Italy, Sweden, and France since the early 1970s.

The basic plot is that of the 1855 account—somebody thinks he/she has been robbed by a stranger, but to his/her embarrassment finds out later that he/she has unjustly accused some innocent person. Many versions include an extra twist to the tale, as Katharine Briggs' version does, by having the supposed victim "steal back" what they think is their own property.

In a rather more recent variant of the story, which is commonly known as "The Packet of Biscuits" or "The Cookie Thief," a man or woman is sitting at a table in a cafe and imagines the person sharing the table is taking their food (often cookies) and aggressively "shares" it with the stranger. Later they find that their own cookies have fallen on the floor or are lying untouched on the table next to them (they have returned to the wrong table after placing a drinks order). As French folklorist Véronique Campion-Vincent says in her discussion of this story: "A prejudiced and erroneous assessment of a situation and too much confidence in their own rightness, turn honest characters into petty criminals and make them inflict a wrong they cannot redress" (Campion-Vincent 1995, 22). The latest appearance of this story is as a tale of a stolen chocolate biscuit told in Dublin (Ireland) in 2006 and reportedly heard in Derry (Londonderry) "just a few years ago."

The story has featured in a handful of short films—"Blues, Black and White" (1987), "Boeuf Bourguignon" (1988), "The Lunch Date" (1989), "Damned" (1993) and "Cookie Thief" (1998). It also furnished an episode for Douglas Adam's novel *So Long, and Thanks for All the Fish* (1984).

The two stories below are both from the United Kingdom. The first one is the 1912 English story quoted by Katharine Briggs and Ruth Tongue, the second is the 2006 story from Northern Ireland.

Examples

1. An elderly brother and sister lived together, and one day the sister wanted to go to town to do some shopping. So her brother gave her a five-pound note, and she set out. She traveled third class, and the only other passenger was a shabby old woman who sat opposite her and nodded. Miss M. was sleepy too, after her early, hurried start, so she dozed a little too. Then she woke up, and thought it wasn't very safe to go to sleep in a railway carriage, alone with a stranger. She opened her bag to make some notes of what she had to buy, and the five-pound note wasn't there. She looked at her neighbour, who was sleeping heavily with a big old shabby bag beside her. Miss M. bent forward and, very cautiously, she opened the bag. There was a new five-pound note on top of everything. "Old scoundrel!" thought Miss M. Then she thought, "She's poor and old, and I oughtn't to have put temptation in her way." She wondered what she ought to do. It would cause a deal of delay and bother to call the police, and it seemed cruel to get an old woman into trouble, but she must have her money.

   So, in the end, she quietly took the five pounds out of the bag and shut it up again. At the next stop, the old woman got out, and Miss M. got to town and did her day's shopping, and came home laden with parcels. Her brother met her at the station. "How did you manage?" he said, "You left your five-pound note on the dressing-table." (Briggs and Tongue 1965, 101–102)

2. My aunty Maeve was in Florentino's, the wee ice-cream shop. She went in and she got a cup of tea and she got a KitKat. She sat down and there was no other seats anywhere, and a man came up to her and said, "Do you mind if I sit here?" and she was like, "Aye, no problem." So she was sitting with her cup of tea in

front of her. She got the KitKat and broke off a segment and dipped it in her tea and started eating it, and the man did the same. She was like, "Oh my God, he's so cheeky!" And he had a cream bun in front of him as well. She broke off another segment and ate it, and he took the last segment. So they were sitting there in silence and just before she left she ran her finger through the middle of his cream bun, and she walked out. She put her hand in her pocket then and pulled out a full KitKat! I remember hearing it from a taxi man and I told him "That happened to my aunty Maeve!" He had heard it through someone else and he was telling people in the taxi. (Told to Peter McGuire by Mary Rainey. See McGuire 2006)

FURTHER READING

Briggs, Katharine M., and Ruth L. Tongue, eds. *Folktales of England*. London: Routledge and Kegan Paul, 1965.

Brunvand, Jan Harold. *The Mexican Pet: More "New" Urban Legends and Some Old Favorites*. New York: Norton, 1986. For "Packet of Biscuits" variant see pp. 137–140.

Campion-Vincent, Véronique. "Preaching Tolerance?" *Folklore* 106 (1995): 21–30.

Hobbs, Sandy. "The Folk Tale as News." *Oral History* 6.2 (1978): 74–86.

McGuire, Peter. "Two Dublin Legends." *FOAFtale News* 65 (August 2006): 8–9.

Smith, Paul. *The Book of Nastier Legends*. London: Routledge and Kegan Paul, 1986. See pp. 23–24.

See: The Double Theft

GLUED TO THE LOO

In October 2003 a man called Bob Dougherty claimed that he had got stuck to a glue-laden toilet seat at a Home Depot in Louisville, Colorado. In November 2005 he initiated a lawsuit against the store. However the defense claimed that he had reported a similar incident in the town's visitor center bathroom in 2004 and was nothing but a hoaxer. Only days after Dougherty had appeared on TV and gained national attention for his case, a similar incident supposedly befell a man in Bakersfield. He said he was using the public restroom at the Home Improvement store when he realized something was wrong. "I was stuck, so I was like what the hell is going on ... I started yelling and yelling, and nobody came," he said. The Bakersfield City firefighters arrived and unbolted the toilet seat, "and moved the individual to a more comfortable position, protecting his modesty." The victim was taken to hospital and vows that in future he will take more care when visiting restrooms (via e-mail from Brian Chapman).

These unfortunate events allegedly are not confined to the United States. From the United Kingdom in 1979 comes a story which is a politer variation on this theme. In this version a man is standing on the toilet seat trying to fix the valve in an old-fashioned wall-mounted toilet cistern. The seat slides sideways and he slips, lodging one foot in the toilet bowl. The fit is so tight that the toilet has to be dismantled and the man has to go to the hospital with his foot still wedged in the toilet bowl (White 1979, 249).

Superglue incidents were reported from Dublin (Ireland) in February 1992 when vandals supposedly superglued the toilets seats in a pub. Then in May 2004 the *Daily Record* (Glasgow, Scotland) carried a story titled "Bostik? No ... It was my Bottom: Shopper in Glue Ordeal" (McDonald 2004). This may have been the basis of the oral story told to Gillian Bennett recently by a hairdresser (see our example). The hairdresser did not, however, report the retraction which the *Daily Record* printed only two days later. Under the excruciating punning headline "Glue Man is Having a Lav: Claims Won't Stick, Say Airport," this second report alleged that the man was a hoaxer who had "pulled the same stunt" twice before, once at Prestwick Airport (Glasgow, Scotland) and once at a home improvement superstore in Ayr, Scotland (McDonald and Christie 2004).

These stories have equivalents in traditional folktales. Certainly a comparable story may be found in a very old French story compilation, Marguerite of Angoulême's *Heptameron* (sixteenth century). The first story of the second day is called "A Nasty Adventure." It tells how, "Madame de Ronceux, while at the monastery of Grey Friars at Thouars, was constrained to go in great haste to a certain place," and "went alone into a darksome privy. [She] was so hard pressed that she had scarcely time to lift her dress [and] sat down in the foulest, dirtiest spot in the whole place, where she found herself stuck fast as though with glue.... " Like the twentieth-century victims, she found the experience totally humiliating. The poor woman called for her maid to come and rescue her and clean her up, but the message got garbled and all the male houseguests turned up to save her, as they thought, from being raped by the Grey Friars. "And when she came out of that foul place it was necessary to strip her naked and change all her garments before she could leave the monastery" (Chartres 1929, 147–149).

Example

You know what I heard from one of my clients? This man went to use the toilets at Homebase and got stuck to the toilet. Some kids had spread superglue on the toilet seats. I suppose they thought it was funny. Anyway, they had to call the fire brigade to come and rescue him. They tried and tried to get him off the seat but they couldn't. So they had to take the toilet seat off its hinges and lead him out of the store with the seat still stuck to his bottom! They took him to hospital, and they put all this stuff on his bottom, solvents and things, but it took ages before he was eventually freed. (Bennett Collection)

FURTHER READING

Brunvand, Jan Harold. *Encyclopedia of Urban Legends.* New York: Norton, 2001. See pp. 419–420.

Chartres, J. S. (Translator and Editor). *The Heptameron of Margaret of Angoulême, Queen of Navarre: A Complete Translation into English from the Authentic French Text of Le Roux De Lincy.* Philadelphia, PA: J. P. Horn and Company, 1929.

Mcdonald, Craig. "Bostik? No . . . It Was My Bottom: Shopper In Glue Ordeal." *Daily Record* [Glasgow] (May 4, 2004).

McDonald, Craig, and Michael Christie. "Glue Man is Having a Lav: Claims Won't Stick, Say Airport." *Daily Record* [Glasgow] (May 6, 2004).

White, David. "There's Something Nasty in the Fridge: Urban Folk Beliefs Take up Where Fairy Tales Left Off." *New Society* 1 (November 1979): 248–249.

See: Accidents Galore; The Exploding Toilet; Framed; Stuck on You; The Superglue Revenge

THE KILKENNY WIDOW

This legend is sometimes called "Promiscuity Rewarded" or "The Unexpected Inheritance." In his *The Choking Doberman* (1984) Jan Brunvand includes it as one of his examples of legends about sex-without-strings. As an example, he gives a story about a sailor in a foreign port who is asked by a rich old man to sleep with his beautiful young wife, then rewarded with a bag of gold coins. The explanation for this strange behavior is that the old man wants an heir so that he can cheat his grasping relatives of the inheritance they so greedily crave (Brunvand 1984, 133).

The title story, collected at the Department of Irish Folklore in Dublin (Ireland) in the early 1980s, has a special Irish flavor. Versions of the same story were printed in the *Reader's Digest* in August 1989 and repeated in the *New York Times* in 1985. Some are located in the Irish town of Kilkenny, like the example below; others feature two American tax agents whose car breaks down, or are located in a sleeping car on an Italian train.

We know that the story has been around since at least the 1940s because it appears in a compilation of stories by anthologist and humorist Bennett Cerf (1945, 179–180).

Example

Two men, John and Mick, went to Kilkenny for the day. Evening came and as they were enjoying themselves they decided they would put off the journey back to Dublin until the following day. They proposed to stay the night in the pleasant hotel they were in, which belonged to an attractive widow whom they were getting to know. They spent an enjoyable evening in the bar and made their way to their separate rooms. However, when all was quiet, Mick made his way to the widow's room and would have been seen, if there were anyone to see him, returning to his room in the early morning.

When they were leaving the widow called Mick aside. "Now I know," says she, "that you have put your names in the register, but I want to be sure who's who," taking out a notebook and pen. Mick, a quick thinker, gave John's name and address.

Mick had forgotten all about Kilkenny until, nine months later, he had a telephone call from John, who seemed to be highly excited. "Hello! Hello! Is that Mick? Listen, do you remember that outing we had to Kilkenny? Hello! To Kilkenny, yes. Well, I don't know what to make of it. I've had a letter from a Kilkenny solicitor. Do you remember that nice widow whose hotel we stayed in? Well, the solicitor says she has died and left me the hotel and a lot of money as well. I don't understand it." (Ní Dhuibhne 1983, 65)

FURTHER READING

Brunvand, Jan Harold. *The Choking Doberman and Other "New" Urban Legends.* New York: Norton, 1984.

Cerf, Bennett. *Laughing Stock: Over Six-hundred Jokes and Anecdotes of Uncertain Vintage.* New York: Grossett and Dunalp, 1945.

Dhuibhne, Eílís Ní. "Dublin Modern Legends: An Intermediate Type List and Examples." *Béaloideas* 51 (1983): 55–70.

See: The Will

KILLER CACTI, STATUES, AND STONES

Since at least the mid-1980s stories have been circulating on the Internet and by word of mouth about a man who was killed by a cactus. This is one of many legends with the theme of poetic justice, in which bad behavior is punished in some ironic and fitting, but totally unplanned, way. Briefly, the cactus story is that a man keeps shooting at a suguaro cactus (these are the giant cacti that look like human beings holding their arms above their heads). The suguaro cactus is a protected species, but the authorities fail to catch the man and nothing seems able to stop him shooting at the plants. Nature, however, does what the law had failed to do, and the plant-killer gets his just deserts (see our example).

Though it seems an essentially modern story, there are precursors in both folk tradition and classical literature. In his work on the theory of drama, the *Poetics*, the Ancient Greek philosopher Aristotle (384–322 B.C.) referred to the story of Mitys of Argos who met his death when the statue of a man whose death he had been responsible for fell on him and killed him. Apparently, the story was well known in Aristotle's day, and he was not the only ancient writer to mention it in his work (Hansen 1999). Another parallel can be found in a local legend attaching to the famous prehistoric stone circle at Avebury (southwest England), which a contributor to *FOAFtale News* heard in 1964. Supposedly the remains of a man were found under one of the stones: it seems he was digging away trying to bring it down, when it fell on him and caused his death (Barksdale 1999).

Example

There was a ne'er-do-well around the Tucson, Arizona, area who continually shot up suguaro cacti in defiance of the law. (Shooting these giant cacti will eventually kill them via the entrance of disease and insects.) The authorities were totally frustrated in their attempts to catch him in the act or garner enough evidence to send him to jail. Then one day they found the guy dead. He had been crushed to death when he shot up a cactus with a disease-weakened root system. The force of the impact had been just enough to break the cactus free of its anchor and send its thousand-pound body down on top of him. (Mongold 1999)

FURTHER READING

Barksdale, Alan F. "Cactus Standing Stone." *FOAFtale News* 45 (November 1999): 4–5.

Hansen, William. "Poetic Justice: The Murder of Mitys of Argos." *FOAFtale News* 45 (November 1999): 4.

Mongold, Roger. "Poetic Justice: Cactus Murder." *FOAFtale News* 44 (May 1999): 11.

See: Killer Suicides; Thieves Get Their Just Deserts

KILLER SUICIDES

These stories have been around in some form or other since at least the late 1960s, and are more or less worldwide. They have turned up in newspapers as true experiences, in story compilations and magazines, on the Internet, and in urban legend collections. There are two main variants.

The first variant, many accounts of which may be factual, tells how a would-be suicide leaps from a window and kills a passerby. Newspaper accounts of this occurrence include: a man who jumps from a window and kills a motorist (UK 1969); a woman who jumps from a twelfth-floor window and kills a food-seller in the street below (Taiwan 1986); a man who jumps from the Eiffel Tower in Paris and kills a woman tourist (France 1989); a man who jumps from a balcony and injures a woman sitting at an outdoor cafe below (Israel 1997); a would-be suicide who jumps and lands on a policeman (Hong Kong 2000); and a man who, after killing his wife, attempts suicide by jumping from a Century Freeway connector in Los Angeles and crashes through the roof of a car below killing the driver (USA 2001). Other accounts come from Australia, Thailand, Brazil, Russia, and Austria; the most recent is a 2004 story from Japan (examples via e-mail from Brian Chapman).

A handful of these stories tell of a suicide who falls on his/her faithless spouse. These bring us nearer the second variant of "The Killer Suicide." This variant is much more legend-like in that it has an element of irony and black humor, and a clear "just deserts" moral. It is impossible to say whether these accounts are factual or not, but the style and structure of most accounts indicate they have at least been "legend-ized"—they appear to have been told many times and to have traveled far and wide. In these stories the would-be suicide is usually the wife of an unfaithful husband. In her misery and despair she decides to end it all by jumping from a window. The person she falls on is, of course, her husband. He is killed, but she survives.

Versions also exist in which the falling woman kills both the cheating husband and the other woman, or in which the would-be suicide is a worker who falls on his bullying boss, or a man who has been fired who falls on the man who has fired him (Brunvand 1993, 86–87). The most absurd version comes from the *Weekly World News* of November 14, 2000. These events were supposed to have happened in Vienna (Austria). The reporter tells how: "An outraged, 190-pound wife leaped from a third-story window and landed on her cheating husband, killing the puny skirt-chaser and breaking both her legs—as he was on his way to spend the night with his 326-pound mistress!" (Anders 2000).

Example

I heard about this woman whose husband told her he was leaving her for another woman. She was so hurt she decided to kill herself by jumping out the window. After he left, she gulped down a drink and then took a good run at the window.

Now, he was coming *out* of the building just as she was coming down. She landed on top of him, and killed him outright. But because he had broken her fall, she walked away with nothing worse than a few bruises. So there! (Bennett Collection)

FURTHER READING

Anders, Drake. "Look Out Belooooooow!. Fat Wife Leaps Three Stories—& Crushes her Hubby like a Bug!" *Weekly World News* (November 14, 2000): 16.

Bishop, Amanda. *The Gucci Kangaroo*. Hornsby, Australia: Australasian Publishing, 1988. See p. 81.

Brunvand, Jan Harold. *The Baby Train* and other Lusty Legends. New York: Norton, 1993.

Mikkelson, Barbara. "Fallen Angel." http://www.snopes.com/love/revenge/suicide.htm

See: Killer Cacti, Statues, and Stones; Thieves Get Their Just Deserts

THE MOLE HILL AND THE JAGUAR

This British story from the 1980s was first reported in the prestigious British newspaper *The Guardian* on January 2, 1988. It shares motifs with legends about exploding toilets and freak accidents, but combines them in an individual way. The example below was told to Paul Smith as a true story.

Example

There was this man who had trouble with moles. They would keep on digging up his garden! So he decided to poison them. He got some potion or other and went out at night to tip it over the molehills. He went out at night so as not to alarm the neighbours, right?

He mustn't have thought this out properly because, of course, it was too dark for him to see what he was doing. So he got into his car, a beautiful new Jaguar, and turned on the lights. But he had left the car in reverse, and the vibration from him getting into the car set it sliding backward into the front of his house, causing £6,000 worth of damage.

To make matters worse he hit an electric heater on his front porch and it ignited the petrol in his car. So his car was a write-off!

In desperation he covered his lawn with a ton of ready-mixed cement. No lawn, no moles! (Smith Collection)

FURTHER READING

Goss, Michael. "Serendipitous Detritus." *Folklore Frontiers* 13 (1991): 4–11.

See: Accidents Galore; The Exploding Toilet; The Solid Cement Cadillac

NOT MY TEETH

Known also as "The False Teeth on the Fishing Line," this international comic tale has been collected since the 1980s from as far apart as Belgium, Holland, and northern Germany in the northern hemisphere, and Australia in the southern hemisphere. There are slight differences between northern and southern versions. The northern versions feature two friends who go on a sea fishing trip together. One friend loses his teeth when he is seasick and, in an attempt at restitution, the other ties his own false teeth to the fishing line and pretends to fish his friend's teeth out of the sea. Australian versions are set at surfing resorts on the Gold Coast or Bondi Beach and feature a husband and wife surfing or swimming. In these stories, a sneering husband gets his just reward for playing a cynical trick on his wife.

The story has appeared in several collections of urban legends between 1972 and 1991, five from northern Europe, and three from Australia.

The example below comes from Australia and seems to be the basic story from which the two other Australian versions derive.

Example

There is the story of the husband who was always trying to score off his wife. This went on for years until both were middle-aged people. Then on one weekend they went to the beach with friends for the day. Husband was a keen surfer still, and he persuaded his wife to go swimming with him despite the big surf running this particular day. The inevitable happened, and the wife was caught by a dumper and rolled helplessly up the beach. In the process she opened her mouth to shout, and lost her false teeth, much to her dismay. Her husband went ostensibly to help her find the missing dentures, along with their friends who accompanied them on the excursion, and, winking hugely at them, slipped his own false teeth out and pretended to find them. He offered them to his wife, who rinsed them in the sea, and tried to fit them in. They wouldn't fit, of course, and to the husband's horror she flung them far out into the breaking waves, saying, "It's no good, those aren't mine!" (Scott 1981, 369)

FURTHER READING

Scott, Bill. *Complete Book of Australian Folklore*. Sydney: Lansdowne, 1981.

Scott, W. N. *The Long and the Short and the Tall: A Collection of Australian Yarns*. Sydney: Western Plains Publishers, 1985. See pp. 235–236.

Top, Stefaan. "Modern Legends in the Belgian Oral Tradition: A Report." *Fabula* 31.3/4 (1990): 272–278. See p. 276.

See: The Teeth in the Cod

THE SKI RUN

This story is one of many urban legends about bizarre, hilarious (and slightly risqué) accidents. It suddenly appeared on both sides of the Atlantic in the mid-1970s and continued to be popular through the 1980s in various forms with various punch lines all involving a second accident. It even found its way into a respected British Sunday paper, *The Observer*, on May 6, 1984.

It was reported as news on January 10, 2003 by *Newsday* (Long Island, NY) (Lowe 2003a); then three days later the writer admitted it was an apocryphal story that to his knowledge had never been reported as news in the media despite claims to the contrary. At various times the scene had been set in Switzerland, the Leksand Slalom Hill in Sweden, the Scottish Cairngorms, the Australian Snowy Mountains, the French Alps, Silver Springs (Pennsylvania), Aspen (Colorado), and Utah (Lowe 2003b).

Example

A girl had gone with some friends on a skiing holiday to Switzerland. She'd never been skiing before. Her nervousness coupled with the cold made her want to "spend a penny." She felt she couldn't wait till she got back to the hotel, so she looked round, edged over to a clump of trees, and pulled her pants down.

OK so far. But when she tried to pull her panties back up, she started to slide, faster and faster down the slope, ski pants and panties still round her ankles. Her journey was broken by a tree stump and she broke a leg.

Traveling home she found herself sitting next to a young chap who also had a broken leg. "What a coincidence! Was it a skiing accident?" she said. "Not really," he replied, "I never even got on the ski slopes. I was in the bar, sitting on one of those tall stools they have, enjoying a drink when some crazy woman shot past the window on skis, with her panties round her ankles. I laughed so much I fell off the bar-stool and broke my leg." (Bennett Collection)

FURTHER READING

Lowe, Ed. "Tale of a Slippery Slope." *Newsday* [Long Island, NY] (January 10, 2003a): A08. http://pqasb.pqarchiver.com/newsday/access/27564451.html?dis= 27565441:2756544518FTM=ABS&FMTS&date=Jan+10%2C+2003&author_

ED+LOWE&pub=Newsday&edition=combined+editions&startpage=A.08& desc=tale+of+a+slippery+slope

———. "Admitting the Naked Truth." *Newsday* [Long Island, NY] (January 15, 2003b): A08.

Scott, Bill. *Pelicans and Chihuahuas and Other Urban Legends.* St Lucia, Queensland: University of Queensland Press, 1996. See p. 155.

Smith, Paul. *The Book of Nastier Legends.* London: Routledge and Kegan Paul, 1986. See p. 30.

See: Accidents Galore

THE SOLID CEMENT CADILLAC

In 1960 a series of newspaper articles appeared in Denver, Colorado telling how a car was accidentally filled with concrete. Within a short time the story achieved legendary status, the "accident" now being reported as the deliberate act of a jealous husband. Soon 43 versions had been collected and published in folklore journals in the United States. At first it seemed that the legends were copycat stories based on the Denver newspaper articles, then it became clear that the oral legends had preceded the newspaper stories and it was either a case of life copying legend or that the newspaper articles were false—planted, some said, as an advert for a local cement company (Attebery 1970; Ed. 1961; J.B.T. 1962; Toelken and O'Bryant 1961).

However, the story continued to be reported throughout the 1970s and into the 1980s, not only in the United States but also in Germany, Norway, Sweden, Australia, and the United Kingdom. A new variant appeared in the early 1980s when a British newspaper reported a story from San Francisco; in this version the cement was dropped into the lover's house through an open bedroom window. In yet another version from about the same date, the lover comes out of the house and gets on his bicycle, leaving the jealous husband worrying about whose car he has wrecked (Smith 1983, 87–88).

In 2002 a very similar story began appearing in newspapers about a guy who turns up at a construction site and asks for his car to be filled with concrete. This was first reported as having happened in Dublin (Ireland) then in Oakland and several other places in California. In the California reports the guy is said to be getting back at his wife (via e-mail from Brian Chapman).

Example

The way I heard it was like this. There was a bloke who thought his wife was being unfaithful to him. He was sure someone was visiting her in the afternoon when he was at work (he drove a cement truck). So, one day he thought he'd come back early and wait round the corner in his cement-truck to try and catch him.

Well, when he arrived at his house he saw a very smart new car parked in front. Thought the lover must have arrived already. "AH-hah!" he thought, "Gotcha!" So he filled up the car with the load of concrete he was carrying (it was an open-top sports car), and sat there waiting for the man to come out of the house. He waited and waited. Nothing happened.

Eventually his wife came out, saw the car, started screaming and shouting, "My husband's new car! My husband's new car!"

It turned out that his wife had bought it for him as a surprise birthday present. So he had ruined his own car! What's more, there never had been a secret lover. She'd been faithful all along! (Bennett Collection)

FURTHER READING

Attebery, Louie W. "It was a DeSoto." *Journal of American Folklore* 83 (1970): 452–457.
Ed. [Barre Toelken] "Notes and Queries." *Oregon Folklore Bulletin* 1.2 (1961): 3.
J.B.T. [Barre Toelken] "The Return of the Cement Truck Driver." *Oregon Folklore Bulletin* 1.3 (1962): 2–4.
Smith, Paul. *The Book of Nasty Legends*. London: Routledge and Kegan Paul, 1983. See pp. 87–88.
Toelken, J. Barre, and Joan O'Bryant. "Notes and Queries." *Oregon Folklore Bulletin* 1.1 (1961): 5–6.

See: The Philanderer's Porsche

THE STOLEN SPECIMEN

Reported since the 1930s, this modern tale has roots in traditional comic narrative. The story concerns thieves who get their come-uppance when they find that what they thought was tasty food or drink is actually some disgusting human body fluid.

The story most commonly told concerns somebody who takes a specimen of urine to hospital in a whiskey bottle; the bottle is stolen and the thief drinks the urine thinking it's whiskey. Other stories feature people traveling on trains who see an old woman keep taking sips from a jug; when the old woman goes to the restroom, the person takes a sip from the jug and discovers that it is full of phlegm (the old woman is tubercular and has been spitting her contaminated mucus into the jug).

Versions have also emerged (from the fall of 1999 onward) which are a cross between "The Stolen Specimen" and "The Cat in the Package." In these stories, the specimen may be stolen from the open window of a car or by opening an unlocked car door. Alternatively, a man may see a shaking woman sitting in a car and ask if she is OK; she replies that she is OK but someone has just stolen her urine sample. In other stories, it is dog poop that is stolen by thieves who think a poop-bag contains something valuable (Singh 2003). In a recent British story, a bag of dirty diapers is stolen by someone who thinks it has been put out for a charity-shop collection and may contain something saleable ("Dirty Nappies Thief . . .").

As far as we are aware the oldest story on this theme comes from sixteenth-century France. A story called "The Nasty Breakfast" in the *Heptameron* of Marguerite of Navarre is told as the second story of the sixth day. It is a complicated tale, but briefly what happens is that a trickster overhears an apothecary against whom he has a grudge telling one of his cronies that he would like a good breakfast but he'd rather have somebody else pay for it. So the trickster goes into the street and picks up a turd which has frozen hard (it is midwinter and very cold). With its coating of frost, the turd looks just like a large sugar loaf. He wraps it up in nice white paper and then "accidentally" drops it in front of the two men as he pretends to saunter by. The apothecary picks it up thinking he is getting something for free, hides it inside his jacket, and he and his crony go into the inn. The "sugar loaf" begins to melt and stink the whole place out. The pair are forcibly ejected and realize that the tables have been turned on them, and that it is they who have been tricked (Chartres 1929, 193–198). This story shares, not only the same plot outline as the modern stories, but the same moral message that thieves may not get what they bargained for.

Example

Have you heard the one about this man who stole a woman's specimen? Well, this woman was pregnant and she was going for a checkup at the hospital. She was on a bus. And she had her purse open on her knee, with her pocket-book, handkerchief, things like that—and her urine sample in an old whiskey bottle. Well, a drunk man got on the bus, and started staring at her purse. As the bus was slowing down at the next stop, he suddenly he leaned over and snatched the whiskey bottle out of her purse. He jumped off the bus, and started running down the street with the urine sample in his hand! (Smith Collection)

FURTHER READING

Brunvand, Jan Harold. *Encyclopedia of Urban Legends*. New York: Norton, 2001. See pp. 412–413.

Chartres, J. S. (Translator and Editor). *The Heptameron of Margaret of Angoulême, Queen of Navarre: A Complete Translation into English from the Authentic French Text of Le Roux De Lincy*. Philadelphia, PA: J. P. Horn and Company, 1929.

"Dirty Nappies Thief Shows a Whiff of Desperation." *Evening News* [Scotland] (November 25, 2005).

Doyle, Charles Clay. "Roaming Cannibals and Vanishing Corpses." *Indiana Folklore* 11 (1978): 133–39. See pp. 137–138.

Singh, Anita. "Mugger's Poop Scoop." *The Scotsman* (October 8, 2003).

See: The Cat in the Package; Grandma's Ashes; Thieves Get Their Just Deserts

THE TEETH IN THE COD

In 1994 a local newspaper in Holland published a story about a man who became seasick during a fishing trip and lost his dentures overboard. Three months later a trawlerman gutting fish found a set of false teeth inside a nineteen-pound cod. The story went on to tell how news of the strange find reached the ears of the man who had lost his dentures at sea, so he went to see the trawlerman. The dentures found in the fish appeared to be his.

These bizarre events were hailed as "the story of the year." The Dutch national press first took it up, then the tale was sold to the Associated Press agency. The story was retold by Swedish newspapers, and by British and Canadian news networks; there were also suggestions that a German film crew were planning to make a documentary about it. Only three weeks later, however, it became apparent the events were a hoax: a well-known practical joker came forward saying he had put the dentures in the cod (they were his wife's spare pair); simultaneously, the man who had lost his dentures in the sea confessed that his dentist had told him the dentures found in the cod were not his. The revelation of the hoax then went round the world again, inspiring headlines such as "Cod Still Good for Laugh" in the Newfoundland *Evening Telegram* [Canada] (Venbrux and Meder 1995, 123).

As in the case of the "Kentucky Fried Chicken" scandal in Sheffield (UK) in 1983 (Smith 1984), the consequences for the people at the center of the story were serious. In the case of "The Teeth in the Cod" both men became social outcasts for a while, one portrayed as a crook, the other as a fool. In revenge, the hoaxer's wife's false teeth were taken out to sea and thrown overboard in a reenactment of the original accident. By the beginning of 1995, however, the man who had lost his dentures at sea seems to have recovered some of his dignity and appeared on national TV telling the story as a tall tale, exaggerating all the ingredients of the story—a huge storm was now supposed to be raging, and the dentures were said to have been vomited twelve feet into the air.

Apart from seeing how a story may be taken up by the media and presented in several different modes—true experience, news, hoax, joke, legend, and tall tale—the interest of this story is the way it combines motifs (that is, story elements) from both urban legend and traditional folktale. From urban legend comes the motif of the teeth lost at sea (compare "Not My Teeth"), and from traditional tales comes the motif of a valuable item recovered from the body of a fish. In folktales the valuable item is usually a ring, the most famous story of this kind being "The Ring of Polycrates" by Herod (c. 484–425 B.C.). In this story King Polycrates throws a valuable ring into the sea as a sacrifice to the gods. The gods refuse his sacrifice and return it to him in the body of a fish. Thereafter he is dogged by misfortune. Arab and Jewish traditions have similar stories about holy men who throw the key to their penitential chains into the sea; in this case, the key is returned in the fish as a sign that the penance is over and the holy man may unlock his chains.

The example below was collected during a survey of urban legends conducted in 1991 by the Meertens Instituut, Amsterdam (Netherlands) by a man who had heard the story from his brother at a birthday party in November of the previous year.

Example

The society of cheesemongers went out fishing at the North Sea for the day. More time was spent drinking than fishing. Cheesemonger Baas Baars not only became drunk but also seasick. Consequently he had to vomit. While he was feeding the fish, his false teeth followed the contents of his stomach.

Some time afterward a huge cod was caught. When returning to the harbor, the anglers started gutting their catch.

Guess what was found in the cod's stomach? Right, Baas Baars's dentures! (Venbrux and Meder 1995, 116)

FURTHER READING

Smith, Paul. "On the Receiving End: When Rumour Becomes Legend." *Perspectives on Contemporary Legend: Proceedings of the Conference on Contemporary Legend*, Sheffield, July 1982. Ed. Paul Smith. Sheffield: CECTAL, 1984. pp. 197–215.
Venbrux, Eric, and Theo Meder. "'The False Teeth in the Cod': A Legend in Context." *Contemporary Legend* 5 (1995): 115–131.

See: Not My Teeth

THIEVES GET THEIR JUST DESERTS

This is a complex of humorous morality stories about tricksters, shoplifters, and petty criminals who are caught in the act in humiliating circumstances.

For example, in several nineteenth-century stories a thief tries to steal a pat of butter. American folklorist Richard Dorson found such a tale in the *Spirit of the Times* (January 23, 1841) which he reprinted in his collection of traditional stories *Jonathan Draws the Long Bow* (1946). It tells how a Vermont storekeeper was closing his doors for the night when he spotted Seth, a "lounging, worthless fellow," grab a pound of butter and hide it under his hat. Rather than confront the thief, the wily storekeeper invited Seth in for "a little something warm," sat him down beside a roaring fire and kept him talking until "streak after streak of the butter came pouring from under his hat" (Dorson 1946, 89–91). Dorson points out that another version of the story, localized to a grocery store in Rutland, Vermont, was printed in Charles M. Skinner's *Myths and Legends of Our Own Land*. Skinner speaks of the trick as "formerly common in school-readers, in collections of moral tales for youth, and the miscellany columns of newspapers" (Skinner 1896, vol. 1 p. 54).

From a similar period, Mark Twain included a similar episode in *The Adventures of Huckleberry Finn* (1885). In chapter 40, Tom and Huck set out for a midnight feast, then remember that they have forgotten the butter for their bread. Tom creeps downstairs to the cellar to get it, but is waylaid by Aunt

Sally. He hides the butter under his hat. The outcome is the same—Aunt Sally has seen the theft and plays the same trick on him as the Vermont storekeeper plays on Seth (Mikkelson).

From the 1970s onward, when the deep-freeze had become commonplace in stores and homes, butter began to be replaced in the legends by frozen meat. Hats, though, remained the favorite place to store the stolen booty, so variant endings began to appear in the stories. Sometimes the meat was said to defreeze in the warmth under the hat so that the thief was covered in dripping blood. This ending remains truer to the earlier versions, but other storytellers follow a different logic to a different outcome; now the frozen food is said to freeze to the thief's head and cause fainting, hypothermia, or fatal "chilling of the brain." Stories with this ending were common in the Scandinavian press from 1966 through to 1974 (Klintberg 1989, 83), in the United Kingdom in the 1970s and 1980s, and in the United States in the 1990s.

Modern versions often show up in collections of humorous stories such as David Hardy's *What a Mistake!* (1987, 109), and Stuart Trueman's tales from Canadian border posts *Tall Tales and True Tales from Down East* (1979, 41–42); in news reports (Anders 2000); and in online form—an item from Anova's "Quirkies," for example, tells a tale from Italy about a man with a frozen chicken drumstick stuck down his pants ("Shoplifter Caught with Frozen Drumstick in his Pants").

Example

During the middle of last summer an old lady wearing a thick coat and a large hat was walking out of the supermarket when she collapsed. A doctor who happened to be going through the checkout at the time rushed forward to see if he could do anything.

Expecting her to be suffering from heatstroke he was very surprised to find it was actually a case of hypothermia! The riddle was finally solved when, to make the lady more comfortable, they removed her hat only to find she had been attempting to shoplift a frozen chicken under it. (Smith 1986, 53)

FURTHER READING

Anders, Drake. "Suspected Shoplifter Collapses—After Hiding A Frozen Chicken Under Her Hat—And Winds Up With Brain Damage From The Cold!" *Weekly World News* (September 12, 2000): 3.

Dorson, Richard M. *Jonathan Draws the Long Bow*. Cambridge, MA: Harvard University Press, 1946.

———. "How Shall We Rewrite Charles M. Skinner Today?" *American Folk Legend: A Symposium*. Ed. Wayland D. Hand. Berkeley, CA: University of California Press, 1971. pp. 69–95. Hardy, David. *What A Mistake!* Secaucus, NJ: Castle, 1987.

Klintberg, Bengt af. "Legends Today." In *Nordic Folklore: Recent Studies*. Eds. Reimund Kvideland and Henning K. Sehmsdorf in collaboration with Elizabeth Simpson. Bloomington, IN: Indiana University Press, 1989. pp. 70–89.

Mikkelson, Barbara. "The Meathead." http://www.snopes.com/crime/dumdum/meathead.asp

"Shoplifter Caught with Frozen Drumstick in his Pants." http://www.ananova.com/news/story/sm_717097.html?menu=news.quirkies.

Skinner, Charles M. *Myths and Legends of Our Own Land*. 2 vols. Philadelphia, PA: Lippincott, 1896.

Smith, Paul. *The Book of Nastier Legends*. London: Routledge and Kegan Paul, 1986.

Trueman, Stuart. *Tall Tales and True Tales from Down East*. Toronto: McClelland and Stewart, 1979.

See: The Cat in the Package; Killer Cacti, Statues, and Stones; The Stolen Specimen

---

THE WILL

This story of an unexpected inheritance has been around in America, Australia, and Europe probably since the 1970s. Like its cousin, "The Kilkenny Widow," it tells of somebody accidentally inheriting a fortune, but it lacks the sex element. "The Will" is the story of a person who finds himself or herself at the funeral or wake of a complete stranger, or in a church in the presence of a coffin. Out of politeness or confusion he/she signs the condolence book; later he/she discovers that the dead person has left a legacy to everybody who signs the book or has prayed for the dead man's soul. By accident a total stranger has become very wealthy.

Jan Brunvand published an account of this story in 1986 and pursued it from Spain to Germany; correspondents wrote in claiming that the events had happened in Chicago or Honduras up to 15 years previously (Brunvand 1999, 86–88; Brunvand 2001, 481–482).

In 1995 a story went round about a woman who needed to use a restroom whilst traveling and, unwilling to use a public toilet, slipped into a funeral home hoping to use the one on the premises. She panicked when asked which funeral she was attending and said she was there for the man without any mourners. Then she signed a condolence book, used the bathroom, and left. Two months later she got a letter announcing that, as the only mourner, she had been left a legacy of $50,000. Similarly in 1998 a series of stories hit the Internet in which a "Spanish guy" traveling in Poland came across a funeral home displaying an open casket and was surprised to find no one there. Feeling sorry for the friendless man, he signed the book of condolence. A while later he got a call from the dead man's lawyer. As the only person to have signed the book, he got the whole of the man's considerable estate.

It has been suggested that the story is an update of a tale from the 1940s about a man who leaves his fortune to whichever of his "loving children" turns up to see him buried. Only one of them, his daughter, comes for the funeral. So she inherits the lot (Mikkelson).

Similar tales are still reported (see, for example, "This Life" 2002). One such story tells how "a professional mourner" attended a man's funeral and cried for a complete stranger. The man's lawyer took him aside and told him that his client, who had been mean and eccentric, had earmarked $20,000 for anyone shedding a tear at his funeral. "I was the only one," he said (Cunningham 2001). There is also at least one "real life" story on this theme. In October 2004 a South African citizen died and stipulated in his will that anybody who attended his wake should share in a legacy of a million rand. Ninety-two guests attended and each received 1,100 rand (about US$170) (Wyckoff-Wheeler 2004).

The example below was sent from Australia by folklorist Bill Scott in January 1999. He said that the story had arrived in Australia about a month previously and was supposed to have happened in a town about 60 miles from his home in Warwick, Queensland.

Example

A young woman was asked to attend her aunt's funeral at the local crematorium. When she got to the place she found there were no less than four chapels and that services were being held. In her haste she entered the wrong one just as the service began. Too embarrassed to leave, she stayed to the end; and as the mourners were leaving they were asked to sign a book, name and address; and still being shy, she added hers to the list. Imagine her surprise when about two months later she received a cheque for several thousand pounds from a solicitor, for the dead man had insisted in his will that his estate should be equally divided among those who attended his funeral. (Bill Scott, personal communication)

FURTHER READING

Brunvand, Jan Harold. *Too Good to Be True: The Colossal Book of Urban Legends*. New York: Norton, 1999.

———. *Encyclopedia of Urban Legends*. New York: Norton, 2001.

Cunningham, Robert. "What A Way To Make A Living! Funeral Groupie Lives Life of Luxury." *Weekly World News* (August 28, 2001): 6.

Mikkelson, Barbara. "Last Writes." http://www.snopes.com/luck/will.asp

"This Life." "Improbable Luck: Mysterious Workings from the 'Other Side.'" *The Age* [Melbourne, Australia] (November 25, 2002). http://www.theage.com.au/articles/2002/11/24/1037697992330.html

Wyckoff-Wheeler, Donna. "A Legendary Funeral." *FOAFtale News* 60 (November 2004): 1.

See: The Kilkenny Widow

4

THE BODY AND DISEASE

A large number of urban legends are about bodily harm. In these stories people are shown as constantly open to threats beyond their control. Danger comes from both inside and outside, from other human beings and from the natural world. The body may be violated by people who deliberately contaminate it with disease, or steal bodily fluids or organs. It is also at risk from accidental invasion by other organisms. Snakes, insects, toads, and other noxious creatures may somehow get into the body by accident or through careless hygiene, foreign travel, or medicines. Even plants may invade the vulnerable tissues and orifices of the body via food or dust.

In this world of threats and dangers, no one is safe.

For other tales of bodily harm see: *The Castrated Boy; The Exploding Toilet; Framed; Glued to the Loo; The Hair-Curler Revenge; Mall Slashers; The Mutilated Shopper; The Poisoned Dress; Spiders at Large; The Superglue Revenge*

AIDS AGGRESSORS 1: INTRODUCTION

For over twenty years rumors and legends have circulated by word of mouth, in the media, and on the Internet about HIV-positive people deliberately infecting others as a form of revenge for their own condition. Over time, the basic plot of the legend has undergone changes that have updated it and made it relevant to changing attitudes and information. These changes are documented in the entries for "AIDS Aggressors" 2–5. Meanwhile this section looks at some famous cases.

One such case was the hoax perpetrated on the magazine *Ebony* and a Dallas talk show in September 1991. A 15-year-old girl from Dallas, Texas, calling herself "CJ" wrote to *Ebony* claiming that, after contracting AIDS, she had become obsessed with picking men up in nightclubs in order to pass the HIV virus on. Her letter concluded "I feel if I have to die of a horrible disease, I won't go alone." Later a woman who identified herself as "CJ" appeared on a local talk show and reaffirmed that she had been haunting nightclubs in the Dallas-Fort Worth area picking men up and having unprotected sex with them. She showed no remorse, saying: "I blame it on men, period. Not just one. I'm doing it to all the men because it was a man that gave it to me." The whole episode was later found to be a fraud; both the "CJ" who wrote to *Ebony* and the woman who claimed to be "CJ" on the talk show were hoaxers. Though both "CJ"'s were exposed as frauds, the Dallas Deputy Police Chief was not reassured: "Our attitude is that there is no CJ as purported to be. However, there are lots of CJ's out there, either knowingly or unintentionally spreading HIV." (Bird 1996).

A case that caused a media frenzy in Britain and Ireland in September 1995 occurred when an Irish priest claimed in a sermon that a "promiscuous, tattooed, HIV positive blonde" had been "marauding through Dungarvan near Cork, Ireland, liberally spreading sexual favours among the village's young men and knowingly infecting up to 80 of them. The girl, 25, who had recently arrived in the village from London, is reported to be 'demented' by her condition." Unfortunately for him, the priest took the allegations seriously, and for this misjudgement he suffered a week of mockery and media attention and was reprimanded by his bishop. Days later, though, he was still insisting that he was "110% sure" the story was true ("AIDS Mary in Ireland"; Bennett 2005, 111–112).

Indeed, some sick, malicious, or misguided people did appear to be acting out the legends in their own lives. Among several cases which were brought to court was the one that Jan Brunvand spotted in 1990 in the *Cincinnati Post* entitled "'AIDS Mary' Murder," that told the story of a man charged with murder who claimed that he had picked up his victim in a bar. After having sex with him she allegedly said, "Welcome to the world of AIDS." The man freaked out, attacked her, and killed her (*Cincinnati Post* January 30, 1991; quoted in "'AIDS Mary' Murder"). In Kenya, during the spring of 2005 it was reported during an AIDS panic fuelled by reports on the Internet that a nurse from Nairobi, having been diagnosed as HIV positive ten years ago, was determined to infect as many men as possible. Reportedly she was heard saying: "Wasn't I young and innocent when I was infected by my boyfriend? Don't men and women deserve to pay for what has happened to me? Why not, my boyfriend must have gotten the infection from a woman and his mother is a woman!" (Oyaro 1999).

Perhaps the most notorious "real life" AIDS aggressor was a man from Newfoundland (Canada). Diane Goldstein's study of this case, in which she became involved when the Senior Crown Prosecutor realized that he needed a folklorist's input, is a classic of its kind. In 1991 a 28-year-old man from Upper Island Cove, Newfoundland was tried under the Common Nuisance section of the Criminal Code for endangering the lives, safety, or health of the public through unprotected sex while knowingly carrying the AIDS virus. He was found guilty and sentenced to $2^1/_2$ years in prison, later increased to 11 years and 3 months (Goldstein 2004, 116–138). More recently, in June 2006, a similar, but less high-profile, case was heard in a British court, and a woman was jailed for 32 months for inflicting grievous bodily harm on her boyfriend. Her offence was that she had not revealed her HIV-positive status to him, with the consequence that he had become infected with the virus. More significant than the charge against the woman was the way the case was treated in the tabloid press. The woman was depicted in terms of the AIDS Aggressor legend as a dangerous sexual predator liable to harm every man she could find:

> Blonde, female, and with a sexual history [wrote an outraged journalist in one of the respectable dailies] she is the ultimate red-top baddie, given the kind of treatment usually reserved for child killers and pedophiles. The reporting of her character is strikingly one-dimensional: she is "Pure Evil" (*The Daily Mail*), a "Bitter Blonde" (*The Sun*), and a "Heartless Blonde Maneater" (*The Express*). The subtext of her depiction is that . . . her HIV status is a punishment (Pool 2006).

Meanwhile, AIDS Aggressor legends were making their way into film (for example "Via Appia," 1992) and television. The story featured, for example, in an episode of the popular British police drama "The Bill" on August 12, 1999. The plotline centered on a man who wrote "Join the Club" on prostitutes' backs and, after using their services, told them, "I have AIDS and now you do too." One of the interesting things about this episode of "The Bill" was the way it used its legend-based plot to explore legal issues such as the difficulty of proving intention to transmit disease and problems in identifying whether the attacker actually has the disease or is maliciously using the legend to provoke anxiety.

FURTHER READING

"Aids Mary in Ireland." *FOAFtale News* 38 (December 1995): 8.

"Aids Mary Murder." *FOAFtale News* 22 (June 1991): 9.

Bird, Elizabeth. "CJ's Revenge: Media, Folklore, and the Cultural Construction of Aids." *Critical Studies in Mass Communication* 13 (1996): 44–58.

Goldstein, Diane E. *Once Upon a Virus: AIDS Legends and Vernacular Risk Perception.* Logan, UT: Utah University Press, 2004.

Oyaro, Kwamboka. "Aids Killers on the Prowl," "On the Web" column. Or *The Daily Nation* (Kenya) (October 20, 1999).

Pool, Hannah. "Porter's Real Crime: She Slept with Black Men." *The Guardian* [London and Manchester UK] (June 21, 2006). http://www.guardian.co.uk/aids/story/0,1802279,00.html

Smith, Paul. "Rumour, Gossip and Hearsay: The Folklore of a Pandemic." *Talking Aids: Interdisciplinary Perspectives on Acquired Immunity Deficiency Syndrome.* Ed. Diane E. Goldstein. Memorial University of Newfoundland: ISER, 1991, pp. 95–121.

See: AIDS Aggressors 1 (Introduction); AIDS Aggressors 2 (Kissing, Biting and Spitting); AIDS Aggressors 3 (Mirrors); AIDS Aggressors 4 (Caskets); AIDS Aggressors 5 (Needles)

AIDS AGGRESSORS 2: KISSING, BITING, AND SPITTING

Since the early 1980s rumors started circulating in the gay community of San Francisco about a "strange guy" at a bathhouse who would have sex with other men, then point out his Kaposi's sarcoma lesions (one of the giveaway signs of AIDS) and announce, "I've got gay cancer. I'm going to die and so are you." However, it was in the form of rumors about random attacks on complete strangers that the legends really took off. By 1986 they usually took the form of stories about infected gays biting or spitting at passersby in the street. In Sheffield (UK) a journalist working on the local paper called Paul Smith with a story he had heard about male homosexual prostitutes who had deliberately given AIDS to their clients. In the same year a member of the Police Committee of the Lothian region of Scotland was reported as having said, "I've heard of rent boys who can infect a hundred or more people in a year. It's a lethal weapon they're carrying in their bodies and it's being allowed to run free" (Smith 1991, 101). The tabloids were also carrying defamatory jokes and stories about gay stars such as Rock Hudson, alleging for example, that he had "French kissed" "Dynasty" star Linda Evans while he had open sores on his mouth (Smith

1991, 118). The example below, published by a British tabloid, is typical of this coverage. The rumor mill in the United States was also busy with stories about HIV-positive cooks masturbating into fast food and so infecting their customers (Langlois 1991; see also Brunvand 2001, 252).

In Poland, too, where AIDS paranoia was rife, folklorist Dionizjusz Czubala reported that people were supposedly being deliberately infected through food and drink. A high school student he recorded in October 1989 told him that, "There was a drug addict who learned he had AIDS, so he threw a party for his friends and treated them to some soup in which he had mixed some of his blood. In this way he infected 30 people out of sheer revenge for being ill himself." Tales also circulated among teenagers about rape-like attacks on young girls by disgruntled carriers, "who hang out in discos to assault unsuspecting victims in secluded spots. Two of them hold a girl's hands, while the third kisses her on the mouth and passes on the virus with his saliva. Rumor has it that hundreds of 14-year-olds have been infected in this way" (Czubala 1991, 2).

However, stories of people deliberately infecting others by their touch, or kiss, or bite are by no means new, though in the past it was likely to be bubonic plague and syphilis that they were accused of passing on. During the plague of London the English diarist Samuel Pepys (1633–1703) recounts how infected people went to burials and deliberately breathed in the faces of the mourners. The *Journal of the Plague Year* written by English novelist Daniel Defoe (1660–1731) purported to be an eyewitness account of the plague of London 1665, and is based on legends, hearsay, gossip, and rumor that were current during the plague. In one episode Defoe tells how a plague-ridden man rushed out into the street and kissed a woman who was passing by, saying that "he had the plague and why should she not have it as well as he?" (Smith 1990, 129–130). A virtually identical story can also be found in French novelist Albert Camus' fictional account of an outbreak of plague (*La Peste*, 1947). Here, the story is that, "a man with all the symptoms [of plague] and running a high fever ... dashed out into the street, flung himself on the first woman he met, and embraced her, yelling that he'd 'got it'" (see Bennett 2005, 118). Again, Camus was a writer who was well aware of folklore and who often incorporated current legends into his novels. So there is a good deal of evidence for earlier traditions of deliberate infection with deadly disease.

Example

A young man of our acquaintance has suffered the most nightmarish of attacks outside a seamy Edinburgh nightclub known to be frequented by all manner of persons of a homosexual inclination. Our chum's superficial wounds, one fears, could yet turn out to be of a quite fatal nature.

As our friend walked past the establishment, a bearded and extremely agitated drunk came tottering out of the premises and grabbed him by the hand.

"Have you got AIDS, dearie?" he asked.

"No, no, I haven't," replied our startled acquaintance.

His attacker seized his arm and sank his teeth into it.

"Well—you have now!" he said. And ran off. (Smith 1991, 100)

FURTHER READING

Bennett, Gillian. *Bodies: Sex, Violence, Disease, and Death in Contemporary Legend.* Jackson, MS: University Press of Mississippi, 2005. See pp. 104–141.

Brunvand, Jan Harold. *Encyclopedia of Urban Legends.* New York: Norton, 2001.

Czubala, Dionizjusz. "Aids and Aggression: Polish Legends About HIV-Infected People." *FOAFtale News* 23 (September 1991): 1–5.

Goldstein, Diane E. *Once Upon a Virus: AIDS Legends and Vernacular Risk Perception.* Logan, UT: Utah University Press, 2004. See pp. 139–158.

Langlois, Janet. "'Hold the Mayo': Purity and Danger in an Aids Legend." *Contemporary Legend* 1 (1991): 153–172.

Smith, Paul. "'Aids: Don't Die of Ignorance': Exploring the Cultural Complex." *A Nest of Vipers: Perspectives on Contemporary Legend V.* Ed. Gillian Bennett and Paul Smith. Sheffield: Sheffield Academic Press for the International Society for Contemporary Legend Research in association with CECTAL, 1990, pp. 113–141.

———. "Rumour, Gossip and Hearsay: The Folklore of a Pandemic." *Talking Aids: Interdisciplinary Perspectives on Acquired Immunity Deficiency Syndrome.* Ed. Diane. E. Goldstein. Memorial University of Newfoundland: ISER, 1991, pp. 95–121.

See: AIDS Aggressors 1 (Introduction); AIDS Aggressors 3 (Mirrors); AIDS Aggressors 4 (Caskets); AIDS Aggressors 5 (Needles)

AIDS AGGRESSORS 3: MIRRORS

By 1986 an "AIDS Aggressor" narrative with a number of traditional motifs had begun to circulate. It featured a woman as the AIDS aggressor and a heterosexual male as her victim. According to Jan Brunvand, Dan Sheridan writing in the *Chicago Sun Times* that year, called it "AIDS Mary" echoing stories of the infamous spreader of another deadly disease, "Typhoid Mary." The name has stuck ever since (Brunvand 2001, 6–7). The story relates how a man picks up a willing and glamorous woman in a bar. He goes back to his room with her, and they spend a night of passion together. In the morning she is gone. But she has left a shocking message scrawled in lipstick on the bathroom mirror, "Welcome to the AIDS Club" (or "Welcome to the wonderful world of AIDS").

A similar story appeared in the *San Francisco Examiner* in January 1987. This time it was said to have happened to a French businessman who spent a weekend with a Jamaican woman (Brunvand 1989, 196). The story was soon well known throughout Western Europe and North America. Paul Smith heard it in February 1987 from a journalist working for *The Sheffield Star* (UK), who called him to say the tale was being told all over the city; the following week, the story was printed in a sensational tabloid newspaper. The legend was featured in Jan Brunvand's syndicated column in March, and again in August and September 1987. It popped up in the Ann Landers column; it was quoted by evangelist Billy Graham on TV; it was "the hottest story going in Toronto"; it was heard in a Welsh hospital; and reported in newspapers from many American states and from Poland, Austria, and Sweden too. It even appeared in *Playboy* in July of that year (Bennett 2005, 106–108). It remained the most-often-told version of tales about AIDS aggressors in Western Europe and North America for about ten years.

By the late 1990s a very similar story was being reported in Kenya. Under the headline "AIDS killers on the prowl" in the "On the Web" column, the [Kenya] *Daily Nation* for October 20, 1999 repeated a story from the web about a man who received compensation when he left his job because he was HIV-positive, and used the money to go on a "sex spree." Supposedly, "He smiled all the way from one unsuspecting woman to another. Before he died, he asked for a paper and pen and wrote down 100 names of women who he had had sex with. The note read: 'Behold these women will also die like me!' (Oyaro 1999).

Examples

1. A British industrialist visiting Miami hired a lady of the streets to keep him company for the night on his stopover. The following morning when he woke, his companion had gone. On entering the bathroom—so the legend goes—he found the following horrific message scrawled in lipstick on his mirror: "Welcome to the AIDS club," (Smith 1991, 98)

2.

   Narrator 1. I have a couple of friends in those circles, so I heard that a lot of them are sick. They all got the virus from a girl that had come from Warsaw. She slept around with a few guys from Katowice. And she got paid with dope. When she was leaving, she told them jokingly about her disease. Quite possible she did this on purpose.

Narrator 2. I heard a similar story. A girl slept with a guy and did not ask for money: instead she left a farewell message on the mirror. When the boy woke up, he read "Welcome to the AIDS club." (Czubala 1991, 3)

FURTHER READING

Bennett, Gillian. *Bodies: Sex, Violence, Disease, and Death in Contemporary Legend.* Jackson, MS: University Press of Mississippi, 2005. See pp. 104–141.

Brunvand, Jan Harold. *Curses! Broiled Again! The Hottest Urban Legends Going.* New York: Norton, 1989.

Brunvand, Jan Harold. *Encyclopedia of Urban Legends.* New York: Norton, 2001.

Czubala, Dionizjusz. "Aids and Aggression: Polish Legends About HIV-Infected People." *FOAFtale News* 23 (September 1991): 1–5.

Oyaro, Kwamboka. "Aids Killers on the Prowl." "On the Web" column. or *The Daily Nation* (Kenya) (October 20, 1999).

Smith, Paul. "Rumour, Gossip and Hearsay: The Folklore of a Pandemic." *Talking Aids: Interdisciplinary Perspectives on Acquired Immunity Deficiency Syndrome.* Ed. Diane. E. Goldstein. Memorial University of Newfoundland: ISER, 1991, pp. 95–121.

See: AIDS Aggressors 1 (Introduction); AIDS Aggressors 2 (Kissing, Biting and Spitting); AIDS Aggressors 4 (Caskets); AIDS Aggressors 5 (Needles)

AIDS AGGRESSORS 4: CASKETS

This version of legends about "AIDS Aggressors" seems to have been current since April 1989, when Canadian folklorist Diane Goldstein saw an article in the Newfoundland *Evening Telegram* headed "Bizarre AIDS story likely a concocted tale." It became the dominant form that AIDS Aggressor legends took in America, Canada, and the United Kingdom for about five years. A typical story would tell how a friend-of-a-friend had a holiday romance in a foreign country. Her holiday boyfriend escorts her to the plane and gives her a little gift-wrapped package as a parting gift. When she opens it she finds, not the engagement ring or sweet memento she expected, but a miniature coffin and a chilling message. The casket is sometimes said to contain just the note or sometimes a toy skeleton; sometimes the "casket" is said to be a miniature coffin, or in some versions—thanks to the "Chinese Whispers" effect of oral tradition—a coffeemaker or coffee mug (Goldstein 1992, 209–224).

The first example below comes from Canada c. 1989, the second from the United Kingdom 1990. Typically of contemporary legends, the details in the British version have been updated and adapted to fit a different time and place. The scene is now set in Spain, which is popular with British people as somewhere to escape the climate; and, in a reference to other concerns of the time, the Spanish playboys are said to have formed a "cult."

Examples

1. This girl needed a break and decided to go to Florida for a month or two holiday, I think. While she was there she met a man, who seemed to be . . . the man of her dreams. He had money, he treated her like gold, and he gave her everything she wanted. She fell in love with him and . . . during her last night there they slept together. The next day he brought her to the airport for her return to St John's. He gave her a small gift-wrapped box and told her not to open it until she got home. They . . . said goodbye and she left hoping that someday they would be married and the gift would be an [engagement] ring. The suspense was killing her and . . . she decided to open the gift on the plane. It was a small coffin with a piece of paper saying "Welcome to the World of AIDS." (Goldstein 1992, 24)

2. A British AIDS counselor warned that infected playboys at Spanish resorts had formed a cult devoted to giving the disease to vacationing girls. He said that in two cases British girls, after a holiday affair in Spain, were given little farewell gifts to carry with them on the plane home. The packages contained a small wooden coffin inscribed with "Welcome to the death club. Now you've got AIDS." The two girls are said to be undergoing three months of testing to see if they have in fact caught the disease. ("Legends in the Tabloids")

FURTHER READING

Bennett, Gillian. *Bodies: Sex, Violence, Disease, and Death in Contemporary Legend.* Jackson, MS: University Press of Mississippi, 2005. See pp. 104–141.

Goldstein, Diane E. "Welcome to the Mainland, Welcome to the World of Aids: Cultural Viability, Localization and Contemporary Legend." *Contemporary Legend* 2 (1992): 23–40. Reprinted in *Contemporary Legend: A Reader.* Compiled by Gillian Bennett and Paul Smith. New York: Garland, 1996.

———. *Once Upon a Virus: AIDS Legends and Vernacular Risk Perception.* Logan, UT: Utah University Press, 2004. See pp. 139–156.

"Legends in the Tabloids." *FOAFtale News* 18 (1990): 10. Reprinted from an item in the (UK) *Sun*, March 1990.

Smith, Paul. "Rumour, Gossip and Hearsay: The Folklore of a Pandemic." *Talking Aids: Interdisciplinary Perspectives on Acquired Immunity Deficiency Syndrome.* Ed. Diane. E. Goldstein. Memorial University of Newfoundland: ISER, 1991, 95–121.

See: AIDS Aggressors 1 (Introduction); AIDS Aggressors 2 (Kissing, Biting and Spitting); AIDS Aggressors 3 (Mirrors); AIDS Aggressors 5 (Needles)

AIDS AGGRESSORS 5: NEEDLES

In February 1987, at the height of the AIDS panic in Britain, a freelance journalist told Paul Smith that "a group of friends in a disco in Germany were attacked by a gang of youths who stabbed them with hypodermic needles containing contaminated blood" (Smith 1991, 102). This variant of "AIDS Aggressor" legends became more and more widespread as time went by and was the dominant story of the later 1990s and the first years of the 2000s. Throughout this period notices were circulating on the Internet warning people that drug users were leaving needles contaminated with hepatitis, AIDS, and other diseases in public telephones. Oral stories, and particularly e-mail messages, began to proliferate which warned of infected needles in soda machine coin slots, and on the underside of the handles of gas pumps.

In the early 1990s there was a huge rumor-panic in Poland which was documented by Polish folklorist Dionizjusz Czubala. In May 1990 a student at the University of Silesia told Czubala that a colleague had said that the town of Bielsko had a huge concentration of infected people and they were terribly aggressive: "It is like a vacationland that attracts infected visitors," she said, "and the city becomes really dangerous. Last year they supposedly became so aggressive that they were going after people with their needles, especially children." In the same month another student from the same university told him that there was a madman infected with HIV in Sosnowiec, and everybody was afraid of him because he got on the tram and "gave the needle to" as many young girls as he could (Czubala 1991, 4).

Later in the decade, there was worldwide anxiety about whether infected people were leaving needles in cinema seats. In 1999 the rumor was reported from Canada, the United States, Germany, Finland, the United Kingdom, Australia, India, Hawaii, Mexico, and Costa Rica ("Needles in Vending Machines and Pay Phones"; Hiscock 1999; Brunvand 2001, 285–287). French folklorists, Véronique Campion-Vincent and Jean-Bruno Renard, reported a rumor-panic in France that was rampant for about a month from the end of February to the end of March 2001. A message circulating on the Internet and by e-mail warned people to be extremely careful and to undertake a "minute visual inspection" of seats in public places. Originally circulating in French-speaking Canada, when it reached Paris the story jammed the government communication network for 48 hours (Bennett 2005, 114–115). A similar panic had broken out in Estonia at the end of 2000 and beginning of 2001. Here it was not just cinema seats which were to be feared. Stories proliferated about deliberately contaminated doorknobs and light switches, and sandboxes in children's playgrounds. "People were terrified of getting infected at the manicurist, at the dentist, at the tattoo salon etc." (Kalmre 2001). Then in November 2002, it was reported that the cinema form of the needle legend had resurfaced in Melbourne (Australia) after lying dormant for 4 years and that it had recently appeared in Delhi (India) too (Sircar 2002).

More recently the legend surfaced in Mauritius. In January 2006 the local newspaper, *L'Express*, carried a story that had been circulating the month before via e-mails about someone walking round the market with a syringe of contaminated blood and trying to infect others as revenge for having contracted the HIV virus. The first article was a poignant account in which the journalist told how he had met a distraught mother and daughter duo at the local hospital after somebody had stuck a needle in the girl's arm. The mother was reported as saying, "Yes, I read through the internet that somebody was doing that to people but little did I realize that it would happen to my own daughter. All I can do is pray." The girl's life was said to have been "shattered" and she was too traumatized to go to school. The second article dismissed the story as "a wicked rumour" (see "Killer of Dreams"; "Of Rumour and Nastiness").

The legend has still enough potency for anyone attacked in the street to fear that they have been deliberately injected with disease. In February 2006, for example, two popular tabloid newspapers in the United Kingdom carried a story about a "maniac" who had stabbed a woman and a young man in the leg with a hypodermic needle. They are said to be waiting test results to see if they have been infected with AIDS or hepatitis B ("Nut with Needle"; "Mum's Bar Needle Terror").

Example

This could be life or death for somebody. There are these gangs running round Britain sticking HIV-infected needles into people then handing them a card reading

"Welcome to the world of HIV." This is not a joke or an urban myth, it's actually happened. They've been seen in Brighton, and last night they were active in The Gallery [club]. So you can see why I'm more than a little anxious about this. Any of us could have been in The Gallery last night, and most of us were planning to go. The idea of this happening to anybody I know gives me the shits, hence the warning. These people don't just operate in clubs, they operate on the street, while you're shopping, anywhere, so being paranoid probably isn't the answer. But please, take care. This IS happening and I couldn't take it if it happened to you. (e-mail message 1998)

FURTHER READING

Bennett, Gillian. *Bodies: Sex, Violence, Disease, and Death in Contemporary Legend*. Jackson, MS: University Press of Mississippi, 2005. See pp. 104–141.

Brunvand, Jan Harold. *Encyclopedia of Urban Legends*. New York: Norton, 2001. See pp. 285–287.

Czubala, Dionizjusz. "Aids and Aggression: Polish Legends About HIV-Infected People." *FOAFtale News* 23 (September 1991): 1–5.

Goldstein, Diane E. *Once Upon a Virus: AIDS Legends and Vernacular Risk Perception*. Logan: Utah University Press, 2004. See pp. 139–156.

Hiscock, Philip. "More Needles." *FOAFtale News* 45 (November 1999): 5.

"Killer of Dreams." *L'Express* [Mauritius] (January 24, 2006). http://www.lexpress.mu/display_article_sup.php?news_id=58182.

"Mum's Bar Needle Terror." *The Sun* [London] (February 6, 2006). http://www.thesun.co.uk/article/0,02-2006060056,00.html

"Needles in Vending Machines and Pay Phones." *FOAFtale News* 44 (May 1999): 10.

"Nut with a Needle Stabs Two." *The Mirror* [London] (February 6, 2006). http://www.mirror.co.uk/news/tm_objectid=16670871&method=full&siteid=94762

"Of Rumour and Nastiness." *L'Express* [Mauritius] (January 24, 2006). http://www.lexpress.mu/display_article_sup.php?news_id=581828.

Sircar, Sanjay. "Aids-Needle Legend, 2001." *FLS News* 38 (November 2002): 13.

Smith, Paul. "Rumour, Gossip and Hearsay: The Folklore of a Pandemic." In *Talking Aids: Interdisciplinary Perspectives on Acquired Immune Deficiency Syndrome*. Ed. Diane E. Goldstein. St John's Newfoundland: Memorial University of Newfoundland. ISER research and policy papers, no. 2, 1991, pp. 95–121.

See: AIDS Aggressors 1 (Introduction); AIDS Aggressors 2 (Kissing, Biting and Spitting); AIDS Aggressors 3 (Mirrors); AIDS Aggressors 4 (Caskets)

THE BOSOM SERPENT

Since biblical times, serpents and toads have been symbols of sin and degradation. Imagine how awful it is to have these creatures entering your body, growing there, and stealing your food.

Horrible though it is, stories like this have been known since at least the Middle Ages and have been found almost all over the world, from the United States to Australia, and from Azerbaijan to Ireland. In the Middle Ages and in Ancient Greece and Rome it was medical orthodoxy to believe that animals could indeed get into the human body and live there, causing pain, disease, and death.

It is not only snakes and toads that are said to take up residence in the human body in these stories. Others tell of newts, lizards, flies, and eels; and, in the strangest legends, there are stories about dogs, mice, "live things," "something alive and black," and "something like a monkey" living in the human gut (Bennett 2000, 47–52).

In modern stories the animal is usually removed by surgery (as in the example below), or accidentally discovered or comes out of its own accord but in older legends it usually has to be tricked out. The theory is that the animal can be persuaded to come back up given the right incentive—a tasty snack of bacon or toasted cheese, or a bowl of warm milk. Alternatively the patient (and therefore the animal inside) is not allowed to drink for several hours, and then taken to a stream; the thirsty creature will leap out when it hears the sound of running water.

The fullest examinations of this legend are those by Gillian Bennett who looks at the history of the stories in Chapter 1 of her 2005 book *Bodies*, at its medical aspects in an article of 2000, and at its social aspects in a contribution to a 1997 book on medical history. Other useful surveys are Chapter 1 of Harold Schechter's examination of folklore and popular art (1988, 2nd ed. 2001) and Chapter 2 of Jan Bondeson's history of medical curiosities (1997). Jerome Clark has several good "Bosom Serpent" stories from American newspapers 1840–1910 in his book *Unnatural Phenomena* (2005, 3, 143, 149, 184, 225, 259–260).

The "Bosom Serpent" theme has been reworked in several literary and popular media. The most famous of these is the short story by Nathaniel Hawthorne which has given the legend its name among folklorists. In "Egotism; or, The Bosom Serpent" (1834) Hawthorne uses the story as a metaphor for the destructive effect of pride and selfishness. Another use of the legend can be found in the diary of Henry D. Thoreau, who speaks of having "drunk from a rill" and swallowed a creature which now must be pulled painfully from his innards. Possibly this was an actual occurrence, but it is more likely that Thoreau was using it as metaphor for the creative process. Another American short story that uses the "Bosom Serpent" theme is Hortense Calisher's "Heartburn" (1951). The story also provides an episode in Willa Cather's 1913 novel O, Pioneers! (Barnes and Smith 2001). Schechter has an interesting analysis of the Hawthorne story, and also of the "Bosom Serpent" in the 1979 movie *Alien* (Schechter 2001, 16–20). "*Star Trek 2: The Wrath of Khan*" (1982) also utilizes the idea of the invading animal.

The example below is taken from a recording of a storytelling session involving five friends at a British university in the early 1980s. It seems to be a report of an item in the press or on the radio, but we have not been able to trace the source.

Example

Rob: There was something on the radio or something, about rats—snakes in bodies, in the body of that girl ... It was about three weeks ago now. I heard it somewhere. It's a snake in some girl's body and they had to operate to get it out ... She was only about six. It must have been in *The Daily Mirror* or on Radio One. No but, she was going really thin. Sue, you read that thing about that snake in that girl ... There was this girl with a snake in, and they operated on it.

Sue: Was it all entwined around her?

Rob: It was all in her intestines. It was still alive ... and they operated. It's true, because it was in the paper. Well, it might not have been true because it was in the paper, but—it was in America.

Fiona: I've heard that about tapeworms. They say it was about forty feet long or something—

Rob: Oh, no, not tapeworms—

Fiona: Apparently you can buy tapeworms like pills or something—

Rob: It was a snake. It was about three weeks ago ... and then they took it out and it was alive and they killed it, which I thought was really unreasonable. (Bennett Collection)

FURTHER READING

Barnes, Daniel R., and Paul Smith. "Research Note—The Contemporary Legend in Literature—Towards an Annotated Checklist, Part 4: The Bosom Serpent." *Contemporary Legend* new series 4 (2001): 126–149.

Bennett, Gillian. "Bosom Serpents and Alimentary Amphibians: A Language for Sickness?" *Illness and Healing Alternatives in Western Europe*. Ed. Hilary Marland, Hans de Waardt, and Marijke Gijswijt-Hofstra. Studies in the Social History of Medicine Series. London: Routledge and Kegan Paul, 1997. 224–242.

———. "Medical Aspects of the Bosom Serpent." *Contemporary Legend* new series 3 (2000): 1–26.

———. *Bodies: Sex, Violence, Disease, and Death in Contemporary Legend*. Jackson, MI: University Press of Mississippi, 2005.

Bondeson, Jan. *A Cabinet of Medical Curiosities*. Ithaca, NY: Cornell University Press, 1997.

Cattermole-Tally, Frances. "The Intrusion of Animals into the Human Body: Fantasy and Reality." *Folklore* 106 (1995): 89–92.

Clarke, Jerome. *Unnatural Phenomena*. Santa Barbara, CA: ABC-CLIO, 2005.

Schechter, Harold. *The Bosom Serpent: Folklore and Popular Art*. Iowa City: University of Iowa Press, 1988. 2nd ed. New York: Peter Lang, 2001.

See: Earwigs in Ears and Ants in Eyes; The Girl with the Beehive Hairdo; (Im)planted; The Spider Boil; The Tapeworm Diet

EARWIGS IN EARS AND ANTS IN EYES

One of the most common types of urban legend today concerns contamination of various sorts—of food, and clothing, and of the body itself. Such stories are often about creatures getting into bodily organs through orifices, especially ears, eyes, and mouth.

Recently the Indian press reported that a patient was found dead after ants had eaten her eyes. A post mortem on the woman was said to have shown that "around 1 inch by 1.5 inch of her eyelid was full of abrasions due to ant bites." The newspaper headlines were particularly lurid: "Ant-nibbled diabetic patient dies in Kolkata," "Ants gorge on eye, patient's cries ignored," and so on. In other versions the victim was said to be a visitor from the western world.

Two versions were printed in the *Calcutta Telegraph*, just a few days apart (November 17 and 23, 2005; see "Ant-bite Slap on Nurses" and "Death Probe Met with Silence"). Interestingly, a very similar tale had been told in New Delhi (India) in February 1991, when doctors were supposed to be "baffled" by ants coming out of the eye of a 12-year-old girl. By March 7 the *Times of India* was reporting that the doctors decided to operate and found no trace of ants in the eyelids. They suggested that the ants had been put there deliberately either by the girl herself or by someone else. The girl's parents, however, insisted it was no hoax (via e-mail from Brian Chapman).

A modern variant is the tale of the person who has a persistent itch under a plaster cast and discovers, to everyone's horror, that termites have eaten into her arm; and there is another story of a boy with a terrible headache who in agony jabs a fork into his head and releases a stream of ants. Iain Banks plugs into the same set of images in his novel *The Wasp Factory* (1984) which climaxes in events surrounding the death of a deformed child with a paper-thin skull that has been protected by a stainless steel skullcap. Here the creatures that get under the skullcap and into the child's brain are flies, but the climax is identical to that of oral stories: "What Eric saw when he lifted the plate up . . . was a slowly writhing nest of fat maggots, swimming in their combined digestive juices as they consumed the brain of the child" (p. 142).

Though these legends look modern and are reported as current news, they have been around for some time. For example, Jewish folk tradition tells how God sent a mosquito (or in some versions a gnat) to the Emperor Titus, and it bored into his brain and started to pick and nibble at it (Hasan-Rokem 2005, 36). In medieval times, it was thought possible to be overrun with lice breeding in the body's tissues and eating the flesh away. Though this belief was later discounted, stories of other unpleasant creatures consuming the body still persisted. For example, in the eighteenth century correspondents to the British revue *The Gentleman's Magazine* were swapping examples of "a frightful insect" eating away part of a woman's face and cases where earwigs had supposedly penetrated a patient's brain after getting in through the ear (Anon 1785; H. F. 1798). Similarly, in the early twentieth century, a correspondent to the British journal *Folklore* recounted a story about somebody who was supposed to have beetles breeding in her ear (Aitken 1926): and a folklore collector in 1940s Virginia was told a story he called "A Man Dies of Earwigs" (Barden 1991, 308–309).

Modern "earwig" and "ant" stories sometimes share the same structure as legends about "The Spider Boil" (i.e. foreign travel, itch, horrific discovery). Like that story, they may also be presented as cautionary tales. For example, the journalist reporting the story in our example below commented "What happened to her there should be a warning to any Westerner considering traveling to that part of the world."

Example

A Canadian student, Arlene Simmons, and two girlfriends decide to go sightseeing in India. Arlene starts to suffer from a terrible itch in her right eye. Her friends take her to a local hospital, where her eyes are treated with ointment and bandaged. After a few days the pain becomes excruciating and she tries to rip off her bandages. The nurses have to tie her arms to the bed. However, after a while Arlene feels sufficiently well to leave hospital. So the moment arrived for the bandages to be taken off. When the doctor removed the bandages, her friends watched in horror as hundreds of ants scurried out of her empty eye sockets. (Version based on research notes from a variety of sources such as an article in the *Calcutta Telegraph*, November 17, 2005)

FURTHER READING

Aitken, Barbara. "London. Smothering the Incurable." *Folk-Lore* 37 (1926): 78–79.

Anon. "Medical Cases." *The Gentleman's Magazine* 55 (1785): 52.

"Ant-bite Slap on Nurse." *The Telegraph* [Calcutta, India] (November 23, 2005), http://www.telegraphindia.com/1051123/asp/calcutta/story_5509444.asp

Barden, Thomas E. *Virginia Folk Legends*. Charlottesville, VA: University Press of Virginia, 1991.

"Death Probe Met with Silence." *The Telegraph* [Calcutta, India] (November 17, 2005), http://www.telegraphindia.com/1051117/asp/calcutta/story_5483976.asp

H. F. "Note." *The Gentleman's Magazine* 68, Part 2 (1798): 555.

Hasan-Rokem, Galit. "Rumors in Times of War and Cataclysm." In *Rumor Mills: The Social Impact of Rumor and Legend*. Ed. Gary Alan Fine, Véronique Campion-Vincent, and Chip Heath. New Brunswick, NJ: AldineTransaction, 2005, pp. 31-52.

See: The Bosom Serpent; The Girl with the Beehive Hairdo; (Im)planted; The Spider Boil; The Tapeworm Diet

THE GIRL WITH THE BEEHIVE HAIRDO

In its modern form this story, which is also known as "The Spider in the Hairdo," goes back to the last years of the 1950s and early 1960s when the "beehive" hairdo was in fashion across America, Canada, and Europe. Shoulder-length hair was backcombed to give it bulk, then the top layer was smoothed over the backcombing and built up into a shape on top of the head that resembled a helmet (or beehive), then it was heavily lacquered to keep it in place. Once in place, it couldn't be brushed or combed, and it took so long to get the hair fixed that many girls did not wash it for several days and used to sleep with a hairnet over it. This gave rise to much criticism, and the style was considered unhygienic as well as ugly. The stories about vermin of various kinds being found in these hairstyles flourished in these circumstances.

A variety of creatures were said to have been found nesting in the dirty hair—any small offensive creatures would do, but spiders (especially Black Widow spiders) and "bugs" were the favorites, with cockroaches and bees also featuring in some versions. The outcome of the infestation was said to vary from social shame or loss of the hair (see our first example below), to death because the creature had eaten through to the brain. The heyday for modern stories about pest-infested hair seems to be the late 1960s to late 1970s. This was after that particular hairdo had gone out of fashion, but the stories call it a "beehive" hairdo as often as they simply refer to it as a "bouffant" style.

A little research shows, though, that the story extends both back and forward in time from this point, and has equivalents in non-European tradition. Australian-Indian folklorist Sanjay Sircar, for example, has drawn attention to an old legend about a scorpion nesting in the elaborate headdress worn by Bengali brides. He says he remembers it being discussed by his grandmother (born in 1900), who said that "everyone" in Bengal knew it (see our second example). Sircar suggests that it might be the source for the Western story. In India, he says, it is not told as a cautionary tale warning against vanity, but as a tale of Fate (the bride is killed on her wedding day and by means of her wedding clothes) (Sircar 2001).

Going back further in time but returning to European tradition, one researcher has found thirteenth-century stories that resemble tales about beehive hairstyles and are definitely cautionary tales (Marchalonis 1976). In one story "a lady of Eynsham" was said to have spent so long fixing her hair in the elaborate style of the day that she didn't arrive at church until Mass was almost over. Consequently "the devil descended upon her head in the form of a spider, gripping with its legs" until she almost died of fright. The creature could not be dislodged by any normal means; the only way to remove it was to show it the sacred wafer used at Mass. This and similar stories were used in sermons of the late thirteenth and early fourteenth century; other tales on the theme include a story about a lady that appeared to one of her husband's servants after her death saying that because she had been so vain about her hair during her life she was now condemned in the afterlife to having toads and scorpions put in her hair.

Going forward in time, stories about nasty things in beehive hairdos have been replaced with stories about braiding, hair extensions, and dreadlocks. From Australia in 1999, for example, comes a story about a young man who decides to get his dreadlocks cut off and goes to a barbershop. As the barber cuts into his hair, the young man complains that he is cutting his head. After a while, he falls silent and complains no more. The barber cuts on, then to his horror sees red-back spiders crawling out of the hair. He stops, and goes round the front of his client to tell him the problem. The young man is dead in the chair: the pain he felt when he thought the barber was cutting his head was actually the spiders biting him to death ("Hair Legend Down Under").

Examples

(This story was told to Gillian Bennett sometime in the mid-1980s by her father as a true story he had heard from fellow health workers).

1. When I was at that clinic in Salford [UK], the nursing auxiliaries there had a series of people they had to go round and delouse from time to time. And they told me of one person . . . Now, this was perfectly true, a group experience, that had really happened—

   Anyway, there was this woman—they were treating the children's hair for lice and had to shave some of the hair off—this woman had got a big beehive lacquered hairdo, and she was complaining of itching there, you see. And they said something like, "How long is it since you had it taken down and washed it?"

   "Oh, I don't worry. I keep it like this for about three weeks," something like that.

   So, when they opened it up they found cockroaches inside. There were cockroaches. So they had to shave her head completely, and she was most indignant about it! (Bennett Collection)

2. There was once a bride; she was adorned for her wedding. She kept complaining, "My head itches, my head itches"; no one would listen to her. As she walked the seven circles around the sacred fire behind her husband in the wedding ceremony, on the last circling, she fell to the ground—dead! It was a scorpion nesting in her head, or in the flowers in her elaborate coiffure. (Sircar 2001, 4)

FURTHER READING

Brunvand, Jan Harold. *The Vanishing Hitchhiker: American Urban Legends and Their Meanings.* New York: Norton, 1981. See pp. 76–80.

"Hair Legend down Under." <urban-legends@onelist.com>

Marchalonis, Shirley. "Three Medieval Tales and Their Modern American Analogues." *Journal of the Folklore Institute* 13 (1976): 173–184.

Sircar, Sanjay. "Urban Legends from India." *Letters to Ambrose Merton* 25 (Spring 2001): 1–22.

See: The Bosom Serpent; Earwigs in Ears and Ants in Eyes; The Spider Boil

---

(IM)PLANTED

These are gruesome stories about people who have vegetation growing inside them after they have been scratched by a plant or had a seed pushed up their nose. The stories have been circulating since at least the early 1980s in America and the United Kingdom. The first story below had a widespread circulation around hospitals in the Sheffield (UK) area in 1983. Since then many variants on this theme have been reported over the Internet or in the press. These include: wheat growing in a woman's nose or ear; a bean sprouting in a man's penis; grass sprouting from someone's eye; a tree sprouting in a person's ear; a bean sprouting in someone's bowels; a barleycorn growing in an ear; a twig growing out of someone's leg; a cactus growing in a leg. The latest incidents, reported in December 2005, tell a story about a man who has an apple growing in his eye after the wind blows an apple seed and some dirt into his eye, and a story about "terrible mutations" turning humans into hybrids of plants or animals—in particular, the tragic tale of a young girl who was turning into a cactus ("Terrible Mutations").

A typically grisly story, widely reported in Sheffield (UK) in the early 1980s tells how a pea was pushed up a boy's nose. It germinated, and the tendrils of the plant grew up into his brain, the roots growing down into his lungs. His weird condition was discovered just in the nick of time; if the plant had been discovered even a day or two later, he would have died. The story in our example below also comes from Sheffield and is another example of the way the legend evolved in that city in the 1980s.

Example

A very sick girl was admitted to hospital with a mystery illness contracted after she had scratched herself on a rose thorn while gardening. The doctor took a blood sample only to be further confused, for her blood was contaminated with putrid cellulose fibres which were spreading through her bloodstream. Although she was extremely ill there was little they could do to help her and she eventually died. The postmortem examination revealed that tendrils of vegetable matter were growing through her veins and it was this that had killed her. (Smith 1986, 48)

FURTHER READING

Healey, Phil, and Rick Glanvill. *Urban Myths*. London: Virgin, 1992.
Paul Smith, *The Book of Nastier Legends*. London: Routledge and Kegan Paul, 1986.
"Terrible mutations may turn humans into plants or animals: Herbal cells may settle down and parasitize on the organism of a human or an animal." *Pravda* (February 8, 2006). http://english.pravda.ru/main/18/90/360/16654_mutation.html

See: The Bosom Serpent; Earwigs in the Ears and Ants in the Eyes; The Girl with the Beehive Hairdo; The Spider Boil

THE SPIDER BOIL

This story, or ones like it, have been around since at least the early 1960s and have been disseminated throughout the English-speaking countries and Europe.

The legend spread like wildfire in Sweden in 1975 and was still popular ten years later. Similar stories have been collected in France, Holland, Germany, Australia, Norway, and the United Kingdom from a wide variety of media—oral stories, newspapers, TV, the Internet, collections of "gross" or "scary" stories, and books of "credos" or popular fallacies.

Usually the creature in the boil is a spider, but some stories feature other small creatures—beetles, flies, or fleas. Sometimes, as in our example, the victim (usually a girl) has simply been sunbathing or lying on a beach or tidying up the basement, but more commonly she has been to some exotic location—Jamaica, the Bahamas, Bali, Easter Island, Mexico, Tibet, or Africa.

In spite of these exotic locations and all the trappings of modern travel, these stories are not new. A tale which is quite similar to the familiar urban legend was recorded by Gerald of Wales (c. 1146–1223) in his *The Jewel of the Church* (1197). In a discussion about whether or not one should drink from a sacramental chalice at Mass if one discovers that it is contaminated by a spider (which was then considered to be an evil and polluted creature), he says that he has "personally heard" that a French monk did indeed find a spider in the chalice and drank from it all the same. He was unharmed by it, but three days later his great toe started itching badly; when he scratched it and broke the skin the spider he had swallowed came out alive. Another monk he had heard of had the same experience; this time the spider emerged through his scalp which he had scratched open with his finger because of the unbearable itch (Henken 2001, 97–98).

During the sixteenth, seventeenth, and early eighteenth centuries, physicians believed in a condition they called "the lousy disease." People suffering from this disease were said to experience uncontrollable itching caused by lice spontaneously generating in their bodies. In many cases the sufferer had swellings like boils all over his body, which when they were lanced or burst open of their own accord were found to be full of hundreds of lice. An English woman, for example, was said to have died after she had developed hundreds of small insect-filled boils; King Philip IV of Spain was said to have suffered from abscesses on his chest and knee, from which, when they were opened, insects streamed out instead of pus; and as late as 1808 a Prussian military surgeon was said to have treated a 13-year-old boy with a huge tumor on his head, which was found to contain a solid mass of insects (Bondeson 1997, 52–61).

There is at least one twentieth-century folk story that appears to form a link between these sorts of beliefs and the modern urban legends. Swedish folklorist Bengt af Klintberg has discovered a German short story from 1842 in which villagers make a pact with the devil, which is sealed by a woman receiving his kiss on her cheek. When the villagers try to welch on the deal, a black boil grows on the woman's cheek, spiders crawl out of it, and kill all the livestock (Klintberg 1985, 281).

Example

A girl went out in the backyard to sunbathe and fell asleep. When she woke up her nose itched a bit, but she figured a bug must have bitten her, and she didn't think much of it. But the itching became unbearable.

Her mother was afraid she might really injure herself she was scratching so hard, so she took her to the hospital. By that time the girl was completely hysterical. She went on scratching and scratching till she tore away part of her cheek. And out came a host of little red spiders (Bennett Collection)

FURTHER READING

Bennett, Gillian. "Vermin in Boils: What if it Were True?" *Southern Folklore* 54 (1998): 185–195.

Bondeson, Jan. *A Cabinet of Medical Curiosities*. Ithaca, NY: Cornell University Press, 1997.

Busby, Cylin. "'This Is a True Story': Roles of Women in Contemporary Legend." *Midwestern Folklore* 20 (Spring 1994): 5–62.

———. *The Chicken-Fried Rat: Stories Too Gross to Be True*. New York: Harper Trophy, 1998. See pp. 50–56.

Cohen, Daniel. *The Headless Roommate and Other Tales of Terror*. New York: M. Evans and Company, 1980. See pp. 112–113.

Henken, Elissa R. "Contemporary Legends in the Works of Gerald of Wales." *Contemporary Legend* new series 4 (2001): 93–107.

Klintberg, Bengt af. "Legends and Rumours about Spiders and Snakes." *Fabula* 26 (1985): 274–287.

See: The Bosom Serpent; Earwigs in Ears and Ants in Eyes; The Girl with the Beehive Hairdo; (Im)planted

---

STOLEN BODY PARTS 1: INTRODUCTION

An abiding human fear is, and has always been, that some other person will steal, use, or take control of one's body or parts of it. In the 1880s, for example, in Tsientsin (China), there were massacres and riots after a rumor spread that children's eyes were being stolen to make developing fluid for photography, which was a new technology at the time (Campion-Vincent 1997, 26); in Lyons (France) in 1770 it had been alleged that surgeons captured a child every night in order to take its arm and try to sew it on to the body of a one-armed prince; in Paris in 1750, in the midst of a panic about disappearing children, it was said that the supposedly leprous King Louis XV abducted children and used their blood to try to cure himself (Farge and Revel 1991, 104–113); and anthropologist Luise White has studied stories of vampire firemen in colonial Africa who, since the end of World War I, have been said to capture people in order to take their blood (White 2005).

Recently, stories about organ thefts have thrived amid rising fears about the ethics and social and political consequences of the international trade in organs. It is easy to find dozens of newspaper articles on the Internet reporting stories and rumors of organ trafficking, abductions, and theft; for example, between 1998 and 2004 there were reports from the United States, India, Australia, Thailand, China, Russia, the Ukraine, Egypt, the Philippines, Costa Rica, Columbia, Guatemala, Brazil, Mexico, Turkey, Afghanistan,

Mozambique, and Greece. There were stories that organ thieves were removing organs from Turkish earthquake victims, and an account of a Canadian woman politician who was assaulted and stabbed with a syringe, she thought in order to steal her kidneys while on holiday in Brazil in June 2001 (news reports via e-mail from Brian Chapman).

In the early 1990s, John Shonder, an American working in Guatemala City, remembers his secretary telling him that the body of a little child had been found on the roadside with the chest open and the heart and other organs missing. A note (in English) had been left on the child's thoracic cage. It said, "Thank you for the organs." Shonder recalled that in the following weeks the numbers of corpses said to have been left at the roadside multiplied; some reports said five bodies had been found, others said eight. In some rumours, instead of a "thank you" note, the killers had supposedly left a handful of American dollars. Another story told of a street urchin found dazed and blind. When he was taken to hospital, the doctors found that his corneas had been removed. Again the child's pockets were full of dollar bills. Everybody Shonder encountered thought the rumours were true, and graffiti appeared throughout the city alleging "Gringos child stealers." Violent incidents followed.

Such fears lie at the heart of many horror stories in film and fiction—tales about vampires, werewolves, monsters, zombies, dissection, mutilations, blood suckers, and human sausage factories—too numerous to list. Films specifically featuring organ theft include "Coma" (1978), "The Harvest" (1992), "The Donor" (1995), and "Dirty Pretty Things" (2002). Literary treatments include the books of the movies "Coma" and "The Harvest," Will Christopher Baer's *Kiss Me, Judas* (1998), and Patrice Jasion's *Unholy Harvest* (1999). Under the heading "Stolen Body Parts," we shall deal with urban legends in current circulation—"Baby Parts," "The Black Volga," "Eye Thefts," and "Kidney Thefts." Readers should also consult the entry on "The Blood Libel."

FURTHER READING

Bennett, Gillian. *Bodies: Sex, Violence, Disease, and Death in Contemporary Legend.* Jackson, MS: University Press of Mississippi, 2005. See pp. 188–246.

Campion-Vincent, Veronique. "Organ Theft Narratives." *Western Folklore* 56 (1997): 1–37.

———. *Organ Theft Legends* (Trans. Jacqueline Simpson.) Jackson, MS: University Press of Mississippi, 2005.

Farge, Arlette, and Jacques Revel. *The Vanishing Children of Paris*. Trans. Claudia Miéville. Cambridge, MA: Harvard University Press, 1991.

Shonder, John. "Organ Theft Rumors in Guatemala: Some Personal Observations." *FOAFtale News* 35 (October 1994): 1–4.

White, Luise. "Social Construction and Social Consequences: Rumors and Evidence." *Rumor Mills: The Social Impact of Rumor and Legend*. Ed. Gary Alan Fine, Véronique Campion-Vincent and Chip Heath. New Brunswick, NS: AldineTransaction, 2005, pp. 241–254.

See: The Blood Libel; Stolen Body Parts 2 (The Black Volga); Stolen Body Parts 3 (Baby Parts); Stolen Body Parts 4 (Eye Thefts); Stolen Body Parts 5 (Kidney Thefts)

STOLEN BODY PARTS 2: THE BLACK VOLGA

In the 1970s and 1980s stories began circulating in Poland, Byelorusse, the Ukraine, Mongolia, and Russia that children were being abducted in black Volga cars and their organs taken for spare-part surgery for rich foreigners. Between 1977 and 1989 the story was so widespread, says Polish folklorist Dionizjusz Czubala, "that you could hardly meet a Pole who was not familiar with it. It was a time of panic among children, teachers and parents, intensified by the media" (Czubala 1991, 1). Common elements included children coaxed into a black or red car or otherwise abducted, their blood being drained, or their organs being taken for spare-part surgery for rich Arabs or Westerners.

Though the legend was best known as "The Black Volga" in Eastern Europe, in other times and places these abduction legends have attached to other cars and/or modes of transport. These include, black coaches in nineteenth-century Britain and Holland (Thorpe 1852, 290), Russian Pobedas in postwar Estonia (Koïva 1998, 7), motorcycles in Cuba in 1995 (Dimmick 1995), Volvos driven by people dressed as clowns in Honduras, red ambulances or large blue or yellow vans driven by Japanese or Americans in Brazil in the mid-1980s (Campion-Vincent 2005, 16), cars and ambulances driven by "Killer Clowns" in Scotland in 1992/3 (Hobbs and Cornwell 1992; 1993), green or white Mercedes trailing children on their way to school in Belgium, and black ambulances driven by women dressed as nurses accompanied by men dressed as *carabinieri* in Bologna (Italy) (Stilo and Tosselli 1991).

Example

Do you know what has happened in Bedzin? Staska told us yesterday. Near the castle there was a black Volga. Some guests were visiting the castle, the hill, and maybe the church. There was a nun with them. They are building a new road and the place looks ruined. Not far from there a group of children were playing. The nun took one of them by the hand and went to an empty house. The men followed her. They came out without the child. They got into the Volga and went away.

When the mother learned about that they started to look for the child and found it dead. The blood had been removed and the body left behind. "I heard that the blood is taken to West Germany to cure leukaemia," said Teresa. "Yes, it is true. It is similar to a story from Czeladz. A child was kidnapped and dustmen found it in a garbage site somewhere in Katowice." (Czubala 1991, 1)

FURTHER READING

Campion-Vincent, Véronique. *Organ Theft Legends*. (Trans. Jacqueline Simpson.) Jackson, MS: University Press of Mississippi, 2005.

Czubala, Dionizjusz. "The 'Black Volga': Child Abduction Urban Legends in Poland and Russia." *FOAFtale News* 21 (February 1991): 1–3.

Dimmick, Adrian. "Cannibals and Stolen Organs." *FLS News* 21 (June 1995): 10.

Hobbs, Sandy, and David Cornwell. "The Clowns." *Dear Mr Thoms* 24 (January 1992): 2–9.

———. "The Clowns: Further Notes." *Dear Mr Thoms* 31 (July 1993): 9–12.

Köiva, Mare. "Bloodsuckers and Human Sausage Factories." *FOAFtale News* 43 (February 1998): 7–9.

Stilo, Guiseppe, and Paulo Tosselli. "The Kidnappers and the Black Ambulance: Child Abduction Legends from Sicily." *FOAFtale News* 23 (September 1991): 5–6.

Thorpe, Benjamin. *Northern Mythology*, vol 3 *Netherlandish Traditions*. London: Edward Lumley, 1852.

See: Stolen Body Parts 1 (Introduction); Stolen Body Parts 3 (Baby Parts); Stolen Body Parts 4 (Eye Thefts); Stolen Body Parts 5 (Kidney Thefts)

STOLEN BODY PARTS 3: BABY PARTS

During the time that stories about organ thefts have been commonplace, they have gone through several versions at different times and in different places. To begin with they proliferated mainly in Central and South America, and centered, as urban legends often do, on threats to children. The earliest form the stories took was about a "death strip" of road between Rio de Janeiro and Sao Paulo (Brazil) where children were mown down so their little bodies could be stripped of organs (Pukas 1995, 16). However, it was a story about hijacked adoptions in 1987 that really got the rumor mill going.

An article appeared in an Honduran newspaper alleging that orphaned children from Guatemala, Honduras, and Costa Rica were being sold to Western Europe, Israel, and the United States for use in the organ transplant trade. In April of 1987 the respected Soviet newspaper *Pravda* and the official Soviet news agency, Tass, both gave credit to the rumor. This led to the story being taken up by the press worldwide. Despite denials by official organizations in Latin America, Israel, and the United States, the rumors continued to be believed and widely disseminated through 1988. The rumor mill went relatively quiet for a while, then burst into life in 1990 when it was alleged that 3,000 Brazilian children had "disappeared" on their way to Italy for adoption (in fact, the figure of 3,000 was simply a computational error). In 1999 it was reported that Egypt's general prosecutor was investigating allegations that an organization north of Cairo charged with caring for homeless children was killing them and selling their body parts for profit.

This particular scare seemed to be over, but then in May 2003 another child organ stealing story surfaced in the press. The British newspaper *The Sunday Telegraph* reported a story from Italy about "a female gang [who] auctioned off a newborn child ... possibly so that its organs could be used for transplants" (Johnston 2003). The following month the BBC printed a story online about a Romanian woman, smuggled into Italy and forced to work as a prostitute, whose baby was taken away within seconds of being born. She thought it had been taken for its organs, and alleged that her experience was not unique: "I know that this has happened to many, many girls," she said "[They have been] put on the streets and got pregnant and then been forced to have the babies induced, for organs" (Thomson 2003). In September 2004 the *Manila Standard* (Philippines) reported "5 Dead Kids; Organs Missing," and in Israel in October the same year, journalists reported that kidnapping rumors were shaking Bedouin towns. Residents were confident that local children were being kidnapped in order for their organs to be "harvested" (Hasson and Ettinger 2004).

Example

The first accusation (January 1987) was that a "fattening house" had been discovered where thirteen handicapped children who had been abducted or bought from impoverished families awaited adoption. But the adoptions never happened because the children were actually sold for $10,000 apiece to be dissected and used in organ transplants. A month later the story appeared in Guatemala. This time fourteen children had supposedly been found in a fattening house (some of them newborns): the fee was now said to be $20,000. In April of that year the story was taken up by *Pravda*, which alleged that "thousands" of Honduran children had been sent to the United States where their organs had been donated to save the lives of children from rich families. The official Soviet news agency, Tass, took the story up and then, as Campion-Vincent puts it, the story "went on a world tour." In Latin America itself the rumors received apparent confirmation from official or quasi-official sources. A Guatemalan police officer claimed to have uncovered an illicit adoption network run by two Israelis selling children for $75,000; and a Paraguayan judge alleged that there was a secret orphanage where Brazilian babies were kept until they could be killed and dissected in U.S. hospitals, their organs being kept in cold storage for future transplants. (Bennett 2005, 194–195)

FURTHER READING

Bennett, Gillian. *Bodies: Sex, Violence, Disease, and Death in Contemporary Legend.* Jackson, MS: University Press of Mississippi, 2005.

Campion-Vincent, Véronique. *Organ Theft Legends.* (Trans. Jacqueline Simpson.) Jackson, MS: University Press of Mississippi, 2005.

Hasson, Nir and Yair Ettinger. "Kidnaping Rumors Shake Bedouin Towns." *Haaretz* [Israel] (October 18, 2004).

Johnston, Bruce. "Italy Rushes in Law to Ban 'Spare Part' Baby Sales." *Sunday Telegraph* [UK] (May 18, 2003). http://portal.telegraph.co.uk/news/main.jhtml?xml=/news/2003/05/18/worg18.xml&sSheet=/news/2003/05/18/ixworld.html

Pukas, Anna. "The Global Lie That Cannot Be Silenced." *Folklore Frontiers* 27 (1995): 16–17.

Samper, David. "Cannibalizing Kids: Rumor and Resistance in Latin America." *Journal of Folklore Research* 39 (January–April 2002): 1–32.

Thomson, Mike. "Woman Tells of 'Stolen Babies'" BBC Radio 4 "Today" program. BBC News (June 11, 2003). http://news.bbc.co.uk/1/hi/world/europe/2981692.stm

See: Stolen Body Parts 1 (Introduction); Stolen Body Parts 2 (The Black Volga); Stolen Body Parts 4 (Eye Thefts); Stolen Body Parts 5 (Kidney Thefts)

STOLEN BODY PARTS 4: EYE THEFTS

Legends began to appear in the mid-1980s about children abducted, and sometimes killed, in order to use their eyes for spare-part surgery. Unlike the "Baby Parts" rumor, which had been largely put about by the mass media, the "Eye Theft" story was mainly transmitted by word-of-mouth through rumors. The media did not take the stories up until they resulted in attacks on foreigners.

The stories began in Latin America, and initially, like the "Baby Parts" legend, involved children. There were slight regional differences. In Central America, the child was usually said to have been abducted then thrown on the side of the road blinded and scarred. In its pocket there were a few dollars and a note saying "Thank you for your eyes." The abductions were said to have been carried out by strangers dressed in black leather and armed with machine guns, who burst out of big black shiny cars or red ambulances (compare "The Black Volga" variant). In Brazil, however, the child was said to have been killed before being dumped. Large blue or yellow vans driven by Japanese or Americans were supposed to be patrolling the poorer districts looking for victims nobody would miss—not only children now, but also delinquents, poor people, and the mentally ill. Rumor had it that the victims were thrown in the back of the van, and their mutilated corpses were later dumped beside the road, or thrown over the walls of the municipal cemetery, or put out with the hospital garbage. The fear was so acute that children were kept out of school, or sent away to relatives in the country, or locked up while their parents went to work.

In Lima, the capital of Peru, for about ten days at the end of 1988 there were rumors that groups of men dressed like doctors but carrying machine guns were driving round the poor districts of the city abducting children. It was said that the children's eyes were being sold to pay off the National Debt. Two attempted lynchings of foreigners resulted from this panic. These, and other, attacks were serious enough for America to recall Peace Corps volunteers to the capital and advise tourists to leave the country altogether.

Two sensational articles published simultaneously in Britain and France at the end of 1991 told the (totally false) story of a poor little Argentinian boy, one of several from the barrios, whose kidneys were stolen and sold on the black market for $45,000 to Americans, Brazilians, or rich people from their own country (Radford 1999, 36). In Mexico in 1989, David Schreiberg heard a story about a traveling salesman "who boarded a bus with a leaky suitcase. When a suspicious bus driver opened it, he found it full of children's eyes and kidneys, wrapped in plastic and chilled with melting ice." He reports that police chiefs said that similar stories had been circulating for at least two years. Official enquiries launched by the Mexican authorities in 1990 and 1992 in light of persistent rumours such as these concluded that there was indeed an illegal trade in children, but for adoption or prostitution, not for organ transplants. The rumors continued, however.

At the end of 2001, similar horrific stories surfaced in Afghanistan. In reports from the news agency Reuters, it was alleged that in September of that year several children had been killed by a gang of Pakistani organ traffickers (officials at the Afghan interior ministry said they had heard the rumors but had no evidence that these crimes were being committed). In one such story a 4-year-old girl from a poor neighborhood had supposedly been abducted while out at play, her eyes had been cut out and her head smashed in, then the body dumped at the roadside near a cemetery. In another, later, account it was said that two women and a man dressed as a woman were abducting children for their eyes and other organs (see example below).

Example

KABUL (Reuters)—No one seems to know who abducted Roma and Maqbula, nor why they were killed in a manner so brutal that it stood out in a city where war and disease have stacked the odds on the side of death.

But whoever snatched and murdered the two little Afghan girls, both aged four and killed some two years apart, took out their eyes and, in Roma's case, her kidneys, according to their families.

And in doing so, the mystery killers spread fear through Kabul that kidnappers trafficking in human organs were on the prowl when the city was under the sway of the Taliban.

Roma went missing four months ago while playing on the street outside her home in the District Nine area close to downtown Kabul at around 10 in the morning

Five evenings later, a pickup truck with its headlights switched off drove past the house and dumped the body on the street, said Najibullah, a 35-year-old relative of the girl and member of the extended family that lives in the home.

"The eyes were missing and there were no kidneys. We couldn't look more closely to see what else was missing," said Najibullah. The girl's abdomen appeared to have been cut open and then stitched up with surgical thread, he said.

Unconfirmed reports, spread by the brush fire of rumor and gossip in this devastated city, speak of many more children who may have met the same, grisly fate (Holmes 2001).

FURTHER READING

Campion-Vincent, Véronique. *Organ Theft Legends* (Trans. Jacqueline Simpson.) Jackson, MS: University Press of Mississippi, 2005.

Holmes, Paul. "Mystery Child Murders Spread Fear in Kabul." Yahoo! News (December 8, 2001). http://uk.news.yahoo.com/011208/80/ckw03.html

Radford, Benjamin. "Bitter Harvest: The Organ-Snatching Urban Legends." *Skeptical Inquirer* 23 (May/June 1999): 34–39, 48.

Schreiberg, David. "Dead Babies." *The New Republic* (December 24, 1990): 12–13.

See: Stolen Body Parts 1 (Introduction); Stolen Body Parts 2 (The Black Volga); Stolen Body Parts 3 (Baby Parts); Stolen Body Parts 5 (Kidney Thefts)

STOLEN BODY PARTS 5: KIDNEY THEFTS

Legends about kidney thefts evolved from about 1990 and became a dominant form of the "Stolen Body Parts" legend in America and Western Europe. They have three points of difference from the organ-snatcher legends that went before. First, it is more usual for the victim to be an adult than a child; second, the victim is usually somebody from a developed country, not the third world; thirdly, as the stories spread they become more rounded as narratives and acquire more traditional motifs.

An early story told how a couple from Sweden had gone on holiday to Brazil and been approached by a small boy who asked them to sign a petition against the denuding of the tropical forest. The "petition" was, in fact, a consent form to donate their kidneys for a transplant. Similarly, there was a story about a woman holidaying in Goa, India, who contracted appendicitis and had to be operated on. Later, it was discovered that, though her appendix was still intact, one of her kidneys was missing. In Italy, rumors circulated that women shopping in boutiques in Bari and Palermo had vanished from changing rooms. It was said that they had been taken to a secret basement room equipped as an operating theater, or removed to a truck parked outside the shop (similarly equipped for surgery), where their organs were removed. A criminal gang was thought to be carrying out organ thefts to order (Bennett 2005, 119–206).

Then folklorists began hearing more elaborate stories. From the United States, Canada, England, Northern Ireland, the Republic of Ireland, Australia, Germany, Sweden, and Denmark stories began coming in between 1991 and

133

1996 that told of a person (usually a man) who had been discovered wandering about with a mysterious scar, and was later found to have had a kidney removed. English folklorist Roy Vickery heard one of these stories in 1992 in the Natural History Museum in London, where he works ("Contemporary Legends: Old? New?"), Danusha Goska heard a similar story in New York which ends with the victim finding himself alone in bed next morning with a 6 inch scar on his back (Goska 1997, 196–197).

By 1996, the story was even more elaborated and started to resemble "AIDS Aggressor" stories by the addition of a message left by the attacker (see our example, which was sent by e-mail to Canadian folklorist Philip Hiscock by a California hairdresser in July of that year). Often now the story ended with the victim waking up in an ice-filled bathtub with a note stuck on his chest or scrawled in lipstick on the bathroom mirror. This motif featured strongly in versions that started appearing in 1997, largely as the result of a warning circulated via e-mail entitled "Travelers Beware!!" which claimed that an organized gang of kidney thieves was operating in the United States, drugging business travelers, removing their kidneys, and selling them on the black market.

Example

[My co-worker] called me at home [a few months ago]. He said, "You are not going to believe what I heard, it really gives me the creeps, it actually has me freaked out." I said, "What?" An acquaintance of his had a nephew or cousin that went to Las Vegas for a little fun. While he was there he met a very friendly and attractive woman in the bar. They really hit it off, and after many hours drinking and flirting, they went up to his room. He woke up some days later in the bathtub that still had some ice in it, naked. He found a note attached to him (how I don't remember) that said, "If you are reading this you have managed to survive. Call 911 immediately, stay calm and don't move out of the tub. Your kidneys have been surgically removed and you are in critical condition." (Hiscock 1996)

FURTHER READING

Bennett, Gillian. *Bodies: Sex, Violence, Disease, and Death in Contemporary Legend.* Jackson, MS: University Press of Mississippi, 2005.

Brunvand, Jan Harold. *Encyclopedia of Urban Legends.* New York: Norton, 2001. See pp. 227–228.

Campion-Vincent, Véronique. *Organ Theft Legends* (Trans. Jacqueline Simpson.) Jackson, MS: University Press of Mississippi, 2005.

"Contemporary Legends: Old? New?" *FLS News* 15 (July 1992): 7.

Goska, Danusha. "'Waking Up Less Than Whole': The Female Perpetrator in Male-Victim Kidney-Theft Legends." *Southern Folklore* 54 (1997): 196–210.

Hiscock, Philip. Footnote to Mazo, Jeff. "Melded Motif: Lipstick and Kidney." *FOAFtale News* 40–41 (December 1996): 18.

Mazo, Jeff. "Melded Motif: Lipstick and Kidney." *FOAFtale News* 40–41 (December 1996): 18.

See: Stolen Body Parts 1 (Introduction); Stolen Body Parts 2 (The Black Volga); Stolen Body Parts 3 (Baby Parts); Stolen Body Parts 4 (Eye Thefts)

THE TAPEWORM DIET

From roughly 1920 to the present time, many legends and rumors have cropped up about people who accidentally swallow the eggs of some sea creature or amphibian. A typical British rumor of the 1920s was that a batch of specially large eggs were crocodile eggs and would hatch out inside anyone who ate them. In the 1950s there was a similar scare about people swallowing octopus eggs while swimming in the sea. And of course, in many stories of "The Bosom Serpent" the terrible infestation comes about because the victim has accidentally swallowed the eggs of toads, newts, or frogs (Bennett 2005, 3–59). In tapeworm tales, however, the person has knowingly swallowed the eggs in the form of "diet" pills (though, in most cases, the woman—it is nearly always a woman—doesn't know her pills have tapeworm eggs in them).

The stories were current between the 1920s and the 1980s in Europe and the United States (Tucker 1978). Barbara Mikkelson reports rumors that the famous opera singer Maria Callas (1923–1977), whose weight problem was as well known as her fiery temperament and her stunning voice, knowingly took tapeworm pills to try to slim down (Mikkelson). A more recent sighting comes from France and the date is given as 1989. The story can be found in two French collections of urban legends (Campion-Vincent and Renard 1992; Le Quellec 1991). Example 1 is a translation from Le Quellec's French text. The second example came in a letter from British folklorist Jacqueline Simpson in 1994.

Examples

1. There's the one about the woman who wanted to slim, she wanted to slim, and she'd tried every imaginable diet. Eventually at the end of her tether she came

across a leaflet, you know, a rapid slimming thing. So she ordered the stuff, and after a while she got a packet of pills. Good stuff these pills!

Well, some of them got left in a corner of the packet. Time passed. Meanwhile the weather got very humid, the air was really heavy and damp, and she noticed that one of the pills was moving. Had grown, you know? Bizarre to say the least! So she sent it to be analyzed, and found out it was a tapeworm egg. Well, you know, people will do anything to get slim! (Le Quellec 1991, 59 translated by Gillian Bennett)

2. Today I was chatting with a retired GP who is a friend of mine, and talk turned to contemporary legends and I chanced to mention the "tapeworm slimming pill" one. He knew it as one which was very, very widespread in the early 1930s. At that time there was a slimming pill called "Silf," and a rumour sprang up that it contained a tapeworm egg, which would hatch inside you, so that the slimming was dramatically quick. The rumour proved unstoppable, and sales of "Silf" collapsed so badly that the product was withdrawn pretty soon. (Jacqueline Simpson, personal communication)

FURTHER READING

Bennett, Gillian. *Bodies: Sex, Violence, Disease, and Death in Contemporary Legend*. Jackson, MS: University Press of Mississippi, 2005.

Campion-Vincent, Véronique, and Jean-Bruno Renard. *Légendes urbaines: Rumeurs d'aujourd'hui*. Paris: Payot, 1992.

Le Quellec, Jean-Loïc. *Alcool de singe et liqueur de vipère . . . plus quelques autres recettes*. Vouillé: Geste Editions, 1991.

Mikkelson, Barbara. "As the Worm Squirms." http://www.snopes.com/horrors/vanities/tapeworm.htm

Tucker, Elizabeth. "The Seven-Day Wonder Diet: Magic and Ritual in Diet Folklore." *Indiana Folklore* 11 (1978): 141–150.

See: The Bosom Serpent; Earwigs in Ears and Ants in Eyes; The Girl with the Beehive Hairdo; (Im)planted; The Spider Boil

5

ANIMALS

Alongside children and crime, animals are one of the most popular subjects to tell urban legends about. Roughly 20 percent of the stories documented in Contemporary Legend: A Folklore Bibliography (Bennett and Smith 1993) relate in some way to animals. Birds, bugs, amphibians, reptiles, spiders, rodents, worms, and wolves all make an appearance somewhere in legend collectors' files. In tales of bodily infestation, for example, spiders erupt from boils and blisters on the skin, and frogs and toads take up residence in the human gut. In stories about contaminated goods, plants, blouses, and blankets are invaded by snakes, and rats, mice and worms are found in take-out food. These sorts of tales can be found in Chapters 4 and 7 of this volume.

The stories in this chapter are about pets or tame animals. The more unfortunate of them come to a grisly end. They are microwaved, squashed, skinned, eaten, exhumed, carried off, and blown up. The few that avoid these fates are either heroes or villains. As heroes they protect their owners from burglars; as villains they turn out to be wolves in sheep's clothing and consume the resident pet.

For other stories about pet animals see: The Doggie Lick; The Double Whammy; The Nude Bachelor; The Peanut Butter Surprise

THE BATTERED BUDGIE

This tale of misadventure, sometimes known as "The Pet Under the Carpet" or "The Bump in the Rug," has probably been around in America and the United Kingdom since the 1960s. Usually the pet that comes to a sticky end is a budgerigar, but sometimes it is a parakeet, a hamster, a pet mouse, or a tame white rat as in the cartoon featured in Paul Smith's "Read all about it!" (Smith 1992, 60). Here, a three-frame strip entitled "Born Loser" in frame 1 shows a guy laying carpet and a bump in the carpet behind him. Frame 2 shows him pounding the bump with a hammer and a jet of fluid flying in the air. Frame 3 shows a little girl saying, "If you see a white rat around here, it's Hurricane's." Usually the mistake is uncovered by another member of the family asking where the pet is, as in the example below, but sometimes it is not discovered until a mysterious dark stain appears on the carpet.

Example

This guy had just finished laying a carpet on the bedroom floor when he noticed that his cigarettes were no longer in his pocket. As he stood up he saw that there was a sort of bump in the carpet, and thinking it must be his pack of cigarettes and not wanting to go to the bother of taking the carpet up and relaying it, he hit it a sharp blow with his hammer. Imagine his surprise when he went out to his car later that day and saw his cigarettes lying on the floor beside the driver's seat.

It gets worse! Think of his horror when his wife reported that Bertie, their pet budgie, had mysteriously gone missing after she'd let it out of its cage to get a little exercise! (Bennett Collection)

FURTHER READING

Brunvand, Jan Harold. *The Choking Doberman and Other "New" Urban Legends*. New York: Norton, 1984. See pp. 93–94.

Dale, Rodney. *The Tumour in the Whale: An Hilarious Collection of Apocryphal Anecdotes*. London: W. H. Allen, Universal Books, 1978. See pp. 61–62.

Smith, Paul. "'Read All About It! Elvis Eaten by Drug-Crazed Giant Alligators': Contemporary Legend and the Popular Press." *Contemporary Legend* 2 (1992): 41–70.

BUNNY BOUNCES BACK

Closely related to "The Cat and the Salmon" and sometimes referred to as "The Hare Dryer," this is a group of related stories that began to circulate at the beginning of the 1990s. What the stories have in common is that somebody thinks he/she has killed a family's pet and, wracked with anxiety or guilt, replaces it, only to find the animal was already dead. For example, there is the story told in the "reader's letters" column of the *Holiday Inn Traveller* (Coetzee 1991). A man finds his German shepherd dog with the mangled body of his neighbor's rabbit, and assumes that the dog has killed it. So he washes the rabbit, fluffs its fur up with a hair dryer, and puts it back in its hutch, only to find that the rabbit was already dead and the German shepherd had merely dug up its corpse.

Then there is a story currently circulating on the Internet about a man who discovers his neighbor's rabbit lying dead on his drive, and thinking that he is responsible for its death, buys another and puts it in the rabbit cage. A version like this was sent by a reader to the "Dear Abby" column in September 2004 (Mikkelson). The neighbor is shocked and horrified when they find the "dead" rabbit alive in its hutch; in a few versions they think they must have buried the animal alive and it has clawed its way to the surface and found its way back to its cage; in other versions it is interpreted as the sick joke of a "demented" person.

Jan Brunvand has an earlier version of the legend in *The Mexican Pet* (1986, 34) which he says combines elements of the tale of "The Cat in the Package." Baggage handlers at Chicago airport find a dead poodle in a crate they are loading. Fearing they may be sued for letting the dog die, they get a similar one from a kennel and substitute it. When the owner comes to recover her crate at Rome, she faints in terror when the dog bounds out of the crate and licks her face. She was shipping her dead pet home for burial.

Almost limitless variations on this theme—told as jokes or true occurrences—have circulated for many years pretty much worldwide in the oral tradition, in newspapers and magazines, in books of comic stories, and on the Internet; and events based on these stories have often been dramatized in episodes of TV comedy dramas and soap operas.

Example

Mrs M. of Lenzie heard a scraping at her back door one night last week. There, on the doorstep, was her pet retriever, Gyp. In his jaws he held a big rabbit.

"Oh no," gasped Mrs M. For the rabbit wasn't a wild one from the field across the avenue. It was a huge white angora.

Gently, she prised the rabbit from the dog's jaws. It was mud-splattered, bedraggled—and very dead. Suddenly the full horror struck. A neighbour's wee boy two doors down had a white angora.

What could Mrs M do?

Mrs M cleaned it up and, with the corpse hidden away under her coat, walked to the neighbour's house. She slipped round the back, opened the empty rabbit hutch, popped poor bunny in a corner and cosied him up with straw. Then Mrs M made good her escape. Back in her kitchen she made a cup of tea and sat down to calm her nerves.

She'd just finished her cuppa when she heard a scream outside. She rushed out to find her neighbour in a terrible state.

"Look at this," the neighbour screeched. "Our rabbit died two days ago. We buried him in the garden, but now he's sitting up at the back of his hutch!"

Yes, it sounds a good yarn. But there isn't a word of truth in it. It's the latest story sweeping the launderette and the coffee mornings. We first heard it about a Mrs M of Lenzie. Next day we were told it had happened to a Mrs B of Bearsden.

So if you hear the white rabbit story, don't tell us! ("How Could She Break It To Her Neighbour?")

FURTHER READING

Brunvand, Jan Harold. *The Mexican Pet: More "New" Urban Legends and Some Old Favorites*. New York: Norton, 1986.

Coetzee, Marie. "Bunny Bounces back." *Holiday Inn Traveller* (Spring 1991): 3.

"How Could She Break It To Her Neighbour?" *The Sunday Post* [Glasgow, Scotland] (January 17, 1988).

Mikkelson, Barbara. "The Hare Dryer." http://www.snopes.com /horrors/ gruesomediscoveries/haredry.asp

See: The Cat and the Salmon

THE CAT AND THE SALMON

This story, which is sometimes called "The Poisoned Pet at the Party," is the tale of a woman who mistakenly thinks that the salmon she has put in her husband's sandwiches or served to her dinner guests must have been contaminated since the cat that ate the leftovers has been found dead. The husband or dinner guests are rushed to the emergency room of the local hospital and have their stomachs pumped. Things, however, are not as they seem. An Irish version, for example, tells how the family cat has eaten paté left over from a big dinner party and now lies dead outside: fearing the salmon has poisoned the cat, the hosts and all their guests have their stomachs pumped out. When they return home, the neighbor calls round to confess that he ran over the cat in his car (Ní Dhuibhne 1983, 68). Featured in a story compilation based on Art Linklater's TV shows from the 1940s and 1950s (Linklater 1967, 72–73) and widespread throughout the 1980s, the story of "The Cat and the Salmon" is closely related to "Bunny Bounces Back," and may perhaps be a forerunner of that legend since its popularity faded at about the same time "Bunny Bounces Back" emerged on the Internet.

The story below was told to Gillian Bennett in Manchester (UK) in the summer of 1981 by a neighbor who had heard it from her hairdresser. At first she believed it; later, she said, she felt very foolish because she began to hear it over and over again. "So I knew it was just a tale."

Example

A woman I know always makes sandwiches for her husband's lunch. Anyway, one day she makes him salmon sandwiches and gives the left-overs to the cat, and goes out shopping. When she comes back she finds the cat unconscious on the back doorstep. She panics, rings her husband at work, and tells him to go to hospital 'cos the salmon must be contaminated. So off he goes, has his stomach pumped out, poor man! Later that evening a neighbor calls, says, "Sorry, I was working on the roof and I dropped a brick on your cat." (Bennett Collection)

FURTHER READING

de Vos, Gail. *Tales, Rumors, and Gossip: Exploring Contemporary Folk Literature in Grades 7-12*. Westport, CT: Libraries Unlimited, 1996. See p. 146.

Dhuibhne, Eílís Ní. "Dublin Modern Legends: An Intermediate Type List and Examples." *Béaloideas* 51 (1983): 55–70.

Linklater, Art. *Oops! Or, Life's Awful Moments*. Garden City, NY: Doubleday, 1967.

See: Bunny Bounces Back

CARRIED OFF

Tales of children and pets being taken by large birds proliferate worldwide. The birds are said to be eagles, vultures, owls, or—in Australia—pelicans.

Australian folklorist Bill Scott began collecting stories about pelicans in October 1984 when an acquaintance sent him a newspaper clipping about a Chihuahua dog that tried to share a pelican's meal and was carried off in the pelican's beak pouch. By January 1991 Scott had collected a number of such stories from Brisbane, Sydney, Kalbarri (Western Australia), Nowra, Bribie Island, Port Philip, and the Gold Coast (Scott 1996, 5–9 and 95). He had also collected a couple of stories from countries where pelicans were not native species: from Germany, for example, there came a story about a dachshund dog carried off by an eagle and from the United States a story about a cat being carried off by a giant owl (Scott 1996, 6–7).

In the United States, it was often vultures, owls, or eagles that featured in stories about pet abductions. In the winter of 1993/1994, for example, there were media scares in Washington DC Maryland, and Virginia about flocks of vultures supposedly "herding" family pets, or attacking farmyard animals, or hovering over groups of schoolchildren. In 1994 Associated Press released a story about a vengeful husband who let a bald eagle carry off his wife's Chihuahua dog. According to the reporter, "When the bald eagle snatched up the dog and flew off with the yelping dog, the horrified wife put her hands to her face, saying 'Oh, my God!' But the husband . . . cheered the bird on, shouting, 'Yeah! Yeah!'" (Ed. 1994, 13–15).

In 1995 it was reported that a game warden had shot a horned owl near Greenville, Maine, after the bird had seized a small dog (a poodle-Pekinese cross), maybe mistaking the little creature for a snowshoe hare. Press reports of similar incidents in the same year came from Ontario (Canada) and from Corinth, Maine, where a little white dog was attacked twice in one hour by "an owl with a wing-span of over one meter" (Ellis 1995, 9). The earliest American account (1977) seems to be a story about a 10-year-old boy from Illinois who was carried 40 feet by a bird with a 10-foot wingspan (Ed. 1994, 14).

Among other reports came a story from South Africa about spotted eagle owls stalking cats, a 1993 story about an Argentinean boy being snatched by a harpy owl, a 1763 story about a 3-year-old girl being carried 1400 feet by an eagle, and historical legends from the United Kingdom about an infant being abducted by an eagle and thus singled out as a child of destiny.

Example

A Chihuahua dog has come to a sticky end on North Stradbroke Island off Brisbane.

The Chihuahua, owned by tourists, became excited when a pelican landed at the end of the jetty on the island.

The Chihuahua raced up to the pelican and barked repeatedly. Onlookers were stunned when, after the dog refused to back off, the bird opened its bill and grabbed the Chihuahua. (Scott 1996, 7; quoting from an Australian Broadcasting Corporation bulletin June 20, 1991)

FURTHER READING

Bord, Colin and Janet. *Alien Animals*. London: Grenada, 1985. See pp. 109–112 and 131–133.

Clark, Jerome. *Unexplained!* Detroit, MI: Gale Press, 1993. See pp. 370–375.

Ed. [Bill Ellis]. "This May Be the Last Issue of *FOAFtale News*." *FOAFtale News* 33/34 (June 1994): 10–15.

Ellis, Bill. "Raptor/Pet Encounters." *FOAFtale News* 36 (January 1995): 9.

Scott, Bill. *Pelicans and Chihuahuas and Other Urban Legends*. St Lucia, Queensland: University of Queensland Press, 1996.

THE CAT IN THE PACKAGE

This gruesome-funny story of poetic justice has been widely told from the 1940s onward in Europe and North America, as an oral story, on the Internet, and in the mass media. It has always been a favorite with compilers of scary stories (for example, Cohen 1983, 107–111; Schwartz 1984, 52–53), and it has been used as the plot of a short story by classic writer of detective fiction Dorothy L. Sayers (see the Appendix). It remains popular to this day, and is told in many forms. Sometimes the cat is discovered already dead on the road by a passerby who kindly wraps it up in newspaper intending to take it and bury it; she puts it on the roof or hood of the car and it's stolen. Sometimes the story goes on to tell how the thief takes the package into a restaurant and it is stolen by a second thief. Overcome by curiosity the second thief takes a look in the package to see what goodies she's acquired. On finding the dead cat, she faints.

Yet other versions develop like a "shaggy dog story," a narrative joke with a long series of increasingly incredible episodes ending in an unlikely punch line. In stories that take this form the cat dies; its owners live in an apartment and have no garden to bury it in; it's wrapped up in paper and the husband is sent to dispose of it. The husband puts the parcel on the rack of a subway train intending to forget all about it, but a helpful stranger retrieves it for him. The husband keeps on trying to get rid of it, and people keep on giving it back. Eventually he looks inside the package to say a last farewell to Pussy, and finds, not a dead cat, but a boiled ham. Somewhere in the course of its many adventures the package containing the dead cat has been swapped for one containing a nice ham! (Brunvand 1986, 31–34).

As well as dead cats and dog droppings, stolen packages may be said to contain dead babies, diapers, maggots, horse manure, potato peelings, and other kitchen waste (Law 1988). Recently (March to May 2005) versions began to appear in newspapers and on the Internet in which the stolen dead pet is a dog that has been boxed-up in the packaging from a TV set or lawn mower (see, for example, Anders 2005). Versions have also emerged (from the fall of 1999 onward) that are a cross between "The Cat in the Package" and "The Stolen Specimen." In these stories it is dog poop that is stolen by thieves thinking the box or bag a dog-walker puts the dog's droppings in contains something valuable (see, for example, Singh 2003).

The most curious incidence of the legend is a nineteenth-century literary story in which a corpse is concealed in a piano which is then stolen (Goss 1993). The story, "The Wrong Box," was written by Robert Lewis Stevenson and Lloyd Osbourne in 1889. It tells how an artist sends for a statue of Hercules but instead receives a headless corpse. Aided by a friend, he stows the corpse in a grand piano which is then promised to a third person; the deal is that this man will dispose of the corpse in the river Thames and take the piano as his reward. The artist puts the piano on a cart to be transported. But, during the journey, a vagrant gets the driver drunk, dumps him in a ditch, and makes off with the cart, the piano (and the corpse).

The story below was told in Stockport (UK) in 1965, and follows the usual plot.

Example

I read this story about a woman whose cat dies. I think it was run over on the road. Well, she decided to have a little private ceremony for it and bury it in Heaton Park. So she got a nice box for a coffin—you know, a gift box left over from Christmas or something—and wrapped the cat up carefully and put it in the box. To make it more special, she tied it all up with white ribbon so it looked really pretty—she was terribly fond of this cat, you see.

She put the box under her arm and set off for the park after dark—it had to be after dark because you're obviously not allowed to go burying things in a park! Anyway, she was just getting near the park gates when a car drew alongside and a man jumped out and snatched the box, jumped back in the car, and drove off at speed.

Well, she was very upset but everybody else thought it was very amusing—just think of the nasty surprise that the thief would have when he opened the package and found the mangled corpse of a dead cat! Serve him right, eh? (Bennett Collection)

FURTHER READING

Anders, Smiley. "Smiley Anders" column. *The Advocate* [Baton Rouge, LA] (May 26, 2005). http://2theadvocate.cm/stories/052605/smi_smiley001.shtml

Brunvand, Jan Harold. *The Mexican Pet: More "New" Urban Legends and Some Old Favorites*. New York: Norton, 1986. See pp. 31–34.

Cohen, Daniel. *Southern Fried Rat and Other Gruesome Tales*. New York: M. Evans and Company, 1983.

Goss, Michael. "Two Literarised Legends." *Dear Mr Thoms* 32 (October 1993): 1–9.

Law, Alan. "Anything Goes." *Daily Mirror* [London] (March 29, 1988): 6.

Schwartz, Alvin. *More Scary Stories to Tell in the Dark*. New York: Harper Rowe, 1984.

Singh, Anita. "Mugger's Poop Scoop." *The Scotsman* (October 8, 2003). http://www.nes.scotsman.cm/latest.cfm?id=2030661

See: The Stolen Corpse; The Stolen Specimen; Thieves Get Their Just Deserts

CATS OUT OF THEIR SKIN

This is a modern story that updates, or at least reflects, older European folklore. Among traditional folk beliefs about animals is the idea that if you nail the tail of an animal to a tree then startle it, it will literally jump out of its skin, leaving the whole pelt still nailed to the tree. The Estonian Folk Archives have several examples of tall tales about hunters who make themselves fabulously rich by selling the pelts of wolves trapped and skinned in this manner.

In the 1990s Estonian children began telling sadistic stories about stray cats. The ending of these stories seemed to be based on this old belief. For example, one tale that sounds like a juvenile boasting story tells how a group of children first try to set a cat alight, then tie a rope round its neck. Holding tightly on to the rope, they throw it out of the window. What they are left with is the complete skin of the cat on the end of a rope. The cat's body, now just a piece of meat, falls into the street.

Estonian folklorist Eda Kalmre reports that this callousness reflects the low status cats have today as pets in her country. The children's tall tale is one of many urban legends about dead cats that are popular nowadays in Estonian tradition.

Example

In 2005 the Estonian police launched an investigation on the basis of an article published in a regional newspaper. The article described incidents of skinning cats in Pärnu, a resort with a population of 52,000 on the Baltic coast in Southwest Estonia. . . . [S]ome boys reportedly cut a T–shape into a cat's face, tied a rope to its tail, and threw the cat from the roof so that all the skin came off over its ears. Reportedly, the boys killed at least six cats this way.

The results of police investigation were published as a Baltic News Service news piece entitled "Article on Cat-Slaughter Based on an Urban Legend" ("*Artikkel kasside tapmisest põhines linnalegendil,*" March 9). According to the police PR officer, the article was inspired by a conversation between two girls, during which one girl had told her friend such stories about cats and blowing up frogs. The friend passed on the horror tale she heard to her mother, who was so shocked by the cruelty of children that she wrote an article in the local newspaper, which, in turn, became the cause of the police investigation. The police averred that they had consulted with experts, who had explained that the animals could not be skinned in this manner (Kalmre 2006, 1).

FURTHER READING

Kalmre, Eda. "Cat out of its Skin!—The Return of an Old Munchhausen Tale in Estonia." *FOAFtale News* 64 (April 2006): 1–2.

See: The Cat in the Package; The Cat and the Salmon

THE CHOKING DOBERMAN

This very popular animal story has been told in this form since at least 1981 when—according to Jan Brunvand—it popped up in an Arizona newspaper in the spring then was spread nationwide during the summer and fall through other newspaper features (Brunvand 1984). He describes the story as follows: "Dog found choking on two or three chewed fingers; burglar found passed out, sans fingers, in closet" (Brunvand 1982). He found it so typical and so modern that he named the second of his compilations after it. In a conference paper on the legend, he did, however, tentatively suggest that the story might be an update of the legend of "The Witch who was Hurt," a story in which a witch is injured while in animal form and so can be identified when she returns to her human form. Possibly, he said, there were links to an even older story, the Welsh legend of Prince Llewellyn's dog Gelert.

While not everyone thinks this is likely, it is certainly true that there are many stories predating the 1980s that could be seen as forerunners of the modern tale. For example there is a story from a book of Scottish folklore published in 1824 that seems very similar to both "The Choking Doberman" story and its cousin "The Severed Fingers." A lady living in Edinburgh Old Town was disturbed one night by a group of drunken revelers banging continuously on the doorknocker. In the morning the doorknocker was shattered but "part of a finger was left sticking in the fragments, with the appearance of having been forcibly wrenched from the hand." Scottish folklorist Sandy Hobbs, who drew attention to this story, says that it was probably old by the time it was recorded, and maybe dates from the mid-eighteenth century (Hobbs 1978, 75). Classical folklorist Adrienne Mayor has suggested that the story is prefigured by narratives from Ancient Rome about dogs that vomit severed fingers as omens of danger (Mayor 1992).

More recently, the legend has appeared in several works including Rick Boyes' 1984 novel *The Penny Ferry*, and Judith Gorog's short story "Juno" (1991).

The story below was told by a high-school student in the southwest of England in the 1990s.

Example

> There was this woman and she got home from work and she had a dog, a doberman, and when she got home it was choking.

So she was a bit concerned, so she took the dog to the vet.

"Well," the vet said, "You'll have to leave the dog here for a couple of days for observations."

So she left the dog there and went home.

When she got home the phone was ringing. So she answered it and the vet said, "Get out of the house immediately."

The police came round and were searching the house and in her wardrobe was this man with his three fingers missing. The dog had bitten the fingers off the man and was choking on the fingers. (Wilson 1997, 253)

FURTHER READING

Brunvand, Jan Harold. "The Choking Doberman Story." *American Folklore Newsletter*, 11.2 (1982): 2.

———. *The Choking Doberman and Other "New" Urban Legends.* New York: Norton, 1984.

Hobbs, Sandy. "The Folk Tale as News." *Oral History* 6.2 (1978): 74–86.

Mayor, Adrienne. "Ambiguous Guardians: The 'Omen of the Wolves' (A.D. 402) and the 'Choking Doberman' (1980s)." *Journal of Folklore Research* 29 (1992): 253–268.

Wilson, Michael. *Performance and Practice: Oral Narrative Traditions among Teenagers in Britain and Ireland.* Aldershot, UK: Ashgate, 1997.

See: The Severed Fingers

THE ELEPHANT THAT SAT ON A CAR

This legend seems to have surfaced first in the United Kingdom, then spread to Europe and the United States. In the United Kingdom it was the second most common legend phoned in to the news desk of British daily newspapers during the period 1957–1966 (McConnell 1982). At one time the legend was so popular that a Swedish garage arranged to have photographs taken of an elephant sitting on a Volkswagen car as a publicity stunt. Jan Brunvand dates its appearance in America from the early 1960s (Brunvand 2001, 130–131). It has since been reported pretty much worldwide. The make of the small car varies from country to country: in England it is usually said to be a Mini and in the United States and other parts of Europe it is supposedly a Volkswagen or

Fiat. It has been reported from all over Western Europe, from Canada and the United States, and from Australia too.

From about 1970 it was regularly featured (and often debunked) in American newspapers, for example, the *San Francisco Chronicle* (February 1971) and the *New York Times* (May 5, 1975). It has been used as an interlude in a handful of novels and short stories including a police procedural crime story, *The Corpse on the Dike* (1976); a crime novel by Dick Francis (*Smokescreen*, 1974); a children's illustrated storybook, *The Elephant who Liked to Smash Small Cars* (1967); a novel *Bliss* (1981), and the 1985 film based on the novel.

In some tellings, like the example below, the story is a very simple one with just one episode; other tellings are embellished with another episode. It may be told, for example, that, after the elephant has sat on the car, the police pull the driver over and when he explains what has happened they arrest him on suspicion of driving while under the influence of drink. In one such story the driver is that symbol of propriety, a nun (Brunvand 1984, 58–61). In Australia tellers concentrate on this ending but sometimes give different reasons for the damage to the car. As well as the familiar motif of the elephant being trained to sit on a red box, several Australian versions feature families at wildlife parks who accidentally trap an elephant's trunk in the window of the car, causing it to rampage and kick the car (Scott 1985, 226–230).

Example

Bill's car, a small VW, had recently been involved in an accident and he had just had it resprayed bright red. Heading for town he was surprised by the number of people about—he had forgotten that it was the day the big circus parade was due to pass through.

Parking in the main street, Bill went to do his weekend shopping. Shortly afterwards the circus parade came into view. There were the clowns, acrobats, horses, a brass band and, at the rear of the procession, a large performing elephant.

One of the tricks the elephant had been taught to do was, when the band played a particular tune, to rear up in the air and, standing on his hind legs, turn in a full circle. The trick culminated with the elephant sitting down on a large drum painted bright red.

The elephant had just drawn level with Bill's VW when the bandmaster, for no particular reason, instructed the musicians to strike up the tune for this trick. Up in the air went the elephant, round and round it went, then, as it always did, it sat on the nearby bright red object—unfortunately, in this instance it Bill's VW. (Smith 1983, 27).

FURTHER READING

Brunvand, Jan Harold. *The Choking Doberman and Other "New" Urban Legends*. New York: Norton, 1984.

Brunvand, Jan Harold. *Encyclopedia of Urban Legends*. New York: Norton, 2001.

McConnell, Brian. "Urban Legends in Fleet Street." *Folklore* 93 (1982): 226–228.

Scott, W. N. *The Long and the Short and the Tall: A Collection of Australian Yarns*. Sydney: Western Plains Publishers, 1985.

Smith, Paul. *The Book of Nasty Legends*. London: Routledge and Kegan Paul, 1983.

THE LOADED DOG

The title usually given to this sick-humorous tale, "The Loaded Dog," is taken from an 1899 short story by Australian writer Henry Lawson, and it has been suggested that Lawson's story was the origin of the urban legend. Lawson's story is set in an Australian mining camp; somebody throws a lighted explosive charge and the dog retrieves it, so blowing up the camp.

During its life as an urban legend, the basic story has acquired an ironic "animal's revenge" ending. The legend tells how an animal—not only a dog, but in some stories a horse, a cat, a rat, a possum, a coyote, a hawk, and even a rabbit (see Seal 1995, 690)—has been wired up by a sadistic prankster or had a stick of dynamite put in its mouth by a misguided owner wishing to give it a quick and painless death. It runs after its tormentor and blows him up too. So, in 1986 an online story told of a person commissioned to humanely destroy a sick cat who hit on the idea of blowing it up and attached a stick of dynamite to it. He lit the fuse and ran away; the cat, fuse burning brightly, chased after him. He ran to a neighbor's home, the cat followed, took refuge under the woodshed, and blew it up (Goudy 1986).

A very similar tale was told in Rolf Harris's compilation of animal stories (Harris, Leigh, and Lepine 1996, 65–66). Here a lazy and greedy Sicilian fisherman decides to blow up the fish rather than trawl for them. A large fish jumps out of the water, catches the dynamite in its mouth, and dives down under the boat. The fisherman loses his boat as well as his catch. More recently the story appeared in the *Weekly World News* of October 2002. A policeman from Moscow (Russia) was said to have got into an argument with some kids on the street, and threw a grenade at them. Their dog, thinking it was a game of "Fetch!" brought it back to him ("Dog Blows Up Owner!").

However, the story has recently been located most often in the United States and adapted to American society by being set during a duck-shoot. A group of hunters from Arkansas (or Michigan, or Tennessee, wherever) set out in the middle of winter on a duck-shoot. The lake is frozen over, so they toss out a lighted stick of dynamite to make a hole in the ice. Their gundog (retriever or Labrador) does what gundogs are trained to do; he fetches it back for them. In some versions the dog, "Napoleon," is blown to pieces, and in a sick twist, is buried with a headstone reading "Here lies Napoleon Blown-Apart" (see, for example, report from the Lewisburg *Tribune* February 1990, quoted in Scott 1996, 86). In other versions, the hunters try to shoot the dog and fail, and in others the dog destroys the "blind" they are sheltering behind. The most truly legend-like, however, in that it features cars, destruction, and revenge, is the e-mail version in our example.

This story was also reported by the "Outdoors Columnist" in the Springfield *News-Leader* (January 18, 2002), and a very similar tale had appeared several times on the Internet in April 1997. In one typical tale, a "young couple" go duck-hunting with their "Labrador retriever" and their new Jeep Cherokee on which they have only just paid their first installment of $475. The dog "retrieves" the dynamite and destroys the beloved vehicle ("Can't Keep a Good Dog Down"). The insurers won't pay up.

Example

Finally, we have an allegedly true e-mail account that may best be filed under the heading of nonurban legends. It involves two Michigan duck hunters, a brand new Lincoln Navigator with $560 per month payments, a Labrador retriever, and dynamite.

Apparently late in the duck season, with local waters iced over, the intrepid hunters drove out onto a lake with the intent of blasting a watery hole into which ducks might be lured with decoys. They lit a stick of dynamite with a 40-second fuse and threw it as far away as possible.

Unfortunately, the highly trained Lab knew all about that game and caught the dynamite just about the time it landed, whirling to bring it back. Rightly alarmed, one of the hunters raised his shotgun and fired at the dog, momentarily stunning the poor animal.

Of course, bird shot was not enough to bring down a large retriever, which again tried to return the hissing dynamite to its owner. Another shot, and the panic-stricken Lab dove under the Lincoln.

At the kaboom, the dog and the $42,500 SUV were destroyed as the ice crumbled and the whole works plummeted to the bottom of the lake.

If the loss of a faithful dog was not enough, the owner of the Navigator was informed by his insurance company that sinking a vehicle by the illegal use of explosives was not covered by his policy. Regrettably, the $560 payments would remain in force. (Stout 2002)

FURTHER READING

Brunvand, Jan Harold. *Encyclopedia of Urban Legends*. New York: Norton, 2001.

"Can't Keep a Good Dog Down." *FOAFtale News* 42 (May 1997): 12.

"Dog Blows Up Owner!" *Weekly World News* (October 22, 2002): 5.

Goudy, Karin. "Andy Devine," 1986. http://www.ctaz.com/~mocohist/museum/andy.htm

Harris, Rolf, Mark Leigh, and Mike Lepine. *True Animal Tales*. London: Century, 1996.

Scott, Bill. *Pelicans and Chihuahuas and Other Urban Legends*. St Lucia, Queensland: University of Queensland Press, 1996.

Seal, Graham. *Great Australian Urban Myths*. Sydney: Angus and Robertson, 1995.

Stout, Byron. "Perilous Turns Part of Hunting." *The News-Press* [FLA] (January 30, 2002). http://www.news-press.com/sports/today/020130stout.html

THE MEXICAN PET

Mistakes of one kind or another provide one of the regular themes in urban legends. In this story, a person (usually a woman) mistakes a rat for a small dog. "The Mexican Pet" has come to be the usual title for this story because the earliest versions told of a couple who went to Mexico on vacation and fell in love with an endearing little Chihuahua dog, only to find out later that the little dog was in fact a "Mexican beach rat," or a "Mexican water rat."

Storytellers customarily go into great detail about how and where the "dog" was found, the way it was smuggled out of the country, and the loving care lavished on it when it was installed in its new home. The denouement varies. In an early version collected by Jan Brunvand from Texas, the animal falls into the toilet, the owners take it to the veterinarian, who reveals its true identity (Brunvand 2001, 258–259). However, most times the ending is a grisly one: the couple realize that their pet is not a dog when it chews the ear of one of their children, or eats the cat.

Since the 1980s, when the legend first came to folklorists' notice, it has spread pretty much worldwide. So stories have been reported about Dutch tourists bringing back a pet from Egypt, Italians and Spaniards smuggling animals from Thailand, Ukrainians bringing home Pakistani rats, Germans bringing back Spanish rats, Canadians bringing back Australian rats, and New Zealanders adopting Korean or Taiwanese rats. Among the strangest accounts is a story from Italy. Here the animal is a crossbreed between a dog and a mouse: the animal has to be put down and the house fumigated (Ed. 1991).

Among the latest sightings of the story are newspaper reports from New Zealand in 1998 and 1999. The quarantine officer for New Zealand's South Island, where the events are supposed to have happened, was reported as saying, "[The story] has been driving us mad. We have not been able to catch up with anybody who has actually been involved in this . . . The more we hear the less likely it is becoming. It started off as a Korean rat, then it became a Korean freezer rat, then a Taiwanese rat, and the latest is that it's an otter" (van Bynan 1998). In the most recent version, told in 2006 by a woman from Northern Ireland, the strangely aggressive "puppy" is a water rat from Londonderry (McGuire 2006, 8–9).

The fullest discussion of the story is Helmut Fischer's 1991 anthology *Der Rattenhund* (the Rat-Dog) which concludes with 36 oral versions of the story. A shorter discussion, with 25 oral texts of "The Mexican Pet" and a careful analysis of the legend, can be found in an English translation (Fischer 1996).

Example

This couple went on holiday to Mexico, and they lay on the beach every day, and every day this dear little dog kept them company and shared their food. The wife was besotted with it. The husband didn't like it at all (it was a miserable-looking little thing, only as big as a fair-sized rat), so he was furious when he found out that his wife had smuggled the dog out of the country in her hand luggage. Anyway it was done and he couldn't do anything about it. His wife adored it. It had a special basket in front of the fire, and she fed it the best of everything, treated it like a baby.

So he decided that he'd buy a pet of his own—something large and strong and masculine. So he went down to the cat sanctuary and got himself a cat—a big old thing, a real fighter, all scars, both ears torn—but he liked it. When he got it home he wrapped it in an old sweater and put it in front of the fire next to his wife's little dog. His cat was twice the size of her dog!

Next morning came downstairs, the cat's missing. Gone! Nowhere to be seen, but the wife's dog is looking pretty sleek and pleased with itself sitting in its basket with a pile of fur and bones in front of it.

Later they were looking at a program about Mexican wildlife and there was an item about Mexican beach rats. They said they were ferocious predators that could take on animals twice their own size, though they were very tame and friendly round humans. They looked at the TV, they looked at their little dog. No doubt about it, they looked exactly the same! (Bill Scott, personal communication)

FURTHER READING

Brunvand, Jan Harold. *Encyclopedia of Urban Legends*. New York: Norton, 2001.
———. *The Mexican Pet: More "New" Urban Legends and Some Old Favorites*. New York: Norton, 1986.
Bynan, Martin van. "Rat Rumour Baffles MAF." *The Press* [Christchurch, New Zealand] (May 22, 1998): 1.
Ed. [Paolo Tosselli]. "Vecchia Leggenda, Nuova Versione" (Old Legend, New Version) *Tutte Storie* 1.1 (1991): 12. (Italian text, English summary).
Fischer, Helmut. "The Rat-Dog: An Example of a 'New' Legend." In *Contemporary Legend: A Reader*. Compiled by Gillian Bennett and Paul Smith. New York: Garland, 1996, pp. 187–207. Translated by Jack Hall from an article appearing in *Rheinisches Jahrbuch für Volkskunde* 26 (1985–1986): 177–195.
Holt, David. "Legends Have a Familiar Ring: Modern Folklore Addresses Universal Concerns with Stories That Are as Old as the Ages and Are Regularly Brought up to Date." *Atlantic Insight* 9.8 (1987): 11–13.
McGuire, Peter. "Two Dublin Legends." *FOAFtale News* 65 (August 2006): 8–9.

THE MICROWAVED PET

The microwave oven was invented by Percy LeBaron Spencer in 1945, the patent was filed in 1946, and the first commercial product marketed in 1947. The earliest domestic microwave oven, the "radar range," cost over $2,000 and was the size of a refrigerator. Initially there was no great enthusiasm for the appliance, but by 1976, 52 million homes in the United States had one. It was not long until folklorists began to collect stories of people who had misused their microwave in ingenious but potentially fatal ways.

Stories about people who have accidentally microwaved their pets are known all over the English-speaking world and in most European countries too, and have been used as episodes in films such as "Gremlins" (1984), "Medium Rare" (1978), and "The Wild Life" (1984). But tales about cooked pets are not new. Thomas Barden found one such about a cooked pet which predates the microwave age, but is plainly an analogue of the modern legend, in a 1937–1942 collection of folklore from Virginia. Titled "Roast Cat for Breakfast" it tells the tale of a woman in a hurry to cook biscuits for her grandson's breakfast. Hardly looking at what she is doing, she shoves the dough into the oven and slams the door shut. When the door is opened again, she finds the cooked biscuits in the front of the oven and "a fine roasted tom cat" in the back (Barden 1992, 157).

Probably, the earliest story featuring a microwave, rather than a conventional oven, was a "true" story from 1949 which Australian folklorist Ron Edwards had heard. Though it did not feature an animal, it seemed to him to be an obvious forerunner of stories about microwaved pets. The story had been told by an engineering student from an Australian technical college: he reported that a machine had been invented that used a new form of energy to give off heat. It had no door, so when somebody put a plate into it, he found that the heavy gold signet ring he was wearing melted and fused to his finger, causing such terrible burns that he lost the finger ("The Microwaved Signet Ring"). Stories continued to be reported about people who had cooked their kidneys or other organs by standing in front of a microwave when it was running.

However, it was stories about microwaved pets that really took the popular imagination by storm. One of the first reports came from Arizona in 1978 when nearly 60 percent of American homes had a microwave in their kitchen but the appliance was still relatively new to the domestic market. It is a simple story about an old lady whose children gave her a microwave as a present. Not understanding the technology, the old lady attempted to dry her dog in it after she had bathed it (Ed. 1979).

Dogs are not the only pets said to have met their deaths in a microwave oven (though poodles are a favorite); cats, turtles, and birds also feature in some stories. For cats, see our example below; for birds see Smith 1992, 58–62. At times, legend has imitated life, or vice versa. There have been reported cases that seem quite genuine. Smith's bird story, for example is taken from an article in the (UK) *Sun* (October 19, 1985) that supposedly reports a court case in which two British students were accused of killing a budgerigar: as the headline put it, "Budgie Cooked Alive in Microwave: Lads Giggled When the Oven Went 'Ding'." The same issue of the *Sun* published a cartoon which depicted a woman reading the instructions for her microwave oven which gave the cooking time for hamsters, goldfish, budgies, mice, and sausages. In 1990 an Ontario court found a young woman guilty of killing her roommate's cat by cooking it in a microwave, and in 1991 when a California girl was arrested for housebreaking and torturing animals. Her crimes were said to include baking a cat in a microwave ("Nuking the Poodle"). In the same year the *Journal of the American Animal Hospital Association* published a case report of the damage done to a toy poodle after the owner's daughter had put it in the microwave and baked it for 30 seconds (Reedy and Clubb 1991).

Example

I heard one about an elderly lady who bred pedigree cats and entered them in cat shows. She specialized in Persian cats and it was always a difficult task to clean and groom them for show purposes. So the old lady had got it down to a fine art: she would wash the cat, towel it dry, then give it a very brief warm-up in her electric oven.

One Christmas she had a show coming up and her cooker developed an electrical fault, but she was an enterprising sort of lady. For a Christmas present she had been given a brand new microwave oven, so she washed the cat as usual, towelled it dry, and put it in the microwave to finish drying. Well, she might have been enterprising, but she didn't know much about the new technology. You can guess what happened—there was no miaow, not any noise at all, but the poor creature exploded the instant the power was switched on. (Smith Collection)

FURTHER READING

Barden, Thomas E. "Early Virginia Analogues of Some Contemporary Legends." *Contemporary Legend* 2 (1992): 155–164.

Belanus, Betty J. "The Poodle in the Microwave Oven: Free Association and a Modern Legend." *Kentucky Folklore Record* 27 (1981): 66–75.

de Vos, Gail. *Tales, Rumors, and Gossip: Exploring Contemporary Folk Literature in Grades 7–12*. Westport, CT: Libraries Unlimited, 1996. See pp. 102–104.

Ed. [Keith Cunningham]. "Hot Dog! Another Urban Belief Tale." *Southwest Folklore* 3.1 (1979): 27–28.

"The Microwaved Signet Ring." (Query from Ron Edwards) *FOAFtale News* 12 (February 1989): 13–14.

Reedy, Lloyd M., and Fred J. Clubb Jr. "Microwave Burn in Toy Poodle: A Case Report." *Journal of the American Animal Hospital Association* 27 (September/October 1991): 497–500.

Smith, Paul. "'Read All About It! Elvis Eaten by Drug-Crazed Giant Alligators': Contemporary Legend and the Popular Press." *Contemporary Legend* 2 (1992): 41–70.

See: The Baby Roast

PARROT TALK

Since about the year 2000 there has been a huge number of stories circulating on the Internet and in the newspapers about telltale parrots. These include: a parrot who shrieks "Quick, hide" whenever the doorbell rings; an escaped parrot who sings "Long live liberty"; another who taunts his owner with "I can talk. Can you fly?"; a parrot who repeats the final words of a murder victim and whose evidence is accepted in court; a parrot who tells a depressed woman to "End it all" because "Life is not worth living"; a parrot who calls "Come in" to the police and gets its owner arrested. And many more.

Older stories on the same theme include legends about a parrot belonging to British wartime leader Winston Churchill. Reputedly Churchill's parrot attended all crisis meetings and his favorite sayings were "****the Nazis" and "****Hitler" (Borrows 2004). From Scotland in 1861 comes a story about a parrot that was trained to call out the names of every station on the Glasgow to Edinburgh run because the train conductor kept on forgetting this task ("Another Parrot Story"). There is also a much older parallel from Ancient Rome. It is said that, after his victory over Anthony and Cleopatra, the Emperor Octavian bought a parrot that had been trained to say "Hail Caesar, Conqueror and Leader!" He then discovered that its owner had hedged his bets by training a second bird to say "Greetings to Anthony, our Victorious Commander" (Boehrer 2002, 11).

Below is our current favorite, told by a friend in January 2005. This version would appear to be based on a newspaper article by Sam Jones (2005), but the tale goes back to rumors and stories from the 1990s. In March 1990 the *Toronto Sun* reported the supposedly true story of an Argentinean divorce case in which the principal witness was a parrot who imitated the unfaithful husband's love talk with his beautiful mistress. Then a similar story was reported from Florida in 2001, and from China, Shanghai, Singapore, and Trinidad in the same year.

Example

I read this in the paper last week. Apparently a Yorkshire couple had a talking parrot called Ziggy. One day Ziggy started saying "Hi Gary!" every time the phone rang.

Then it started making kissing noises every time the name Gary was mentioned on the TV. Then it started moaning, "Oh, it's so good! I love you Gary!" You'll understand the husband was NOT called Gary! So he got a bit suspicious and confronted his wife. It turned out that she was having an affair with a work colleague—who WAS called Gary—so he threw his wife out and got rid of the parrot too.

"I wasn't sad to see the back of my wife after what she did," he said, "but it really broke my heart to let Ziggy go." (Bennett Collection)

FURTHER READING

"Another Parrot Story." *FOAFtale News* 11 (October 1988): 11.

Boehrer, Bruce Thomas. *Parrot Culture*. Philadelphia: University of Pennsylvania, 2002.

Borrows, Bill. "F*** the Nazis, Says Churchill's Parrot." *The Mirror* [London] (January 19, 2004). http://www.mirror.co.uk/news/topstories/tm_objectid=13832640%26method=full%siteid=94762-name_page.html

Jones, Sam. "How Talking Parrot Spilled Beans on Owner's Cheating Girlfriend." *The Guardian* [Manchester and London] (January 17, 2005): 8.

"Pillow Squawk!" *The Sunday People* [London] (May 19, 2002). http://www.People.co.uk/hoempage/news/page.cfm?objectid=11882627&method=thepeople_full&siteid=79490

See: "Out of the Mouths of Babes . . ."

THE PENGUIN STORY

This humorous story seems to have begun in the United Kingdom sometime in the 1970s and to have recently spread to the United States. It appeared in British writer Rodney Dale's *The Tumour in the Whale* (1978), which was one of the first compilations of urban legends to be published. In Dale's story a child visits an (unspecified) zoo. When they return, his mother notices a strange movement in the tote bag the child has been carrying all day. She investigates, and finds a baby penguin. The child denies stealing it, but the mother decides to check with the zoo to make sure he is telling the truth. The zoo staff say they have no reports of missing penguins and go off to do a penguin head-count. Sure enough, all the penguins are present and correct. The mystery is—who does the baby penguin belong to and how did it get into the child's bag? (Dale 1978, 134).

By 1993, when British writers Phil Healey and Rick Glanvill reported the story in their popular collection *Urban Myths*, the story had become more elaborated. Now the zoo is named (it is Dudley zoo in the English West Midlands), the child is hyperactive, and the penguin has been stolen, and is found splashing about in the child's bath (Healey and Glanvill 1993, 203–204). This is the form that the legend took when it became more widespread. In 2005 it was reported on at least a couple of occasions on the Internet, on both occasions as having occurred in the United Kingdom at a theme park in the West Midlands; in one story, the penguin-thief is a normal active 12-year-old boy, in the other story he is a grown man with the mental age of a 12-year-old (see Mikkelson).

By 2005 the story was turning up in the United States and being recognized as an urban legend by staffers at zoos and aquariums. It had been reported from places as far apart as New England, Arkansas, and California. In these accounts the child is autistic and has slipped the penguin into his backpack.

Example

A 12-year-old boy with autism visits the New England Aquarium and gets lost in the crowd. When his mother finds him, he seems agitated. So she takes her son home and puts him in a bath to calm down. When she checks on him, she finds a penguin splashing with him in the tub. The boy admits that he slipped the penguin out of the aquarium in his backpack . . .

In an attempt to squash [the story] once and for all, aquarium officials invited reporters yesterday to a penguin head count . . .

All 61 penguins residing at the aquarium are safe and accounted for, [a spokesman] said. They waddle around an ocean tank with steep walls and zip through water, kept at a chilly 50 degrees, so fast they appear to be flying. No child could scale the tank railing . . . drop 6 feet into the water, scoop up a penguin, and leave, at least not without being noticed (extract from Tench 2005).

FURTHER READING

Dale, Rodney. *The Tumour in the Whale: An Hilarious Collection of Apocryphal Anecdotes*. London: W. H. Allen, Universal Books, 1978.

Healey, Phil, and Rick Glanvill. *Urban Myths*. London: Virgin, 1993.

Mikkelson, Barbara. "Birdnapped." http://www.snopes.com/critters/farce/smuggled.asp

Tench, Megan. "Penguin Story Is a Fishy Tale." *Boston Globe* (December 2, 2005). (Extract reprinted in *FOAFtale News* 64 (April 2006): 6–7.)

SERVING THE DOG

Almost everybody knows a story about somebody who finds a severed finger in a Chinese meal, or a dead rodent in a package of take-out chicken, or a dead dog in an ethnic restaurant kitchen—and such tales have certainly been around for some time. However, there is an older story that combines the elements of ethnic food, restaurants, and animals in a slightly different way. In this legend, known since at least 1850, the story is that a couple go to a restaurant somewhere in the Far East (usually mainland China or Hong Kong). They take their dog with them, and order a meal for themselves and a meal for the dog. The waiter takes the dog away (as they think, to be fed in the kitchen), and they enjoy a wonderfully tasty and totally unfamiliar dish of food. When they are ready to leave they ask for their dog to be returned to them; they are met with blank stares for, of course, they have eaten the dog. Misunderstanding their instructions—and being accustomed both to eating dogs and to customers choosing their food from a selection of still-living creatures—the chef has cooked the dog and served it up to its owners.

The story appears in a 1973 movie "Theater of Blood," and as a climactic incident in a 1932 Hitchcock film, "Rich and Strange," released in the United States as "East of Shanghai." Hitchcock's film was based on a 1930 novel with the same title by Dale Collins. In the film an English couple on a luxury cruise in the Far East are rescued from their sinking ship by the crew of a Chinese junk. They are starving, so really appreciate the excellent meal the crew serve up to them. Then they see the skin of the ship's cat nailed up to dry, and realize what they have just eaten. More than 80 years earlier a story of an eaten pet had featured in a novel by the Victorian writer William Makepeace Thackeray, *The History of Pendennis* (1850). Its first modern appearance in the press was in an item from Reuters press agency in 1971 purporting to relate events that had happened in Zurich, Switzerland. Soon after that date it began to be recorded in the oral tradition on both sides of the Atlantic (Buchan 1992, 91). So it appears that the story began life in literary-popular media, then gradually spread into the popular press, and from there into informal channels by word of mouth.

Today, the story still turns up in a variety of media—for example, in collections of "urban myths" (see Healey and Glanvill 1992, 70–71), or humorous anecdotes (Brandreth 1982, 136), or outlandish occurrences (Train 1978, 60), or as news. One of the most recent sightings was in June 1996, when a correspondent wrote to *FOAFtale News* saying he had heard several versions of a supposedly "true" story and asking for information. He had seen stories about eaten pets in the "Dear Abby" and "Ann Landers" columns, and, to his knowledge, they had recently been reported from Germany, Italy, and the United States. More recently, local newspapers in Valencia (Spain) where he was currently living, had reported it as a true occurrence (McGuire 1996).

Example

An English couple went out one evening for a Chinese meal. As they did not want to leave their dog in the car they took it into the restaurant with them. The waiter, who didn't appear to know much English, showed them to a table and they indicated that they would like him to take the dog to be fed. He smiled and went away taking the dog with him

Another waiter came to their table, so they ordered their meal and sat back relaxing while they waited for the food to arrive.

Then the first waiter came back bearing a large platter which he placed in the centre of the table. When he lifted the lid the couple were mortified to find their dog—cooked and served with full trimmings (Smith 1986, 95).

FURTHER READING

Brandreth, Gyles. *The Book of Mistakes*. London: Futura, 1982.

Buchan David. "Folkoristic Methodology and a Modern Legend." In *Folklore Processed in Honour of Lauri Honko on his 60th Birthday 6th March 1992*. Ed. Reimund Kvideland in collaboration with Gun Herranen, Pekka Laaksonen, Anna-Leena Siikala, and Nils Storå. Translated from the Finnish by Susan Sinisalo. Helsinki: Suomalaisen Kirjallisuuden Seura, 1992, pp. 89–103.

Healey, Phil, and Rick Glanvill. *Urban Myths*. London: Virgin, 1992.

McGuire, Tom. "Circulating in Valencia: Pet Food and Filched Child." *FOAFtale News* 39 (June 1996): 5–6.

Smith, Paul. *The Book of Nastier Legends*. London: Routledge and Kegan Paul, 1986.

Train, John (Compiler and Annotator). *True Remarkable Occurrences*. New York: Clarkson N. Potter., 1978.

See: Fingers in Take-Out Meals; Kentucky Fried Rat; Urban Cannibals and Human Sausage Factories

6

SEX AND NUDITY

With just a few exceptions—all of which are tales of revenge for infidelity—these are the most lighthearted urban legends. Endlessly inventive, the stories tell of people of both sexes who find themselves in the most ridiculous predicaments— they fart in public, they expose themselves naked in the street, they zip themselves to tablecloths, they unwittingly engage in sex play with total strangers, they broadcast their ecstatic lovemaking to a bar full of drinkers: the list of their embarrassments is seemingly endless. If bad luck and/or bad timing can expose somebody to sexual humiliation and cause maximum amusement for others, it will happen and it will be told of in these stories.

For other tales of sex and nudity see: *Accidents Galore; The Body in the Bed; Glued to the Loo; The Kilkenny Widow; Parrot Talk; The Ski Run; White Slavers*

ALL ZIPPED UP

This story of social embarrassment has been known in Europe and the English-speaking world since the time zips replaced buttons as fastenings for men's trouser flies. As far as we are aware, the first time this story was noted by folklorists was in Roger D. Abrahams 1977 essay "The Most Embarrassing Thing that Ever Happened." In this essay Abrahams relates an incident that initially he says he witnessed at first-hand, then confesses really happened to the ubiquitous friend-of-a-friend. During an evening of dancing and dining in Philadelphia, he says, he noticed that a friend's fly was undone. When he warns him, Abrahams' friend hastily zips up, but he zips the tablecloth into his trousers. He doesn't notice what he's done, but when he gets up to dance, he pulls the cloth and all that was on it onto the floor. Carrying the tablecloth in front of him he has to retire to the men's room to disentangle himself. All the other diners applaud.

Similar events are recorded as supposedly happening in the United Kingdom (see our example below), in Belgium, Scandinavia, Australia, and Ireland as far back as the 1960s. Other versions increase the embarrassment and introduce a sexual element by having the unfortunate man zip an item of women's clothing into his trouser fly. The earliest of these was recalled as having been told in Denmark in the late 1960s or early 1970s, and a version also appeared in the United States in Art Linkletter's book of humorous anecdotes *Oops! Or Life's Awful Moments* (1967, 58). Obviously the story must have already been familiar in the oral tradition by this date.

This version continued to be popular until well into the 1990s. The story goes that a man at the theatre discovers that his flies are open and hurriedly starts to zip up. Just then a woman in a floaty chiffon dress, or a long lace gown, or a trailing fox-fur wrap pushes past him and he catches the hem of the dress or edge of the wrap in his zipper. These stories, too, end with the man having to edge to the restrooms with the dress and its wearer still firmly attached to his trousers. Other versions set the scene on a crowded bus and end with the man and the woman being forced off the bus and being last seen "struggling to get free of each other" ("Stop Me if You've Heard," 11). In a version from Belgium, "In order not to tear the dress, the man and woman decide to leave the room together. First they make another try [to get free] in the corridor, but because the task seems so arduous, they move on to the restrooms. They go into the ladies' together. There they are caught by the police and are fined for an act of indecency" (Top 1990, 5).

A further variant of the story was contributed to *FOAFtale News* by Canadian folklore collector Brian Chapman who found two stories about gloves caught in zippers, one in the *Victoria Times Colonist* [British Columbia, Canada] of November 1996, and one in Heinz Hammer's *Routes: The Lighter Side of Public Transit* (1989, 155–156). The scene is a crowded bus, and the characters are a shy young woman and a man whose flies are, unknown to him, unzipped. The girl drops her gloves at exactly the same moment as the man discovers his plight. In his haste to zip up, he catches up one of the girl's gloves and zips it into his fly where it dangles suggestively until he checks that he is decent. Feeling the glove, and seemingly mistaking it for his shirt tails, without looking he stuffs it down his trousers (Chapman 1997).

Example

Ian was very anxious to impress his girlfriend's parents so he was particularly pleased when they invited him round for dinner. They all seemed to get on very well and the meal was a really sumptuous spread. Their hospitality knew no bounds and they constantly pressed him with extra helpings. In fact it was probably a mixture of their hospitality and his willingness to please that led to his downfall.

After the second helping of the main course he was feeling so full that he decided he had better secretly loosen his waistband a little. Unfortunately in doing so his zip fly came open. He wasn't too worried as no one could see it under the table. As the meal finally came to a close he surreptitiously zipped up his fly and prepared to adjourn with his girlfriend's father for a drink.

It was as he stood up when the ladies left the table that the incident occurred. He had unfortunately zipped the table-cloth into his fly, and, not realising, as he walked away he made a pretty fair job of clearing the table. (Smith 1986, 26)

FURTHER READING

Abrahams, Roger. D. "The Most Embarrassing Thing that Ever Happened: Conversational Stories in a Theory of Enactment." *Folklore Forum* 10.3 (1977): 9–15.

Bregenhøj, Carsten. "From Zipper to Briefcase: Recycled Legends in Advertising." *FOAFtale News* 24 (1991): 6–7.

Chapman, Brian. "Glove Caught in the Zipper." *FOAFtale News* 42 (May 1997): 8.

Linkletter, Art. *Oops! Or, Life's Awful Moments*. Garden City, NY: Doubleday, 1967.

Mikkelson. "Man of the Cloth." http://www.snopes.com/love/dating/tblcloth.htm

Smith, Paul. *The Book of Nastier Legends*. London: Routledge and Kegan Paul, 1986.

"Stop Me if You've Heard." *FOAFtale News* 26 (June 1992): 10–12.

Top, Stefaan. "Modern Legends in the Belgian Oral Tradition: A Report." *FOAFtale News* 17 (March 1990): 3–6.

See: Stuck on You

BATMAN FROLICS

This is one of a pair of stories that can be told two ways—either as a tale of a comic accident, or as a horror story about rape (compare "The Batman Rape").

The comic version, which we call "Batman Frolics"—and elsewhere has been referred to as "Super Hero Hi-Jinks"—seems to have started up sometime in the 1980s and spread very rapidly in America and the United Kingdom. Paul Smith heard it repeatedly told in Sheffield (UK) and included it in his *Book of Nastier Legends* (1986, 103–104). Gillian Bennett heard it told in Stockport (UK) at about the same time as a true story about an attractive local politician living in her neighborhood (see our example below). It was encountered in New Zealand in 1988. It spread widely throughout the United States after two radio personalities used it in their programs in the summer of 1989. By January 1990, it had turned up in the Ann Landers column in a letter from a Minnesota reader ("Superhero Sexual Accidents"). It appeared in *The Joy of Sport* (1991), and in the "Confessions" column of the magazine *Cosmopolitan* (September 2002). Batman is not the only superhero to feature in these stories—there are also versions about sexy frolics involving Tarzan, or Spiderman, or Superman costumes.

The story continued to be told, at least intermittently, on the Internet until November 2004, when Canadian legend collector Brian Chapman was sent a version from Indiana. This version begins like the Stockport story and the woman's lover is the local mayor. He has a head wound that he got when trying some sexy antics and hitting his head on the ceiling fan. It was said that, "the mayor begged and pleaded and ordered that no-one should talk. But, a few days later, when he stopped at a local diner for breakfast, the customers began humming the Batman theme" (via e-mail from Brian Chapman).

These stories very often tag on an ending that characterizes "Accident Galore" stories. An ambulance is sent for, but when they hear the tale the paramedics laugh so much they can't hold the stretcher steady. They drop "Batman," or "Superman," or "Tarzan," or "Spiderman," and he breaks his ankle.

Example

A man with a broken ankle and dressed in a Batman suit was admitted to the emergency room of the local hospital. Whatever could have happened?

Well, it seems this man was the lover of [Mrs X, a local politician] and one afternoon her neighbors heard shouts and cries coming from her house. They banged on the door but could get no reply so they rang the emergency services.

The police broke in and found her lying manacled to the bed and the man trapped under a wardrobe. He was dressed as Batman and she was dressed as Robin. He confessed that they liked to play sex games and Batman had been about to leap from the wardrobe on to the bed to rescue the Boy Wonder when the wardrobe collapsed and fell on top of him. (Bennett Collection)

FURTHER READING

Brunvand, Jan Harold. *Too Good to Be True: The Colossal Book of Urban Legends*. New York: Norton, 1999.

Smith, Paul. *The Book of Nastier Legends*. London: Routledge and Kegan Paul, 1986.

"Superhero Sexual Accidents." *FOAFtale News* 17 (March 1990): 10

See: Accidents Galore; The Batman Rape

THE CYBERSEX SURPRISE

In May 1997 *FOAFtale News* printed an urban legend which they called the "Cybersex Surpriser Surprised" and which seemed to be entirely a product of our modern age. It had been passed to Bill Ellis who was the editor at the time, by a student at North Western University, who, in turn, had had it via a long chain of e-mailers. Reportedly, it was the true experience of a girl at Colorado University, Boulder. Briefly, what happened was that, after breaking up with her boyfriend, the girl made use of a sex chat line and met a man who called himself "Jeremy." She told him her name was "Katie," and soon they were having cybersex. For a year they exchanged sex fantasies and their intimate thoughts, then they planned to meet in person. They booked a room in Vale, Colorado. The girl was the first to arrive. She climbed into bed, put out the light, and lit a candle. "Jeremy" came in, whispered "Katie," and put on the light. She recognized him. Of course she did—he was her father.

Bill Ellis said that he'd seen a similar story in a collection of "white slavery propaganda" at the University of Reading (UK). "In that version," he wrote, "it's a Victorian epicure whose thing is sex with preadolescent girls, whom his contact provides him by kidnapping them off the street." The current editor of *FOAFtale News*, Philip Hiscock, added a note saying that he had heard a similar story in the mid to late 1970s. Hiscock's story provides us with Example 1.

Since then, the "cybersex" story, with names and places changed has been told in Melbourne (Australia), in Singapore, and in France, where the man finds he has been engaging in cybersex with his mother ("Man Dates Gal On Internet For Six Months—And It Turns Out She's His Mother!").

In a variant which must be the older form, a man who books a stripper or hires a prostitute for a bit of fun discovers to his horror that the girl he has employed is his sister, his wife, or his ex-girlfriend. Modern examples of this version come from Greece ("Paternal Nightmare"), and Israel ("Father's Surprise: Call-Girl Daughter"). Older versions include anecdotes supposedly told by a British aristocrat, the Marquess of Aberdeen and Temair. After his death, an obituary written by a political journalist included a story that the Marquess liked to tell about a "private hotel" in Elvaston Place, Kensington (London), where—so the story went—a Guards officer being shown into a bedroom discovered that the girl assigned to him was his sister (Roth 2002). As the Marquess was 82 when he died, this tale must go back to the 1940s or 1950s.

These legends are part of a complex of morality stories about unpleasant surprises involving sexual misbehavior; they could be grouped together under the Biblical warning, "Be sure your sins will find you out." They date from the 1940s to the present day and are very widely distributed, ranging from the horrific to the absurd. At the "horrific" end of the scale, they include the Victorian account of the girl kidnapped for prostitution that Bill Ellis refers to, an account of a gang rape where the victim turns out to be the sister of one of the rapists, and another where a rapist kills himself after finding out that his victim was his own mother. At the comical end of the spectrum, there are stories about people who put personal ads in the paper and find that the only reply comes from a member of their own family (see Example 2 which dates from the 1940s). In between these extremes are stories about men who call a sex chat line offering conversation with "Hot Housewives," but who find they have called their own wives, men who hire an exotic dancer or stripper for a male-only party, only to find she is their own daughter, or their childhood sweetheart, or ex-wife (news reports via e-mail from Brian Chapman)

Examples

1. [A] friend . . . passed on a story he had heard at work in St John's Newfoundland, in a Canadian federal government department. I recently asked [him] to retell me the story. He said: "an old guy" at work had a friend from Corner Brook (about 500 miles west of St John's) who had to visit St John's on business.

When he checked into the Holiday Inn he asked the desk clerk to help him by procuring a hooker. "A short time later, someone knocks on his room door, and lo and behold, it was his daughter, who was going to university in St John's (and of course did not know he was in town)" (Hiscock 1997)

2. A lady who was worried at the failure of her twenty-eight-year-old daughter to find a husband persuaded her to insert a classified ad in the "personal" columns, reading: "Beautiful, exotic young heiress seeks correspondence with devil-may-care gentleman who wants to go places fast." Two days later after the ad appeared, the mother asked anxiously, "Well? Any answers?" "Just one," sighed her daughter. "Who wrote it?" demanded Mama. "I can't tell you," said the daughter. "But this was my idea," shouted Mama, "and I insist upon knowing." "All right," said the daughter wearily. "It was Papa." (Cerf 1959, vol. 2, 299–300)

FURTHER READING

Cerf, Bennett. *Bennett Cerf's Bumper Crop of Anecdotes and Stories, Mostly Humorous, about the Famous and Near-Famous.* 2 vols. New York: Garden City Books, 1959.

"Cybersex Surpriser Surprised." *FOAFtale News* 42 (May 1997): 11–12.

"Father's Surprise: Call-Girl Daughter." BBC News (October 11, 2002). http://news.bbc.co.uk/1/hi/world/middle_east/2319863.stm

Hiscock, Philip. Footnote to "Cybersex Surpriser Surprised." *FOAFtale News* 42 (May 1997): 11–12.

"Man Dates Gal On Internet For Six Months—And It Turns Out She's His Mother!" *Weekly World News* (May 16, 2005).

"Paternal Nightmare." *Fortean Times* 198 (August 2005): 9.

Roth, Andrew. Obituary. "The Marquess of Aberdeen and Temair: Mischievous Peer Who Liked to Shock with Tales of His Times in the World's Better Brothels." *The Guardian* [London and Manchester] (August 23, 2002). http://www.guardian.co.uk/obituaries/story/0,3604,779365,00.html

DEAR JOHN'S REVENGE

This humorous revenge story has been around since at least 1881. It tells of a man's witty but cruel response to a letter from his girlfriend telling him their relationship is at an end. The climax of the story is that the girlfriend asks her rejected lover to return his photo of her. His reply is the ultimate put-down.

He says he has forgotten what she looks like so is sending her his collection; perhaps she can find her own picture and return the others?

The story appeared recently in the joke column of *La Vie Outre Manche* (Life on the other side of the [English] Channel), a magazine for students of French; it was also in *The Arizona Republic* of January 8, 2003, as an event that had supposedly happened at the officer candidate school at the U.S. Coast Guard Academy in Groton, Connecticut in 1959.

Other versions come from the United States and Canada in the World War II years and from the first decade of the twentieth century. Most of these are in the form of humorous press stories or in compilations of comic anecdotes. But, like legends, they are "told as true" or located to real places and/or to seemingly real people. Like legends, too, it is apparent that these stories are told at second or third hand and are in common circulation. For example, a story reported in *The Washington Post* on July 13, 1901 had been reprinted from *The Chicago Tribune*, and a story (involving a sailor rather than a soldier) that was published in *The Los Angeles Times* on February 3, 1941 credited *The Montreal Star* as the source. A very similar, if not identical, story was also printed in *The Wall Street Journal* in April of the same year (via e-mail from Brian Chapman).

Our first example, one of the earliest versions of the tale, printed in *The National Police Gazette* (January 1881), has a slightly different but no less demoralizing put-down as its climax. Our second example comes from a 1945 compilation of humorous anecdotes.

Examples

1. Not long since, a young lady who had been engaged to a fine young man for some time met a richer person and soon put off the old love for the new. She wrote to the old lover requesting him to return her photograph. Here was a chance for revenge, which he took by sending her the following note: "I would gladly comply with your request, but if I do so it will spoil my euchre deck. I have a collection of photographs which I use for playing cards, and I do not wish to break it by giving away the deuce of diamonds." (Article in *The National Police Gazette* [January 15, 1881]; XXXVII: 173, 2)

2. When Private Jones left for the South Seas, his girl cried as though her heart would break and vowed that she would be true to him. For two years he carried her image in his heart. Then, one day, he received a curt note which began, "Dear Mr. Jones: I have decided I can't wait for you," she wrote. "The banker's

son wants to marry me, and he has already given me a mink coat. Please return my picture."

Jones burned for two days. Then he collected every picture in the camp, including mothers, grandmothers, movie pin-up girls, and naked natives. He sent the whole collection to his ex-girl with a penciled note: "I don't remember exactly who you are, but if your picture is among these, please take it out and send the rest back to me." (Cerf 1945, 131–132)

FURTHER READING

Cerf, Bennett. *Laughing Stock*. New York: Grosset and Dunlap, 1945.

DING, DONG, DINNER BELL

Mistaken identity is a recurring theme in stories of every kind, and the same is true of urban legends. One of the best-known comic legends is about a wife who mistakes a stranger for her husband, with dramatic and hilarious consequences. The plot relies on two elements, a playful wife and a man whose head cannot be seen for some reason—he is a mechanic working under the family car, he is a plumber come to fix the kitchen sink or the shower, he is pulling a sweater over his head, and so on. It is time for tea, or lunch, or dinner, and seeing the headless man and assuming it is her husband, the wife reaches out and (in the words of one commentator) "visits some familiarity upon his person" calling out "Ding, dong, dinner bell!" The startled mechanic, or plumber, or dinner guest leaps from under the car or sink or wherever, bangs his head, and knocks himself out. Like "Accidents Galore," "Glued to the Loo," and many "Exploding Toilet" legends, the story often ends with the paramedics who come to attend to the man's injuries laughing so much that they drop him and inflict further damage.

A similar story, with a slightly different setup and a different witticism from the wife, was sent in a letter to Australian folklorist Bill Scott and retold in his book of Australian yarns (1985, 236–237). In Scott's story two men have been out fishing and return to the home of one of them for a meal and a shower. While the homeowner gets to work in the kitchen his friend takes a shower. It is while he is doing this that the other man's wife returns, leans into the shower, and tugs at him shouting "Gotcha!" The friend faints with shock. Scott comments that the man who had sent him the story said he had read it in a newspaper that was wrapped around take-out fish and chips in Cardiff (Wales) and was reported as a true local occurrence. He also notes that he himself heard a variant of the story where the friend is so startled that he falls over and concusses himself (Scott 1985, 236–237).

With yet another punch line, "Tinkle, tinkle, time for tea," and lacking the multiple accidents ending, this story has been popular for a long time. Collector of erotic folklore Gershon Legman says that it circulated as "absolutely true" on the West Coast of the United States in 1940 (Legman 1968, 710).

The version that forms our second example was printed in the [London] *Weekend Telegraph* in 1989. It is told with the writer's tongue firmly in his cheek, and is set in an English country house after a fox-hunting expedition in (or so it is implied) days gone by. Scott's Australian story forms a bridge between this and the more familiar version. The setup is similar to the older tales (though with fishing substituted for hunting), but the ending is similar to the more recent stories.

Examples

1. I have heard that one about a woman from Pennsylvania. She was a raunchy sort of person, full of fun, you know? Well, it was time for lunch, and she saw her husband—what she thought was her husband—working on the car in the yard. He was under the car with just his lower half sticking out. So she skipped out, grabbed hold of him I needn't say where, and pulled, saying "Ding, Dong, Dinner Bell!"

   But it wasn't her husband! It was a stranger, just a guy her husband had asked to look at the engine of his car. Well, he was so shocked, he jumped up, slammed his head into the car, and knocked himself out.

   When he recovered consciousness, he was on a stretcher. He told the ambulance attendants how he'd hurt his head. They laughed so much they dropped the stretcher and broke his arm. (Smith Collection)

2. Mind you, the old days had their moments. A certain man went hunting with a pack of hounds ... It was day of teeming rain. They had a great hunt and finished up miles away. In the course of the day the Visitor had conversed with a Native of that Country. He suggested that the Visitor should return with him to his house nearby, where bed, board and dry clothing would be available.

   On arrival at the Native's house, the Visitor was taken up to the dressing-room, where dry clothes were laid out ... The Native's lady had been absent when the hunters arrived. On her return, loving spouse that she was, she went at once in search of her mate.

The Visitor had gladly removed his sodden nether garments, and was struggling to get his wet clinging shirt over his head when he heard the door open. A wife entering her husband's dressing-room and seeing there a man naked except for a shirt over his head is likely to make certain assumptions; especially if what she sees does not differ greatly from what she is accustomed to seeing. A humorous lady may feel that a little conjugal jape is in order.

The Visitor, still struggling with his shirt, found gentle advantage being taken of his person, and heard a soft voice saying: "Tinkle, tinkle, time for tea," followed by peals of silvery laughter. The silvery laughter continued all the way down the stairs and into the drawing room—where the lady found her fully-clothed husband leaning against the mantelpiece.

There may be those among you so dull of soul to doubt the truth of this story. I can vouch for its veracity. How do I know? Ah, well now, surely you know that a gentleman never tinkles and tells. (Poole 1989)

FURTHER READING

Brunvand, Jan Harold. *Encyclopedia of Urban Legends*. New York: Norton, 2001. See pp. 81–82.

Legman, Gershon. *Rationale of the Dirty Joke: An Analysis of Sexual Humor*. New York: Grove Press, 1968.

Poole, R. W. F. "A-Hacking We Will Go." *Weekend Telegraph* [London] (January 28, 1989): 9.

Scott, W. N. *The Long and the Short and the Tall: A Collection of Australian Yarns*. Sydney: Western Plains Publishers, 1985.

White, David. "There's Something Nasty in the Fridge: Urban Folk Beliefs Take up Where Fairy Tales Left Off." *New Society* (November 1, 1979): 248–249.

See: The Nude Bachelor; The Nude Housewife

FRAMED

This is a companion-story to the "Glued on the Loo" legend. "Framed" tales frequently appear in story compilations and consequently are very much more worked and rounded than the usual "Glued on the Loo" story. However, they are clearly related.

In "Framed" the victim is glued to the toilet seat in his or her own bathroom and has to be rescued with the toilet seat still stuck to his/her bottom. In many of them the victim is a woman and the closing dialogue between the victim and the male physician is the perfect excuse for a punch line that has served in many other comic narratives. "Did you ever see anything like this before, doctor?" the embarrassed girl asks. "Well, yes," says the doctor, "but I believe this is the first time I've ever seen one framed." Stories with this punch line were printed in J. M. Elgart's collection of saucy stories *Over Sexteen* (1951, 161), and in *Playboy* (1954).

The story below was told to Paul Smith in December 2003; his informant said she had read it on the Internet.

Example

Well, the story is that this woman stayed up late redecorating the house. She had used up all the paint except for a bit in the bottom of the can, so she decided that she would use it to paint the toilet seat before she went to bed. Her husband arrived home a little while later—he was a shift-worker—and sat on the toilet. The wet paint stuck to his bum, and made "the prettiest frame you ever saw round his ass." (Smith Collection)

FURTHER READING

Elgart, J. M. *Over Sexteen*. New York: Grayson Publishing Company, 1951.
Mikkelson, Barbara. "Frame Job." http://www.snopes.com/embarrass/doctor/framed. asp

See: Accidents Galore; The Exploding Toilet; Glued to the Loo; Stuck on You; The Superglue Revenge

GYNO GLITTER

This comic tale of sex and embarrasment has been around since about 1994 and is probably an update of an older story from the 1960s.

In its contemporary form it tells of a respectable older woman who sprays herself with feminine deodorant before visiting the gynecologist, only to find that what she has actually used is glitter spray. Alternatively, she takes a washcloth with her to the restroom at the clinic, only to find out later that her child has used it to wipe glitter spray off his hands. In its older form the story goes back to the days when "green stamps" were issued with a variety of goods to encourage sales. In this variant the woman uses the restroom before her gynecological examination, and finding there is no toilet paper, pulls out a tissue from her purse, only to discover later on that a green stamp which was stuck to the tissue is now stuck to her bottom. The gynecologist exclaims, "My! I didn't know they gave green stamps with that!"

Example

A young woman returned from her annual visit to her gynecologist in a state of some humiliation. She almost tearfully recounted to her roommate (another woman, it seems) that when the doctor viewed her . . . on the examining table, he exclaimed "Fancy! Faaannnnncyy!!" She reported she was too embarrassed to ask what inspired the outburst and just skulked away after the exam.

Her roommate asked if he'd ever acted weird like that before and was assured that he certainly hadn't—he was the soul of discretion. She next asked her distraught friend if she had done anything different in preparation for her exam, "No, not at all. Well, I did borrow some of your feminine hygiene spray." She gestured to an aerosol can on the dresser.

"That's not feminine spray! It's glitter spray for my hair!" Fancy alright. (Roland 1996, 4)

FURTHER READING

Brunvand, Jan Harold. *Encyclopedia of Urban Legends*. New York: Norton, 2001. See p. 179.

Mays, Alan. "The Glittering Gynecological Examination." *FOAFtale News* 39 (June 1996): 5–6.

Mikkelson, Barbara. "All the Glitters is not Bold." http://www.snopes.com/embarrass/feminine/glitter.asp.

Roland, Kathy. "Fancy!" Query in *FOAFtale News* 39 (June 1996): 4.

See: Framed

THE HAIR-CURLER REVENGE

One of several legends about a wife's grisly revenge for her husband's infidelity, this story circulated during the late 1980s and early 1990s in Canada and the United States. In all but the wife's chosen method of torture, the tale is more or less identical to the better-known legend of "The Superglue Revenge." In its details of deviousness, "kinky sex" and bondage, it also resembles "The Batman Rape."

The story was known in British Columbia, Canada about the year 1988, and versions were attached to a local chiropractor, who, some months later, was accused of sexually abusing his patients ("Hair Curler Revenge"). In central Ohio, where it surfaced in the spring of 1994, it was likewise attached to a named citizen, this time the rich and successful owner of a car dealership. The rumor appears to have started in May, and by June it was being debunked in a local "alternative press" newspaper (Russell 1993). On July 4 the annual "Doo Dah Parade" was held in Columbus, Ohio, and one of the floats featured a banner which read: "First he was dealin'; then he was squealin'; now he's healin'." Anyone who hadn't already heard the "Hair Curler Revenge" story went about asking, "What's all that about?" By the end of the day, everybody had heard the legend (Wyckoff 1994, 6).

Example

The "hair curler revenge" legend ... surfaced, almost intact, in central Ohio this past spring, attaching itself to a local car dealership celebrity ... The basic story here is that [the man's] wife arrived home one evening to find him in bed with another woman (or, in some versions, another man). She leaves without letting him know she has seen what is going on, comes back later and suggests some "kinky sex," which involves [her husband] being tied up. Once he is firmly bound, she sticks a curling iron in his rectum, turns it on, and leaves. She, or someone else, then phones the 911 emergency number. The rescue squad and police arrive, and [the man] is transported to a local hospital. The legend-teller's source is frequently either a friend of "a nurse" in the hospital [he] is taken to, or "one of the guys" on the police or emergency squad who responds to the call for help. (Wyckoff 1994, 5)

FURTHER READING

"Hair Curler Revenge." In the "Have You Heard?" column. *FOAFtale News* 30 (June 1993): 11. Contributed by John Betts.

Russell, Danny. "The Curling Iron Rumor." *The Other Paper* [Columbus, Ohio] (June 3–9, 1993): 4.

Wyckoff, Donna. "Getting the Point in Central Ohio: A Localized 'Hair Curler Revenge' Rumor." *FOAFtale News* 32 (February 1994): 5–7.

See: The Batman Rape; The Superglue Revenge

THE HAIRDRESSER'S SURPRISE

This entertaining tale sometimes called "The Hairdresser's Error" has been around at least since the late 1970s, and continued to be told intermittently until well into the 1990s. We first heard it in Sheffield (UK) told as a funny-but-true story by a secretary in the Department of English Language at the University of Sheffield. Since then it has been reported from places as far apart as New Zealand and the United States. Its latest appearance is as a newspaper story appearing in *The Australian* in January 2004. It is clear that the journalist knows it is an urban legend. The item begins, "My hairdresser sucked me in. She told me it had happened only last weekend. Her best friend . . ."; and it ends, "I howled with laughter and naturally spread the story far and wide. Three months later I read about it in *The New Yorker* . . ." (Fraser 2004).

Like this Australian story, most versions take place in a hairdressing salon, and the situation depends on the hairdresser mistakenly thinking that a customer is masturbating under the sheet or gown she has wrapped round his neck. Most often, the man has simply been cleaning his glasses, but in a few versions he is said to have been winding his watch. The hairdresser attacks her customer with a mirror, a hair dryer, a bottle of shampoo, a hairbrush, or some other handy implement. Sometimes she verbally abuses him as well, and sometimes she calls the police. In a few recent versions, the customer sues her for damages. Some storytellers turn the legend into a little morality tale about judging by appearances.

Jan Brunvand has a version from 1996 which is set on a passenger jet. A female flight attendant sees "suspicious" movements under an airline blanket wrapped round a male passenger, and calls the pilot, only to find the passenger was trying to un-jam a roll of film. A similar, supposedly true, story was reported in the Chicago *Sun-Times* in September 2000. Allegedly a man is suing United Airlines for a quarter of a million dollars after he was arrested on an unfounded charge of public indecency. He had been flying from St Louis to Chicago when he began to feel ill, and, on doctor's orders, began to rub his stomach two inches above his navel to make himself feel better. The cabin crew misinterpeted his movements (Pallasch 2000).

Example

A friend of my neighbour's owns a hairdresser's and last Friday just as she was closing, this chap came along and asked her if she could possibly cut his hair. He apologised for being so late, but went on to explain that he was to attend a wedding next day and it would be too early to get it done before. My neighbour's friend relented and decided to do it. She put him a gown on him and proceeded to cut his hair. After a few minutes she saw a violent movement under his gown and thought, "Oh, my giddy aunt! I have a pervert here!" With no hesitations she lifted up a mirror and hit him over the head. She was horrified to find he was only cleaning his glasses! After apologising, she took him to the hospital, where he had eight stitches put in a head wound. (Walkden 1990)

FURTHER READING

Brunvand, Jan Harold. *Encyclopedia of Urban Legends*. New York: Norton, 2001. See pp. 183–184.

Fraser, Jane. "Cutting Stories of Black and White." *The Australian* (January 7, 2004), http://www.theaustralian.news.com.au/common/story_page/0,5744,8335082%255 E28737,00.html

Pallasch, Abdon M. "Man Sues Airline over Stomach Rub." *Chicago Sun-Times* (September 3, 2000), http://www.suntimes.com/output/news/wu03.html

Smith, Paul. *The Book of Nasty Legends*. London: Routledge and Kegan Paul, 1983. See p. 30

Walkden, M. D. Letter to the Editor, *Dear Mr Thoms* 14 (January 1990): 3.

THE HALLOWEEN PARTY

This perennial favorite about unwitting adultery whilst in disguise has been repeatedly told in Europe and on the North American continent. In essence, it is an updating of a traditional theme, that of the man who is tricked into sleeping with his own scorned or neglected wife under the impression she is a new lover. In modern stories, the roles are switched: a woman now is the chief character and she sleeps with a stranger mistaking him for her husband.

According to the modern story, she can do this because the events take place at a Halloween party and, unknown to her, her husband has loaned his costume to a friend. Unlike the old stories, the modern tales involve no intentional infidelity and there is no implication that either husband or wife has been scorned or neglected. In the old tales, the husband is taught how to love his wife and the wife has a happy night of lovemaking. In the modern stories the wife is taught to trust her husband, and a stranger has the night of a lifetime.

The story has been a favorite in compilations of humorous anecdotes (Cerf 1965, 183–184) and collections of jokes for "after-dinner" speakers (see our example). It has also appeared in photocopied joke sheets (Dundes and Pagter 1987, 125–126), in online humor lists (Koven 1996), in the press (Chiron 2001), and of course in collections of urban legends (Brunvand 1989, 209–212).

Example

One gentleman used to go to a convention each year, but his wife was never invited. He always said there was too much work to be done there for spouses to be invited. Instead her job was to pick out and rent a costume for him for the masquerade ball that was the highlight of the convention activities each year.

So one year she rented him a bunny costume, and just for the hell of it, she rented one for herself, too. She was going to find out just how much work and how much play was done at this convention.

Without his knowing it, she snuck off to the convention, got dressed in the bunny outfit, and went to the masquerade ball.

She spotted the other bunny costume, struck up a conversation, got a little flirtatious, and finally the "other bunny" propositioned her. She agreed to go to his room provided they both agreed not to take their masks off.

She stayed the night and they made passionate love many times over.

When her husband returned from the convention, she asked how it went. He said, "Fine. We got a lot of work done." She said, "Did you have a good time in your bunny outfit at the masquerade ball?" He said, "Oh, I was much too busy to go to that, so I lent the costume to Charlie. He said he had the greatest time of his life." (Perret and Perret 1990, 134–135)

FURTHER READING

Brunvand, Jan Harold. *Curses! Broiled Again! The Hottest Urban Legends Going.* New York: Norton, 1989.

Cerf, Bennett. *Laugh Day: A New Treasury of Over 1000 Humorous Stories and Anecdotes.* New York: Doubleday, 1965.

Chiron, Michael. "I Slept with Wrong Hubby." *Weekly World News* (October 2, 2001): 12–13.

Colman, Nina, ed. *The Friars Club Bible of Jokes, Pokes, Roasts, and Toasts.* New York: Black Dog and Leventhal, 2001.

Dundes, Alan, and Carl R. Pagter. *When You're up to Your Ass in Alligators: More Urban Folklore from the Paperwork Empire.* Detroit, MI: Wayne State University Press, 1987.

Koven, Mikel J. "And About That Halloween Party . . ." *FOAFtale News* 40/41 (December 1996): 14–15.

Perret, Gene, and Linda Perret. *Gene Perret's Funny Business: Speaker's Treasury of Business Humor For All Occasions.* Englewood Cliffs, NJ: Prentice Hall, 1990.

LEFT AT THE ROADSIDE

This is one of many legends about people caught in the nude or scantily dressed. Alternative names for this story are "The Wife Left at the Roadside," "The Locked-Out Nude," and "The Nude in the RV." The story below was told to Gillian Bennett in 1981and features a caravan being towed along the highway. The legend has been very popular and widely recorded on both sides of the Atlantic since at least the 1950s. It was reported as a true story in a 1973 book *The Weekend Camper.* It was used as a climatic episode in a Doris Day movie "With Six You Get Egg Roll" (1968), and it appeared in an episode of the long-running 1960s British TV comedy series "The Likely Lads." The English version in our example is very similar to a story an Australian correspondent sent Brunvand in 1989: in the Australian version a lady simply referred to as "Auntie" dressed only in her panties hitches a ride on the pillion of a motorcycle driven by a leather-clad biker (Brunvand 1999, 381).

Brunvand believes that, in its tamer versions, this is an example of a legend that really happened but that has probably been embroidered upon in its various retellings. From 2001 to 2005 the Internet was awash with stories of motorists (in America, Canada, Australia, New Zealand, and Bangkok) who had left family members behind in restrooms and at truck stops; some of these seem real enough, others—where the husband or the wife is stranded on the highway wearing only night clothes, and/or is rescued by a youth in a small car—sound very similar to the legendary events (see, for example, "Driver Strands Pyjama-Clad Girlfriend").

However, there is at least one very much older parallel. A story in Islamic tradition tells how the Prophet Mohammed's favorite wife, Ā'ishah Bint Abī Bakr accompanied him on an expedition into the desert. On the last day of the return journey orders were given to break camp in the early hours of the morning. Ā'ishah left the others "to satisfy a natural need," but when she returned to camp she found she'd lost a precious necklace she had been wearing. So she retraced her steps and went in search of it. When she returned to camp a second time, she found that everyone had already left. There was nothing she could do but wait for them to come back for her. So she sat down where she was, and soon fell asleep. She wakened some time later to find an embarrassed young man looking down at her. Gallantly, the young man put her on his camel and took her all the way to Medina. Her absence had not been noted by Mohammed and the others; the first suspicion that they had left her behind was when they saw the young man arrive with Ā'ishah on his camel (Abbott 1944, 30–31; Shojaie Kawan 2005, 140–144).

Example

This is very funny, but this is absolutely true. It was my aunt's neighbour who we knew very well. This just reminded me—"Someone's wife left at the roadside during a vacation journey." They went on a caravan holiday. It, it was a long time ago, because I believe nowadays you're not allowed to sleep in a caravan while you're driving it. But in those days there was no law about it. I should say it's about twenty to twenty-five years ago, and—er—they were coming home from Wales. It was late at night and she was tired. Her husband said. "Oh, I'll drive. You go and sleep". So she went in the caravan, got undressed and put herself to bed, and they'd been driving about half an hour. She wasn't settled, and the car stopped, and she looked through the window. She saw her husband get out and go in the field, so she wanted to go in the field as well! She got out and—um—didn't tell him because he had gone by the side of the road and she went behind a tree or something, and he came back jolly quick and got in the car and drove off, and she'd just gone behind this tree, so she sort of ran out in her nightdress and shouted him, but on he went!

Anyway, she was there on the roadside for ages in her nightdress, and a young boy came along, and he was only about eighteen, on a motorbike, and she sort of flagged him down, and he stopped, and she told him what had happened. Said could he take her home as her husband had gone, and he said, "I can't, because I'm out late and my mother will kill me anyway!" So she said, "But I'll come and explain to your mother. Please! You can't leave me here in the road!" She'd only got her nightie on. So anyway, he did take her, and they overtook this caravan.

Her husband was absolutely staggered to see her, to see this woman on the back of the pillion. Hayes, their name was. That reminded me of that, but that's true, you know. There's no doubt about that. (Bennett Collection)

FURTHER READING

Abbott, Nabia. *Aishah: The Beloved of Mohammed*. 2nd ed. Chicago: University of Chicago Press, 1944.

Bennett, Gillian. "Legend: Performance and Truth." In *Monsters with Iron Teeth: Perspectives on Contemporary Legend III*, ed Gillian Bennett and Paul Smith. Sheffield. Sheffield Academic Press 1988, pp. 13–36. Reprinted in *Contemporary Legend: A Reader*. Compiled by Gillian Bennett and Paul Smith. New York: Garland, 1996, pp. 17–39.

Botkin, B.A., ed. *Sidewalks of America: Folklore, Legends, Sagas, Traditions, Customs, Songs, Stories and Sayings of City Folk*. Indianapolis, IN: Bobbs-Merrill, 1954. See pp. 522–523.

Brunvand, Jan Harold. *Too Good to Be True: The Colossal Book of Urban Legends*. New York: Norton, 1999. See pp. 111–112 and 378–381.

"Driver Strands Pyjama-Clad Girlfriend at Gas Station." *Victoria* [British Columbia, Canada] *Times-Colonist* (July 24, 2001): A1.

Shojaie Kawan, Christine. "Legend and Life: Examples from the Biographies of 'A'ishah Bint Abī Bakr, Mary Carleton, and Friedrich Salomo Krauss." *Folklore* 116 (2005): 140–154.

Smith, Paul. *The Book of Nasty Legends*. London: Routledge and Kegan Paul, 1983. See p. 36.

See: The Nude Bachelor; The Nude Housewife; The Surpriser Surprised 1 (The Blushing Bride); The Surpriser Surprised 3 (Not His Lucky Night)

LOVERS DIAL M (FOR MAXIMUM EMBARRASSMENT)

These stories have circulated at least since the 1960s and drew legend scholars' attention during the 1980s/1990s. The stories tell how a pair of lovers accidentally broadcast their lovemaking to the world at large, sometimes by failing to switch off the baby alarm in their holiday hotel or accidentally switching on the intercom, sometimes by activating the redial button on their bedside table, and sometimes by inadvertently e-mailing a private video clip to all their friends and colleagues. An alternative scenario is for the couple to be making enough noise to alarm the neighbors, who then call the police.

An apparently true incident of this nature took place in the south of England in 2001, when people taking a stroll near some woodland heard screams and moans coming from the bushes and alerted the police. Having also received accounts from local teens that they had seen a man carrying a naked "dead body" into the woods, the police sent out a search team to scour the woods and a nearby lake. Though the couple were not found after a 6-hour search, the police concluded that the noises had been made by a "courting couple." A spokesman laconically announced that "We are just very grateful that we are not dealing with a more sinister incident" ("Passionate Woman's Sex Screams Spark Murder Hunt").

A story printed in 1994 in the British newspaper, *The Independent*, blends all these themes. Here, a girl in the throes of passionate lovemaking accidentally presses the redial button on her bedside telephone with her big toe. The phone rings in her mother's house. When the mother picks up the phone she hears her daughter shouting, "Oh God, What are you doing to me!" Believing that an attacker is in her daughter's bedroom, the mother calls the emergency services (Macdonald 1994). A variant from the early 1990s tells how a man's sentimental baby-talk to his infant son is picked up by the baby-monitor which is switched into a hotel bar; unfortunately his words are ambiguous and are taken to be intimate love-talk between him and his partner (Healey and Glanvill 1992, 22–24).

Other related legends are stories that tell of girls who do a video-strip for their boyfriends and accidentally e-mail it to everyone in their address book ("New Video-Strip Legend"; "More on the Video/e-mail Strip"); and a story about an airline pilot's suggestive remarks about an attractive female member of the cabin-crew being broadcast to the passengers when he forgets to turn off the intercom after having made a public announcement (Smith 1986, 112). A very similar story to the tale in Paul Smith's compilation appeared in Art Linkletter's *Oops! Or Life's Awful Moments* (1967, 4). A recent, apparently real life, story was that of a TV host who took a toilet break and whose gossiping about her husband and family to a colleague in the restroom was broadcast as a background to President Bush's speech on the anniversary of the Hurricane Katrina disaster. The whole nation, it seems, heard her commenting on her sex life and the trouble she was having with her sister-in-law (Markham-Smith 2006).

Example

A couple who went to bed and made love after a few relaxing drinks in a hotel bar forgot to switch their baby alarm off.

For the next hour, fellow guests in the bar chortled happily as ecstatic moans and groans wafted down from the lovers' room.

One of the eavesdroppers said last night, "Some people wanted to go up and tell them, but we decided it might spoil their fun—and ours.

"We listened for ages before everything went quiet."

The couple, from the Paignton area of Devon booked into the Blackpool hotel with two young children.

The father, who prefers not to be named, said, "We found out in the morning that people had been listening in. It was very embarrassing." ("Baby! What an Earful!")

FURTHER READING

"Baby! What an Earful!" *The Mirror* [London] (October 19, 1988): 3. Reprinted in *Dear Mr. Thoms...* 25 (April 1992): 19–20.

Healey, Phil, and Rick Glanvill. *Urban Myths*. London: Virgin, 1992.

Jennings, Karla. *The Devouring Fungus: Tales of the Computer Age*. New York: Norton, 1990. See p. 134 for an Internet version.

Linkletter, Art. *Oops! Or Life's Awful Moments*. Garden City, NY: Doubleday, 1967.

Macdonald, Marianne. "Lovers Dial M for Maximum Embarrassment." *The Independent* (UK) (June 6, 1994): 1. Reprinted in *Dear Mr Thoms ...* 35 (August 1994): 26–27.

Markham-Smith, Ian. "How a Newsgirl's Gossip in the Loo Drowned out Bush." *The Daily Mail* [London] (August 31, 2006): 11.

"More on the Video Strip." *FOAFtale News* 39 (June 1996): 11.

"New Escaped Video Legend." *FOAFtale News* 38 (December 1995): 5.

"Passionate Woman's Sex Screams Spark Murder Hunt." http://www.ananova.com/news/story/sm_329147. html?menu=news.quirkies, filed: 10:42 Sunday, June 17, 2001).

Smith, Paul. *The Book of Nastier Legends*. London: Routledge and Kegan Paul, 1986.

"Why the Big Toe?" *FOAFtale News* 39 (June 1996): 11–12.

See: Parrot Talk

THE NOTE

In its classic modern form this story spreads mainly among lawyers, and is perhaps part of their occupational folklore. Versions recorded in legend compilations come from Australia (Scott 1985, 231), the United Kingdom (Dale 1984, 75–76), and the United States (Brunvand 2001, 482–483). The Australian one dates to 1980. The United Kingdom and Australian versions are very similar and both made their way into the mass media. Bill Scott's informant told him that only four days after he had heard the story from one of his students it was featured on TV as a true story.

The plot of these modern versions revolves round a witness giving evidence in a rape trial. She is too embarrassed to repeat the actual words the rapist said to her, so she is permitted to write it down. The judge reads the note then passes it to the jury. However, one juryman has been dozing and does not wake up until the note is thrust into his hand by the lady sitting next to him. He reads the note, smiles, and stuffs it into his pocket. The judge is surprised by his conduct and asks him to return the note. "Your honor," the juryman replies gallantly, "This note is a private matter between this lady and me."

Few legends are entirely new, so it is no surprise to find a story based on the same sort of misunderstanding in the *Cassell Dictionary of Anecdotes* (1999). Here it is related that the owner of a stately home in England had a butler who was a bit too fond of a drink. On one occasion his employer was hosting a grand dinner-party for the great and famous and discovered that the butler had had too much to drink. So she wrote him a note that said, "You are drunk. Leave the room immediately." She was horrified to see her butler lurch across the room and hand the note to one of her guests (Rees 1999, 69). Another tale about a note was printed in *Fun Fare: A Readers' Digest Treasury of Wit and Humor* (1949), and relates to the Hollywood actress Jane Wyman. It was said that once, when she was expecting guests, she laid pretty guest towels out on the bed with a note to her husband, "If you use these I'll murder you." After the guests had gone, she found the towels unused exactly as she had left them with the note still attached (Chapman 2000, 6). The story in our example below was circulating among New York newspapermen in the 1930s and was printed by *New Yorker* columnist Alexander Woollcott who had a good eye for an urban legend. The setting is different but the embarrassing misunderstanding is the same.

Example

A very stiff and very elaborate dinner, we hear, was given not so long ago to entertain the singer, Rosa Ponselle, on a visit to the West. Before the dinner, the hostess, a little doubtful about the ability of her Filipino head houseboy to cope with the situation, went over his duties with him carefully. Coming to the matter of glasses, she showed him each kind to be set out, and when, and where. "These are for the cocktails," she explained, "these are for the wine, these for the champagne, and these go to the men in the library after dinner." The dinner was going off very well and the hostess was congratulating herself when she heard a slight gasp from Miss Ponselle. The lady had just raised her glass, and noticed a small strip of paper stuck to its rim. "Go to the men in the library after dinner," it read. (Woollcott 1931)

FURTHER READING

Brunvand, Jan Harold. *Encyclopedia of Urban Legends*. New York: Norton, 2001.

Chapman, Brian. "Excerpts from *Readers' Digest Fun and Laughter*." *FOAFtale News* 46 (May 2000): 6–7.

Dale, Rodney. *It's True, It Happened to a Friend: A Collection of Urban Legends*. London: Duckworth, 1984.

Rees, Nigel. *The Cassell Dictionary of Anecdotes*. London, 1999.

Scott, W. N. *The Long and the Short and the Tall: A Collection of Australian Yarns*. Sydney: Western Plains Publishers, 1985.

Woollcott, Alexander. "Instructions." "The Talk of the Town" column. *The New Yorker* (September 26, 1931): 10.

THE NUDE BACHELOR

"The Nude Bachelor" is a popular and typical legend of accidental male nudity that has been known in Europe (especially Eastern Europe) and the United States since at least the early 1960s. In this story a naked man gets locked out of his house or stuck up a tree after a set of absurd circumstances that usually begin when he takes a shower. The story may also be told with the "Accidents Galore" ending where the ambulance men inflict further injuries by dropping the stretcher because they are laughing so much. Jan Brunvand reports that the story was the basis for a "Garfield" comic strip in 1987. The strip depicted Garfield's owner smacking him for some misdemeanour, then Garfield getting his revenge by slamming the front door on his owner when he goes to collect his newspaper clad only in a towel (Brunvand 1999, 147–148).

A bizarre variant was originally posted on an Internet site in November 1996. The location was said to be Bremen in Germany and the story told how a man who had been gardening outside lost his keys and tried to get back indoors through the cat-flap. He managed to get his head and shoulders in but got stuck round the waist. After a while a group of students came by but, instead of helping him escape, they took his pants and underwear off, stuck a daffodil between his buttocks, and put up a sign reading "Germany resurgent. Please give generously" ("The Cheeky Daffodil").

"The Nude Bachelor" occurs as an incident in *The Twelve Chairs* (1928) by Russian novelists Ilya Ilf and Evgeny Petrov; a similar incident is reported as a true occurrence in John Kenneth Galbraith's 1969 book *Ambassador's Journal*.

Example

Early one morning a friend of my brother went downstairs in his short karate-style dressing-gown to collect the post. As he bent forward he suddenly felt what he thought was a hand on his bare backside—what he did not know was that it was the cold wet nose of the family's pet dog.

So great was the shock of the young man that he catapulted forward and went straight through the glass door and into the street—well, that is what he told the police when they found him. (Smith 1983, 37)

FURTHER READING

Brunvand, Jan Harold. *Too Good to be True: The Colossal Book of Urban Legends*. New York: Norton, 1999.
"The Cheeky Daffodil." *FOAFtale News* 40/41 (December 1996): 22
Mikkelson, Barbara. "Nude Awakening." http://www.snopes.com/embarrass/buff/lockout.asp
Smith, Paul. *The Book of Nasty Legends*. London: Routledge and Kegan Paul, 1983.

See: Accidents Galore; The Nude Housewife; The Surpriser Surprised 1 (The Blushing Bride); The Surpriser Surprised 3 (Not his Lucky Night)

THE NUDE HOUSEWIFE

There are a large number of comical legends about nudity and mistaken identity. This complex of stories is one of them. It is not a single legend but a group of stories related by the same theme and details and a similar cast of characters—a naked wife, alone (as she thinks) at home, who misinterprets the situation and displays herself nude.

In a story from 1950s Britain, the wife has just seen her husband off for work and starts running a bath for herself. She is just about to get in it when she begins worrying about whether she has locked the back door. So, not bothering to put her clothes back on, she runs downstairs to check the door. She is just crossing the kitchen when she hears somebody coming to the door. Thinking it is the milkman and he will soon go away, she shuts herself from view in the broom cupboard. However, it is not the milkman but the gasman who has come to read the meter. As the meter is in the broom cupboard, the gasman has quite a surprise when he opens the door. His surprise turns to amusement when the wife blurts out, "I thought you were the milk man" (Smith 1986, 27–28). A story from 1930s United States has the same situation, except that the wife has forgotten to leave the door open for the iceman. Again, she goes down to the kitchen stark naked and finds a man who has come to read the gas meter. In her confusion she announces, "I was waiting for the ice-man" (Brunvand 2001, 473). These versions have been very widespread in the United Kingdom since the 1950s, and often turns up in "after dinner" speeches at social functions.

An up-to-date equivalent can be found in *Cosmopolitan* magazine (May 2005, 38). It is a supposedly true story of a teenage couple who were spending an evening alone at the young man's place, watching porn films and generally misbehaving. The young man went to the kitchen to get a drink of water. When the girl heard footsteps coming down the hallway, she struck a sexy pose and said, "Want bottom or top this time, Cowboy?" The person who stood in the open door was her boyfriend's father.

Our example is taken from an essay which first brought this story to folklorists' attention alongside tales of "The Surpriser Surprised."

Example

There was this Baptist couple who were real important people in the church. It was the woman's birthday and her husband had planned a surprise birthday party for her. While she was upstairs taking her shower that night, the minister and the rest of the church people were led in by the husband and hidden behind chairs in the living room. The wife, upon finishing her shower, walked down the stairs and stood naked at the bottom and hollered, "Come and get it while it's clean." (Jansen 1979, 78)

FURTHER READING

Brunvand, Jan Harold. *Encyclopedia of Urban Legends*. New York: Norton, 2001. See pp. 294–295 and 437; see also entries under "Nudity" p. 296.

Jansen, William Hugh. "The Surpriser Surprised: A Modern Legend." *Folklore Forum* 6 (1973): 1–24. Reprinted *Readings in American Folklore*. Ed. Jan Harold Brunvand New York: Norton, 1979, pp. 64–90. See pp. 64–72, and 82–88.

Smith, Paul. *The Book of Nastier Legends*. London: Routledge and Kegan Paul, 1986.

See: The Nude Bachelor; The Surpriser Surprised 1 (The Blushing Bride)

"OUT OF THE MOUTHS OF BABES . . ."

This humorous-yet-moral sex story has spread in a variety of media—newspapers and magazines, compilations of comic anecdotes, cartoons, collections of traditional stories, and as word of mouth. It tells how an unfaithful wife is exposed by the unguarded comments of her small child. French folklorist Jean-Bruno Renard, who has studied this story closely, believes that modern versions may have originated in 1953 and been given credence by a real-life incident which happened during a French chat show in the 1980s. However, he says, there are many parallels in traditional narrative from as early as the thirteenth or fourteenth century (Renard 1995), including references in the massive and authoritative French *Dictionaire Larousse* (1866–1886).

The earliest American version of "Out of the Mouths of Babes . . ." probably comes from Kermit Schafer's 1953 book *Your Slip is Showing!* Schafer relates an incident, supposedly true, that happened during a showing of the popular TV series "Strike it Rich," during the Korean War. The interviewer asked a 5-year-old girl what she would like as her prize and she answered "an apartment big enough for me to have my own bedroom." Surprised, the interviewer said, "But surely, with daddy away in Korea there's lots of room?" The child told him that during the week she slept with mommy, "but when Uncle Charlie comes, they make me sleep in the kitchen" (Schafer 1953, 15). With slight variations, this incident was later (1978) reported by Art Linklater as having happened on his own show. In Linklater's version, he was interviewing a young boy during World War II. When he tried to console the boy for his father's absence, the child supposedly responded, "Oh, no, I think it's great. I get to sleep with mommy every night except Wednesday when Uncle Bob comes over!" (Linklater 1978, 120–121).

European versions of the story date from a little later (1980s and 1990s). About 1987 or 1988 a story began to spread throughout Italy relating to a live TV show called "Piccoli Fans" in which children sang in front of an audience of family and friends. Supposedly when the host of the show asked one young performer if he had a fiancée, he replied "yes"; and when the presenter went on to ask him what he did with his fiancée, he replied, "I do what Mama used to do with Uncle Antonio," or "What Mum and Uncle Giovanni do when Dad isn't in" (Renard 1995, 77).

A virtually identical story had circulated earlier in France and related to a similar show called "L'école des fans," on air since 1977. Renard believes that the French stories may have developed by rumor and word of mouth from a true happening on this show. The presenter of the show told Renard that one young boy had been asked who accompanied him to the show and replied, "Mum and Uncle Johnny." When asked who Uncle Johnny was he had replied, "The man who comes to see my mum when Dad is at the restaurant." The show was not live, and the question-and-answer sequence was removed from the broadcast at the request of the family. However, the studio audience had heard it all and repeated it to their friends, with the result that the story (with the wording changed to "the man who sleeps with Mum when Dad is at the restaurant") was told in a high-circulation TV magazine. Renard believes that the Italian story is a simple redressing of the French event, with "Uncle Johnny" changed to "Uncle Giovanni" and "L'école des fans" changed to "Piccoli Fans."

In another French version, the presenter asks the child what he has for dinner each day. The child replies, " On Monday steak and chips, on Tuesday ham and mash, on Wednesday sandwiches." Wednesday, of course, is the day when "Mum has a rest with Nunky."

But the tale cannot have been entirely new in the 1980s—or, indeed, the 1950s—since Antti Aarne and Stith Thompson's classic *The Types of the Folktale* (1961) includes "Child unwittingly betrays his mother's adultery" in the list of traditional European tale types, and gives seven examples from Finland. From much earlier times there is a medieval French "fabliau" (a story in verse), "De celui qui roula la pierre" ("[a story] about the one who rolled a stone"). It tells how a priest approaches a peasant woman who is standing at her door idly rolling a stone about with her foot. The priest tells her that if he sees her rolling the stone about again he will lay her down and punish her. She rolls the stone again. Some time later the woman's husband comes home from the fields, picks up the stone, and is about to throw it away, when his little boy comes running out of the house, shouting, "Leave the stone alone or the priest will punish you like he punished mother!" (Renard 1995, 80).

Renard says that the "Out of the Mouths of Babes" story constituted a sequence in a 1969 film "Le clan des siciliens," which was adapted from a detective novel of 1967. In this sequence a young boy watching TV sees a couple lying on a beach, kissing passionately. The child points and announces,

"Looks like Auntie Jeanne and Mr Sartet!" Auntie Jeanne being a married woman, this remark triggers a vendetta which ends with the murder of the guilty lovers.

Our example is a modern story said to be "currently circulating in Manhattan."

Example

It seems that a group of 6-year-old girls from an elite private school were at a birthday party, and the conversation turned to their mommies' trainers. As the proud mothers listened nearby, one youngster piped up: "My mommy has a trainer, and every time he comes over, they take a nap" (Ali and Miller 2004).

FURTHER READING

Ali, Lorraine, and Lisa Miller. "The Secret Lives of Wives." *Newsweek* (July 12, 2004): 50.

Linklater, Art. *The New Kids Say the Damnedest Things!* Aurora, IL: Caroline House, 1978.

Renard, Jean-Bruno. "Out of the Mouths of Babes: The Child Who Unwittingly Betrays its Mother's Adultery." *Folklore* 106 (1995): 77–83.

Schafer, Kermit. *Your Slip is Showing! A Collection of Radio and TV's Most Hilarious Boners.* New York: American Book—Stratford Press, 1953.

THE PHONE BILL REVENGE

This modern tale of rejection and revenge—sometimes called "Dial R.E.V.E.N.G.E." or "The Lover's Telephone Revenge"—has been around since the early 1980s. The story goes that a man decides to separate from his wife or live-in girlfriend and one day announces over breakfast that he is off to the Far East and when he comes back he wants her gone. When he comes back she has indeed gone, but before she left she dialed long-distance to an automated line and left the phone off the hook. He now faces a telephone bill that runs to thousands of dollars.

The story often circulates by word of mouth but is also a favorite with the mass media. One such version is a comic poem that was printed in the British revue *The New Statesman* in 1986 (Brunvand 1989, 216–217), another is a Garfield cartoon printed in June 1996, and yet another a Valentine's Day article in the *Chicago Tribune* entitled "Nifty Ways to Leave your Lover" (for both these, see Brunvand 1999, 80). The automated message line is usually said to be the speaking clock in Tokyo or New York, or the weather report from Hong Kong or Australia.

Example

A young couple living in the Bristol area had been having marital problems. Most of it was caused by the husband's bad temper and the fighting and constant arguing had been going on for several months. Things finally came to a head one morning when the husband, just before he left for a three week business trip, told his wife they were finished and she had better get out of his house for good before he returned.

When he arrived home his wife had gone, leaving the house in an awful mess. While he was clearing up he noticed that the telephone was off the receiver. He replaced it and thought no more about it. Several weeks later the quarterly telephone bill arrived. It was astronomical—running into several thousands of pounds. He immediately queried it, only to be told that the phone had been connected to the speaking weather report in Australia for a three week period. (Smith 1986, 85)

FURTHER READING

Brunvand, Jan Harold. *Curses! Broiled Again! The Hottest Urban Legends Going.* New York: Norton, 1989.

———. *Too Good to Be True: The Colossal Book of Urban Legends.* New York: Norton, 1999.

Smith, Paul. *The Book of Nastier Legends.* London: Routledge and Kegan Paul, 1986.

See: The Hair-Curler Revenge; The Superglue Revenge

STUCK ON YOU

This humorous sex story, sometimes called "The Stuck Couple," has almost endless variations depending on how and where a love-dazed couple are said to get stuck together. The funniest, and politest, is the story below which was first broken by Reuters news agency, then appeared in many compilations of humorous stories in the 1970s and 1980s. Other stories feature superglue, or muscle spasms caused by shock or sudden surprise, and in one case, even a story about a burglar stuck in a life-size latex female-shaped sex toy ("Burglars Having Sex"). Newspapers worldwide continue to print articles (whether true or false, who knows?) about newlyweds or illicit lovers trapped in an embrace. For example, between 1992 and the present day, stuck couple incidents have been reported from Swaziland, Kenya, Namibia (Tenthani 1999), Singapore, and China. At times these stories have collected details from the legend of the superglue revenge and tell of couples superglued together by a vengeful spouse ("Legends in the Tabloids").

It is not, however, altogether a modern story. There is something similar in the works of a fifteenth-century Italian writer, Giovanni Francesco Poggio Bracciolini (usually known as Poggio), a young student from Tuscany who traveled to Rome hoping to get employment with Pope Boniface IX. Tale number 170 of his "Facetie" collection of stories published in 1450 concerns a licentious monk who seduces a girl. To spare her blushes he suggests that they should do it through a hole in a wooden board. He underestimates the size of the hole and gets himself stuck (Ellis 2001, 80). In the previous century Robert Mannyng's 1303 poem "Handlyng Synne" contains a story about an amorous couple stuck together as a punishment for making love close to a church. Even older are stories from the classics that, allowing for the passage of 27 centuries, are very similar to African ones such as that reported by Raphael Tenthani in the 1990s. The Greek poet Homer tells the story of the illicit love affair between the goddess Aphrodite and the god Ares whilst Aphrodite was married to the god Hephaistos. Learning of the affair Hephaistos straightaway made a net of unbreakable and invisible chains and suspended it from the ceiling of the bedroom like a spider's web. He pretended to leave. Ares arrived, the lovers went to bed, and the net fell over them and bound them together so they could not separate (Hansen 1995).

Example

A young couple were parked in a tiny car on the common one night doing a spot of courting when all of a sudden the young man let out a scream; he had slipped a disc in his back. Try as he might he could not sit upright so he lay there naked in the back of the car. In desperation the girl called the ambulance service.

When they arrived they tried to ease his pain but nothing they could do could get him upright and out of the car. In a final attempt to free the poor man, the ambulance man called the fire brigade, and they arrived with special cutting equipment. Before the panic-stricken girl could say or do anything, the firemen had cut off the top of the car and freed her lover.

At this point the girl broke down in tears, and a friendly fireman reassured her saying, "Well, look on the bright side, your boyfriend's been released and is now on his way to hospital."

"Yes," she sobbed, "but how will I explain the state of the car to my husband?" (Smith Collection)

FURTHER READING

Brunvand, Jan Harold. *The Choking Doberman and Other "New" Urban Legends.* New York: Norton, 1984. See pp. 142–143.

"Burglars Having Sex." *Letters to Ambrose Merton* 9 (March 1997): 13–14.

Ellis, Bill. "*Haec in Sua Parochia Accidisse Dixit*: The Rhetoric of 15th Century Contemporary Legends." *Contemporary Legend* new series 4 (2001): 74–92.

Hansen, William. "The Stuck Couple in Ancient Greece." *FOAFtale News* 36 (January 1995): 2–3.

"Legends in the Tabloids." *FOAFtale News* 18 (June 1990): 10.

"Stuck on You." *FOAFtale News* 44 (May 1999): 12–13.

Tenthani, Raphael. "Couple Remain 'Lovelocked' after Secret Tryst." *The Namibian* (October 21, 1999). http://www.namibian.com.na/Netstories/October99/secret.html

See: Glued to the Loo; The Superglue Revenge

THE SUPERGLUE REVENGE

This grisly story of infidelity and revenge seems to have begun some time in the late 1970s. It peaked as an oral story in the 1990s, and as a media story in the early years of the twenty-first century. It is a legend that puts a modern twist on traditional tales of castration as a punishment for infidelity. Instead of the cheated wife taking a knife to her man, she takes a symbolic revenge by gluing the offending part of the man's body to his leg or stomach.

The earliest study of this legend is Mark Glazer's essay on 22 versions from the Rio Grande Folklore Archive (1988). Between 1989 and 2005 Canadian legend-collector Brian Chapman's accumulated 19 further versions, mainly from the media, some of which were reprinted in *FOAFtale News* ("The Superglue Revenge"). Many of the newspaper reports are told as true stories; the most recent of these is a Pittsburgh court case, reported worldwide, in which a man was purportedly suing his vengeful ex-girlfriend for damages of $16,000 ("Man Sues ex-Girlfriend"). It is hard to know whether these reports are based on fact or folklore.

There is at least one newspaper report about an alleged case where the roles are reversed and it is the husband who takes revenge on his cheating wife by gluing her private parts shut. Supposedly this was a court case in Newport, Tennessee, in August 1997.

An article printed in the Pittsburgh *Post-Gazette* reported an interview with Harry Coover, the inventor of superglue. It seems that the story of "The Superglue Revenge" was nothing new to him. "I heard some of those stories. We had a small group that was collecting all these stories from papers and publications and all that." It was his impression, he said, that until five years ago the story "existed largely as urban legend" (Roddy 2005).

The example quoted below comes from an oral source. It was collected from a Mexican-American informant who had first heard it around 1983.

Example

This really happened in ... the names are withheld because they are very well known people in the community. [They] were having some problems in their marriage, nothing outstanding. The wife worked outside the home, and the man was a very wealthy businessman. One day the wife decided she was really going to try to talk to her husband ... so they could work out their problems. She decided to leave her work early and surprise him. When she got home, she heard voices coming out of the bedroom. A little frightened she tiptoed upstairs, and to her surprise, grief, and amazement, she heard the voices of her husband and her next door neighbour (a not-too-good-looking woman in her early thirties). She was ready to barge in, but she decided against it. She tiptoed out of the house and drove away, her humiliation, pain and grief immeasurable. In a few minutes she decided what to do. This time she walked upstairs, and found her husband drunk and fast asleep. She went to the bathroom and found a tube of superglue which her children had bought for a school project. She took the tube and spread his legs with it, walking out of the house. When the man woke up he couldn't move. He yelled and screamed until one of his young sons walked in, called an ambulance, and took him to his doctor. The doctor sent him to Houston so he could be operated on. The woman had her revenge, and the man could not prosecute her because of the scandal (Glazer 1988, 141).

FURTHER READING

Glazer, Mark. "The Superglue Revenge: A Psychocultural Analysis." *Monsters with Iron Teeth: Perspectives on Contemporary Legend III.* Ed. Gillian Bennett and Paul Smith. Sheffield: Sheffield Academic Press for the International Society for Contemporary Legend Research in association with CECTAL, 1988, pp.139–146.

"Man Sues Ex-Girlfriend for Super-Gluing Genitals." *The Irish Times* (November 5, 2005). Reprinted in "The Superglue Revenge." *FOAFtale News* 63 (December 2005): 3–5.

Roddy, Dennis B. "It's Just Another Tacky Story In Super Glue Inventor's Book." *Pittsburgh Post-Gazette* (November 5, 2005), http://www.post-gazette.com/pg/05309/601174.stm

"The Superglue Revenge." *FOAFtale News* 63 (December 2005): 3–5.

See: Glued to the Loo; The Hair-Curler Revenge; The Phone Bill Revenge; Stuck on You

---

THE SURPRISER SURPRISED 1: THE BLUSHING BRIDE

The "Surpriser Surprised" legend tells how somebody throwing a surprise party gets more than they expected; the person they were hoping to surprise instead surprises them with a display of nudity or indecency. The basic plot has been shaped into several identifiable types, but this one, which tells of a young couple caught naked or making love, is perhaps the most popular one. It often turns up in photocopied joke sheets, in compilations of jokes, "after dinner" stories and tall stories, and—of course—on the Internet. Altogether, it has been around for the best part of 70 years in one form or another.

The first and most complete analysis of the story is a 1973 article by William Hugh Jansen. His "Blushing Bride" stories come from all over the United States and date from 1935 to 1970. Many of them from this period end with a typical urban legend coda—the girl is now in a lunatic asylum and can recognize nobody, she has had a nervous breakdown, the boy has left town, or the engagement has been broken, and so on.

The story below is typical except that it lacks the going-mad ending.

Example

A young couple, who were just about to be married, stayed in one night to babysit for the girl's younger brother. After a session of petting on the couch, the young man managed to persuade the girl to go upstairs to bed with him—for after all they were to be married soon.

They were both naked in bed when the girl suddenly remembered that she had forgotten to put the laundry in the washing machine as her mother had instructed. Rather afraid that her mother would be cross, she jumped out of bed to run downstairs and quickly load the machine. Her boyfriend said he would come and help so, in the nude, they both charged downstairs to the kitchen. As they ran through into the kitchen all the lights came on and they heard someone yell "Surprise!"

To their dismay her parents had arranged a surprise party and the kitchen was filled with a horde of relatives and friends and, last but not least, the vicar who was to marry them. (Smith 1983, 31)

FURTHER READING

Jansen, William Hugh. "The Surpriser Surprised: A Modern Legend." *Folklore Forum* 6 (1973): 1–24. Reprinted in *Readings in American Folklore*. Ed. Jan Harold Brunvand New York: Norton, 1979, pp. 64–90. See pp. 64–72, and 82–88.

Smith, Paul. *The Book of Nasty Legends*. London: Routledge and Kegan Paul, 1983.

See: The Nude Housewife; The Surpriser Surprised 2 (The Fart in the Dark); The Surpriser Surprised 3 (Not His Lucky Night); The Surpriser Surprised 4 (The Peanut Butter Surprise)

THE SURPRISER SURPRISED 2: THE FART IN THE DARK

In this popular form of the "Surpriser Surprised" legend, the indelicacy the poor victim accidentally commits is not sexual and does not involve nudity as other versions do. However, it is almost as embarrassing; the victim's offence is to fart loud and long not knowing he/she is in company. William Hugh Jansen first wrote about this group of legends in 1973; his earliest story was told by a 10-year-old boy and dates to 1935.

The details vary from story to story and are virtually endless—sometimes the person who lets out a series of giant explosions is hidden behind a curtain not knowing his/her friends are throwing a surprise party; sometimes he/she is blindfolded waiting for a "surprise," not knowing all his/her friends have come into the room; sometimes he/she has eaten too many beans and gets rid of surplus gas by farting several times out of an open window only to find that the guests at a surprise party have hidden underneath the window; sometimes he/she is in a car and his/her friends have hidden in the back intending to surprise him/her. The victim faints, "wants to climb up the wall," almost dies of embarrassment, and so on.

This story is often told orally, but almost as often it is spread via joke sheets and cartoons (Smith 1984, 149). It features in Carson McCullers's 1940 novel *The Heart is a Lonely Hunter*. The example below lacks the twist that the flatulent person farts at his/her own surprise party, but it is otherwise very typical. It comes from one of the earliest collections of urban legends, Rodney Dale's *The Tumour in the Whale* (1978).

Example

A Fulham lass my wife's sister knows is always getting herself into scrapes, usually over new boyfriends. This occasion was no exception. She had just met a really dishy posh bloke, who had invited her to a party with his friends. Determined to impress him, she dolled herself up in a classy little black number.

At the party, though, she was so nervous that a certain amount of biliousness welled up inside her and threatened to make itself heard in a loud trumpet, so that she couldn't relax at all. What made it worse was that every time she tried to give vent to her flatulence in private, her guy sought her out with a smile and sidled up next to her. The queue to the lav stretched down the stairs, so no point in waiting for that either.

Eventually, the boyfriend came over to her and said, to her relief, that they were going now. Holding in the noxious wind for just a little longer while the bloke escorted her to the car and let her in, she was even more relieved when he finally left her side, saying he'd forgotten to get someone's telephone number.

With immense satisfaction, she sat in the passenger seat and let fly the most enormous rasping fart.

A minute later, her man opened the driver's side to get in. "Sorry, I've been terribly rude—have you met Carol and Peter?" he said, pointing to two embarrassed friends holding their noses in the back of the car. (Dale 1978, 195–196)

FURTHER READING

Dale, Rodney. *The Tumour in the Whale: An Hilarious Collection of Apocryphal Anecdotes*. London: W. H. Allen, Universal Books, 1978.

Jansen, William Hugh. "The Surpriser Surprised: A Modern Legend." *Folklore Forum* 6 (1973): 1–24. Reprinted in *Readings in American Folklore*. Ed. Jan Harold Brunvand New York: Norton, 1979, pp. 64–90.

Smith, Paul. *The Complete Book of Office Mis-Practice*. London: Routledge and Kegan Paul, 1984.

Smith, Paul. *The Book of Nastier Legends*. London: Routledge and Kegan Paul, 1986. See pp. 31–32.

See: The Surpriser Surprised 1 (The Blushing Bride); The Surpriser Surprised 3 (Not His Lucky Night); The Surpriser Surprised 4 (The Peanut Butter Surprise)

THE SURPRISER SURPRISED 3: NOT HIS LUCKY NIGHT

"Not His Lucky Night" is one of the most popular of the identifiable types into which the basic "Surpriser Surprised" plot has been shaped. It first came to folklorists' attention in William Hugh Jansen's 1973 paper, and corresponds to his stories A9 to A12 (pp. 72–76). These were collected from the late 1950s to the early 1970s, and by that time they seem to be already international and to have appeared in print as well as in oral versions. For example, though two of his versions were collected from American college students, another was told by a girl in Newfoundland (Canada) who had heard it at the University of Wales (UK) about twelve years earlier. Similarly, though these three stories were told orally, another version came as a photocopied joke sheet, and yet another from a compilation of slightly risqué stories published in 1953 (Elgart 1953, 50).

Several versions circulated in joke books (Brann 1976, 98–99), newspapers, and on the Internet. The story was used recently, in a tamer form, on British TV in a series of advertisements for a headache cure.

Example

It was the day of the boss's birthday, and, quite out of the blue, his secretary invited him round to her place for a drink after work. She was an attractive woman and the boss had always fancied her, so he was hopeful that something might come of it. By the time he arrived at her apartment he had persuaded himself that she was giving him the come-on. When she gave him a large whisky, and said she was just going to slip into the bedroom to see to a few things, he got very excited and was convinced this was going to be his lucky night. So, in a mad moment, he took all his clothes off and waited for her to come back, as he thought, in a flimsy negligée.

So there he was in just his socks, when the door opened and his wife, his kids, and all his work colleagues burst in carrying a cake and shouting "Happy Birthday!" (Smith Collection)

FURTHER READING

Brann, Christian. *Pass the Port: The Best After-Dinner Speeches of the Famous.* Cirencester, England: C. Brann, 1976.

Elgart, J. M. *More Over Sixteen.* New York: Grayson Publishing Company, 1953.

Jansen, William Hugh. "The Surpriser Surprised: A Modern Legend." *Folklore Forum* 6 (1973): 1–24. Reprinted in *Readings in American Folklore.* Ed. Jan Harold Brunvand New York: Norton, 1979, pp. 64–90.

Smith, Paul. *The Book of Nasty Legends.* London: Routledge and Kegan Paul, 1983. See p. 34.

See: The Surpriser Surprised 1 (The Blushing Bride); The Surpriser Surprised 2 (The Fart in the Dark); The Surpriser Surprised 4 (The Peanut Butter Surprise)

THE SURPRISER SURPRISED 4: THE PEANUT BUTTER SURPRISE

This gross variant of "The Surpriser Surprised" legend emerged in online discussion groups in June 1994. "Surpriser Surprised" legends usually feature someone caught out in some sort of indelicacy (sex, nudity, farting) by people who have come along to give the victim a surprise party. In this variant, the would-be surprisers are surprised—not to say disgusted—by finding the girl they had hoped to surprise engaged in a sex act involving her dog and a tub of peanut butter.

Accounts on the online discussion group varied as to the details of the story. The most common version was the dog and peanut butter story, but other accounts featured margarine, whipped cream, and dog food (and even a cat and tuna fish). The dog was often called Lucky or Skippy; the woman was said to be a newlywed wife, a nurse who lived alone, or a pet-loving work colleague. Like other "Surpriser Surprised" stories, "The Peanut Butter Surprise" ends with the shaming of the central character—she quits her job, leaves town, calls off the wedding, or sells her home, and so on.

The legend was first published in a Canadian satirical magazine, and a correspondent later wrote in to say it had originated in a private American telephone service that allows callers to listen to confessions or to record stories of their own humiliations or misdeeds. It also surfaced in radio call-in programs, including Dr. Judy Kuriansky's "Love Phones" show (A. E. M. 1994).

According to Snopes website, there are accounts which predate the 1994 online discussion. Barbara Mikkelson cites correspondents who claim to have heard it from about 1980 onward in Canada and the United States. These versions come from Chicago (1980/1981), California (1981), Texas (early 1980s), Australia (1984, this one features a horse and a lump of sugar), Michigan (1986), and Alberta, Canada (1987) (Mikkelson). Ten complete versions posted online between June and October 1994 can be found in an item by "A. E. M." [Alan Mays, News Editor of *FOAFtale News* 1991–1996].

Example

This guy decided to have a surprise party for his wife. So my friend and everyone hid in the living room and waited for this woman to show up. They heard her come into the kitchen, and they waited a few minutes. Then they all ran into the kitchen and shouted "Surprise!" The woman was laying on the floor. She had spread peanut butter all over herself, and the family dog was going down on her. She ran out of the house. That was three weeks ago, and she hasn't been heard of since (A. E. M., 9)

FURTHER READING

A. E. M. "The Peanut Butter and Dog Surprise." *FOAFtale News* 35 (October 1994): 8–11.

Mikkelson, Barbara. "The Lap Dog." http://www.snopes.com/risque/animals/peanut-butter.asp

See: The Surpriser Surprised 1 (The Blushing Bride); The Surpriser Surprised 2 (The Fart in the Dark); The Surpriser Surprised 3 (Not His Lucky Night)

THE TAGGED LADY

Since at least the 1950s an amusing story has circulated by word of mouth and a variety of other media about a lady who embroidered a motif on her sweater based on Chinese characters she had seen and had thought were attractive. A passing person from Hong Kong or mainland China broke into a fit of giggles when he/she saw them—apparently the characters meant, "Bargain price—$6.95."

There are almost endless variations on the meaning of the Chinese characters. Jan Brunvand, for example, was sent an item from an issue of the *Saturday Review* (November 27, 1965). It told the story of a "dress designer who liked to knit," and who copied some letters from a menu in a Chinese restaurant, and wove them into the design of a sweater she was making. Along came somebody whose parents had been missionaries in China; he took one look at the sweater and burst out laughing. The Chinese characters read, "This dish cheap but unmistakably good" (Brunvand 1993, 223–224). Similarly, a story in one of J. M. Elgart's collections of saucy tales tells how a "very proper dame" was sent a brooch by an "unknown admirer" in China. She wore it a great deal, until one day she was at a party with an eminent Chinese scholar and she asked him to translate the inscription. It read "Licensed prostitute—City of Shangai" (Elgart 1954, 78; Cerf 1959, 203–204).

In other variants, a tag with a compromising message is left on a garment. Our example comes from the mid-nineteenth century, and was recorded by celebrated American writer Nathaniel Hawthorne on March 23, 1854 in his *English Notebooks.*

Example

Mr Bright told a funny story of the lady of a former American Ambassador to England. In London, one day, she went to a cheap shop, where the articles are ticketted, and bought a shawl, which she wore pretty extensively about town.

She had not taken care to remove the ticket from the shawl; so that she exhibited herself to the eyes of the metropolis with this label—Perfectly Chaste, 15 s[hillings] (Hawthorne 1853/56, vol. 2, 84).

FURTHER READING

Brunvand, Jan Harold. *The Baby Train and other Lusty Urban Legends.* New York: Norton, 1993.

Cerf, Bennett. *Bennett Cerf's Bumper Crop of Anecdotes and Stories, Mostly Humorous, about the Famous and Near-Famous,* 2 vols. New York: Garden City Books, 1959.

Elgart, J. M. *Still More Over Sexteen.* New York: Grayson Publishing Company, 1954.

Hawthorne, Nathaniel. *The English Notebooks 1853–1859,* 2 vols. Ed. Thomas Woodson and Bill Ellis. Columbus, OH: Ohio State University Press, 1997.

MERCHANDISE

This chapter brings together a number of legends about products, corporations, and goods offered for sale both privately and in shops. Here we find tricks, cheats, deceptions, and conspiracies of various kinds. Food, drink, and luxury items on sale may be contaminated with poisons or foreign bodies, and cars and jewelry offered at bargain prices always come with a catch. Large corporations allegedly conspire to defraud the customer; alternatively, they are said to be in league with the devil or secret supporters of some religious or political group seen as dangerous or antisocial.

Most of the stories are serious in tone, but there are occasional humorous stories of unusual good luck or clever trickery—and even one story about intelligence rewarded.

For other stories about merchandise see: The Mole Hill and the Jaguar; The Solid Cement Cadillac

COBRAS AT K-MART/RATTLERS AT WAL-MART

There is a large group of legends that tell about horrified customers finding snakes in goods they buy in downtown stores. These sorts of stories may be found throughout the North American and European continents (see, for example, Klintberg 1985), but it is American folklorists that have taken most interest in them and tried to interpret them (see, for example, Fine 1992). One theory is that the stories reflect distrust of foreign imports, but since many tales specifically mention discount stores it is just as likely that, if they have a "message" at all, it is about the dangers of cheap goods.

Some of the earliest studies of these sorts of legends date from the period 1969 to 1975 when rumors of snakes in produce were being spread about stores in the K-Mart chain. People were said to have been bitten by snakes hiding in garments (fur coats, sweaters, blouses, and so on), or plants from the garden and lawn department, or in mattresses and blankets in the household department. Nearly always the victim was a woman; the produce came from some exotic foreign country; and the consequences of the bite were serious (death, amputation, paralysis, and so on). Early studies of this spate of rumormongering in the United States were undertaken by Xenia Cord (1969), Patrick Mullen (1970), and Ann Carpenter (1976). At the height of the rumor, Cord interviewed managers of K-Mart stores. The consensus among the managers was that the story had originally come from somewhere in the south, it was widespread, and it had been started either by someone with "a nasty sense of humor," or by a disgruntled ex-employee or other troublemaker.

More recently the focus of the legends has shifted to Wal-Mart stores, and tends to feature rattlesnakes supposedly hiding in the same sorts of produce as the "Cobras at K-Mart." Reports have included: a story from St Petersburg, Florida (August 1987) about a customer bitten by a pygmy rattlesnake hidden in a plant; a story about a man who supposedly won over $8,000 in damages against a Wal-Mart store in a town near San Antonio, Texas, after being bitten by a rattlesnake (1996); a story about a Wal-Mart store rumored to have been built over a "rattler den" in a Wisconsin town (September 2002); and reports of rattlesnakes found in Wal-Mart stores in Hammond, Louisiana (2001), and Brownwood, Texas (2003) (news reports via e-mail from Brian Chapman).

Example

In a story that has gone nationwide, Douglas Hatchett of Bangs told Wal-Mart store officials a small rattlesnake bit him on the hand Monday in the shoe department [...]

Wal-Mart officials have questioned the validity of Hatchett's claim of being bitten, but have not said specifically why.

"There are just too many inconsistencies for us and too many things that just don't add up," Wal-Mart spokesman Tom Williams said from corporate offices in Bentonville, Ark. "We continue to look at it. We do have some concerns where things don't add up as they were told by the individual.

"It's just an issue that's fraught with a lot of inconsistencies." (Nash 2003)

FURTHER READING

Carpenter, Ann. "Cobras at K-Mart: Legends of Hidden Danger." *What's Going On?* In *Modern Texas Folklore*. Ed. Francis Edward Abernethy. Austin, TX: The Encino Press, 1976, pp. 37–45.

Cord, Xenia. "Department Store Snakes." *Indiana Folklore* 2.1 (1969): 110–114.

Fine, Gary Alan. *Manufacturing Tales: Sex and Money in Contemporary Legends*. Knoxville: University of Tennessee Press, 1992. See pp. 164–173.

Klintberg, Bengt af. "Legends and Rumours About Spiders and Snakes." *Fabula* 26 (1985): 274–287.

Mullen, Patrick B. "Department Store Snakes." *Indiana Folklore* 3 (1970): 214–228.

Nash, Steve. "Report Claims Snake Bite Never Happened." *Brownwood Bulletin* [Texas] (October 3, 2003), http://www.brownwoodbulletin.com/articles/2003/10/03/news/news01.txt

See: Snakes in Bananas; The Snake in the Garment; Spiders at Large

CORPORATE CONSPIRACIES

Corporate conspiracy legends mainly circulate through informal channels, for example by word of mouth as rumors or via the Internet as e-mailed warnings. The usual claim is that some corporation or organization is, as sociologist Gary Alan Fine describes it, "directly in league with" some other body that "the general public believes is outside of the mainstream of legitimate political or religious discourse" (Fine 1992, 175), and somehow conspires to destabilize social values and cohesion. Because they are aimed at specific social, religious, or ethnic groups and plug into existing prejudices and/or anxieties, they are often widely believed. The bodies the corporations are supposedly conspiring with may be religious groups (today these may be the Church of Satan or the Unification Church; in the past it was more likely that members of the Catholic or Jewish faiths would be singled out); or they may be political groups such as the American Nazi Party, the Palestine Liberation Organization (PLO), or the John Birch Society.

Among numerous examples are unfounded allegations about prominent companies or multinationals being funded by the Ku Klux Klan. Among these, are the Troop clothing company, Marlboro cigarettes, Kentucky Fried Chicken, Coors Beer, Uncle Ben's Rice, and Church's Fried Chicken. From the 1980s, Church's Fried Chicken have been accused of putting an additive in their food that will sterilize black men (Turner 1993, 57–107), so too, supposedly, have the manufacturers of the "Tropical Fantasy" drink (Brunvand 1999). Coors Beer has at one time or another also been said to have links with Nazis, the Contras, arms sales to Iran, and the "Moral Majority," and Uncle Ben's Rice with the PLO. There is, of course, no evidence for these claims.

Other companies have been said at one time or another to be in league with the devil or to support "cults" of various types. Among these are rumors that McDonalds, Exxon, Liz Claiborne clothes, and Johnson & Johnson have links to Satanism, and Wendy's have links with the Unification Church. Again, these claims have no discernible basis in fact.

The most persistent legend of this type concerns the soap and detergent manufacturer Procter and Gamble. In November 1980 it began to be alleged that the logo they had had since 1882 was a satanic symbol. The logo showed a crescent-shaped man-in-the-moon with a face, horns, and curly beard surrounded by thirteen stars. The thirteen stars, so rumor said, represented members of a satanic coven, curly hairs in the man-in-the-moon's beard were the number 666 the so-called "sign of the beast," and the horns of the moon were plainly the horns of the devil himself. By 1985 Procter and Gamble were receiving over a hundred thousand calls a month, and had filed half a dozen law suits against people it believed were spreading the rumors. Some of the callers alleged that a Procter and Gamble executive had announced on national TV that the company habitually donated 10 percent of its profits to satanic cults. Despite a vigorous anti-rumor campaign, the stories continued to proliferate and in 1985 the company decided their only option was to modify their logo.

Examples

1. Television is slaughtering blacks on drug abuse. They never show the whites. But in reality 80% of crack users are white. Television shows the blacks in poverty.

Troop clothing and shoes are allegedly manufactured by the KKK because they know black teens and drug dealers will buy the products. I always hear drug abuse is genocide to blacks. (Turner 1993, 183)

2.

ATTENTION!! ATTENTION!! ATTENTION!!

.50 cent sodas

BLACKS AND MINORITY GROUPS

DID YOU SEE (TV SHOW) 20/20???

PLEASE BE ADVISED "Top Pop" & "Tropical fantasy".50 cent sodas are being manufactured by the Klu Klux Klan

Sodas contain stimulants to sterilize black men, and who knows what else!!!!

They are only put in stores in Harlem and minority areas.

You won't find them down town . . . Look around . . .

YOU HAVE BEEN WARNED

PLEASE SAVE THE CHILDREN

(Flyer posted in stores March 1990. Bennett Collection)

FURTHER READING

Brunvand, Jan Harold. *Too Good to Be True: The Colossal Book of Urban Legends*. New York: Norton, 1999. See pp. 386–392.

"Devilish Logo." "Strange Days" column. *Fortean Times* 59 (September 1991): 17.

Fine, Gary Alan. *Manufacturing Tales: Sex and Money in Contemporary Legends*. Knoxville, TN: University of Tennessee Press, 1992. See pp. 174–188.

Kapferer, Jean-Noël. *Rumors: Uses, Interpretations, and Images*. New Brunswick, NJ: Transaction Publications, 1990.

Turner, Patricia A. *I Heard It through the Grapevine: Rumor in African-American Culture*. Berkeley, CA: University of California Press, 1993.

THE DEATH CAR

This classic automobile legend has been popular since the 1930s or 1940s. American folklorist Richard M. Dorson discovered a version dated to 1938

(Dorson 1959, 250–252), but the heyday of the story in the United States seems to have been the 1950s and 1960s. Though widely collected on both sides of the Atlantic, there are slight variations between American and British versions. In both cases the car is for sale because someone has died in it, but British versions are often more gory—often the dead man's blood is still wet, whereas in the typical American versions it is only the smell of death that lingers.

Polish folklorist Dionizjusz Czubala published thirteen Polish and Russian versions of the story in 1992, and he says the story is known in at least four former Soviet countries (Russia, Belorusse, the Ukraine, and Lithuania). The majority of his informants place the events, which they nearly all allege are true, in the late 1980s. The deaths are either unexplained or are attributed to heart attacks or automobile accidents; the smell is caused by the body lying decomposed in the car for some time before being found. The car is usually named as a Polonez, though one account mentions a Volga, and another a Honda. In some cases, the widow or other family member offers it at a remarkably low price, as in most Western versions, but sometimes the narrator just says it is impossible to sell it.

This legend is thematically related to Stephen King's novel *Christine*, his story "Riding the Bullet" (2002), Elizabeth Jane Howard's short story "Mr Wrong" (1979), and films of the same name (see Appendix).

The first of our examples is taken from Czubala's Polish and Russian research; the second one was collected in Leeds (UK) in the early 1960s, and like many others was told as a true occurrence that happened to a friend-of-a-friend. In other English versions, the man is said to have died of a heart attack or carbon-monoxide poisoning or in "a messy accident." The vehicle in which this death has occurred is always a prestigious and expensive model.

Examples

1. A man was driving a Polonez through a wood where he stopped for a while. At that moment he had a heart attack and died. The body decomposed in the warm weather for several days. When it was taken out, the car had a terrible smell. It could not be removed. The family wanted to sell it, but no-one wanted to buy: potential buyers were driven off by the smell. The family asked a famous professor from Warsaw to remove it, but he failed to do so. The car is for sale for 150,000 zloty.

Another student says that its price is 50,000zl and no-one wants to buy it. (Czubala 1992, 3)

2. My brother-in-law's friend saw an advert in the *Argus* offering a top-of-the-range motor at an incredibly low price. He went to the address in the advert and the door was answered by a red-eyed woman dressed head to foot in black. She shows him the car, hands over the keys, and offers to let him test-drive it. It's great! He loves it! But as he's getting out of the front seat he just glances into the back. The back seat is soaked with blood! It's still wet!—well, sort of tacky. The woman sees his look of horror and explains that it was her husband's car and he has shot himself in it, the body has only just been taken away by the police. She can't bear to have it round, she wants to get rid of it NOW. He buys it. (Bennett Collection)

FURTHER READING

Brunvand, Jan Harold. 2001. *Encyclopedia of Urban Legends*. New York: Norton. See pp. 107–108.

Czubala, Dioniszjusz. "The Death Car: Polish and Russian Examples." *FOAFtale News* 25 (March 1992): 2–5.

Dorson, Richard M. *Modern Folklore*. American Folklore. Chicago: University of Chicago Press, 1959.

McKelvie, Donald. "Aspects of Oral Tradition and Belief in an Industrial Region" *Folk Life* 1 (1963): 77–94. See esp. pp. 90–91.

See: The Philanderer's Porsche

DRUGGED CHILDREN: LSD TATTOOS, MICKEY MOUSE ACID, BLUE STAR ACID, ETC.

This is a story, or series of stories, that began slowly, then burst into sudden flame. At its height it was known all over the Western world, then it gradually faded away and was reported much less frequently. The story seems to have begun in 1980 or thereabouts in French-speaking Canada and the northern United States (Hadjian 1989/1990). By April 1988 it had reached France and between 1988 and 1990 it was a major scare in the countries of Western Europe from Holland to Italy, and in the United States, the United

Kingdom, and Australia. After about 1991 it was gradually replaced with scares about child sex abuse and Satanism. As legends sometimes do, however, the story has burst into life again at least twice since then, in 1995 and 2000. It is still being reported today from South Africa, Australia, and the United Kingdom.

The story was, and continues to be, transmitted mainly through the written word—in newspapers, letters, posters, and flyers—and from official as well as informal sources. Among those initially spreading the story were schools and educational authorities, parent groups, hospitals and medical experts, national and local government officials, the military, businesses, and pharmacies (Hadjian 1989/1990). All these groups were later in the forefront of debunking the story and reassuring parents.

The basic story of the legend is that drug-pushers are trying to get young people hooked on drugs by means of drug-laced stickers or "tattoos." The drug is almost always said to be an hallucinogenic, usually LSD (Lysergic Acid Diethalylamide). Initially, there were three main variants. The tattoos were said to be passed out with entrance tickets to "acid house" parties (Mucklow 1990); or passed to children in school playgrounds; or stuck on the arms of passing children ("Update: LSD Transfers"). Nowadays, little is heard about the first and third of these methods.

The stickers are said to look like postage stamps, to be brightly colored, and to have pictures of Bart Simpson, Superman, clowns, butterflies, blue stars, red pyramids, Mickey Mouse or other Disney characters, or a "window pane" design. Often they are said to be wrapped in foil or in a red box.

When the story resurfaced in 1995 and 2000 it seems to have been either the original flyer, or something very similar circulating online (Anderson 1995; "Blue Star Redux Redux"; Garnett 1992; Hiscock 1995). In a recent outbreak of the legend in England and Scotland, the story has circulated either in the form of typed notices headed "Important Information From the Metropolitan Police" or as letters and e-mails (see, for example, Puttick 2001 and "Alert Over Bogus 'LSD Tattoos' Letter").

Our example is a flyer circulating in the United Kingdom in 1990, and sent to *Dear Mr Thoms* (see "Update: LSD Transfers," which also features newspaper clippings and photocopies of letters sent to or by schools and public bodies). Though the flyer was circulating in the United Kingdom its source was obviously the United States because the spelling is American, not British-style; also, English children would call this kind of sticker a "transfer" not a "tatoo."

Example

WARNING
DRUG LACED TATOOS
WARNING TO FELLOW OFFICERS AND PARENTS

A form of TATOO called the "BLUE STARS" is being sold to school children

DESCRIPTION

1. It is a small sheet of paper containing "BLUE STARS"
2. They are the size of pencil erasers
3. Each star is soaked with LSD

THE DRUG CAN BE ABSORBED THROUGH THE SKIN SIMPLY BY HANDLING THE PAPER!!
There are also brightly colored paper tabs resembling postage stamps. They have pictures of the following:

SUPERMAN   CLOWNS   BUTTERFLIES
MICKEY MOUSE BART SIMPSON OTHER DISNEY CHARACTERS

EACH ONE IS BOX WRAPPED IN FOIL
This is a new way of selling acid by appealing to young children.

A young child could happen upon these and have a FATAL TRIP. It is also believed that little children could be given a free "TATOO" by other children who want to have some fun by cultivating new customers without the child's knowledge.

A "STAMP" called "RED PYRAMID" is also being distributed along with microdots in various colors.

Another kind of "WINDOW PANE" which has a grid that can be cut out is another kind that is being distributed.

THESE ARE LACED WITH DRUGS
Please advise your neighbors, friends and relatives, daycare, and children about these drugs. If your child gets any of the above DO NOT HANDLE THEM. These are known to react quickly and some laced with STRYCHNINE.

. . . .

SYMPTOMS

1. HALLUCINATIONS   4. MOOD CHANGES
2. SEVERE VOMITING   5. CHANGE IN BODY TEMPERATURE
3. UNCONTROLLED LAUGHTER

PLEASE FEEL FREE TO REPRODUCE THIS ARTICLE AND DISTRIBUTE IT WITHIN YOUR COMMUNITY AND WORKPLACE. GET THE WORD OUT ABOUT THIS DANGER TO OUR CHILDREN.

FURTHER READING

"Alert Over Bogus 'LSD Tattoos' Letter." *Manchester Evening News* (June 12, 2001): 25.

Anderson, Alan. "More Blue Stars." *Foaftale News* 37 (June 1995): 10.

"Blue Star Redux Redux." *FOAFtale News* 39 (June 1996): 10.

Ellis, Bill. "Mickey Mouse LSD Tattoos: A Study in Emergence." *FOAFtale News* 14 (June 1989): 3–4.

Garnett, Chris. "Store falls for Sick Drug Hoax." *Stockport Times* (May 28, 1992): 9.

Hadjian, Joseph. "Le Syndrome de la Rumeur: Des Lycéens de Pierrelatte Enquêtent." *Documents pour l'enseignement économique et social [Dees]* 78–79 (1989–1990): 165–168.

Hiscock, Philip. "More LSD Tatoo Rumours." *FOAFtale News* 38 (December 1995): 9.

Mucklow, E. S. "New Drug Danger for Children." *The Lancet* (December 8, 1990): 1444.

Puttick, Helen. "Drug Tattoos Hoax Warning Sparks Panic." *The Evening News* [Scotland] (August 20, 2001): 14.

"Re Mickey Mouse LSD Rumor." *FOAFtale News* 13 (March 1989): 5.

Schmidt, Sigrid. "*Bild* and the Mickey-Mouse LSD Rumor." *FOAFtale News* 16 (December 1989): 1–4.

"Update: LSD Transfers." *Dear Mr Thoms* 21 (June 1991): 11–15.

FINGERS IN TAKE-OUT MEALS AND OTHER TALES OF CONTAMINATED FOOD

Folklorists have kept track of several persistent rumor-and-legend complexes about contaminated fast food since the 1960s. Stories circulating in the press in the mid-1960s often claimed that a human finger had been found in a Chinese take-out meal. Soon claims were being made about dogs and cats being found in the deep-freeze at a number of ethnic restaurants. In the summer of 1973, folklorist Bengt af Klintberg heard a story about a man who had found a rat's tooth in his take-out pizza in Stockholm and rumors were rife that Chinese restaurants in Sweden were using dog and cat food in their meals. He further reported that, in the following summer, a Chinese restaurant had lost so much business because of these sorts of rumors that it had to close down (Klintberg 1989). At that time, the British press were running a series of related stories from around the United Kingdom claiming for instance that one shop's French fries had contained cockroaches, that another shop was putting horsemeat in its pies, and another was using kangaroo meat; a Welsh bakery allegedly had sold a pasty with a bird's head in it.

In 2004 Elizabeth Tucker was told a story by a Chinese student at Binghamton University NY. A girl had a room exactly above her boyfriend's room at the Chinese University of Hong Kong. The exams were coming, the boy was studying very hard, and the girl cooked him soup every evening, letting it down through the window to his room below. After the exam the boy wanted to get in touch with the girl again but was told she was dead. He couldn't believe it—after all, she'd been serving him soup every evening. Then he found out that what he'd been eating was a soup made from her decomposing eyes and hair (Tucker 2005, 105).

Like so many contemporary legends, these modern horror stories have parallels with older legends. Klintberg points out that during the war and the postwar years of the 1940s there were persistent rumors throughout Europe about dogs, cats, and foxes being served in local restaurants and rats being ground up to make sausages. Apparently, too, there were stories about cat meat being used instead of beef in cafes along the Mexican-American border. Jacqueline Simpson has traced many parallel stories in Charles Dickens's *Pickwick Papers* which seem to be based on contemporary rumors and legends. These are mostly about stray cats and kittens baked into pies (Simpson 1983). Old though such legends may be, they continue to circulate to the present day.

Example

Though I heard this story a long time ago, I actually remember it quite clearly. What's made it stick in my mind is that I really believed it at the time, then when I started on the folklore course I realized that it was a classic urban legend.

The story was that a friend of one of the teachers had gone to a local Chinese restaurant. I forget which, but I'm pretty sure it was mentioned by name, and while she was eating her meal she found a lump of chicken she couldn't chew properly. She didn't want to make a fuss, so she pretended to wipe her nose and slipped the piece of meat into her handkerchief and surreptitiously dropped it into the pocket of her coat which was hanging over the back of the chair.

Anyway, she forgot all about it, but a couple of days later there's a knock on the door and it's the police. They ask her if she has recently had a meal at the Chinese restaurant, and she says, yes, she has. They ask her whether she had noticed anything odd about the food. She's just beginning to say no when she remembers the unchewable lump of meat. "Well," she says, "The food wasn't very nice and there was a lump of something unpleasant in it." The police seem very interested in this lump of meat, and she suddenly realizes that she has forgotten to take it out of her coat pocket.

So she finds the coat, and the hanky is still there. She unwraps it—and there's half a human finger, bitten off at the knuckle!

Now, I see now that it doesn't make any sense. But I believed it implicitly. It made a real impression on me at the time! (Bennett Collection)

FURTHER READING

Busby, Cylin. "'This Is a True Story': Roles of Women in Contemporary Legend." *Midwestern Folklore* 20 (Spring 1994): 5–62.

Klintberg, Bengt af. "Legends Today." *Nordic Folklore: Recent Studies*. Ed. Reimund Kvideland and Henning K. Sehmsdorf in collaboration with Elizabeth Simpson. Bloomington, IN: Indiana University Press, 1989, pp. 70–89. See pp. 75–77.

Simpson, Jacqueline. "Urban Legends in the Pickwick Papers." *Journal of American Folklore* 96 (1983): 462–470.

Tucker, Elizabeth. *Campus Legends: A Handbook*. Westport, CT: Greenwood Press, 2005. See pp. 101–106.

See: Kentucky Fried Rat; Urban Cannibals and Human Sausage Factories

GENIUS

The story of the cleaning lady or janitor who comes up with a simple but brilliant idea about a famous firm's product has been told of several companies, including Swan Vestas matches and Coca-Cola (Mikkelson), and is still popular today. Here it is told about the toothpaste firm Colgate.

Example

Top management at Colgate toothpaste were having a brain-storming session about how they could sell more toothpaste. Nobody had any idea—toothpaste was toothpaste, you could only use so much, couldn't you? Then a little voice was heard over the din, "Why not make the hole bigger? If more toothpaste comes out of the tube every time you squeeze, then you'll have to buy a tube more often."

"Brilliant!" said the Managing Director, "Who was the genius who thought of that?"

"It was me," said the cleaning lady from the back of the room where she'd been dusting shelves. Nobody had noticed she was in the room.

The cleaning lady was promoted and given a place on the Board of Directors. She is now Head of Sales. (Bennett Collection)

FURTHER READING

Mikkelson, Barbara. "Blue Collar Innovation." http://www.snopes.com/business/genius/innovate.asp

See: The Fatal Cleaning Lady

KENTUCKY FRIED RAT

This is one of several persistent rumor-and-legend complexes about contaminated fast food. In the United States stories began circulating in the early 1970s about rats being served at Kentucky Fried Chicken (KFC) franchises, and it was said that in 1979 Johnny Carson told the audience in his "Tonight" show that a fast food chain was being sued for serving rats. By the early 1980s similar claims were being made in the United Kingdom, Australia, Germany, and Scandinavia. In the early 1990s a researcher was able to collect twenty "true" stories in the Berkeley and San Francisco area (Busby 1994).

The legend does not only attach itself to KFC franchises; almost any fast food outlet can be targeted. Similarly, rats are not the only contaminated food said to be served at fast food chains. But the story about rats in KFC has been virulent enough for the legend to be usually referred to as "The Kentucky Fried Rat."

In 1981 Paul Smith investigated a case where such a rumor brought despair and nearly ruin to a couple who ran a KFC outlet in Sheffield (UK) (Smith 1984). The story in our example was recounted at this time by a group of teenagers who claimed to know the girl who had started the rumors.

Example

Elaine: My friend, my friend told me about, two or three years ago, and she claimed that her friend went down to Kentucky [Kentucky Fried Chicken] once—her friend and her boyfriend went down to Kentucky and they got themselves a Kentucky Chicken, like, and chips, and they were walking along Middlewood Road, and they got up to one of the lights and they said they were going to sit on't wall and eat their chicken, like, before they went on't bus, and, er, they're sat on't wall and this girl bit into her chicken and it were a MOUSE! They said it were, she told ME that it were a mouse in this chicken in batter, instead of chicken, and it'd still got all its FUR and everything on! I heard it were all in't

PAPER. Because then they said it were a scandal and they'd never HEARD of it and nothing like this had happened. Because it were in't [Sheffield] *Star* there were a big ARTICLE about it.

Tracy: I heard that this, er, WOMAN she went in and she got, like, chicken and chips and then she went out, and it were half a RAT! I heard it, that! Everybody were TALKING about it and that, and, like, publishers got to know about it and they went down to't place—to shop—and they denied everything, and they can't find anybody that says it's happened to THEM. And there were a big ARTICLE up in paper about it, but this. They denied it all and just told everybody to FORGET about it!

Interviewer: Do you think it's true?

Tracy: It's DIFFICULT really because that many people have heard about it but they hear about it in different ways. It's like ANY STORY that goes round, it gets CHANGED. Everybody ADDS a bit to it.

Interviewer: She got BLOOD on hers?

Elaine: Yeah! My friend told me when she bit INTO it all blood went all over her. She were covered in BLOOD, all her FACE and that.

Interviewer: It wasn't even cooked properly? It was a RAW MOUSE, uh?.

(Field recording made by Ervin Beck at a school in Sheffield, UK, c. 1984)

FURTHER READING

Brunvand, Jan Harold. *Encyclopedia of Urban Legends*. New York: Norton, 2001. See pp. 226–227.

Busby, Cylin. "'This Is a True Story': Roles of Women in Contemporary Legend." *Midwestern Folklore* 20 (Spring 1994): 5–62.

Fine, Gary Alan. *Manufacturing Tales: Sex and Money in Contemporary Legends*. Knoxville, TN: University of Tennessee Press, 1992. See pp. 120–140.

Klintberg, Bengt af. "Legends Today." *Nordic Folklore: Recent Studies*. Ed. Reimund Kvideland and Henning K. Sehmsdorf in collaboration with Elizabeth Simpson. Bloomington, IN: Indiana University Press, 1989, pp. 70–89.

Smith, Paul. "On the Receiving End: When Rumour Becomes Legend." In *Perspectives on Contemporary Legend: Proceedings of the Conference on Contemporary Legend, Sheffield, July 1982*. Ed. Paul Smith Sheffield: CECTAL, 1984.

See: Fingers in Take-Out Meals and Other Tales of Contaminated Food; The Mouse in the Coca-Cola Bottle

THE MOUSE IN THE COCA-COLA BOTTLE

Leading drinks manufacturer Coca-Cola has been the object of very many urban legends. Among many other unfounded beliefs: it is said that Coca-Cola is brewed to a secret formula only two people know, and that its logo is an attack on Islam; it is also claimed it can be used as a contraceptive or a hangover remedy, and that "crushed cockroaches" in the secret formula cure back pain (for these, and many other popular beliefs about Coca-Cola, see Smith 1991).

One typical, and at one time very widespread, legend concerning Coke is the story of "the Mouse in the Coca Cola Bottle." It seems to have been circulating since the later 1940s and peaked in the late 1970s. The story was a simple one—an unwary drinker found a dead and decomposed mouse in his bottle of Coke. Though stories about dead mice in drinks bottles were also being told about Seven Up, Coors Beer, and Pepsi, they stuck most readily to the brand leader, Coca Cola, through the "Goliath Effect" whereby the most prominent company attracts any legend that is going the rounds (Fine 1992, 141–163).

The most complete study of this legend is Gary Alan Fine's "Cokelore and Coke Law" in which he compares legend versions to law suits actually brought against the company for contaminated produce. Fine discovered that the first case of this sort was brought in 1914 in Mississippi, and that from then to 1976 a total of 45 cases were heard in court (the figure does not include those settled out of court). As well as mice, the contaminants found in the bottles included cockroaches, cigarette butts, and hairpins. Fine does not claim that these real events were the origin of the legends; his contention is that the real and the legendary events support each other and the legends help express "real fears about the industrialization of America" (Fine 1992, 79–85). The example below comes from this essay; the narrator dates these events to 1948 and they are said to have occurred in Norfolk, Virginia.

Example

This is a true story but I am including it because of what was said in class about foreign objects dissolving in Coca Cola. It was mid-night when me and a buddy of mine had just gotten off watch. We went down to the mess hall where we had a Coke machine and got two Cokes. This buddy of mine had his just about half gone when he noticed something in the bottle. We looked and seen this small mouse.

We ran up to sick bay to get the doctor and he gave him some white stuff to drink to make him heave. He did, and was sick for the next three days. (Fine 1992, 80)

FURTHER READING

Bell, L. Michael. "Cokelore." *Western Folklore* 35 (1976): 59–65.

Fine, Gary Alan. *Manufacturing Tales: Sex and Money in Contemporary Legends.* Knoxville, TN: University of Tennessee Press, 1992. See pp. 79–85 and 141–163.

Smith, Paul. "Contemporary Legend and Popular Culture: 'It's the Real Thing'." *Contemporary Legend* 1 (1991): 123–124. Reprinted *Popular Culture Theory and Methodology*. Ed. Harold E. Hines Jr, Marilyn F. Motz, and Angela M. S. Nelson Madison, WI: University of Wisconsin Press/Popular Press, 2006, pp. 318–343.

See: The Corpse in the Cask; Fingers in Take-Out Meals; Kentucky Fried Rat; The Snake in the Garment; Snakes in Bananas; Spiders at Large

NEW LAMPS FOR OLD: REDEMPTION RUMORS

People regularly collect a variety of objects in the hope of recycling them or putting them to some good use. To an extent, this hope has been harnessed by manufacturers to aid sales. Coupons and other incentives have been a recognized marketing tool since the last half of the nineteenth century. Many redemption offers are perfectly genuine, but totally imaginary ones have grown up alongside the real ones and news of them spreads in the form of rumors. So stories have proliferated that all sorts of useless things can be redeemed for something genuinely desirable or in aid of some charitable cause.

In 1883, for example, a note appeared in the long-running British correspondence magazine *Notes and Queries* about children collecting used stamps without any clear idea why: "Some thought the Post Office authorities would pay something for a million; others said that poor people etc could be got into hospitals, almshouses etc by collecting a certain number" (Sawyer 1883). A similar rumor was reported in *The Illustrated London News*. Here, the story was that "a certain young lady . . . was to be placed in a convent, by her father, if she did not procure, before the 30th April last, one million of used postage stamps . . . In March last, a lady . . . residing not many miles from Derby, mentioned this condition to her friends, and in a short time the lady began to receive packages by post and railway from every quarter, which poured in in such numbers that, in

10 days, during last April, she received parcels containing millions of stamps." This huge response included a packet with 240,000 stamps, and a hamper, a clothes chest, and a tea-chest, all crammed with stamps. The consequence was that, not only could the mail man not cope with the amount of mail and an additional mail man had to be hired, but so many packages arrived by rail that notices had to be printed asking the public not to send any more stamps ("Extraordinary Postage Stamps Contribution").

Nearer our own time (in April 1947) the New York *Herald Tribune* had to explode the popular myth that Ford Motors would trade a brand new car for a 1943 copper cent. The rumor went that only 200 such coins were minted; Ford had 180 of these coins and wanted twenty more (no one explained why). In actual fact, a call to the Mint revealed that no copper coins at all had been minted in 1943 ("Penny Myth Exploded"). Alternatively, Ford were rumored to be giving away a Model T in exchange for four dimes with mint-marks F., O., R., and D. (Miller 1947). These stories were so widespread that they became the subject of jokes. One story went that a thrifty housewife saved all her empty cans and shipped them off to Detroit. After a few weeks she was delighted to get a nice letter from Ford: "Dear Madam, In accordance with your instructions we have made up and are shipping to you today, one Ford. We are also returning eight cans which were left over" (McConnell 1989, 239).

In 1959 stories were circulating among British schoolchildren that an eccentric millionaire had left his vast fortune to anyone who could collect a million bus tickets. Other such stories prevalent among schoolchildren at that time told about fortunes to be won by collecting a million cigarette cards, or bus tickets the serial number of which ended with the number 7, or a million milk bottle tops, or a million candy wrappers (Opie and Opie 1959, 306–308).

One particularly persistent form of redemption rumor which has surfaced from time to time since the mid-1930s is that various useless things (especially cigarette packets) can be redeemed for medical equipment, or guide dogs for the blind, or to help sick children. The Ladies Auxiliary of an Albany, New York area American Legion post, for example, reportedly collected "tons and tons" of used cigarette packs, teabags, and old postage stamps which they took to the Veterans Hospital in Albany. The hospital staff, however, just "looked at [them] as if [they] were crazy" (Fine 1992, 196).

Example

According to the *Evening Times*, Glasgow, 3rd December, 1986: Voluntary worker Stan Kilna's plans to help a handicapped youngster have gone up in smoke. Three times a week the voluntary driver picked up his disabled passenger, John Purden, in his wheelchair. Stan said, "Everybody knew John would benefit from an electric wheelchair. And everyone knew it would cost a lot of money to get him one." Then Stan hit on a bright idea to raise the necessary £1,900. He collected cigarette packets to raise the funds. Stan said, "I read about an appeal for cigarette packets and thought it was a good idea. It wasn't till four months later that somebody told me the appeal had been a hoax." Now Stan has been left with 100,000 cigarette packets, and dashed the hopes of 24-year-old wheelchair bound John Purden. A spokesman for the giant tobacco firm, Gallaher, said, "This man appears to be the latest person to be taken in by this cruel hoax. It has been happening from time to time in the last few years, and almost every person has heard about this appeal for cigarette packets by word of mouth." She revealed other tobacco companies had been involved in the hoax too. (McConnell 1989, 240)

FURTHER READING

Brunvand, Jan Harold. *The Mexican Pet: More "New" Urban Legends and Some Old Favorites.* New York: Norton, 1986. See pp. 169–174.

"Extraordinary Postage Stamps Contribution." *The Illustrated London News* (May 18, 1850): 349.

Fine, Gary Alan. "Redemption Rumors: Mercantile Legends and Corporate Beneficence." *Journal of American Folklore* 99 (1986): 208–222. Reprinted as Chapter 10 of *Manufacturing Tales: Sex and Money in Contemporary Legends.* Knoxville, TN: University of Tennessee Press, 1992, pp. 189–204.

McConnell, Brian. "The Corporate Folk-Legend: Marketing Invention or Consumer Response?" *The Questing Beast: Perspectives on Contemporary Legend IV.* Ed. Gillian Bennett and Paul Smith. Sheffield: Sheffield Academic Press for the International Society for Contemporary Legend Research in association with CECTAL, 1989, pp. 231–247.

Miller, William Marion. "Henry Ford and Four Dimes." *New York Folklore Quarterly* 3 (1947): 86–87.

Opie, Peter, and Iona Opie. *The Lore and Language of Schoolchildren.* Oxford: Clarendon Press, 1959.

"Penny Myth Exploded." *Western Folklore* 6 (1947): 283.

Sawyer, Frederick E. "Juvenile Pursuits." *Notes and Queries* 6th series VIII (1883): 355.

See: The Dying Child's Wish

THE PEARLS

This humorous morality tale was popular in America and the United Kingdom between 1940 and 1990. It comes in several versions. In version 1 a shoplifter steals a valuable pearl necklace and hides it on the counter of a discount store, only to see a woman purchase the necklace at a fraction of its real value (Cerf 1959, vol. 1, 543). In version 2 a woman buys a cheap imitation pearl necklace to wear at a dance, and is astonished when another guest at the dance tells her the pearls are genuine and very valuable (Buchan 1984, 87). In version 3, the plot is reversed. A woman is invited to a smart ball but has no jewelry suitable for the occasion; a friend lends her a beautiful necklace that appears to be very valuable; the woman loses the necklace and spends a fortune on having an exact copy made, only to find out that the friend's "valuable necklace" was a fake (Mays 1995 quoting *The Village Voice* 3 January 1989). The third version follows the plot of an 1884 short story, "La Parure" [the jewelry], by French writer Guy de Maupassant (1850–1893). It is possible therefore that the Maupassant story was the origin of the legend. It is equally possible, however, that the legend was known in the late nineteenth century in France and that Maupassant simply reworked the traditional material as often he did in his short stories.

Example

This woman, it seems, walked into a discount store and bought a cheap imitation pearl necklace. She wore it at a dinner dance. There was a jeweller at the dance and he told her that it was a perfectly matched set of pearls "worth a small fortune." The woman didn't believe him of course and told him they were fakes. "No," he said, "They're real enough. If you don't believe me let me get them valued for you." So she did and to her amazement, the experts said they were worth £20,000. Apparently what had happened was that the pearls had been stolen, and when they'd got too hot for the thief to handle, he'd dropped the necklace on the discount store counter to get rid of it. (Bennett Collection)

FURTHER READING

Buchan, David, ed. *Scottish Tradition: A Collection of Scottish Folk Literature*. London: Routledge and Kegan Paul, 1984.

Cerf, Bennett. *Bennett Cerf's Bumper Crop of Anecdotes and Stories, Mostly Humorous, about the Famous and Near Famous.* 2 vols. Garden City, NY: Garden City Books, 1959).

Mays, Alan E. "New Jewelry Legends: Some Tracks." *FOAFtale News* 36 (January 1995): 6.

THE PHILANDERER'S PORSCHE

This classic tale of revenge has been popular in Europe, Australia, and North America for at least 60 years. The basic story varies very little from the account in the example below, which tells how a husband deserts his wife and tells her to sell his expensive car and send the proceeds to him; she does as he asks, but has her revenge by asking a ridiculously low price for it. In some versions the husband is dead and in his will has instructed his wife to sell the car and give the proceeds to his mistress. A story with this twist was circulating in Edinburgh (Scotland) and the north of England as early as the 1940s. It was printed in the Wakefield (UK) *Evening Standard* in 1948 and picked up by the national daily papers (Sanderson 1969, 249). The journalist believed it to be true. Anne Landers also thought the story was true when she reported it in 1979 after a reader said he had read it in the *Chicago Tribune* (the *Tribune* denied printing it) (Brunvand 2001, 316–317).

There is a very much older story that shares the same plot. When Marguerite of Angoulême, Queen of Navarre (1492–1549) the sister of Francis I of France, was compiling her famous collection of stories, *The Heptameron*, she included several stories which we now would call urban or contemporary legends. One of these, "The Spanish Horse," follows much the same plot as "The Philanderer's Porsche," but with an additional clever twist. On his deathbed a rich merchant of Saragossa told his wife that, after his death, he wanted her to sell a "fine Spanish horse" he owned and distribute the money among the poor. She had been fond of her husband, the story goes, but she was no fool about money and thought that her husband had given enough to the poor in his lifetime. So she sent her servant out to dispose of the horse and to sell a cat at the same time. The price of the Spanish horse would be one ducat, the price of the cat 99 ducats—the catch was that the buyer had to buy both.

The editor of the English translation of these stories thinks that Queen Marguerite had heard this little tale at the time of her journey to Spain in 1525. He remarks, "The example set by the wife of the Saragossa merchant has been followed in modern times in more ways than one." Indeed, a very similar story was reported in 1990 from Austria. Here it is told how a "pious Miser" leaves his widow the task of selling a rooster and a cow. The money for the cow is to be donated to the church, but she may keep any proceeds from the sale of the rooster. The woman's response is the same as that of the widow of the Saragossa merchant: she offers the cow for five florins and the rooster for fifty, the catch being that the purchaser has to buy both (quoted in de Vos 1996, 117).

The story below, which was collected in Nottingham (UK) in 1962, tells of another wily woman's plan to foil her husband's inappropriate plans.

Example

A teacher is driving along the road to school when he sees a notice on a tree outside a house, "Car for sale. Very cheap." He drives slowly past, the garage doors are open, and he can see a very nice car parked up inside. He returns along the same road in the evening. The notice is still there, so he stops and goes to the house. He knocks on the door and the door is answered by a woman. The car is a new-ish Rover, top of the market in those days. The woman says he can take a look at it and test-drive it if he likes. He likes. It's great.

"How much?"

"Half a crown" [about 50 cents]

"Why only half a crown?"

The car belongs to the woman's husband who has left her for someone else and has instructed her to sell it and send the proceeds to him. The motorist turns down the deal . . . says it sounds like trouble to him. (Bennett Collection)

FURTHER READING

Brunvand, Jan Harold. *Encyclopedia of Urban Legends*. New York: Norton, 2001.

Chartres, J. S. (Translator and Editor). *The Heptameron of Margaret of Angoulême, Queen of Navarre: A Complete Translation into English from the Authentic French Text of Le Roux De Lincy*. Philadelphia, PA: J. P. Horn and Company, 1929. See pp. 215–219.

de Vos, Gail. *Tales, Rumors, and Gossip: Exploring Contemporary Folk Literature in Grades 7–12*. Westport, CT: Libraries Unlimited, 1996. See pp. 116–117.

McKelvie, D. *Some Aspects of Oral, Social and Material Tradition in an Urban Industrial Area*, unpublished PhD thesis, Leeds, 1963. See pp. 349–362.

Morgan, Hal, and Kerry Tucker. *More Rumor!* New York: Viking Penguin [Steam Press], 1987. See pp. 197–198.

Sanderson, Stewart. "The Folklore of the Motor-Car." *Folklore* 80 (1969): 241–252.

Scott, Bill. *Complete Book of Australian Folklore*. Sydney: Lansdowne, 1981. See pp. 360–361.

See: The Death Car

THE POISONED DRESS

This very well-known legend, sometimes referred to as "Embalmed Alive," first circulated in America during the 1930s. By the mid-1940s it was taking the mid-West by storm. It seems to have begun as a student horror-story, then been adapted as a commercial legend attacking large stores and/or unscrupulous morticians. In most of the American stories the dress has been removed from a corpse and resold. The poison which kills the girl is formaldehyde, which has soaked into the dress while it was on the embalmed corpse. The story has spread, not only by word of mouth, but via compilations of scary stories such as those of Cohen (1983, 23–27), Schwartz (1981, 56–66), and Young and Dockery Young (1993, 160–162).

Like most urban legends it is part of a wider story-tradition. Many historical legends from Europe, for example, tell of death from poison-soaked clothing or accessories (rings, scarves, boots, stockings, and gloves, as well as dresses), and there are parallels in the Greek classics in the stories of Nessus' shirt and Glauke's gown (Mayor 1997).

Example

A girl was invited to a grand banquet and decided that she had to have a new dress. So she bought a stunning white gown at a local department store. It was a real bargain—almost impossibly cheap but nothing wrong with it. It was beautiful.

During dinner she began to feel faint and the dress began to smell very peculiar. She went to the cloakroom and took the dress off, but nothing seemed to be wrong with it, so she put it back on again and returned to her table. Before long she passed out and she had to be taken home. The doctor was called but she died before he got there. He could do nothing to save her, but he thought he recognized the strange smell on her dress.

He ordered an autopsy and they discovered that the girl had formaldehyde in her veins. When she perspired and her pores opened, she took in the formaldehyde and it had coagulated her blood, and killed her.

They investigated the department store where she had bought the dress and found out that the dress had been sold to dress a corpse for a funeral. After the funeral the dress had been removed and sent back to the store, who had sold it on to the girl. Isn't that dreadful! (Bennett Collection)

FURTHER READING

Baughman, Ernest. "The Poisoned Dress." *Hoosier Folklore Bulletin* 4.1 (1945): 19–20.

Bennett, Gillian. *Bodies: Sex, Violence, Disease, and Death in Contemporary Legend*, 2005. See pp. 60–103.

Cohen, Daniel. *Southern Fried Rat and Other Gruesome Tales*. New York: M. Evans and Company, 1983.

Himelick, Raymond. "Classical Versions of 'The Poisoned Garment'." *Hoosier Folklore* 5 (1946): 83–84.

Mayor, Adrienne. "Fiery Finery." *Archaeology* (March/April 1997): 55–58.

Reaver, J. Russell. "'Embalmed Alive': A Developing Urban Ghost Tale." *New York Folklore Quarterly* 8 (1952): 217–220.

Schwartz, Alvin. *Scary Stories to Tell in the Dark Collected from American Folklore*. New York: Lippincott, 1981.

Young, Richard, and Judy Dockery Young. *The Scary Story Reader*. Little Rock, AR: August House, 1993.

THE SMUGGLER

This is a traditional humorous story—a "trickster tale"—which continues to be told today and is now usually considered to be an urban legend. Earlier versions circulated chiefly by word of mouth or in compilations of humorous stories and anecdotes, later ones via the Internet.

A correspondent to the British revue *New Society* remembers that it was given as a dictation exercise in his French class during the 1950s, but guesses that it is older than that (Hobbs 1987). In fact, the father-in-law of one of us (Bill Bennett) used to tell a very similar tale as a personal experience story relating to his wartime service in Italy. Early in 1944 Italy's second-highest volcano, Mount Vesuvius, erupted. During the month of March Bill, as a military policeman with the occupying British forces, was responsible for keeping open a single-track road round the volcano. Only essential traffic was allowed to pass. One of his stories was that he turned back the King of Italy; another was that he turned back a peasant farmer with a horse and cart. When the farmer failed to convince Bill that he was "essential traffic," the farmer turned back, only to return a little while later with an armful of planks. As a pedestrian, he was allowed to pass. A little while later still, he passed through the roadblock again with another armful of planks, then another; then he came through with a wheel, then another and another until he had passed through four times with four wheels. Eventually he sauntered through leading a horse.

Bill's story recalls other legends of wartime tricksters. From the Vietnam war comes a similar story of soldiers trying to mail guns home piece by piece (Barden 1995). And from World War I more smuggling stories such as the one about the boy who wheeled a bicycle bearing a sack of sand past Mexican or German border guards every day. The guards diligently searched the sack of sand for contraband, not recognizing that it was bicycles that the boy was smuggling. In a similar story a man was said to have crossed a frontier every day leading a donkey loaded with a sack of rice; the guards searched the bags of rice but found nothing—it was rice and donkeys that the man was smuggling (Mikkelson).

In a tale told on the United States–Canada border, a boy was said to cross the bridge between St Stephen and Calais every day riding a bicycle. Every day he was stopped by American customs and asked what was in the sack he was carrying. "Nothing but sand," was the reply. And every day there was indeed nothing but sand in his sack. The story ends when the, now-retired, customs officer meets the now-grown man and asks him what he was smuggling. The answer is "bicycles." Also from the same frontier comes a story (told in the 1970s but relating to former times) about an "apple-cheeked" youth who crossed the border every day in a horse and cart: he was, of course, smuggling horses and carts, not the tobacco he was suspected of taking over the border (Trueman 1979, 45 and 11).

Versions of the legend are also attached to Juan Peron (President of Argentina from 1946 to 1955) and his wife Eva. It was said that during the construction of a luxurious villa on the outskirts of Buenos Aires, the Perons set up a strict guard round the project to prevent building materials being stolen. Every day at the same time a man appeared wheeling a barrow-load of straw. The guards searched the straw for stolen goods but found nothing. Sometime later, after the building was completed, the guard met the man and asked him to confess what he had been smuggling past him for so long. The answer—of course—was "wheelbarrows" (Cerf 1952, 64). A virtually identical story, but lacking the Peron connection and located in a factory, was circulated on the Internet in 1994 (Mikkelson).

With their ironical twist, these stories also recall post–World War II stories about German hyperinflation. The situation was so bad that shoppers needed literally hundreds of banknotes to make a simple purchase. Legend has it that a woman was on her way to the store to buy some groceries, using a wheelbarrow piled high with the bank notes. While her back was turned, someone dumped the pile of notes and stole the barrow.

Example

Since partition in 1922 the rambling, 200-mile border between north and south [Ireland] . . . has provided a modest living for smugglers. Anyone prepared to take a small risk of running into a patrol could make a few pounds on commodities like petrol, spirits, cigarettes, livestock and contraceptives . . .

The most famous local smuggler . . . had been fined no less than five times in the last year. After his fifth fine he completely gave up trying to get anything past the border in his lunch bag, but the [police] kept searching him. Every day he would cycle past the lonely border post, and every day they would make him get off. But every time they would find nothing and he would cycle, whistling, on his way.

In the end the [police] had lost all patience with the man. They knew he was carrying something but they couldn't figure out what. So they took his bicycle and opened the tyres and the inner tubes. They took off the handlebars and saddle, and they sawed open the frame tubes, and they found—nothing.

So the [police] bought the man a new bicycle and sent him on his way, still whistling. "And d'ye know," said my friend, "They never did work out that what the man was smuggling, was bicycles" (Hobbs 1987).

FURTHER READING

Barden, Thomas, and John Provo. "Legends of the American Soldiers in the Vietnam War." *Fabula* 36.3/4 (1995): 217–229.

Cerf, Bennett. *Good for a Laugh*. New York: Hanover House, 1952.

Healey, Phil and Rick Glanvill. *Now! That's What I Call Urban Myths*. London: Virgin Books, 1996. See. pp. 34–35.

Hobbs, Sandy. "One or Two Legends in *New Society?*" *Forum* 3 (April/May 1987): 19.

Mikkelson, Barbara. "Wheel of Fortune," http://www.snopes.com/crime/clever/wheelbarrow.asp

Trueman, Stuart. *Tall Tales and True Tales from Down East*. Toronto: McClelland and Stewart, 1979.

THE SNAKE IN THE GARMENT

There is a large group of legends that tell about a horrified customer finding a snake in goods she buys in a downtown store. According to the stories, the contaminated goods may be blankets, mattresses, bananas, grapes, or exotic plants (Mullen 1970).

Among these there is the story of "The Snake in the Garment," which folklorists have collected since the late 1960s and which became particularly popular in the 1980s in Europe and North America. Sometimes the garment is supposedly sent as a gift from the Far East or Indian subcontinent, and sometimes it is for sale in a downtown store (often the store is named by the storyteller). Sometimes the snake is in a coat and sometimes in a blouse or dress. The victim is always a woman. Many versions just stop with the horrific discovery, and others go on to tell of the consequences—usually death or the amputation of a limb.

For example, a series of rumors broke out in Omaha, Nebraska in March 1991 when a woman supposedly became "deathly ill." Doctors trying to diagnose what was wrong with her persuaded her to recount her every action the day before, and she told them that she had been trying on coats in a (named) factory outlet. Police investigated, it was said, and found young poisonous snakes in the fur decorating imported coats. Callers to the local newspaper confirmed the story (including a nurse, a doctor, and a lawyer). Local health authorities said they had had numerous calls, but could never substantiate the claims. "We had people say that they knew a person that it happened to" an investigator said, but they never heard from anyone who claimed to have been bitten themselves. The vice president of the company said that, though it was detrimental to business, "there's not a lot that can be done except to let the stories die" ("Department Store Snake").

The story is older than this, however. Gillian Bennett's mother told her the tale in the 1980s and said she had heard it told in the 1930s when she was in domestic service at a baronet's "stately home," Attingham Hall, in Shropshire (UK). The story was spread by the servants, she said: "I heard it in at least three or four different situations. Slightly different but essentially the same and it has always been true, it has always happened to the lady they were with in a previous situation" ("Snake Bite"). This is our first example. Our second example comes from a collection of scary stories.

Examples

1. The story of the fur coat. I've heard it in several variations. But essentially, it's always the same. The lady of the house, her husband has brought her a very

beautiful fur coat and sometimes he's bought it direct from India where he's a high-ranking soldier out there, but anyway he bought her this beautiful fur coat. She takes it out of the wardrobe and gloats over it and lays it flat on the bed ready to wear and while she's getting dressed, she looks at the coat and to her horror, it's moving up and down, and it stops moving and she gets a bit scared, puts it back in the wardrobe and as she puts it in the wardrobe, she sees the sleeves waggling as if there's an arm in it, screams and shuts the wardrobe door and sort of runs out. Later, persuaded that she's imagined it all, goes to put the coat on, puts her arm down the sleeve and out slithers a great big huge snake. ("Snake Bite")

2. A woman went into one of the big discount department stores in Columbus, Ohio, to buy a coat. While she was trying on coats she felt a sharp pain in her arm. It was like a pin prick, so she assumed that there had been a pin left in the coat, and forgot about it. Later that night she began to feel very, very, sick, and her arm became badly swollen.

The condition worsened very quickly, and within a matter of a few hours she was completely delirious. Her husband became extremely worried and rushed her to the hospital. At first the doctors had no idea what was wrong with her, but there was one doctor at the hospital who knew about snakebites. He thought the woman's symptoms were those of a person who had been bitten by a poisonous snake.

Naturally the health department got in touch with the store and they examined the coats. In the lining of one of them they found a whole nest of baby snakes. The coat been imported from Hong Kong, and it seems that a snake must have gotten into the coat while it was on the dock awaiting shipment. The snake laid its egg in the lining, and the eggs hatched after the coat arrived in the US.

In a way the woman was lucky, because the type of snake that was found in the coat was poisonous. If the snake had been full grown the bite would have killed her without a doubt. (Cohen 1980, 114–115)

FURTHER READING

Carpenter, Ann. "Cobras at K-Mart: Legends of Hidden Danger." *What's Going On? (in Modern Texas Folklore)*. Ed. Francis Edward Abernethy. Austin, TX: The Encino Press, 1976, pp. 37–45.

Cohen, Daniel. *The Headless Roommate and Other Tales of Terror*. New York: M. Evans and Company, 1980.

"Department Store Snake." *FOAFtale News* 22 (June 1991): 12.

de Vos, Gail. *Tales, Rumors, and Gossip: Exploring Contemporary Folk Literature in Grades 7–12*. Westport, CT: Libraries Unlimited, 1996. See pp. 196–197.

Morgan, Hal, and Kerry Tucker. *More Rumor!* New York: Viking Penguin [Steam Press], 1987. See pp. 194–196.

Mullen, Patrick B. "Department Store Snakes." *Indiana Folklore* 3 (1970): 214–228.

"Snake Bite." *Dear Mr Thoms* 19 (February 1991): 24.

See: The Poisoned Dress; Snakes in Bananas; Spiders at Large

SNAKES IN BANANAS

Rumors of snakes infesting bananas are one of the more popular forms which legends of snakes in produce take. Such stories have appeared intermittently in oral tradition and the press in the Western world since the 1930s and continue to surface today. A correspondent to *FOAFtale News* said that in the 1930s she had heard that small black snakes would breed in imported bananas when they were picked. The young snakes would come to maturity when the fruit warmed up, and bite the hand of any unsuspecting person handling the fruit. This particular version seems to have been current until the 1950s. Folklorist Linda Dégh also sent in a Hungarian newspaper article dated August 1992 about a woman who claimed to have found a snake's fang in her bananas ("Snakes and Bananas").

Example

My brother's wife told me this. A friend of hers had gone shopping with her little boy and bought a bunch of bananas. The boy was making a bit of nuisance of himself so when she got home she plonked him down at the kitchen table, gave him a banana, and said, "Now sit there, shut up, and eat that!" Then she went into the kitchen.

Suddenly she heard him shout, "Mummy, the banana bit me!" The mother took no notice because she was really fed up with his tricks, but when she went back into the kitchen, the boy was lying on the floor unconscious. He had been bitten by a miniature cobra.

Now I always check before I eat a banana to make sure there isn't a snake in it. (Bennett Collection)

FURTHER READING

de Vos, Gail. *Tales, Rumors, and Gossip: Exploring Contemporary Folk Literature in Grades 7–12*. Westport, CT: Libraries Unlimited, 1996. See pp. 195–201.

Klintberg, Bengt af. "Legends and Rumours About Spiders and Snakes." *Fabula* 26 (1985): 274–287.

Mullen, Patrick B. "Department Store Snakes." *Indiana Folklore* 3 (1970): 214–228.

"Snakes and Bananas." *FOAFtale News* 28 (December 1992): 10–11.

See: The Snake in the Garment; Spiders at Large

SPIDERS AT LARGE

Under this heading we have grouped a selection of legends and rumors about spiders in produce, airplane toilets, restaurant restrooms, and American prisons since 1990. Tarantulas, black widow spiders, blush spiders, and brown recluse spiders are the rumor-mongers' special favorites. The stories have been passed by word of mouth or have appeared as newspaper reports or as e-mail warnings (that are usually later debunked as "hoaxes"). These reports are often quite specific—the spider is named and the effects of its bite are described; if it has been found in produce, then the store the goods were bought at is named, and so on.

For example, in the summer and fall of 1991, there were widespread rumors about black widow spiders being found in green seedless grapes (deVos 1996, 201). This particular story was reported from Maine and Massachusetts. The grapes were said to have originated in California's Coachella Valley, just north of the Mexican border (Fullerton 1991).

Then there were persistent rumors in the United Kingdom in the mid-1990s about tarantulas being found in imported yucca plants, often linked to a named, high-profile department store chain. A little later, in 1998, stories circulated in the United States about tarantulas being found in cactus plants imported from Mexico. Here, the story was that "plate-size," tiger-striped, bird-eating tarantulas regularly laid their eggs in that type of cactus and, when they grew to their full size, the cactus would explode and fling large numbers of hairy spiders everywhere. An Australian version of the same story circulated on the Internet in January 2001.

These stories all end very dramatically. After the owner of the cactus sees the spider emerging, he rings the Public Health authorities, and is asked to describe the creature. There is silence on the line for a moment, then the whole family is warned to leave the house immediately. A few minutes later fire trucks, cop-cars, and ambulances come "screaming up," and men in masks and protective clothing leap out in a frenzy and destroy the cactus with hoses or flame-throwers. Sometimes it is said that the house and the adjoining houses have to be evacuated, fumigated, and sealed up for two weeks.

In August 1999, a story surfaced on the Internet about a deadly spider being found under toilet seats on airplanes and being responsible for several deaths in Chicago. Then in the fall of 1999 e-mail warnings originating in South Africa or the United States circulated about spiders in toilets—"Warning!" it said, "Spider in the toilet!"—and told how nine women in Pretoria and Johannesburg (or five women in Chicago) turned up at hospitals over a five-day period complaining of fever, chills, and vomiting. Muscular collapse was said to follow, then paralysis and death. It was said that an immediate inspection of the toilets on all flights had been ordered and that nests of blush spiders had been discovered on four different planes. The rumor was quickly debunked as a "hoax" ("'Spider Death' email a web of lies"). It was said that a web page prepared by university entomologists drew 49,000 hits in its first two weeks ("Internet Spider Hoax").

In July 2001 a story circulated on the Internet about a tarantula that crawled out of one of the vents of a brand-new PT Cruiser "on special order from a faraway dealership." Then another spider crawled out and scurried over the dashboard. The new owners turned round straight away and returned to the dealership only to be told that many PT Cruisers had been found to harbor tarantulas but nothing could be done about it since the vehicle was manufactured in Mexico.

In December 2002, "panic" was supposed to have "gripped" inmates "in the 12-story downtown county lockup," according to the San Diego *Union Tribune*, when "mystery symptoms" were attributed to spider bites. A staff reporter related how "about a dozen inmates say they have been bitten by dangerous brown recluse spiders, whose venom can cause gruesome, painful lesions. They say sheriff's deputies know what is happening but won't do anything about it. The inmates say they are afraid to sleep at night and that when they shake their clothing in the morning, spiders fall out. The Sheriff's Department says the inmates are working themselves into a ridiculous and baseless panic" and that "neither the medical staff nor the [jailers] have been able to sight or find any spiders" (Jones 2002). Similar complaints and panics were reported from prisons in Davisborough, GA, in September 2003 and Pittsburgh, PA, in November 2004. Though the medical authorities attributed the prisoners' symptoms to a skin infection, the prisoners themselves believed they had been bitten by spiders.

The example below features spiders, pot plants, and the United Kingdom's best-known department store.

Example

I heard about somebody who bought a pot plant in Marks and Spencer's, and it died after two days. So she took it back and they offered her a replacement. She said, "I just want to know why the plant died." So they investigated, and they found that there was a dead male tarantula in the pot. So people from Public Health came, and they found a living female under her bed. They had to fumigate everything—the whole place—the curtains, the upholstery, everything. Everything was ruined! (Bennett Collection)

FURTHER READING

de Vos, Gail. *Tales, Rumors, and Gossip: Exploring Contemporary Folk Literature in Grades 7–12*. Westport, CT: Libraries Unlimited, 1996.

Fullerton, Linda. "Shop 'n Save pulls grapes from shelves." *Press Herald* [Portland, ME] (July 9, 1991): 1A, 8A. Quoted in *FOAFtale News* 23 (September 1991): 14.

"Internet Spider Hoax." Department of Entomology, UC Riverside. http://cnas.ucr.edu/~ento/Spiders/debunk.html

Jones, J. Harry. "Spider panic grips inmates: Officials say brown recluse not behind mystery symptoms." San Diego *UnionTribune* (December 7, 2002). http://www.signonsandiego.com/news/metro/20021207-9999_7m7spider.html

"'Spider Death' email a web of lies." *Independent* [South Africa] (April 25, 2002). http://www.iol.co.za/index.php?click_id=139&art_id=ct20020425092855696F3421678&set_id=1

See: Cobras at K-Mart/Rattlers at Wal-Mart; The Snake in the Garment; The Spider Boil; The Girl with the Beehive Hairdo; The Mouse in the Coca Cola Bottle

THE SUPPRESSED PRODUCT

Stories of suppressed enterprise of one sort or another are a regular part of the folklore of products. For example, it was alleged in a German newspaper, the

Neue Presse of Hannover, in November 1993 that somebody had invented a "washing ball" that could clean clothes without the use of detergents and that a detergent company were offering to buy the patent for over two and a half million marks in order to suppress it (Lassen 1995, 24). In the late 1980s and early 1990s, the favorite story in the United Kingdom, Germany, and Scandinavia was that an everlasting lightbulb had been invented and the patent had been bought up to protect the sales of the ordinary sort of bulb (Smith 1983, 67). In the 1960s and 1970s rumors abounded of suppressed inventions—carburettor designs that would halve fuel consumption, revolutionary car lights, everlasting razor blades and vehicle tires (Brunvand 1986, 161–163; Lassen 1995, 11–24). One of the most persistent stories was that somebody had invented an additive that could be put in gasoline to get hugely improved mileage from cars (Ainsworth 1976).

In occupied France during World War II it was being told that the Germans had a sort of pill that could be added to water to produce gasoline. There is no suggestion in these stories that the product was suppressed; indeed, in a development of the legend the story was that kindly German soldiers were giving out their magic pills to aid fleeing refugees (Bonaparte 1947, 94–95).

In the early 1940s the famous American song collector Alan Lomax told how he had met a blues singer who said that he had invented a machine that would generate 250 volts of current without using fuel but "they" had tried to steal his idea so he had had to destroy his only model (Lassen 1995, 21).

But these are by no means either the earliest or the only legends of suppressed products. In a brilliant essay that explores these themes, Danish folklorist Henrik Lassen finds stories about the suppression of the discovery of malleable glass in late seventeenth-century France, early seventeenth-century Spain, and in a famous thirteenth-century collection of sermon stories, the *Gesta Romanorum*. The tales in the *Gesta Romanorum* seem to have originated in Ancient Rome, for Lassen has found stories about the Emperor Tiberius in Pliny the Elder's *Natural History* (written c. A.D. 77) and Petronius' *Satyricon* (written c. A.D. 60). They were apparently in oral circulation during that time. In these stories a man brings his invention to the Emperor; his invention is a type of glass that, as he demonstrates by wielding a little hammer, is both bendable and unbreakable. The emperor has him beheaded and/or his workshop destroyed so that the value of Rome's precious metals will not be undermined (Lassen 1995, 3–5).

Lassen also provides a comprehensive checklist of films, novels, short stories (even a "Peanuts" cartoon) which make use of this legend type. These include: the film "The Man in the White Suit" (1951); Robert A. Heinlein's short story "Life-Line" (1939); John Wyndham's short story "The Flying Machine" (early

1950s); and Lionel Davidson's novel *The Sun Chemist* (1976). Stephen King uses the story in his *The Tommyknockers* (1998), and it formed an episode of the popular British TV series from 1971, "The Persuaders."

Example

It was around 1920, shortly after he had married, when the old man originally purchased the light bulb from a small store in town. It appeared to be a normal light bulb. However, when after sixty years it was still going strong, he decided to write to the manufacturers and tell them about the remarkable phenomenon. By return a reply came from the company indicating they were very interested in the bulb and would like to send someone to see it. Eventually, one of the directors of the firm called and, instead of just showing interest, offered to buy it for £1,000.

The old man, of course, refused, as the light bulb had given him good service. However, his curiosity was certainly aroused—why so much money for his light bulb? The director could provide no plausible explanation as to why they were willing to offer so much for the bulb, so the old man decided to explore this mystery further.

With the help of a solicitor friend he did a little investigating and discovered that in the 1920s this particular light-bulb manufacturer had bought and tested the patent for an everlasting light bulb. Only a few of these bulbs were made and the company, finding the invention worked, destroyed the bulbs and suppressed the idea—after all, it would have put them out of business. Unknown to the company one of the lights had accidentally become mixed up with a batch of ordinary bulbs and this was the light bulb which had lit the old man's kitchen for the past sixty years. (Smith 1983, 67)

FURTHER READING

Ainsworth, Catherine Harris. "Gasoline Folklore." *New York Folklore* 2 (1976): 111–113.

Bonaparte, Marie. *Mythes De Guerre*. Paris: Presses Universitaires de France, 1946. Translated by John Rodker as *Myths of War*. London: Imago, 1947.

Brunvand, Jan Harold. *The Mexican Pet: More "New" Urban Legends and Some Old Favorites*. New York: Norton, 1986.

Lassen, Henrik. "'The Improved Product': A Philological Investigation of a Contemporary Legend." *Contemporary Legend* 5 (1995): 1–37.

Smith, Paul. *The Book of Nasty Legends*. London: Routledge and Kegan Paul, 1983.

8

MURDER, DEATH, AND BURIAL

Once more, we are in the heartland of urban legend. The majority of these tales are horrific, but even here there are lighter moments. On the one hand there are black comedies such as "Dead Again" and "The Failed Suicide." On the other hand we have "The Blood Libel Legend," which is probably the most disturbing legend of all time, and worse for having been believed and acted upon over several centuries. Between these extremes there is the story of "The Murdered Son," an ironic tale of mistaken identity resulting in death, and sick stories such as "The Stolen Corpse," "The Corpse in the Cask," and "Grandma's Ashes."

Despite the grim and unlikely content of the stories in this chapter, "The Blood Libel Legend" is not the only one to have been believed, at least for a time. Stories of "Killer Clowns" caused near panic among British and American schoolchildren, and stories about "Halloween Sadists" resulted in a nationwide rethink of how "Trick-or-Treat" visits should be conducted.

For other stories of murder, death, and burial see: "Aren't You Glad You Didn't Switch on the Light?"; The Assailant in the Back Seat; The Babysitter and the Man Upstairs; The Boyfriend's Death; The Doggie-Lick; Killer Suicides; Lights Out!; The Roommate's Death

THE ARCHITECT'S BLUNDER

The usual name for this group of stories, "The Architect's Blunder," is not really an accurate description. In the first place, this is not a single story-type, but a complex of legends held together by the theme of a master-craftsman being murdered, or committing murder or suicide. Secondly, though some of the stories involve blunders, in others what leads to the crime is the architect's success, not failure. Thirdly, just as often as the central character is said to be an architect, he is said to be a sculptor or a civil engineer. However, the title has stuck and it's not easy to find another name that will cover all the variations.

The legends take three principal forms:

1. The master craftsman discovers that his apprentice's work is better than his own, so he kills his apprentice.
2. The master craftsman is killed by his employer so that he will not build a finer building for another client.
3. The master craftsman makes an elementary mistake, which shames him so much that he kills himself.

These legends have been told worldwide for centuries, and have been discussed by folklorists since at least the beginning of the twentieth century, the earliest full-scale treatment of the theme being William Crooke's 1918 article in the British journal *Folklore*. Modern examples come from India, New Zealand, Canada, the United States, France, Germany, and the United Kingdom. Types 1 and 2 are the older forms.

1. The master craftsman discovers that his apprentice's work is better than his own, so he kills his apprentice. One of the earliest example of pupils killed by the master craftsman they are apprenticed to comes from Greek mythology. Talus (or Perdix), the nephew of the famous Athenian craftsman, Daedalus, was a prolific inventor. It was said that Talus's skill and ingenuity aroused the envy of Daedalus, so Daedalus threw him from the top of the temple of Athena on the Acropolis in Athens (Crooke 1918, 219–220).

A story like this is attached to Rosslyn Chapel, the scene of the climax of Dan Brown's 2003 best seller, *The da Vinci Code*. The "Prentice Pillar" at Rosslyn is supposedly so called because the master builder killed his apprentice when he discovered that the pillar the apprentice had built was finer than his own (Crooke 1918, 219). Virtually identical stories are also attached to two rare windows in Rouen Cathedral (France), and to several churches in Greece (Hasluck 1919). A story like this also attaches to a church in Rothenburg (Germany) that has two towers of unequal height. It is said that the architect built one, and his apprentice built the other. When the architect discovered that the apprentice's tower was taller than his own, he killed his pupil (Simpson 1992, 5–6).

2. The master craftsman is killed by his employer so that he will not build a finer building for another client. Another large group of legends tell of patrons who kill (or in some versions mutilate) the master craftsman they have employed so that no finer building will ever be constructed again. A story like this comes from fourteenth-century France where the inventor of an astronomical clock was said to have been murdered by a jealous bishop (Hasluck 1919, 135). Other versions come from Ireland, ancient Arabia, and India.

An Indian tale, recorded by Crooke, tells the story of the architect of the Diamond gate at the thirteenth-century fort at Dabhoi in modern-day Gujarat. There are four exquisitely carved gates leading into the fort, one facing each direction. The most exquisite is the east gate, the "Diamond Gate," created by the architect Hiradhar and called the "Hira" gate in his honor. The story is that the Raja who had employed him was afraid that Hiradhar would take his talents elsewhere after completing the gate, so he had him buried alive under the adjoining Kalika Mata temple. However, Hiradhar did not die; he had a faithful wife who passed milk to him through cracks between the stones. Six years later news came to the Raja that Hiradhar had survived; Hiradhar was released by the remorseful Raja and went on to create other fine works for him (Crooke 1918, 222–223).

3. The master craftsman makes an elementary mistake, which shames him so much that he kills himself. The most common form taken by legends of "The Architect's Blunder" today is a tale of a master craftsman who commits suicide out of shame when he discovers that his building has some elementary error. Often these stories take on the characteristics of place legends and attach themselves to local features such as buildings with grand entrances at the back instead of the front, or churches with twisted steeples, or animal statues lacking ears or feet or tongues. The architect of the Kelvingrove Art Gallery in Glasgow (Scotland), for instance, was said to have committed suicide when he discovered that the building had been built back to front (the Kelvingrove Art Gallery is actually as the architect intended, the imposing rear façade originally leading from a grand pavilion designed to house the Glasgow Exhibition of 1901). There are at least eighteen similar legends attached to buildings and sculptures in Scotland alone (McCulloch 1987, 110).

Churches with crooked spires also attract legends of suicidal builders. In at least three British towns there are local legends that tell how the architect despairingly threw himself off the top of the spire when he saw how badly it had warped (Simpson 1992, 5; Smith 1992, 7 and 11; Harte 2001). Similarly, in Denmark the architect of the Church of our Savior, Christianshavn, was said to have killed himself in shame when he realized that the dramatic external staircase round the spire turned anticlockwise (supposedly a "satanic" direction).

The story in our example was recorded by folklorists Linda Dégh and Andrew Vázsonyi in Budapest (Hungary). This story is known, not only throughout Hungary, but in neighboring Slovenia and the former Yugoslavia too. A very similar story has been reported from Scotland. A statue dedicated to the nineteenth-century writer James Hogg ("The Ettrick Shepherd") was donated to the town of Moffat in 1875 and stands in the High Street. It depicts a ram; if you look closely you will see that the ram has horns but no ears. Legend has it that when the sculptor realized his mistake he killed himself ("Town of the Week: Moffat"). Legends about suicidal sculptors and architects are also attached to sites in France. Guidebooks to Paris state, for example, that the lake in the Parc Montsouris mysteriously emptied itself on the opening day in 1878, and the mortified engineer committed suicide. Likewise it is said that the artist who created the statue of Joan of Arc in the Place Jeanne d'Arc in Chinon killed himself when it was pointed out to him that the stance of the horse Joan was depicted as riding was physically impossible (Hobbs 1992, 3).

Example

[T]he legend is common knowledge to everyone who was born and reared or who lived for a while in the Hungarian capital. It is about the Chain Bridge, the first to connect the two parts of the city, which is divided by the Danube. This bridge, decorated with two lion statues on both ends, was built in 1842 by Adam Clark, a British engineer. At the opening ceremonies, Clark proudly stated that he had completed his work to perfection—not even a nail was missing. A cobbler's apprentice delivering boots to customers happened to pass by and heard what the engineer said. "The lions have no tongues!" yelled the boy in front of the audience of eminent townspeople, whereupon the embarrassed builder jumped into the river and drowned. (Dégh and Vázsonyi 1978, 264–265)

FURTHER READING

Crooke, W. "'Prentice Pillars': The Architect and His Pupil." *Folk-Lore* 29 (1918): 219–225.

Crooke, W. "'Prentice Pillars': The Architect and His Pupil." *Folk-Lore* 31 (1920): 323–324.

Dégh, Linda, and Andrew Vázsonyi. "The Crack on the Red Goblet or Truth and Modern Legend." *Folklore in the Modern World*. Ed. Richard M. Dorson. World Anthropology Series. The Hague: Mouton, 1978, pp. 253–272.

Harte, Jeremy "Suicidal Architect." *FLS News* 34 (June 2001): 12–13.

Hasluck, F. W. "'Prentice Pillars." *Folk-Lore* 30 (1919): 134–135.

Hobbs, Sandy. "Errors, Suicides, and Tourism." *FOAFtale News* 27 (September 1992): 2–4.

McCulloch, Gordon. "Suicidal Sculptors: Scottish Versions of a Migratory Legend." *Perspectives on Contemporary Legend Volume II*. Ed. Gillian Bennett, Paul Smith, and J. D. A. Widdowson. CECTAL Conference Papers Series. Sheffield: Sheffield Academic Press/CECTAL, 1987, pp. 109–116.

Simpson, Jacqueline. "More Suicidal and Homicidal Architects." *FOAFtale News* 28 (December 1992): 5–6.

Smith, Robin. "The Church of the Crooked Spire: St Mary and All Saints, Chesterfield." *Dear Mr Thoms . . .* 28 (November 1992): 1–11.

"Town of the Week: Moffat." *The Sunday Mail* [UK] (September 23, 2001). Reprinted in *Letters to Ambrose Merton* 27 (Spring 2002): 27–28.

See: Backwards Buildings and Other Architectural Errors

THE BLOOD LIBEL LEGEND

This is one of the oldest, most widespread, and most disturbing urban legends of all. It is based on the defamatory and groundless belief that Jews need blood for religious ceremonies and for cures for bizarre physical conditions they alone suffer from. From the twelfth century onward Jews have been charged with these imaginary offences, and all such cases as have come to trial have proved to be wholly unfounded. Many Christian writers and theologians, including a dozen popes, have refuted the "Blood Libel," but it has persisted to modern times. The charges have been very varied and include the crucifixion of Christian children, the abduction and murder of Christian children, the draining of their blood for medical or ritual purposes, and the baking of blood into the Passover bread.

Most scholars of the Blood Libel see the case of William of Norwich in 1144 as the first of a long line of accusations. In this famous English case the Jewish population of a prosperous port were accused of abducting and crucifying a 12-year-old Christian boy on Good Friday. Nine or ten similar accusations surfaced in England between the Norwich case and 1290, the most famous of which is the case of Hugh of Lincoln in 1255.

Accusations of crucifixions were less common in mainland Europe. When the rumors spread from England to the continent they tended to take the form of accusations that Jews had drained Christian children's bodies of blood. In Fulda (presentday Germany) in December 1235, thirty-four Jews were executed because two of them were supposed to have "cruelly killed the five sons of a miller [and] had collected their blood in bags smeared with wax and . . . set fire to them." From then on, cases in which Jews were accused of obtaining Christian blood began to proliferate across Europe. The expulsion of Jews from Spain in 1492 was due in large measure to the case of "El Santo Niño de La Guardia," a high-visibility, but almost certainly entirely imaginary, case "uncovered" by the Inquisition.

Rumors continued unabated. Accusations were brought against Jews at Verona 1603; Venice 1705; Viterbo 1705; Ancone 1711; throughout Poland from about 1650 to 1780; and in Hungary and Transylvania between 1764 and 1791, and many other places. The accusation that surfaced at Iampol in Poland 1756 was typical. A Christian child was murdered and immediately local Jews were accused of having killed him so that they could use his blood in their Passover bread.

If anything, accusations increased during the nineteenth century. Among the most notorious of these were charges brought at Damascus (Syria) in 1840 where "confessions" were extorted by tortures of medieval ferocity, prompting the President of the United States to speak of "heart-rending scenes which took place at Damascus" and to instruct the American Chargé d'Affaires "to interpose his good offices" on behalf of the Jews of Damascus. In the later part of the century accusations arose in Turkey and elsewhere in the Middle East, particularly in Egypt. Blood Libel accusations continued into the twentieth century, famously the Beilis (or Kiev) case from the Ukraine in 1911–1913. There was trouble in Poland in 1918 and again in 1928; in Lithuania in 1929; and in Bulgaria in 1934. The Nazis in Germany used the legend to whip up anti-Jewish feeling during the Third Reich.

The spread of the Blood Libel legend was not confined to the Europe, Asia, and the Middle East. Newspaper reports from the United States 1913–1919 relate scares, rumors, and court cases from Pennsylvania, New York, Fall River, Chicago, and Pittsfield (Duker 1980). There was a very serious outbreak of Blood Libel hysteria in the town of Massena in upstate New York in September 1928, which has been studied by Saul S. Friedman. Friedman took oral testimony from local people living at that time and wove it into a complex narrative which supplies historical background to the libel and is rich in contextual detail (Friedman 1978). Only a few years later, in 1933, anonymous leaflets alleging the reality of Jewish ritual murder were distributed in California (Roth 1959, 327).

The libel resurfaced again in Poland in 1946, where an anti-Semitic rising was well organized and led to killings and mass exodus of Jews (Czubala and Milerska 1999). As recently as the early 1960s the Blood Libel legend was reactivated in Soviet Dagestan, Uzbekistan, Tashkent, Georgia, and Soviet Lithuania. It was used by Muslim states in agitations against Israel, Jews and Judaism, this sort of propaganda appearing in Egypt, Lebanon, and Iraq between 1967 and 1978.

In 1991 the Dowager Lady Birdwood was prosecuted under British race-relations legislation for distributing leaflets containing the Blood Libel. As late as 2002 an article was published in a Saudi newspaper alleging that Jews use the blood of Christian or Muslim children in pastries during Purim. The columnist was sacked (Hobbs 2002). This is altogether a horrifying catalogue of prejudice and unreason that indicates that the history of this ancient slander is not over yet.

The example below is an extract from the work of the Abbé Desportes, "Le mystère du sang chez les juifs de tous les temps" [the blood rite among the Jews throughout the ages] (1890).

Example

Jews have periodic ceremonies for which they choose a very young boy as a sacrifice or, failing that, a young girl, the abduction having been meticulously planned beforehand. The children have to be without sin or stain, their blood pure and free from any polluting contact. They open up the child's veins by inflicting multiple wounds so that the blood spurts out like water spurting out of a sponge. The blood is collected in an urn, shared between those present, and drunk among wild chants. Some of the precious liquid is sometimes used for the Passover bread, and sometimes a little of it is put on one side for each of those present so that they can use it later as a libation. (Translated from the French by Gillian Bennett)

FURTHER READING

Bennett, Gillian. *Bodies: Sex, Violence, Disease, and Death in Contemporary Legend.* Jackson, MI: University of Mississippi Press, 2005. See pp. 247–303.

Czubala, Dionizjusz, and Anna Milerska, paper delivered at the conference of the International Society for Contemporary Research, Newfoundland, June 1999.

Duker, Abraham G. "Twentieth-Century Blood Libels in the United States." *Rabbi Joseph M. Lookstein Memorial Volume.* Ed. Leo Landerman. New York: KTAV Publishing House, 1980, pp. 85–109.

Dundes, Alan. *The Blood Libel Legend: A Casebook in Anti-Semitic Folklore.* Madison, WI: University of Wisconsin Press, 1991.

Friedman, Saul S. *The Incident at Massena: The Blood Libel in America.* New York: Stein and Day, 1978.

Hobbs, Sandy. "Blood Libel" *Letters to Ambrose Merton* 28 (Summer 2002): 7.

Roth, Cecil. "Blood Libel." *The Standard Jewish Encyclopedia.* London: W. H. Allen, 1959.

Strack, Hermann L. *The Jew and Human Sacrifice [Human Blood and Jewish Ritual]: An Historical and Sociological Inquiry.* Trans. Henry Blanchamp. London: Cope and Fenwick, 1909.

THE BODY IN THE BED

This grisly story became very popular between 1988 and 1996 and was reported (usually as true) from various locations in the United States (Atlantic City, Fort Lauderdale, Las Vegas, Miami, New Jersey) and from places as far away as Kyoto, Japan, and Cancun, Mexico. It remains popular, the latest report coming from Kansas City in 2003. As well as featuring in newspaper reports, it has been widely circulated on the Internet. It was said, for example, that at a "love hotel" in Kyoto twelve "ladies of the night" had sex with their customers, unaware that the corpse of a dead woman had been placed under the mattress of the bed (Schreiber 2002). In contrast to the seedy Japanese "love hotel," American versions of the story sometimes feature luxury hotels.

These are the sorts of stories where it is impossible to sift fact from fiction or to say whether life is imitating legend or legend imitating life. In her discussion of the legend in *FOAFtale News*, Barbara Mikkelson argues that there have been several real-life cases in United States between 1987 and 1996, and cites ten newspaper articles.

Example

I heard this or read it somewhere, I forget where. Anyway the story was that two tourists booked into a cheap room at a motel somewhere in America. There was a terrible smell, but they were tired so they put up with it and didn't complain till morning. In the morning they were given another room, and maids were sent in to clean the first one. The smell was coming from the bed itself, and when the maids lifted they mattress the found the body of a man in the box frame underneath. They had been sleeping on top of a corpse. (Smith Collection)

FURTHER READING

Mikkelson, Barbara. "The Body under the Bed." *FOAFtale News* 43 (February 1998): 15–16.

Schreiber, Mark. "Unwitting couples copulate over corpse in love hotel." *Mainichi Shimbun* [Japan] I (January 9, 2002), http://mdn.mainichi-msn.co.jp/waiwai/archive/news/2002/01/20020108p2g00m0dm999000c.html

See: The Death Car

THE CADAVER RELATIVE

Several legends told by medical students concern experiences in the dissecting room, and commentators have suggested that their function is to help students cope with the shock of their anatomy classes by turning the horror into a sick joke (Hafferty 1988). One such story is about the student who discovers that the corpse he is about to dissect, or has already dissected, is that of a relative who has gone missing or who has willed his/her body to medical science.

Such fears and such stories have been common since dissection became an essential part of the education of physicians and surgeons. In the United Kingdom, for example, in the mid-nineteenth century (the age of the infamous body-snatchers Burke and Hare) rumors were rife about what went on in anatomy classes. It was rumored, for example, that sexual indecencies took place, that anatomists fed used body parts to dogs, that dissected bodies were made into soap and candles, and so on. Among these rumors were several stories very like contemporary urban legends. People said that children were stolen and killed, their bodies being transported on the new steamships to be dissected abroad. There were also clear examples of "The Cadaver Relative," stories about anatomists who discovered to their horror that the body they purchased for dissection was that of a member of their own family (Bennett 2005, 227).

Example

A couple of years ago, a guy had gone to anatomy class on the first day of school. When he pulled open the box, there was his mother! She'd been missing a couple of weeks. (Trahant 1981, 46)

FURTHER READING

Bennett, Gillian. *Bodies: Sex, Violence, Disease, and Death in Contemporary Legend*. Jackson, MI: University Press of Mississippi, 2005. See pp. 223–228.

Hafferty, Frederic W. "Cadaver Stories and the Emotional Socialization of Medical Students." *Journal of Health and Social Relations* 29 (1988): 344–349.

Orso, Ethelyn G. "The Cadaver-Relative Legend." *Louisiana Folklore Miscellany* 5.3 (1983): 51–52.

Trahant, Yvette L. "The Oral Tradition of the Physician." *Louisiana Folklore Miscellany* 5.1 (1981): 38–47.

See: The Cadaver Arm; The Cybersex Surprise

THE CORPSE IN THE CASK

Sometimes called "Tapping the Admiral" because one famous version features the remains of Admiral Lord Nelson, the hero of the Battle of Trafalgar (1805), this story tells how sailors or thieves drink from a cask of alcohol not realizing that the alcohol has been used to preserve a dead body and that the body is still in the cask. Apart from the Lord Nelson story, the legend seems to have been most often reported in France, though versions have also turned up in the United States, Germany, and North Africa (Campion-Vincent and Renard 1992, 78–93). The most recent variants appear to be a story about the body of a Mexican worker being found, ground or sliced up, in a vat of pickles in a pickle factory in Michigan (Domowitz 1979), and one about the remains of a worker being found in a beer barrel at a brasserie in Texas. These examples date from the 1950s to the 1980s.

French researchers have found stories from the 1960s to the 1990s which tell of workers falling into vats of vermouth or wine, especially cheap wine from Algeria, and only being discovered when the vat is emptied and the contents have already been bottled and exported. It is often not clear whether the victim drowned in the vat or whether he was killed elsewhere and his body hidden in the vat.

Classic versions flourished in France from the mid-nineteenth until the early years of the twentieth century, in times before refrigeration. In those days meat, and on occasion an animal or human corpse, was preserved in honey or spirits until it could be disposed of. In its most common form the story tells of a cask of very fine liqueur being washed up on the beach. It is not until all the liqueur has been drunk by villagers that they discover that it has been used to preserve the remains of a monkey (Le Quellec 1991, 11–40).

The story may be even older. The fifteenth-century Italian writer Poggio Bracciolini (1380–1459) tells a very similar story as a humorous tale about a Florentine and a Jew (Doyle 1978); even earlier, there is the thirteenth-century Arab tale which provides our example below.

The writer Roald Dahl has used the legend several times in his work—in a novel, *My Uncle Oswald* (1979); in an essay, "Lucky Break: How I Became a Writer" (1977); and in interviews (see Burger 2002, 138–139). A ballad version of the story was still being sung by Irish-American loggers in the twentieth century (Brunvand 1993, 77), and the legend is clearly related to the story of "Grandma's Ashes." For those who read French, the most comprehensive discussions of this legend may be found in books by Jean-Loïc Le Quellec (1991, 146–157), and Véronique Campion-Vincent and Jean-Bruno Renard (1992, 78–90).

Example

A reliable man told me that one time when he and some other people were looking for treasure in the vicinity of the pyramids, they came across a well-sealed jar. On opening it and finding it full of honey, they began to eat it. Then one of them noticed that a hair had stuck to his finger; he pulled, and out came the body of a little child with all its limbs intact. (Abd el-Latif as quoted by Campion-Vincent and Renard 1992, 88. Translated from the French by Gillian Bennett)

FURTHER READING

Brunvand, Jan Harold. *The Baby Train and Other Lusty Legends*, New York: Norton, 1993.

Burger, Peter. "Contemporary Legends in the Short Stories of Roald Dahl." *Contemporary Legend* new series 5 (2002): 136–158.

Campion-Vincent, Véronique, and Jean-Bruno Renard. *Légendes urbaines: Rumeurs d'aujourd'hui*. Paris: Payot, 1992.

Domowitz, Susan. "Foreign Matter in Food: A Legend Type." *Indiana Folklore* 12 (1979): 86–95.

Doyle, Charles Clay. "Roaming Cannibals and Vanishing Corpses." *Indiana Folklore* 11 (1978): 133–139.

Quellec, Jean-Loïc Le. *Alcool de singe et liqueur de vipère . . . et quelques autres recettes*. Vouillé: Geste Editions, 1991.

See: Grandma's Ashes; The Mouse in the Coca-Cola Bottle; The Stolen Specimen

---

DEAD AGAIN

This ironic tale of fate has been popular with writers and journalists since the 1970s. It concerns people who are thought to be dead, but who revive at the very last minute. However, their return from the dead is short-lived—they are immediately killed in a freak accident. A brief story on this theme was told to Gillian Bennett by a lady in a podiatrist's clinic in 1982: "What was it I heard? Somebody was going to be buried and came round and found they were in the hearse. They banged on the coffin lid, jumped out, and got run over by a car!" This story is very like one recorded from Romania, where the woman comes to just as her coffin is being lowered into her grave; again, she jumps out of the coffin, runs into the road and is killed by a passing car (Bondeson 2001, 273).

Similarly, a story which was told to Jan Brunvand by a student, and which he calls "The Second Death," was originally told by a mortuary worker to a group who were touring the premises. Apparently, a mortuary worker was sent to collect the body of an elderly woman who had died in the night. On the journey back to the mortuary he thought he heard a "gurgling noise" coming from the hearse, but put it down to an air bubble escaping from the mouth of the corpse as they went over a number of bumps in the road. However, when they went round to the back of the hearse to take the corpse out, they found that the woman was still alive. An ambulance was immediately called, and set off at top speed to the nearest hospital. Unfortunately, though, the driver went far too fast, collided with another vehicle, and the woman was killed (Brunvand 1989, 67).

Example

In Ontario it was a sad day for the friends and relatives of Mrs Sadie Tuckey. She had been accidentally knocked off her bicycle by a bus and killed. When the funeral was held, scores of mourners came to pay their last respects, but as the coffin was being carried to its final resting place the mourners themselves nearly died of shock when they saw the "body" sit up in the coffin. Sadie was not dead at all! She had merely been stunned into a deep coma. The "body" screamed, leapt out of the coffin with fright and ran off down the road, straight into the path of a bus—which killed her outright. (Brandreth 1982, 139)

FURTHER READING

Bondeson, Jan. *Buried Alive*. New York: Norton, 2001.

Brandreth, Gyles. *The Book of Mistakes*. London: Futura, 1982.

Brunvand, Jan Harold. *Curses! Broiled Again! The Hottest Urban Legends Going*. New York: Norton, 1989.

Sieveking, Paul. "Strange Deaths." *Fortean Times* 56 (Winter 1990): 12–13.

Sieveking, Paul, and Robert. Rickard. "Doomed." *Whole Earth Review* 46 (1985): 58.

See: The Failed Suicide; The Seemingly Dead Revive

DEATH FROM FEAR

Several legends concern people who die through shock caused by fear, often in sham executions. Some of these stories are set in prisons where condemned prisoners supposedly are used as guinea pigs in experiments to test the power of suggestion. It was rumored, for example, that in Copenhagen in 1850 doctors blindfolded a prisoner, cut his arms and legs, and opened the faucets over a sink in the room. When the prisoner heard the sound of dripping water he was convinced that he was bleeding to death and died of a heart attack. Mary Baker Eddy, the founder of Christian Science, refers to a similar story in a book of 1875 and a sermon of 1886; in this case the experiment was said to have been carried out in the United Kingdom by students at Oxford University. Similar heartless experiments were reported to have taken place in India in the 1930s (Sones and Sones 2004). A 14-year-old schoolboy in Sheffield (UK) in the 1980s told a story in which the victim was said to be a dangerous psychopath in a local hospital (see our first story below). Another boy told a version in which the sham execution was a student prank (see our second story).

Deaths after "executions" committed as a prank are probably rather more common than stories about experiments. They come in two main forms and may be set in hospitals, universities, or fraternity houses. Sometimes the prank is malicious, played out for revenge; sometimes it is said to be part of a fraternity ritual (this variant is usually called "The Fatal Initiation").

Stories of sham execution as a malicious prank seem to be more common in the United Kingdom and are certainly older. A famous Scottish legend from the end of the eighteenth century, "Downie's Slauchter" (or "Slaughter"), is set in the University of Aberdeen. It tells how Downie, a university official in charge of student accommodation, became so unpopular that the students decided to punish him. They set up a mock courtroom hung with black drapes, with a "judge" and "witnesses" all clothed in black and wearing black masks. Then they proceeded to try him for various offences, found him guilty, and condemned him to be beheaded. They set him on the "block," an "executioner" stood by with an axe, they struck him on the neck with a wet towel, and he died of shock. Something very similar was said to have happened in the United States in the late nineteenth century to a janitor at an American college; supposedly the case was reported in J. C. Warren's *Surgical Pathology and Therapeutics*, published in Philadelphia in 1895, but we have not been able to trace this reference.

Needless to say, this is not the earliest appearance of stories like this. A very similar anecdote formed part of a sixteenth-century Italian novella in the compilations of Matteo Bandello. Here a nobleman of Ferrara turns the tables on a practical joker by sentencing him to death then faking his execution. The man's neck was placed on the block: "the executioner then emptied [a] bucket of water on his head, while all the people shouted out for mercy. Thinking the bucket of water was the axe, so great was the fear that poor unlucky Gonnella felt at that moment that he rendered up his soul to his creator" (Bandello 1952, 746–750).

Sham executions as a non-malicious prank are usually located in American university fraternity houses. The story goes that fraternity brothers decide to play a trick on a disobedient initiate as part of his initiation ceremony. In some versions the prank consists of the bleeding-to-death trick, in others the pledges say they are going to brand the initiate. They then put an ice-cube on his arm and hold a piece of burning meat to his nose. He dies of shock.

Examples

1. They'd got this patient from a mental hospital, a very dangerous one, put him in prison and they were using him as a guinea pig, and they blindfolded him and they told him that they were going to cut his throat and let all the blood drip out and one of them brought something, put something across his neck, and then they turned tap on to imitate dripping blood. And he DIED! SHOCK! (Field recording Wisewood School Sheffield, UK, courtesy of Ervin Beck)

2. My uncle he works in the hospital and he says that he's heard quite a few stories while he's been there.

   And one of them were about these students that, like, worked in hospital and a new student came, and the other students decided to play a joke on him so they—so they set up all their apparatus and then they went toward him, tied him up, blindfolded him, and told him that they were going to chop his HEAD off. And they'd fixed up a model guillotine, and they told him to put his head on it. Then they took blindfold off, and ONE of them hit him across neck with a wet TOWEL, then he DIED in hospital! (Field recording Wisewood School Sheffield UK, courtesy of Ervin Beck)

FURTHER READING

Bandello, Matteo. *Tutte le Opere di Matteo Bandello.* vol. 2, *Le Novelle,* La quarto parte, Novella XVII. Milano: Arnoldo Mondadori Editore, 1935; Reprint 1952.

Baughman, Ernest. "The Fatal Initiation." *Hoosier Folklore Bulletin* 4.3 (1945): 49–55. See Baughman's Type 3.

Bronner, Simon J. *Piled Higher and Deeper: The Folklore of Campus Life.* Little Rock: August House, 1990. See pp. 64–65.

Hobbs, Alexander. "Downie's Slaughter." *Aberdeen University Review* 45 (1973): 183–191.

Smith, Paul. *The Book of Nastier Legends.* London: Routledge and Kegan Paul, 1986. See p. 50.

Sones, Bill, and Rich Sones. "Loud drips can scare you to death." *Deseret News* (January 5, 2004), http://www.deseretnews.com/dn/view/0,1249,575041154,00.html

THE "DEATH" OF PAUL McCARTNEY

One of the most enduringly popular bands of the late twentieth century was undoubtedly the Liverpool group, The Beatles. Two of the four performers, John Lennon and Paul McCartney, achieved iconic status as singer-songwriters. John Lennon met an early violent death in New York; Paul McCartney, now in his 60s and a multimillionaire, still occasionally performs as a solo artist. However, a rampant rumor swept the United States in October 1969 that Paul was dead, and that evidence of this could be found in the Beatles' album, "Abbey Road."

Though strictly speaking this was a rumor rather than an urban legend, it is usually accepted as a legend, and the way it spread and developed reveals a great deal about the behavior of urban legends. It appeared quite suddenly, spread like wildfire among a group of like-minded people first in the United States then the United Kingdom and wherever there were Beatles fans. It invaded all media, and required active participation. Going in search of clues and sharing them among friends was a necessary part of believing and telling the legend. This aspect of the legend has been insightfully discussed by Donald Allport Bird and his colleagues, who call the story, "a self-deceiving game for multiple players." Bird also speaks of the role of advice columns in spreading urban legends (see Bird 1976; Bird, Holder, and Sears 1976).

Other useful resources are: Morgan and Tucker's entry in *Rumor!* (1984, 82–87), which prints contemporary illustrations; a note by the editors of *Folklore Forum*, which gives a list of press reports from October to November 1969 (Eds. 1969); a short bibliography of the legend in the informal British folklore magazine *Dear Mr Thoms* ("The Living Legend of the Death of Paul McCartney"); Tom McIver's informed article which looks at claims that hidden messages have been inserted into recordings and can be heard if the disc is played backward, among these a message proving that Paul McCartney is dead (McIver 1988); and Andru J. Reeve's *Turn Me On Dead Man* (2004).

Example

LONDON Oct 21—A spokesman for the Beatles said tonight that a rumor sweeping the United States that Paul McCartney was dead was "a load of old rubbish."

"We've been inundated by telephone calls from teenagers in the United States inquiring about the rumor," the spokesman for the company, Apple Corps, Ltd, said. He added that the 26-year-old Beatle was "alive and well in his home in St John's Wood," a quiet residential area in north west London.

"They won't take no for an answer when told Paul's alive and that someone has started something very stupid," the spokesman said. "We're all mystified by the rash of calls which started last Friday."

The callers seem to find evidence of Paul's death in the lyrics of recent songs by the Beatles," the spokesman said. "They say that if you play some of the songs at slower speed or in reverse, you can actually hear Paul say, 'I am dead.'" He added, "I don't know, I've never tried it."

"One caller asked why Paul wasn't wearing shoes on their newest album cover," he said, adding that the calls were becoming " a nuisance." He dismissed the rumor with the statement: "Paul McCartney is alive and well, and if he weren't he'd be the first to know about it" ("Beatle Spokesman Calls Rumor of McCartney's Death 'Rubbish'").

FURTHER READING

"Beatle Spokesman Calls Rumor of McCartney's Death 'Rubbish.'" *New York Times* (October 22, 1969): 8. Newspaper cutting in *Dear Mr Thoms* 34 (May 1994): 33.

Bird, Donald Allport. "A Theory for Folklore in Mass Media: Traditional Patterns in the Mass Media." *Southern Folklore Quarterly* 40 (1976): 285–305.

Bird, Donald Allport, Stephen C. Holder, and Diane Sears. "Walrus Is Greek for Corpse: Rumor and the Death of Paul McCartney." *Journal of Popular Culture* 10 (1976): 110–121.

"The Living Legend of the Death of Paul McCartney." *Dear Mr Thoms* 34 (May 1994): 32–35.

McIver, Tom. "Backward Masking, and Other Backward Thoughts About Music." *The Skeptical Inquirer* 13 (1988): 50–63.

Morgan, Hal, and Kerry Tucker. *Rumor!* Harmondsworth, UK: Penguin, 1984.

Oring, Elliott, Frank de Caro, and James R. Durham. "McCartney's Lyke Wake." *Folklore Forum* 2 (1969): 167–168.

Reeve, Andru J. *Turn Me On Dead Man: The Beatles and the "Paul-is-Dead" Hoax.* Bloomington, IN: Author House, 2004.

THE FAILED SUICIDE

Here is a legend that uses a theme from traditional folktales but adapts it to modern living and turns it into a dark comedy. The climax of several Norse and Celtic folktales is a bizarre series of accidents in which the protagonist dies three times over and thus a riddling prophecy is fulfilled. The modern stories are tragicomic tales that leave out the prophecy motif and concentrate on the bizarre multiple deaths. Typically they concern would-be suicides whose ludicrous failed attempts lead them to give up trying to die.

The earliest of these is a late nineteenth-century story from the *New York Herald* of May 1, 1896. The headlines tell that a woman "Made desperate by a lovers' quarrel" tried three different methods of suicide. First she took laudanum (a tincture of opium in alcohol), then, when this failed, she shot herself and set fire to her clothing. She was said to be "in a precarious condition" (Hodgson 2001, 72). Nearer our own time comes a report from the Reuters press agency about a couple from Zagreb who survived a suicide attempt that included poisoning by gas, sleeping pills, and a gunshot to the temple (via e-mail from Brian Chapman).

A more typical story, in that the bizarre multiple suicide is made to seem ridiculous and ends in abject failure, is the one reported in 1936 in the San Francisco *Mail* and picked up by Curtis MacDougall for his book *Hoaxes* (1958, 6). Our example is a slightly different version of this story and was originally reported in the late 1950s by Sir Sidney Smith (see Appendix).

Example

The story is that a highly pessimistic individual had determined to take his life, and wanted to make sure there would be none of the slip-ups he had read about. He decided that hanging would be an efficient method of self-destruction, and selected a tree with a stout branch overhanging a cliff, the sea being fifty feet below. This, he thought, would make a fitting and spectacular finish. In order to prevent any pain in the hanging process he procured himself a large dose of opium. Although the arrangements seemed fairly complete, he decided that to make sure of a successful result it would be a good idea to shoot himself as well. The noose adjusted, the poison taken, and the revolver cocked, he stepped over the cliff, and as he did so fired. The jerk of the rope altered his aim, and the bullet missed his head but cut partly through the rope. This broke with the jerk of the body, and he fell fifty feet into the sea below. There he swallowed a quantity of water, vomited the poison, and swam ashore a better and a wiser man (Simpson 1989, 3)

FURTHER READING

Brunvand, Jan Harold. *The Baby Train and other Lusty Legends*. New York: Norton, 1993. See pp. 86–87.

Hodgson, Barbara. *In The Arms of Morpheus*. Vancouver: Greystone Books, 2001.

MacDougall, Curtis D. *Hoaxes*. London: Macmillan, 1958.

Simpson, Jacqueline. "A Modern Tale of Fate." *Motif* 7 (February 1989): 3–4.

See: Dead Again; The Seemingly Dead Revive

THE FATAL CLEANING LADY

This story seems to have first surfaced in 1996 in an article in the *Cape Times* [South Africa] ("Cleaning up the Floors"). In only a short time it was widely spread by the Internet. It has also been spread by word of mouth as a humorous anecdote, and it has been used as an incident in "A Touch of Frost," a British detective series based on the novels of R. D. Wingfield (broadcast on January 15, 2001). Other variations on the same theme include the cleaning lady who unplugs a restaurant's deep-freeze and causes an outbreak of food poisoning, the cleaning lady who unplugs a computer and brings a government department to a standstill, and the company whose computers regularly crash at the same hour every day thanks to the secretary who pulls the plug on the server when she plugs in the kettle to make a cup of tea.

Example

The way I heard it was that nurses in some hospital in South Africa kept on finding a patient dead in the same room, in the same bed, every Friday morning. They could find no reason for the deaths, and were really upset and mystified. They checked the bed itself, they questioned the nurses, and they examined the air-conditioning system in case there was a bacterial infection—nothing.

Then somebody had the idea that they should mount a week-long 24-hour watch on that bed, and do you know what they discovered? Every Friday morning this cleaning lady would enter the room, plug her floor polisher into a socket by the bed, and zoom about polishing like crazy. Only problem was that she used the socket that the patient's life-support system was plugged into—took the life support plug out, attached the plug of her polisher, and zoomed off round the ward! Her machine was so loud she couldn't hear the patient screaming and moaning. Then when she finished the polishing, she'd plug the life-support machine back in and leave—totally unaware that she'd killed the patient! (Bennett Collection)

FURTHER READING

"Cleaning up the Floors." *FOAFtale News* 40/41 (December 1996): 21.

McClare, Kate. "Oops! Hospital Maid Accidentally Kills 12 Patients . . . by unplugging their life-support systems!" *Weekly World News* (July 9, 2002): 4.

Mikkelson, Barbara. "Polished Off." http://www.snopes.com/horrors/freakish/cleaner. htm

GRANDMA'S ASHES

It is amazing what can happen to cremated remains. News reports from Canada, America, and the United Kingdom tell how "Potato-Chip Can Found in Place of Woman's Remains in Mausoleum" (*Houston Chronicle* June 10, 2005), how remains are stored in a package and mistaken for drugs, anthrax, or other dangerous substances, or ground up and put into an hourglass (Starnes 1997), or sewn into a widow's breast implants (*Sydney Morning Herald* November 5, 2001).

The story of "Grandma's Ashes" (which is sometimes called "A Mix-Up in the Mail") gives an even more bizarre twist to this gruesome catalogue by adding an "accidental cannibalism" theme. It tells what happens when cremated remains are eaten or drunk in error. This happens when the ashes are mistaken for instant tea or coffee, cake mix, dietary products, or special spices, as in the examples below.

Stories like this have been traveling the world for decades, maybe for much longer. An eighteenth-century chapbook, "The Constant, but Unhappy, Lovers," tells how a dying soldier wrote a letter to his love in his own blood and ordered his servant to bake his heart to a powder after his death, wrap it all up with a bracelet she had given him, and deliver the package. The lady's jealous husband ground the whole lot up and stirred it into her tea. She drank it and took to her bed and died (Ashton 1882, 442).

Examples

1. Grandma had gone out to spend Christmas with her cousins who lived in the Far East. She had not seen them for several years and was very excited about the trip.

They had always been very kind to her and each Christmas they used to send a present of a jar of special spices to go in the Christmas cake her daughter made.

About two weeks before Christmas, a small airmail parcel arrived from the Far East. It had been posted on 1 December and contained what appeared to be the special spices for the Christmas cake. There was no note with it, nor, surprisingly, any Christmas card. Not wanting to delay any longer, the daughter got on with the baking and produced a magnificent cake for the Christmas festivities.

It was the day after Boxing Day that a letter arrived from the cousins in the Far East. Also dated 1 December, it expressed how sorry they were to have to break the news of Grandma's death—the excitement had been too much for her. They also wrote that, because of all the arrangements that had had to be made for the cremation, they would not have time to send over the special spices for the Christmas cake this year. However, they had airmailed Grandma's ashes home and they should arrive shortly. (Smith 1983, 106)

2. The instant coffee a group of friends drank as they tried to sober up after a night out on the tiles tasted a bit odd.

Soon after, they found out why—when one of their companions told them: "That was no coffee . . . that was my grandfather's ashes." (*Daily Mail* Staff)

FURTHER READING

Ashton, John. *Chap-Books of the Eighteenth Century*. London: Chatto and Windus, 1882.

Daily Mail Staff. "You Drank my Granddad." *Daily Mail* [UK] (November 19, 2004). http://www.thisislondon.co.uk/news/articles/14836912?source=Daily%20Mail

Newall, Venetia. "Folklore and Cremation." *Folklore* 96 (1985): 139–155.

Smith, Paul. *The Book of Nasty Legends*. London: Routledge and Kegan Paul, 1983.

Starnes, Richard. "Joker Plans Afterlife As Egg-Timer." *The Ottawa Citizen* [Canada] (July 16, 1997): A14.

See: The Baby Roast; The Corpse in the Cask; The Stolen Specimen

THE HALLOWEEN SADIST

During the 1970s and into the 1980s, America was riven by fears about deviants who supposedly maliciously tampered with the little gifts given to trick or treaters at Halloween. Parents were warned to check any treats given to their children to make sure they contained no poison, or drugs, or razor blades, or needles. This was in addition to routine warnings about inflammable costumes, masks which impair vision, and other things that might cause accidents. In California (in 1971) and New Jersey (in 1982) laws were passed designed to prevent Halloween sadism; schools trained children to inspect their treats; parents restricted their children's trick or treating or arranged indoor parties instead; and at least one hospital initiated a program of X-raying Halloween candy. Another indication of the level of concern is that in 1985, 105 students at California State University Fresno wrote essays for an upper division writing exam advocating the abolition of the holiday, and of these 90 percent cited Halloween sadism in support of their opinion (Best and Horiuchi 1996, 114).

In 1985, Joel Best a leading authority on popular beliefs about violence against children, and a colleague Gerald T. Horiuchi, undertook a survey with a colleague into newspaper reports of Halloween sadism in *The New York Times*, *Chicago Tribune*, *Los Angeles Times*, and *Fresno Bee* between the years 1958 and 1984. In spite of claims that "hundreds" of children had died and that Halloween was a major risk to children, they found only 76 reports of tampered treats during this 27-year period, which indicates that such stories circulated mainly by word of mouth and other informal channels. The majority of the stories Best found (52) came in two surges. Only nineteen stories were reported in the ten years from 1958 to 1968, then, in the first peak of interest, there were 31 stories in the three years 1969–1971. In 1972 the number of reports dropped suddenly to only one. There were nine reports in the four years 1973–1977, and none in the years 1977/1978 or 1980. Then another surge came in 1981/1982 with 21 stories in the press. Only two of these stories were genuine occurrences, and in both cases the children had been poisoned by family members, not by strangers. No other deaths were recorded and only very minor injuries in a handful of cases. After careful checking, Best and Horiuchi concluded that the vast majority of the 76 reports were unfounded and probably had never happened at all (Best and Horiuchi 1996, 116–117).

The earliest folkloristic discussion of Halloween sadists is that by folklorist Sylvia Grider, who interviewed the father of 8-year-old Timothy O'Bryan who died from a poisoned Halloween treat in 1974 (the father was convicted of the poisoning). Grider sees a two-fold relationship between this case and legends about tampered treats. Though beliefs about tampered treats circulated from at least the late 1940s, she says, they were primarily part of the oral tradition of children, not parents, journalists, and legislators. But, by so publicly acting out these traditional beliefs, Timothy O'Bryan's father brought the legend into the mainstream of American consciousness where it became institutionalized by the press. One of the reasons it could thrive so well was that it played to existing cultural fears—a distrust of old customs and traditions, a deep-rooted fear of strangers, and ambivalence toward random violence (Grider 1984, 132). Best and Horiuchi suggest that another reason might have been that the concept of the Halloween sadist combined two themes already established in urban legend, fears about threats to children and fears about contaminated food (Best and Horiuchi 1996, 118–122).

The scare was over by the early 1990s. A report on Halloween 1993 in *FOAFtale News* quoted an announcement by hospitals in Harrisburg, PA, saying that they would no longer X-ray Halloween candy and that the check should be a parental responsibility. Hospitals in the Washington, DC area would continue to X-ray Halloween candy and fruit "as usual," but pointed out that evidence of tampering had been found only in one case (a needle in a candy bar in 1988) and, even so, no arrest had followed; the injuries they treated at Halloween were caused by automobiles not candy. A local mother, who helped check candy at a YMCA party, confessed that it was almost like a superstitious rite "if you don't check, something happens," but in ten years, she said, "we've never found anything, and we don't know anyone who has ever found anything." The National Confectioner's Association claimed that no incident of candy-tampering had ever been verified except the 1974 O'Bryan case ("Tampered Treats").

Our example below consists of extracts from newspaper reports 1970–1983 discussed by Best and Horiuchi (1996, 113–114).

Examples

... that plump red apple that Junior gets from a kindly old woman down the block ... may have a razor blade hidden inside (*New York Times* 1970).

If this year's Halloween follows form, a few children will return home with something more than an upset tummy: in recent years, several children have died and hundreds have narrowly escaped injury from razor blades, sewing needles and shards of glass purposefully put into their goodies by adults. (*Newsweek* 1975)

It's Halloween again and time to remind you that . . . [s]omebody's child will become violently ill or die after eating poisoned candy or an apple containing a razor blade (Van Buren 1983 ["Dear Abby" column *Fresno Bee*])

FURTHER READING

Best, Joel. *Threatened Children: Rhetoric and Concern about Child Victims*. Chicago: University of Chicago Press, 1990. See pp. 131–150.

Best, Joel, and Gerald T. Horiuchi. "The Razor Blade in the Apple: The Social Construction of Urban Legends." *Social Problems* 32.5 (1985): 488–499. Reprinted in *Contemporary Legend: A Reader*. Compiled by Gillian Bennett and Paul Smith. New York: Garland, 1996, 113–131.

Grider, Sylvia. "The Razor Blades in the Apples Syndrome." *Perspectives on Contemporary Legend: Proceedings of the Conference on Contemporary Legend, Sheffield, July 1982*. Ed. Paul Smith. Cectal Conference Papers Series. Sheffield: CECTAL, 1984, pp. 128–140.

"Tampered Treats." "Just In!" column. *FOAFtale News*, 32 (February 1994): 7.

See: Fingers in Take-Out Meals; Kentucky Fried Rat; The Mouse in the Coca-Cola Bottle; The Poisoned Dress

KILLER CLOWNS

Curious incidents of mass panic among schoolchildren broke out in locations across America during the early years of the 1980s, then again in 1985. In 1991/1992 there were similar panics in the United Kingdom and again in the United States. These died down, but reappeared in the United Kingdom and Ireland in 1995. One of the more puzzling elements in these scares was that the panics were caused by fear of characters thought by adults to be endearing, funny, and child-friendly—clowns. The children were convinced that "bad clowns" were patrolling the streets near their schools in vans, giving out candy, and getting ready to do them some dreadful (but unspecified) harm.

These panics resembled similar scares that broke out in various places in the mid-1990s about child abductions. For example, people dressed as clowns were featured in rumors and panics about children being abducted for their organs in Central America; reports were circulating in Britain about bogus social workers; in Belgium there were rumors of "phantom photographers"; and in Italy rumors spread about gypsy women trying to catch children and hide them under their skirts (Bennett 2005, 188–246). But the "Killer Clowns" panics were not quite the same. What made them different was that they were caused by an urban legend that circulated exclusively among children by word of mouth.

The first documented outbreak began in Boston, MA, then spread through New England and on to the Midwest in 1981. Folklorist and "Fortean" Loren Coleman reported widespread alarm among children about clowns supposedly driving vans of various colors and wielding knives, swords, or firearms (Coleman 1983, 211–217). A briefer scare surfaced in Phoenix, Arizona in 1985, died down, then resurfaced in Chicago and New Jersey in 1991 (Brunvand 2001, 314–315).

The British scare as it related to the city of Glasgow (Scotland) was closely monitored by folklorists and psychologists Sandy Hobbs and David Cornwell in the informal folklore magazine *Dear Mr Thoms*. Their first report was of an intense scare in September/October of 1991 in which, not only children, but parents, schools, the press, and the police became involved. Except in one story where the clowns were supposed to be traveling round in police cars and another where the vehicle was said to be an ice-cream van, in Glasgow it was nearly always a blue van that the threatening people were supposed to be driving.

As in the United States, though clowns were the main "baddies," there were accounts of threatening people wearing Bart Simpson or Ronald McDonald masks or dressed as monkeys, turtles, gypsies, or policemen. The threat these bad people posed was generally not defined. There were a small handful of accounts where the candy the clowns were handing out was supposed to be drugged, or rape was hinted at, or facial cuts such as made by "Smiley Gangs" were supposedly inflicted, or where the children said they would be chopped up and put in a deep-freeze and eaten for lunch. However, in most cases the children didn't know why they were supposed to be afraid of the clowns; they just said they were "bad" clowns. Nevertheless, Glasgow children became so fearful that a group of about twelve children at one school threw stones at two workmen who got out of a van near the school, and in other instances children became hysterical if they saw a van or heard a helicopter (Cornwell and Hobbs 1992, 7). The scare seems to have been over as quickly as it blew up; by November the story had dropped out of the press, and by June 1992, though many parents still remembered the panic, it was recalled as an event from the past (Cornwell and Hobbs 1993, 11). At Halloween 1994, however, it resurfaced in an area of Scotland to the southwest of Glasgow (Cornwell and Hobbs 1995).

Example

Yesterday my child was reluctant to go to school and complained of a slight tummy ache. On previous occasions where that's happened, she's gone to school and been fine afterwards. So she went to school as normal. On the way to school in the car, she happened to mention that a friend of hers had told her the previous day that there had been someone going round dressed in a clown's outfit giving sweets [candy] to children [. . .]

A rumour was going round—someone, a person or people, dressed in a clown's outfit, going round in a blue van, giving sweets to children . . . I telephoned the headmaster who said that the rumour was right round the school . . . they had asked five parents to come at the interval into the playground and they had also contacted the . . . police. He . . . thought they had calmed the kids down but at lunchtime two girls had . . . seen the local newspaper with a picture of a clown on the front page. It was in fact a promotional item. The two girls had returned to school in a state he described as near hysterical.

When I . . . went to pick the kids up from school that evening, my son who is eleven, my daughter who is eight . . . told me that in fact there were three individuals that were going round, one with a Bart Simpson mask, one with a Ronald McDonald mask, and one with a turtle mask. They were driving around in a van that was disguised as a police van, throwing out bags of sweets to children, and that in fact the sweets were drugged. And my son became quite irate, quite distressed when it was put to him that really there was very little basis for that story. (Cornwell and Hobbs 1992, 3–4. From a recorded interview September 1991)

FURTHER READING

Bennett, Gillian. *Bodies: Sex, Violence, Disease and Death in Contemporary Legend.* Jackson, MI: University Press of Mississippi, 2005.

Brunvand, Jan Harold. *Encyclopedia of Urban Legends.* New York: Norton, 2001.

Coleman, Loren. *Mysterious America.* London: Faber and Faber, 1983.

Cornwell, David, and Sandy Hobbs. "The Clowns." *Dear Mr Thoms* 24 (January 1992): 1–9.

———. "Up-Date: Abductions. (1) The Clowns: Further Notes." *Dear Mr Thoms* 31 (July 1993): 9–13.

———. "The Clowns: A Further Update." *Letters to Ambrose Merton* 1 (February 1995): 21–22.

See: Drugged Children; The Halloween Sadist; Smiley Gangs

THE MURDERED SON

This story, sometimes known as "The Tragic Mistake" or "The Tragic Homecoming," was born of war and social upheaval, and has had a documented history of almost 400 years. It was circulating in broadsides on the streets of Paris and London in 1618 and has been in continuous transmission from then until at least the 1950s. It has appeared in newspapers, ballads, street literature, plays, and poems throughout Europe and the United States, as well as spreading via the oral tradition in places as far apart as the former Czechoslovakia and Missouri, Norway and Italy. The story was the theme of "The Ballad of Billie Potts" written by the first American Poet Laureate, Robert Penn Warren, and set in rural Kentucky (Warren 1944, 271–284). It was featured in a column written by *New Yorker* journalist Alexander Woollcott in one of the earliest discussions of urban legend (Woollcott 1931). It also appeared in at least twenty European plays from the mid-eighteenth century to the mid-twentieth, including Albert Camus' dark classic of 1944, *Le Malentendu* (the Misunderstanding) (Bennett 2005, 176–183). Its most recent appearances have been in the late 1940s in the United States and Germany. It seems to be dormant at present, but its incredibly long and diverse history, its horror and perennial themes, make it a classic urban legend.

The most comprehensive survey of the legend is Maria Kosko's French-language study (1966); also useful are Chapter 4 of Gillian Bennett's *Bodies* (2005, 142–183), Véronique Campion-Vincent's survey article (1998), and for German treatments of the theme, Chapter 3 of Tom Cheeseman's *The Shocking Ballad Picture Show* (1994, 85–118). American texts can be found in Botkin (1955, 209–212), Dorson (1949), Randolph (1951), and Woollcott (1931).

Example

Mr Alexander Bock had eighteen year old son, little farm—mortgaged. Ten years after, son come home, want to get surprise for his parents. They sent him to America to make money to pay off the mortgage. He comes back with money as a surprise. He comes to the inn and meets old friends, his godfather, mayor of the village, Csanok. Godfather didn't recognize him, now 28, with mustache, whiskers. But when boy tell him, he was awful glad; they drink together. Then Mr Bock invite him to see his parents in the morning, have a big party.

Alexander calls on them, asks for room. They don't recognize him. He asks if his money will be safe. "Oh, yes." That night mother and father can't sleep, thinking of all that money. They get up, cut his throat, bury him in the manure pile. But shepherd boy behind store see everything.

Next morning the godfather comes over, "Where's Alexander?"

"Haven't seen him."

"Why he went to see you last night. I had wine with him at the inn. He was bringing money to surprise you."

Mother faints. Father says, "No, we didn't see anybody."

Chief of police comes around to investigate. He offers shepherd boy an apple. "Did you see anything?" He tells. (Dorson 1949)

FURTHER READING

Bennett, Gillian. *Bodies: Sex, Violence, Disease, and Death in Contemporary Legend.* Jackson, MI: University Press of Mississippi, 2005.

Botkin, B. A. *A Treasury of Mississippi River Folklore.* New York: Crown 1955,

Campion-Vincent, Véronique. "The Tragic Mistake: Transformations of a Traditional Narrative." *ARV* 54 (1998): 64–79.

Cheeseman, Tom. *The Shocking Ballad Picture Show.* Oxford and Providence, USA: Berg, 1994.

Dorson, Richard M. "Polish Tales from Joe Woods." *Western Folklore* 8 (1949): 131–145.

Kosko, Maria. *Le Fils Assassiné (AT 939a): Étude d'un thème légendaire.* Helsinki: Suomalainen Tiedeakatemia. Academia Scientarum Fennica, 1966.

Randolph, Vance. "Bedtime Stories from Missouri." *Western Folklore* 10 (1951): 1–10.

Warren, Robert Penn. *Selected Poems 1923–1943.* New York: Harcourt Brace and Co, 1944.

Woollcott, Alexander. "Folk-Lore." "Shouts and Murmurs" column. *The New Yorker* (December 12, 1931): 36.

THE SEEMINGLY DEAD REVIVE

Alongside newspaper reports of patients who suddenly recover from a coma or a persistent vegetative state after lying for a long period in a death-like trance, there are others, more or less unverifiable, about "corpses" who have revived at the very last minute to the horror, shock, or delight of onlookers. These themes are shaped into stories that may be either humorous or horrific, a lesson in the workings of fate and chance, or an example of someone getting his "just deserts." These stories are commonplace as fillers in newspapers and in compilations of "weird happenings"; they are found worldwide and needless to say, they are not new.

British medical historian, Douglas Guthrie, records three historical cases in his 1945 *History of Medicine*, which fall somewhere between fact and folklore.

The first is connected to Scottish anatomist Alexander Munro (1697–1767) and tells how a fight broke out in an Edinburgh hospital between medical students and the family of a woman criminal who had just been executed. The students claimed the corpse for dissection, the family wanted to bury it. While they were fighting, the corpse came to life, escaped into the street and lived for many years afterwards. Guthrie's second story is about "Half-Hanged Maggie Dickson" who returned to life as her funeral procession was taking her home for burial "to the consternation of the bearers and the delight of the mourners" (Guthrie 1945, 227–228). Guthrie's third story is about the great anatomist Vesalius (1514–1564). Vesalius died during a pilgrimage to Jerusalem, and rumor had it that the reason he was on the pilgrimage was that a "corpse" he had been dissecting came to life on the dissecting table and died for real as the result of the dissection (Guthrie 1945, 139).

A large number of such tales have been collected together by Paul Sieveking, coeditor of *Fortean Times* in articles entitled "Resurrections" and "Cheating the Grim Reaper" (Sieveking 1992 and 1987 respectively), and by historian of medical curiosities Jan Bondeson.

Bondeson points out that such stories grew out of fears of premature burial. Several popular legends on "The Seemingly Dead Revive" theme were going the rounds in the 1700s and by the early 1800s, "books about apparently dead people coming to life were eagerly read by all and sundry" (Bondeson 1997, 105). The oldest of these nineteenth-century stories, he says, is the story of the lady and the ring. It tells how a rich lady died suddenly and was buried in her best clothes and all her jewelry including a large gold ring. In the night a servant digs up the coffin to steal the ring; he cannot get it off her finger, so begins to hack at the finger. The pain brings the lady round, and she is reunited with her husband. There are two possible endings to this yarn. In one, the servant is excused his attempted theft and given a reward: in the other, he is struck dead with terror when the "corpse" comes back to life.

An eighteenth-century tale tells how a lecherous monk stops at an inn and is asked to watch over the corpse of the innkeeper's beautiful daughter who had died the previous day. At the sight of her the monk "forgot the sanctity of his vows and took liberties with the corpse." The monk leaves, and the girl comes back to life. Nine months later, the monk returns to the inn and sees the girl with an infant in her arms. He casts off his monkish robe, renounces his vows, confesses himself the father of the child and offers to marry the girl. The parents are delighted. It is not said what the girl thought of the proposal (Bondeson 1997, 107). This has a modern counterpart in a story from Bucharest (Romania), where an apparently dead girl is revived by the horror of a sexual assault. Again, this story has a happy ending—for the rapist (Klintberg 1992. See our first example).

Another story from a book of 1816 tells the humorous tale of an English squire, Sir Hugh Ackland. Sir Hugh died from a fever, and was laid out, and two servants were set to watch over the corpse. Remembering how much Sir Hugh had liked brandy, they poured out a glass and tipped it down the dead man's throat. He immediately came to life, finished the brandy, and lived for several years. The servants were given a handsome reward (Bondeson 1997, 109). Our second example is a modern story from Italy with a similar sort of ending.

These are not the only old stories with modern equivalents. Guthrie's story about Vesalius is paralleled by stories in British newspapers and magazines, 1988–1996. In one story a corpse revives in a New York mortuary and grasps the throat of the pathologist who was dissecting him; the doctor dies of shock. In another, two doctors die of shock when a "corpse" suddenly sits up and bursts into a drinking song (Bondeson 2001, 273).

In compilations of scary tales and legends, the theme is often treated in a much more sentimental way, and the story is shaped into an example of faithful love and marvelous intuition. Daniel Cohen, for example, has such a story in his 1983 compilation, *Southern Fried Rat*. It tells how an epidemic of typhoid fever struck a small Louisiana town and a young woman fell deathly ill. Her brother, who was devoted to her, was away at the time, was called back to her funeral, but something told him she was not dead. He arrived at the cemetery just as the gravediggers were closing up the grave. He begged them to open the coffin for one last look at his sister. As he looked, the corpse began to move and eventually stepped out of the coffin. She had not been dead at all, but in a coma. If the brother had not heeded his intuition and had not returned in the nick of time, she would have been buried alive. As it was, she lived for many years, and raised a large family (Cohen 1983, 86–88).

Examples

1. Bucharest (Reuter): A Romanian girl who had been declared dead woke up in the mortuary, when a watchman started to assault what he believed was a corpse, a Romanian paper reported yesterday. The girl had taken an overdose of sleeping pills and alcohol. The watchman tried to rape her before preparing her body for autopsy. When the girl suddenly rose, he fainted.

The weekly *Expres Magazin* quotes a doctor in northern Romania for this bizarre story. He tells that the heart of the 18-year-old girl stopped beating after she had taken an overdose of medicine, having had a quarrel with her boyfriend. Doctors tried in vain to revive her and presumed that she was dead. The watchman was arrested, according to the paper. But the girl's parents have interceded on behalf of the 23-year-old necrophiliac, since their daughter "would have been dead for ever, if it had not been for the rape" (Klintberg 1992. Translating from *Det Fri Aktuelt* [Copenhagen] [January 311992]: 10.)

2. During a burial service in Longano, northern Italy, the "deceased," Ernesto Quirino, 60, opened his eyes, looked round in horror, leapt out of the coffin and ran . . . The same scenario played out in Guastalla, central Italy in September 1990. Mourners praying at the open coffin of Rubens Incerti, 78, screamed in terror as he sat up, clambered out and fled. He was found having a stiff drink at a table laid for his own wake. (Sieveking 1992, 37)

FURTHER READING

Bondeson, Jan. *A Cabinet of Medical Curiosities.* Ithaca, NY: Cornell University Press, 1997.

———. *Buried Alive.* New York: Norton, 2001.

Cohen, Daniel. *Southern Fried Rat and Other Gruesome Tales.* New York: M. Evans and Company, 1983.

Guthrie, Douglas. *A History of Medicine.* London: Thomas Nelson and Sons, 1945.

Klintberg, Bengt af. "Rape Wakes Seemingly Dead." *Dear Mr Thoms* 25 (April 1992): 28–29.

Sieveking, Paul. "Cheating the Grim Reaper." *Fortean Times* 49 (1987): 55–60.

———. "Resurrections." *Fortean Times* 63 (1992): 36–38.

See: Dead Again

THE STOLEN CORPSE

Sometimes known as "The Runaway Grandmother" or "The Granny on the Roof Rack," this story is one of the best-known urban legends. It has been repeatedly reported since the 1950s from Canada and the United States and from numerous European countries (England, Ireland, France, Sweden, Denmark, Italy, Spain, Germany, Poland, and the former Yugoslavia). It has also surfaced in Australia, Mexico, Nigeria, Namibia, and the Bahamas. It is a genuine international tale with more than 200 variants reported worldwide (Dégh 2001,

64–66, 197). Recently similar events have been told as news from the Ukraine, and from Iraq, and there was a report in 2003 of a man who drove from South Carolina to Ottawa with the dead body of his mother-in-law on the backseat of his car. This last report recalls the experience of the Joad family in John Steinbeck's 1939 novel *The Grapes of Wrath*, when they crossed the Arizona–California border with "Gramma" dead beside Ma Joad. The story has also featured in Roger Peyrefitte's novel, *Diplomatic Conclusions* (1954), and in a Hitchcock film, "The Diplomatic Corpse" (1958).

The legend is probably older than that: Swedish folklorist Bengt af Klintberg has found a report from a Danish journalist that tells how a Swede and a Dane were fleeing from Paris (France) as Hitler's troops advanced on that city; when the Dane's mother-in-law died, they put her body in a mahogany tea chest on the roof-rack. The tea chest was stolen (Klintberg 1989, 83). A similar wartime story was noted by British folklorist Katharine Briggs in her mammoth folk tale collection. Her story is set during the German occupation of France and tells how the grandma of a refugee family died and was rolled up in a Persian carpet and put on the roof-rack. When they reached a port (the story does not say which one), they left the car to enquire about a boat to take them over the English Channel to safety, but when they got back they found the carpet, and Grandma, gone (Briggs 1991, Part B, 769–771).

Example

I heard this as a repetitive story that was going around and appeared in so many areas, and when I heard it first years ago they were touring in France, in Northern France, and their Granny died and they didn't know what to do about it because they didn't want to bury her there and they couldn't get back to England very quickly, so they wrapped her up in a blanket and put her on the roof rack, and while they were having lunch later on, the car was stolen and Granny with it, and they were never, ever, recovered. (Bennett Collection)

FURTHER READING

Briggs, Katharine M. A *Dictionary of British Folk-Tales in the English Language*. 2 vols. London: Routledge and Kegan Paul, 1991. First published 1970/1971.

Dégh, Linda. *Legend and Belief*. Bloomington, IN: Indiana University Press, 2001.

Doyle, Charles Clay. "Roaming Cannibals and Vanishing Corpses." *Indiana Folklore* 11 (1978): 133–139.

Klintberg, Bengt af. "Legends Today." *Nordic Folklore: Recent Studies.* Ed. Reimund Kvideland and Henning K. Sehmsdorf in collaboration with Elizabeth Simpson. Bloomington, IN: Indiana University Press, 1989, pp. 70–89.

Schmidt, Sigrid. "Coffins on Cars—Three Namibian Adventures: Some Remarks on the Relationship of Contemporary Legends and Jests." *Contemporary Legend* new series 3 (2000): 45–63.

Scott, Bill. *Complete Book of Australian Folklore.* Sydney: Lansdowne, 1981. See pp. 368–369.

See: The Cat in the Package

THEY ARE NOT DEAD

In the final part of Peter Jackson's award-winning film adaptation of J. R. R. Tolkien's epic trilogy *The Lord of the Rings* (2003), Aragorn summons an army of ghosts to follow him and help defeat the evil Sauron. The spectres have lain under a hill for centuries waiting for such a summons; their response to Aragorn's call will purge them of the treachery they committed during their lifetimes.

This is one of many variations on a traditional theme, that of the undead waiting for some final summons which will come in civilization's hour of need. Its most common expression is the idea that a "culture hero" is not dead but lies hidden somewhere ready to return when all other hope is lost. Probably the best-known example is King Arthur who, folklore tells us, is lying on the now-vanished Isle of Avalon waiting to resume his kingship and establish a new Golden Age in a new Camelot.

The concept of "Camelot," and of "the once and future king," found its expression in the twentieth century in the folklore surrounding the death of President John F. Kennedy in November 1963. "Suddenly," one commentator wrote, "the dead Kennedy became what he had been for relatively few in life—the hope for the future, the promise of advancement for the underdog, the notion of grace and magic, the hero, the prince of youth . . ." (Edwards 1984, 413)—in other words, a culture hero. No surprise, then, to find a burgeoning folklore surrounding his death. According to Bruce A. Rosenberg's concise and informative essay "Kennedy in Camelot": "Hardly had the President's remains been buried when the rumor came alive that he was not really dead, but 'only' critically wounded and kept under intensive care away from [his] exhausting responsibilities" (Rosenberg 1976, 52). In some accounts he was secreted away in a persistent vegetative state in Bethesda Naval Hospital, or at Camp David, or on a remote island provided by Jacqueline Kennedy's next husband Aristotle Onassis, or in Parkland Memorial Hospital, Dallas, Texas. The evidence for the latter assertion, according to *Time* magazine, was that Mrs Kennedy had visited the grave of her husband only five times but had called at the Dallas hospital 340 times.

The stories circulated orally as well as in the press, and were picked up by folklore magazines in 1969 and followed through to December 1971 (see Eds. 1969, September 1971, and December 1971; F. de C. and E. L. O. 1969; "New Kennedy Lore"). Our first example below is taken from one of these brief research notes.

Elizabeth Bird followed the "Kennedy is Alive" story through the American tabloid press from 1971 to 1984. She reported, for example, that the *Sun* newspaper (July 3, 1984) claimed that the President had been reincarnated in a 7-year-old German boy, and that psychics could communicate with him through the person of this boy. A month later the *National Examiner* (August 4, 1984) claimed that a "world-respected parapsychologist and professor of antiquities" in India had discovered a 10-year-old girl who "had lived before as President Kennedy." One report Bird quotes is from the *Weekly World News* (August 21, 1990). The source is purportedly the account of a Polish neurosurgeon who was attending Kennedy in a secret location in Poland to which the President had been spirited away to prevent a second attack on his life. Though paralyzed, Kennedy was said to be "lucid" and advising subsequent Presidents (Johnson, Nixon, Ford, Carter, Reagan, and [George] Bush) on affairs of state (Bird 1992, 175–177).

The other "King" supposedly still alive is, of course, Elvis Presley. Presley died in 1977, yet in the spring and summer of 1988 the tabloid press, radio, and TV talk shows, gossip, and conversation were all buzzing with speculation that he hadn't "really" died at all but had faked his death. Among the "evidence" for this belief were friends' comments that the corpse looked like a wax dummy, that some of the mourners wore loud clothing such as Hawaiian shirts, that somebody was seen removing a ring from Elvis' finger during the committal service, that his middle name "Aron" had been misspelt on his tombstone, and that "hundreds" of fans had seen him since his death (at a Rolling Stones concert, at a Burger King at Kalamazoo, shopping in Michigan, buying gas in Tennessee) (see The National Insecurity Council 1992, 75–80). So Elvis was said to be actually alive and well, living as a hermit in the backwoods, or traveling the world unrecognizable in a beard and glasses.

The reasons given for Elvis to fake his own death vary. One theory espoused by the *National Inquirer* is that Elvis was caught up in an FBI scheme to bust a Mafia ring called the "Fraternity." The scheme was only partially successful. Several mobsters escaped, leaving Presley vulnerable. His death was faked by the FBI as a way of protecting him. A more common explanation is that he faked his death himself to avoid the intolerable glare of celebrity.

There are other reasonably modern stories asserting that "they are not dead." In an essay of 1927, the President of the (British) Folklore Society looked at this theme as an example of the similarity of ancient and modern folklore, alongside his nine historical examples listing seven from his own time. Many of these stories related to heroes of World War I—for example, between 1918 and 1921 it was believed in the United Kingdom that inspirational British army officer, Lord Kitchener, had not been killed but was a prisoner in Germany, or had come again driving the German armies before him under an assumed name (Wright 1927, 27–28). Rumors and stories from World War II centered on President Franklin D. Roosevelt, as in the third of our examples below.

Among other culture heroes supposed not to have really died at the time their death was announced are Charlemagne, Alexander the Great, Che Guevara, Barbarossa, and Abraham Lincoln; among celebrities, there are Jim Morrison, Bruce Lee, Buddy Holly, Marilyn Monroe, James Dean, and Oscar Wilde; and among counter-heroes are the Roman Emperor Nero, Adolph Hitler, and former Soviet leader Leonid Brezhnev.

Examples

1. Folklore after J.F.K.'s assassination, perhaps spurred on by a rage of controversy over the murder "plot," and certainly fed by the existing Kennedy mystique, centered around the "myth" of the fallen hero who in reality still lives. John Kennedy, however, was not asleep in a cave awaiting return in time of need, but was existing in a vegetable-like state, in Parkland Hospital or on a Greek island, presumably awaiting a more prosaic end. ("New Kennedy Lore")

2. According to Gallup Canada, Inc, a poll conducted February 8-11, 1989, indicated that 10% of Canadians are not convinced that Elvis Presley has died. Half of this group is uncertain whether he is alive or dead, and the rest (5% of the total) is certain the King is alive. Sex and age seemed to have little to do with the distribution of the belief, but residents of the eastern regions were much more likely to believe that Elvis was living. 15% of Quebecers and 14%

of Atlantic Canadians stated either that he had definitely not died or that they were unsure. ("Elvis Watch")

3. "I remember now that in the summer of 1945 I learned with some surprise and some amusement that there was considerable speculation about the cause of death and even some speculation as to whether the late President [Franklin. D. Roosevelt] was even dead at all. Probably the wildest story of all was that President Roosevelt and Adolph Hitler were hiding out together . . . in South America I believe, and that when they had all their arrangements made, they would return and by surprise take over the whole world. (Baughman 1947)

FURTHER READING

Baughman, Ernest W. "About the Death of President Roosevelt." *Hoosier Folklore* 6.3 (1947): 111–112.

Bird, S. Elizabeth. *For Enquiring Minds: A Cultural Study of Supermarket Tabloids.* Knoxville: University of Tennessee Press, 1992. See pp. 172–193.

Eds. "Notes for Queries." *Folklore Forum* 2 (1969): 82, 76.

Eds. "Notes for Queries." *Folklore Forum* 4.5 (September 1971): 126.

Eds. "Notes for Queries." *Folklore Forum* 4.6 (December 1971): 151.

Edwards, O. D. "Remembering the Kennedys." *Journal of American Studies* 18 (1984): 405–423.

"Elvis Watch." "Just In!" column. *FOAFtale News* 14 (June 1989): 4.

F. de C., and E. L. O. [Frank de Caro and Elliott Oring]. "J.F.K. Is Alive: A Modern Legend." *Folklore Forum* 2 (1969): 54–55.

Goss, Michael. "The (Urban) Legendary Elvis." *Magonia* 31 (November 1988): 6–10.

Moody, Raymond A. Jr. *Elvis after Life.* New York: Bantam Books, 1987.

The National Insecurity Council. *It's A Conspiracy!* Berkeley, CA: Earth Works Press, 1992.

"The New Immortals." *Fortean Times* 65 (October/November 1992): 58, 87.

"New Kennedy Lore." *Folklore Forum* 3.2 (March 1970): 65, 71.

Rosenberg, Bruce A. "Kennedy in Camelot: The Arthurian Legend in America." *Western Folklore* 36 (1976): 52–59.

Wright, A. R. Presidential Address: "The Folklore of the Past and Present." *Folk-Lore* 38 (1927): 13–39.

See: The "Death" of Paul McCartney

URBAN CANNIBALS AND HUMAN SAUSAGE FACTORIES

A wartime legend that was widely known and transmitted in Berlin in the summer of 1946 tells how, when all the city was starving, a young woman was asked to help a blind stranger she met in the street by delivering a letter to an address in the city. She happened to glance back and saw the "blind" man speeding along the street with his cane under his arm, so she decided not to deliver the letter. This proved to be a wise choice, because the house was full of butchered human corpses and the letter would have made her the latest victim of a gang selling human meat to hungry citizens. This story was first told in the *New Yorker* in July of 1946, and was made the subject of a case study in Gordon Allport and Leo Postman's well-known book *The Psychology of Rumor* (Allport and Postman 1947, 201–204). An abbreviated version of this story, sent to a British folklore magazine as recently as 2000, forms our first example below. Other versions of this story have been collected from Germany, France, and Sweden. The Swedish version is slightly different. The scene is still Berlin in the immediate postwar period, but the victims are said to be orphans and the message is "Here is the veal" (Campion-Vincent and Renard 1992, 95–98) (For a virtually identical plot with a slightly different punch line and context consult our discussion of "White Slavers" p. 41).

The *New Yorker* writer plainly recognized the story as what we now call an urban legend: "This story is pure myth," he says. "Yet all the Germans I know in Berlin, as well as a number of others I have questioned, have heard it, and ninety-five percent of them have believed it. Quite frequently, some man I've discussed the story with has given me a hint . . . that he was personally acquainted with the young woman who so narrowly escaped being sold by the pound" (Allport and Postman 1947, 202).

There are many more nineteenth-century examples of people unwittingly eating human flesh. These include, from Europe: a French place-name legend about a pastry-cook whose "secret ingredient" was the flesh of little children (Campion-Vincent and Renard 1992, 97); rumors from London and southeast England between 1829 and 1839 that the broth served to inmates in "work-houses" (refuges for the destitute) was made from the bits left over from hospital dissecting rooms (it was popularly known as "[a]natomy soup") (Richardson 1987, 212–222 and footnote 13 p. 359); and the British legend of "Sweeney Todd, the Demon Barber of Fleet Street," whose barber's chair tipped up and catapulted his victims into the cellars below, to be made into pies by his neighbor (Simpson 1983, who also discusses the unwitting cannibalism theme as it appears in the works of Charles Dickens). Much earlier, there is a legend from 1612 of a Parisian pastry-cook who, aided by his neighbor (who, like Sweeney Todd, was a barber), added human flesh to his pastries because it tasted better than the flesh of other animals (Le Quellec 1991, 139).

Nearer our own time, legends and rumors about bloodsuckers and human sausage factories proliferated in post–World War II Estonia. Stories were told of abductions off the streets of the cities, of people lured into strangers' houses. Soap was supposedly made from the bones of the victims' bodies, sausages from their bowels, and their fat was used to create lather for a scouring paste. In rural areas, the rumors told of farmers who waylaid and murdered travelers, salted them in a barrel and fed them to their pigs, or who hung them up by their feet, and drained their veins to make blood sausages (Köiva 1998, 8).

Still nearer the present day, rumors circulated in Miami in 1994/1995 about Cubans putting human meat into their hamburgers (Dimmick 1995), and it was alleged in some quarters that China was selling aborted fetuses as beauty aids or cures for a range of maladies (item from a listserve for the John Birch Society, via Bill Ellis). In 1996, a correspondent to *FOAFtale News* asked whether other readers were familiar with a shocking story he had heard: was it an urban legend, he asked? Many homeless people in the city were frightened of a group of destitute people who lived under the state Capitol building in Albany, New York. The story was that these people were surviving by killing and eating other homeless people or anybody out on the streets near the Capitol after dark) ("Urban Cannibals").

For some of the many films and works of fiction that have utilized the cannibal theme, see the Appendix.

Examples

1. In Berlin, after World War II, money was short, supplies were tight, and it seemed like everyone was hungry. At that time, people were telling the tale of a young [woman] who saw a blind man picking his way through the crowd. The two started to talk. The man asked for a favor: could she deliver a letter to the address on the envelope? Well, it was on her way home so she agreed. She started out to deliver the message, when she turned round to see if there was anything else the blind man needed. But she spotted him hurrying through the crowds without his smoked glasses or white stick. She went to the police, who raided the address on the envelope, when they found heaps of human flesh for sale. And what was in the envelope? "This is the last one I'm sending today." (Leonard 2000, 10)

2. Many children had been missing [in Tartu, Estonia]. They wanted to make sausages out of us. We called the militia. Only then the militia found out about that factory. It was underground, in a kind of cellar. A father recognized his daughter from her apron. It was after the war, when sausages were made from human flesh. A man found only the head of [his] daughter: a pink ribbon was tied in her hair. (Köiva 1998, 8)

FURTHER READING

Allport, Gordon, and Leo Postman. *The Psychology of Rumor*. New York: Holt, 1947.

Campion-Vincent, Véronique, and Jean-Bruno Renard. *Légendes urbaines: Rumeurs d'aujourd'hui*. Paris: Payot, 1992. See pp. 94–105.

Dimmick, Adrian. "Cannibals and Stolen Organs." *FLS News* 21 (June 1995): 10.

Köiva, Mare. "Bloodsuckers and Human Sausage Factories." *FOAFtale News* 43 (February 1998): 7–9.

Leonard, Paula. "Strange but True." *Letters to Ambrose Merton* 24 (Winter 2000): 9–12. See second item p. 10.

Le Quellec, Jean-Loïc. *Alcool de singe et liqueur de vipère . . . plus quelques autres recettes*. Vouillé: Geste, 1991. See pp. 133–141.

Richardson, Ruth. *Death, Dissection and the Destitute*. London: Routledge and Kegan Paul, 1987.

Simpson, Jacqueline. "Urban Legends in *The Pickwick Papers*." *Journal of American Folklore* 96 (1983): 462–470.

"Urban Cannibals." *FOAFtale News* 40/41 (December 1996): 10.

See: The Baby Roast; The Blood Libel Legend; The Corpse in the Cask; Grandma's Ashes

9

THE SUPERNATURAL

On the whole, the themes and subject matter of urban legend relate to this world not the Other World, but there are a handful of stories of the supernatural among them, including perhaps the most famous urban legend of all—the story of "The Vanishing Hitchhiker." This story is discussed in an introductory section and six separate entries which cover the main variants. Two other legends dealt with in this chapter are also very well known—"The Devil at the Disco" and "Mary Whales I Believe in You" (sometimes known as "Bloody Mary in the Mirror"). Also discussed here is an older legend, "The Ghost in Search of Help for a Dying Man."

THE DEVIL AT THE DISCO

Stories about the devil are not a common sort of urban legend, but they do exist. "The Devil at the Disco" is the most widespread type. It blends traditional motifs with modern settings, so that the deceptively handsome young man is betrayed by his devilish features. These may be cloven hooves, a pointed tail, a horse's hoof, and a chicken's claw for feet. Alternatively he and his partner may rise in the air surrounded with heat, fire, or sulphur. But all this happens at a modern nightclub or discotheque.

The story has been chiefly reported in Mexico and among Mexican-Americans, in Brazil, in French-speaking Canada, and the southern and south-western United States.

A 1994 study of the legend among Mexican-Americans living in the Rio Grande Valley of Texas has revealed interesting patterns in the development of the legend over time. Folklorist Mark Glazer found 353 legends about the devil in the Rio Grande Folklore Archive, which he contextualizes in terms of the role the devil plays in Chicano culture. Of these 353 legends, 86 are of "The Devil at the Disco" type, 59 are actually set in a discotheque, 27 are older stories set in a dance hall. He sees the older legends as more "traditional," and suggests that this sort of story goes back at least to the beginning of the twentieth century, maybe to the time that Europeans first colonized the area (Glazer 1994, 33). The traditional tale, he says, "delineates what is proper and improper conduct in Chicano culture." Proper behavior for a Chicana girl includes obeying one's mother or grandmother, not flirting, and treating religious occasions respectfully. Traditional stories are structured so that a girl is forbidden to go to a dance or specifically warned that, if she does go, the devil will appear to her. She goes, she flirts with a stranger, she enjoys the attention she and her partner receive—and sometimes makes things worse by doing this on Good Friday. The result is death.

Glazer's 59 modern legends (of which he presents seven good texts) are set in the disco. Some of them begin like the traditional legends with the girl being forbidden to go to the dance, though it is less emphasized. The results are the same as the first group—the girl is burnt, her dress is torn, there is panic in the disco, and sometimes the girl later dies of shock. However, girl's disobedience doesn't automatically result in death; instead, she is burnt by the devil's touch, or she becomes hysterical, or faints, or her dress catches fire. In others, the traditional elements are even further downplayed. There is no parental prohibition, and the stories tend to concentrate on how the devil's identity was discovered by his distinctive feet, and his disappearance in smoke. Glazer sees these changes as a cultural adaptation to American life.

Stories collected from Brazil in the early 1990s follow roughly the same pattern. Initially the story told how a girl at a samba dance at a specific dance-hall one Sunday night in a Brazilian town flirtatiously approached a young man and ripped his hat off his head. To everyone's horror, they saw that the hat had been covering a pair of horns. Panic erupted, the girl fainted (or, some said, died on the spot). Later, the story got elaborated: the young man was said to be tall, young, handsome, blond; he was such a good dancer that the women were lining up to dance with him. It wasn't long before other dance-halls in the area reported that the devilish young man had visited them too, and some added the detail that he had a tail as well as horns. A local newspaper identified him as a youth called Aléx, AKA "The Capeta [devil] of Vilarinho," and spoke of him terrorizing the area at weekends. A comic book appeared on news-stands featuring a boy called Aléx who could "dance like the devil": he had died and gone to hell but had now returned to earth disguised as a mortal to captivate the ladies. If they danced with him, their bosoms smoked (Burns 1992). A second report from another Brazilian town told about a superb lambada dancer appearing at a dance; again, all the women wanted to dance with him. Suddenly there was a scream; his partner had looked at his face. He had flaming eyes and the face of a devil. She fainted, and the young man disappeared leaving the smell of sulphur behind. Again, this character started appearing all over the region, and the stories now reported how he had told one of his partners that the lambada was his favorite dance and that he was going to take the best dancing partners down to the depths of hell (Ninevé 1992).

All these stories carry some sort of more or less explicit moral unease about dancing being enjoyed. At its weakest in the traditional Chicano stories it focuses on dancing on a day that should be given to religious activities, or dancing when your mother has told you not to. At its strongest the unease is about the type of dancing (the samba is sexy, intimate: the lambada is often called "dirty dancing" or "the forbidden dance").

The same sort of moral overtones can be found in versions collected among the Ramah Navajo people, New Mexico, in the 1980s. The scene in these tales is a "Squaw dance," a frequent Navajo summer custom which is part of the "Enemy Way" ceremony but which is a major social event and regarded as a time of sexual licence. Here, a dancer (who may sometimes be a female) suddenly disappears from the dance leaving coyote tracks behind (Cunningham and Cunningham 1989, 223).

Similarly, stories from the United Kingdom collected at the turn of the nineteenth and twentieth centuries show the same sorts of moral concerns, though adapted to a different set of cultural norms. In these stories dances are often replaced by card parties as activities in which the devil might participate. One such story, which dates from 1896, tells what happens at a card party held on a Sunday.

This story comes from rural Wales, where the predominant religious tradition until recently was a strict variety of Methodism where "Sabbath Observance" was the norm and card-playing was frowned upon as leading to the sin of gambling. During the course of the evening, a well-dressed stranger arrives and gets permission to dance with the prettiest girl in the room. Then he sits down to play cards with her. She accidentally drops a card, and when she stoops down to pick it up she notices that the handsome stranger has cloven feet. She faints. She never recovers her health and dies shortly after (Winstanley and

Rose 1926, 162). A later story, dated 1926, is set in Manchester, northwest England. It appears to have mutated to suit the secular outlook of an industrial city, but it is still essentially a moral tale. Here some card-players are enjoying a game—and perhaps enjoying some illegal betting because they are alarmed when a knock comes on the door and they think it is the police. A pleasant stranger enters and asks to join the game. A card is dropped as in the Welsh version, and the stranger is seen to have a sinister club foot (see Rose 1926).

There is a story recorded in the French journal *Mélusine* which predates both the British ones and is very like some of the stories from Mexico. It is set in Danzig (now Gdansk in Poland) in 1875, and it seems it was spreading quickly through this conservative Catholic city. It tells how a young girl was forbidden by her mother to go to "The Vineyard" ballroom in the town, but the girl defied her mother and went anyway. At the ball she quickly attracted the attention of "a handsomely dressed stranger with black hair and eyes that glistened like onyx." They danced faster and faster, until one of the musicians noticed the stranger's cloven hooves. The band stopped playing waltzes and began to play hymns, at which the stranger grabbed his partner and whirled her through a window. Next day, the girl was found dead in the garden surrounded by broken glass (Renard 1994, 1–2, quoting Mannhardt 1878).

The story below was recorded in 1985 from a Mexican-American graduate student at UC Irvine.

Example

I met this friend of mine at the Jai Lai whose name is Javier. And he was commenting on an event that happened in Tijuana, especially at the Club Aloha. And he was telling me that a young woman who was a friend of his wanted to go out dancing on a Friday night but her mother told her not to go. And she stubbornly, stubbornly went to the dance. And this happened about midnight. She was sitting in front of the dance area and there was this young man that was dancing. He looked like he was projecting a certain image through his eyes, a certain brilliance. She became interested in dancing with the young man; and she started dancing with him, disco music. And they danced for at least twenty minutes. And the ambience in the Aloha spread like a fire, like a fire. The spectators became aware when she was dancing that she began to rise, see ... she was rising above the ground, see, and all the people around the dance floor began to run. And she was not aware of what was happening. Smoke was coming from the two of them all over. And the following day they found her body had been burnt and the Aloha was burnt down (Herrera-Sobek 1988, 148).

FURTHER READING

Burns, Thomas LaBorie. "On Becoming the Devil at the Disco." *FOAFtale News* 25 (March 1992): 1–2.

Cunningham, Keith, and Kathryn Cunningham. "'The Appearing Hitchhiker': Narrative Enculturation among the Rama Navajo." In *The Questing Beast: Perspectives on Contemporary Legend IV*. Ed. Gillian Bennett and Paul Smith. Sheffield: Sheffield Academic Press, 1989, pp. 213–230.

Glazer, Mark. "'El Diablo en el Baile': Cultural Change, Tradition and Continuity in a Chicano Legend." *Contemporary Legend* 4 (1994): 31–44.

Harmeyer, Alice J. "Devil Stories from Las Vegas, New Mexico." *Hoosier Folklore* 6 (1947): 37–39.

Herrera-Sobek, Maria. "The Devil in the Discotheque: A Semiotic Analysis of a Contemporary Legend." *Monsters with Iron Teeth: Perspectives on Contemporary Legend III*. Ed. Gillian Bennett and Paul Smith. Sheffield: Sheffield Academic Press for ISCLR, 1988, pp. 147–157.

Ninevé, Miguel. "The Devil Does the Lambada: Another Visit to Brazil." *FOAFtale News* 27 (September 1992): 4.

Renard, Jean-Bruno. "Old Contemporary Legends: 19th-Century French Folklore Studies Revisited." *FOAFtale News* 32 (February 1994): 1–4.

Rose, H. J. "The Devil at a Card-Party." *Folk-Lore* 37 (1926): 395.

Winstanley, L., and H. J. Rose. "Scraps of Welsh Folklore, 1." *Folk-Lore* 37 (1926): 154–174.

THE GHOST IN SEARCH OF HELP FOR A DYING MAN

This story, which has been told since at least the late nineteenth century in places as far apart as the United States (Vail 1950) and Russia (Edgerton 1968), is a relative of the much more familiar legend of "The Vanishing Hitchhiker." Here, a ghost persuades a doctor or priest to drive to the home of a relative to bring medical help or to administer the last rites. When the doctor or priest arrives at the house, the ghost disappears, and is later identified as the daughter or wife or mother of the household. The story has been repeatedly revised and reported in popular sources and story compilations (see, for example, Musick 1965, tale number 16, "Help").

A story like this swept through the Russian city of St. Petersburg during December 1891. Under the headline "A Mysterious Fact," the earliest of several newspaper reports of what they called a "miracle" told how a priest was asked to go to a house to administer the last rites to a dying man. When he got there he was baffled because the young man who answered the door said he was the only person who lived there and he was perfectly healthy. The priest insisted that a young lady had approached him in the street and asked him to go to the house. To prove it, he pointed to a portrait hanging on the wall: "This," he said, "is the young woman who brought me here."

"But that's a picture of my dead mother!" said the young man. He was so awestruck that he decided to take communion with the priest, and by the evening he was dead (Edgerton 1968, 31–39).

An English story told in London in the 1940s is a variant on the same theme. A woman dressed in white alights from a taxi and approaches a doctor as he is walking home one night, and asks him to go with her to a certain address. When he gets out of the cab he finds that she has disappeared, but he knocks on the door anyway, and a servant tells him that nobody in the house is ill. Out of curiosity he returns the next morning and finds that the master of the house has died suddenly in the night. A photograph identifies the woman in white as the wife of the man who has died; she herself has been dead for many years (Edgerton 1968, 40).

There is a happier outcome in a story which Gillian Bennett heard told in a church sermon in a village on the Welsh-English border in the 1940s or early 1950s. In this telling it was presented as an example of the efficacy of prayer.

Example

One dark night, very late, a country doctor was surprised to hear a knock at his door. When he answered it he saw a frail-looking young woman standing there. "Come quickly," she said. "My father is dying!" He had never seen the girl before, but she was obviously sincere, so he grabbed his bag and followed her into the night. She took him to a remote cottage, and opened the gate for him, and he went up the path to the door. He expected that she would follow him and let him in, but when he turned to speak to her she wasn't there. He waited a while to see if she'd gone in by some back door and would come round to let him in. But nothing happened. So he knocked on the door.

A woman came to the door, in tears, very distressed. "Oh, doctor!" she said. "Thank God you've come. I think he's dying." She took him upstairs to a bedroom where a man lay in bed, clearly very ill indeed. The doctor stayed with him all night and by the morning the man was out of danger. The doctor took a little breakfast with the woman then got ready to leave the house, sure the man would continue to recover now the crisis was over.

"Thank you so much," said the woman. "You've saved his life. I prayed you'd come but I could find no way of getting a message to you. I couldn't leave him alone."

"Your daughter came for me," he said, puzzled. "Where is she? It's strange I haven't seen her all night."

"My daughter?" the woman said. "My daughter's dead."

"Dead?" he said. "But she came for me and said her father was dying."

"She couldn't have done," said the woman. "She's been dead three years. That's her picture on the mantelpiece" (Bennett Collection).

FURTHER READING

Edgerton, William B. "The Ghost in Search of Help for a Dying Man." *Journal of the Folklore Institute* 5 (1968): 31–41.

Musick, Ruth Ann. *The Telltale Lilac Bush and Other West Virginia Ghost Tales.* Lexington, KY: University of Kentucky Press, 1965.

Vail, R. W. G. "A Philadelphia Variant of the Hitchhiking Ghost." *New York Folklore Quarterly* 6 (1950): 254.

See: The Vanishing Hitchhiker 2 (Home-Going Ghosts)

"MARY WHALES I BELIEVE IN YOU"

Otherwise known as "Bloody Mary in the Mirror," or " I Believe in Mary Worth" (Mary Worthington, Mary Johnson, Mary Weatherby, Mary Lou, Mary Jane, or sometimes even Kathy), this is partly a legend and partly a ritual among teens and pre-teens.

The details of the ritual are almost endlessly variable, and reflect traditional folklore about methods of conjuring ghosts—for example, walking seven times "widdershins" (i.e., counter-clockwise) round a grave—allied to beliefs about the power of ghosts to appear in mirrors. The ritual is performed in groups as a dare, or as a sort of initiation, or as a way of reenacting the legend. The usual procedure is that the participants go to the bathroom, turn all the lights out, and maybe light a candle. Next, they must look in a mirror, and invoke Mary several times using the correct formula (the number of times varies from storyteller to storyteller as does the exact formula). The ghost of Mary will appear in the mirror. She will be maimed or ugly and have long finger nails and maybe scratch one of the participants; or she may appear as blue mist or black smoke and leap out of the mirror; or she may pull somebody down the toilet. However, all the details may vary from account to account; even the mirror is not a constant ingredient.

The "Mary Whales" ritual has featured in the classic horror film "Urban Legend" (1998); it is echoed in the situation which sets up the plot of "Candyman" (1992); and it has formed an incident in the popular TV series "Supernatural."

The legend part of this story is perhaps even vaguer. Mary is sometimes said to be the ghost of a girl who was disfigured in an accident and now is intent on harming other teenage girls; sometimes, as in the traditional Spanish-American legend "La Llorona," she is supposed to be grieving for the murder of her child. She may be a girl killed in a road accident, or a girl whose father would not allow her to become a nun, or a witch burned at the stake in the Salem witch trials of 1692. In a substantial number of "Mary" legends collected by folklorist Janet Langlois in Indiana in 1972/1973, the "Mary Whales" legend merges with "The Vanishing Hitchhiker," and Mary is supposed to be the ghost of a girl killed on the way to a party and doomed to hitch rides from passing motorists (Langlois 1978, 196–197, 199, 204–205, 208–211).

"Mary Whales" is best documented among American teens, especially girls, but it has also been reported from southwest England as told by boys. According to a 12-year-old boy's account, you are supposed to crack a mirror, turn the lights out, and say "Bloody Mary" a hundred times. When you turn the lights back on, you will see the future in the cracked mirror. According to an 11-year-old boy you should all hold hands and go round in a circle saying, "Bloody Mary, I killed your child." If you do this three times, then look at a curtain, you will see a mysterious figure appear there. A 12-year-old girl reported another ritual in which you link hands round a post with a partner, then together go round and round the post saying "Black Jack" 40 times. The result is that a spirit called Black Jack will follow you home from school and squeeze your shoulder (Wilson 1997, 249–250).

The example below was collected from an 11-year-old Vietnamese-American girl who learned it in third grade, in 1992, at Hellyer Elementary School in San Jose.

Example

You go into the bathroom at school, turn out the lights, and close the door. You can go by yourself or with two or three friends. I'm not positive, but I think boys can do it too—if they want to. You light some red candles, like about three, and you put them in front of you in a triangle, two on a side and one in the front. Then you keep on chanting "Bloody Mary" like about three times or something. You're sitting there and looking at the water in the toilet and chanting. And they say she will appear, her face in the water. Then you have a weird reaction or something and she pulls you down into the toilet and flushes your head down the toilet. And you never come back or something (Dundes 2002, 83).

FURTHER READING

Dundes, Alan. "Bloody Mary in the Mirror: A Ritual Reflection of Pre-Pubescent Anxiety." *Western Folklore* 57 (1998): 119–135. Reprinted in Dundes, Alan. *Bloody Mary in the Mirror*. Jackson, MI: University Press of Mississippi, 2002, pp. 76–94.

Langlois, Janet. "'Mary Whales, I Believe in You': Myth and Ritual Subdued." *Indiana Folklore* 11 (1978): 5–33. Reprinted in *Indiana Folklore: A Reader*. Ed. Linda Dégh. Bloomington, IN: Indiana University Press, 1980, pp. 196–224.

Wilson, Michael. *Performance and Practice: Oral Narrative Traditions among Teenagers in Britain and Ireland*. Aldershot, UK: Ashgate, 1997.

THE VANISHING HITCHHIKER 1: INTRODUCTION

The ultimate urban legend classic, this story is known almost worldwide, and updates older traditions of roadside ghosts. Though, since folklorists began collecting and discussing the story in the early 1940s, the hitchhiker is almost always given a ride in an automobile, older legends tell of ghosts taking rides in horse-drawn vehicles or jumping on the backs of horses as benighted travelers ride home through country lanes. The central story is that a motorist gives a ride to a stranded traveler who mysteriously disappears from the vehicle and is later discovered to be an other world personage of some sort—a ghost, alien, prophet, or sacred personage.

If the hitchhiker is a ghost, he/she may be picked up outside a cemetery or on an isolated road. He/she is usually trying to get to a particular destination, most often his/her home or a party. If the hitchhiker is a girl she may conduct a romance with the driver, who only later discovers he has been making love to a ghost. The story will end with the ghostliness of the hitchhiker being established some way. This may be by some sort of evidence being left in the car or on a grave, or by the puzzled car driver calling at the address the hitchhiker gave and being shown a photograph of a dead relative. Ghostly hitchhikers are most often young girls, but there are a few stories in which the hitchhiker is an old woman, or a man, or occasionally even a whole family.

If the vanishing hitchhiker is a sacred or otherworldly personage, he/she is usually said to issue warnings or make a prediction about future events before disappearing from the vehicle.

Stories like this have an almost worldwide distribution and have been collected from places as far apart as Korea and Hawaii, Russia and South Africa. Perhaps one of the reasons for the popularity of Vanishing Hitchhiker stories is that they are easily adjustable to cultural expectations. So the mysterious hitchhiker may be an alien in UFO literature, Jesus in the bible belt of America, a mythological being on a Native American reservation, a malevolent spirit in Guam, and so on. In South Africa and Namibia, the story has been adapted to local cultural traditions about ghosts, so the ghost who hitches a ride beats the motorist about the head before disappearing (Schmidt 1990). In 2005 hitchhiker stories were commonplace in Thailand, where the hitchhiker was identified as a victim of the tsunami that claimed thousands of lives in coastal resorts ("Thai tsunami sparks rash of foreign ghost sightings").

Vanishing Hitchhiker stories turn up in a variety of media as well as in a variety of places. They may be found in literary works, magazines, folklore journals, and popular story compilations. They also circulate as topical rumors reported by newspapers. The story appeared in the pilot episode of the popular TV series "Supernatural," and has featured in several films. These include "Encounter with the Unknown" (1973), "Pee-Wee's Big Adventure" (1985), and in a film set in Ireland and starring Orson Welles, "Return to Glennascaul" (1951). For other films and literary works, see the Appendix.

Because there is so much material on vanishing hitchhikers, we have divided the legends into six major subtypes—Home-Going Ghosts; The Party-Going Ghost; The Coat on the Grave; Jesus on the Thru'way; Hitchhiking Prophets, Saints, and Aliens; and The Double Prophecy.

FURTHER READING

Beardsley, Richard K., and Rosalie Hankey. "The Vanishing Hitchhiker." *California Folklore Quarterly* 1 (1942): 303–335.

———. "A History of the Vanishing Hitchhiker." *California Folklore Quarterly* 2 (1943): 13–25.

Bennett, Gillian. "Alas, Poor Ghost!": *Traditions of Belief in Story and Discourse*. Logan, UT: University of Utah Press, 2005. See pp. 159–166.

Goss, Michael. *The Evidence for Phantom Hitch-Hikers: An Objective Survey of the Phantom Hitch-Hiker Phenomenon in All Its Manifestations*. Wellingborough, UK: Aquarian Press in conjunction with ASSAP, the Association for the Scientific Study of Anomalous Phenomena, 1984.

Jones, Louis C. "Hitchhiking Ghosts in New York." *California Folklore Quarterly* 3 (1944): 284–291.

Schmidt, Sigrid. "The Vanishing Hitchhiker in South Africa: Additional Notes." *FOAFtale News* 17 (March 1990): 1–3.

"Thai Tsunmai Sparks Rash of Foreign Ghost Sightings." *Channel News Asia* [Singapore] (January 14, 2005), http://www.channelnewsasia.com/stories/afp_asiapacific/view/127300/1/.html

See: The Ghost in Search of Help for a Dying Man; The Hairy-Handed Hitchhiker; The Vanishing Hitchhiker 2 (Home-Going Ghosts); The Vanishing Hitchhiker 3 (The Party-Going Ghost); The Vanishing Hitchhiker 4 (The Coat on the Grave); The Vanishing Hitchhiker 5 (Jesus on the Thru'way); The Vanishing Hitchhiker 6 (Prophets, Saints, and Aliens); The Vanishing Hitchhiker 7 (The Double Prophecy)

THE VANISHING HITCHHIKER 2: HOME-GOING GHOSTS

The classic Vanishing Hitchhiker is a young girl dressed in an evening gown encountered on a wild night in a desolate place. This ghost has died far from home and wants to return there. Waiting at home, there is always a grieving mother to burst into tears and identify her daughter, to show the concerned driver a photograph, or to explain that the ghost of her daughter always tries to get home on rainy nights or on the anniversary of her death. Though there are isolated stories in which the Vanishing Hitchhiker is not a young girl—maybe, the spirit of an American serviceman killed in a car crash, or that of an innocent man hanged for murder, or a young husband on the way to see his first child—these are not very common (Bennett 1998).

Stories like this have spread widely in place and time. Though the first systematic studies of the legend were undertaken by American graduate students in the early 1940s (Beardsley and Hankey 1942, 1943), it is likely that the story is rather older than that and can be traced to the days when a horse and cart rather than a car was the commonest means of transport. However, it cannot be much older than the mid-nineteenth century because, before that time, ghosts who could not be distinguished from living people were not a regular part of supernatural folklore (Bennett 2005, 159–166).

The story below was first told as the true experience of a friend, then relayed to Gillian Bennett at third hand in the early 1980s. It is set on the wild and desolate moors that separate the English counties of Lancashire and Yorkshire.

Example

Michael's teacher... they were talking one day about ghosts and she said that her friend at Leeds had been out for the evening with a friend of hers—a gentleman friend—and they'd spent the evening in Leeds and were driving home late, very late, on a very wet, dark night. And they lived on the outskirts of Leeds somewhere and as they were driving home, they passed a bus-stop and there was a young girl—a youngish girl—standing at the bus stop, and they drove straight past and then thought it was odd she should be standing there so late... So the young man said he would take his friend home and then go back and see if the young girl was still at the bus-stop, and if she was still there he would give her a ride home. So he went back to the bus stop and found the young girl still there and asked if he could give her a ride because she was getting very wet and there were no more buses that night.

So he asked her where she lived. She gave him the address. So they set off. Driven a little way when they came to some traffic lights—he had to stop at the traffic lights—and when he looked, she'd gone! Couldn't be seen! He couldn't understand it at all. Next morning he went round for his friend... and told her what had happened. Very perplexed about it.

So they decided they'd go to this address that the young girl had given. Knocked at the door. An elderly lady answered it and they said, did, you know, did a young lady or anybody, live there—because they'd given a ride to this young lady the night before who'd given this address and couldn't find her. She'd just disappeared, didn't know where she was. And the old lady burst into tears and said that was her daughter who had died years earlier on that same day in an accident at the traffic lights! (Bennett Collection).

FURTHER READING

Beardsley, Richard K., and Rosalie Hankey. "The Vanishing Hitchhiker." *California Folklore Quarterly* 1 (1942): 303–335.

———. "A History of the Vanishing Hitchhiker." *California Folklore Quarterly* 2 (1943): 13–25.

Bennett, Gillian. "The Vanishing Hitchhiker at Fifty-Five." *Western Folklore* (1998): 1–19.

———. *"Alas, Poor Ghost!": Traditions of Belief in Story and Discourse.* Logan, UT: University of Utah Press, 2005. See pp. 159–166.

Brunvand, Jan Harold. *The Vanishing Hitchhiker: American Urban Legends and Their Meanings.* New York: Norton, 1981. See pp. 24–46.

Goss, Michael. *The Evidence for Phantom Hitch-Hikers: An Objective Survey of the Phantom Hitch-Hiker Phenomenon in All Its Manifestations.* Wellingborough, UK: Aquarian Press in conjunction with ASSAP, the Association for the Scientific Study of Anomalous Phenomena, 1984.

See: The Ghost in Search of Help for a Dying Man; The Vanishing Hitchhiker 1 (Introduction)

THE VANISHING HITCHHIKER 3: THE PARTY-GOING GHOST

This version of the Vanishing Hitchhiker story has been collected worldwide from at least the 1940s, and continues to appear as a news item and on the Internet. It is a romance with a creepy ending. A car driver sees a girl standing in the street, often at or near the gates of a cemetery, but dressed for a party. Just as the address-giving ghost is desperate to get home, this phantom is determined to get to a dance. The boy is going to the party too and gives the girl a ride. The mode of transport is always suitable for the location—cars in the United States, scooters in Italy, motorbikes in India. They dance together all night—for several nights in one version from New York—"and play and party at the door" afterward (Jones 1944). In one American story the traveler falls in love with the hitchhiker and meets her six nights in succession, and in a South American story that circulated on the Internet it seems like they spend the night together. Eventually something gives the game away and the boy discovers he has been partying with a ghost.

This version often ends with the "Coat on the Grave" sequence of events. The boy loans the girl a warm coat, sweater, or scarf, which he later finds hanging over the tombstone on her grave. For example, a tale from Ruth Ann Musick's popular story compilation *Coffin Hollow* tells how a young man meets a girl at a dance, dances with her all evening, lends her his coat, kisses her goodnight at the door—all without any suspicion. Then when he calls at her home on the pretext that he needs his coat, he is informed she is dead, and finds his coat on her tombstone (Musick 1977, story no 72).

In Indian and South American stories the partying hitchhiker spills wine on her dress and the wine-stained garment is found in the dead girl's closet. One particularly detailed and thrilling rendition with a similar ending comes from *Apparitions and Precognition* by Swiss Jungian psychoanalyst Aniela Jaffe. The book was compiled in 1954 and 1955 from personal experience accounts sent in by readers of a popular twice-monthly paper. In her version three soldiers meet a girl in a restaurant and entertain her all evening. During the meal, she spills wine down her dress. The story progresses in the usual way to the discovery that the girl is dead. Her coffin is opened, and the girl's body is found undecayed, "she lay there in her snow-white dress, on which was visible the wine-stain of the evening before. Her white shoes were covered with mud" (Jaffe 1963, 183).

Some of these stories strongly recall traditions about vampires and she-devils who seduce unwary men. They also have similarities to the "Devil at the Disco" legend about girls who go to dances and unwittingly dance with the devil (though with the roles reversed). This similarity was noted by Beardsley and Hankey, the first writers to discuss Vanishing Hitchhiker stories in a folklore journal. Calling attention to literary versions of this theme, they suggested that this variant was the first, and maybe the original, type of Vanishing Hitchhiker legend.

In fact, there is at least one traditional local legend from the United Kingdom which seems to blend the two types. This story, printed in an issue of the *Buxton Advertiser* and attributed to "an old copy" of a local parish magazine, tells how:

> The White Lady of Longnor comes out of the Black Pool, and flits about the roads. She was disappointed in love, rural gossips say, and so perambulates at the old trysting time, in hope to meet her faithless swain once more...
>
> There used to be a public house called "The Villa" where much junketing, merrymaking, and dancing was in vogue amongst the rustics on high days and holidays.
>
> Here there suddenly appeared amongst the pleasure party a sweet, fresh, love-some girl, dressed all in white, as if for a festal occasion.
>
> She danced with one swain after another, and the fun grew fast and furious till at length the more sedate members of the party began to exchange suspicious glances, and suddenly the whisper went forth, "The White Lady of Longnor."
>
> The whisper had barely gone the round when the place of the strange visitor was void. She had disappeared as suddenly and unaccountably as she came. This was her wont, and the party, in compliance, broke up and dispersed.

As a labourer, who was practically a contemporary of the incident remarked, "Theer was never no more dancin' at 'The Villa'" ("The White Lady of Longnor").

In most English versions of the party-going ghost, however (including the famous legend of Bluebell Hill, in our second example), the girl has been killed on the way to her wedding.

Examples

1. These boys picked up this girl by the roadside, and she was dressed like she was going to a dance. It was raining hard and she didn't have a coat. They were going to the dance too, so they stopped and gave her a ride there. She said she was called—Rosa, I think it was... some flower name like that. She was very pretty, very very nice—they all wanted to dance with her.

   When they were going home, they said they would take her home too. She asked to be put down at the cemetery gates, said she would walk from there. When they got to the cemetery, it was still raining so one of the boys lent her his raincoat, said he would pick it up later from her house.

   Not sure how he knew which house it was, but he went there the next day and asked for Rosa. The lady said she did have a daughter called Rosa but she was killed in an accident. She was buried in the cemetery. They didn't believe her, so they went there to check it out. They found the coat beside a grave. It was her grave and she'd been dead three years. She'd been killed on the way to a dance! (Bennett Collection).

2. The "Blue Bell Hill" ghost? Well, she's supposed to haunt the road between Chatham and Maidstone. Bluebell Hill isn't much of a hill, but it counts as a hill in that part of Kent, and there's something weird about it, it's deceptive somehow, a bit strange, you know?

   Anyway, if you're lucky (or unlucky!) and you're driving at night you might see a girl thumbing a lift on the crest of the hill. She will ask to be taken to Maidstone and give an address in that town; she'll be very excited and talkative and tell you she is going to be married there the next day. However, when you reach the outskirts of Maidstone she'll stop talking and if you turn round she'll have vanished. That's the Bluebell Hill ghost. She was killed in a car crash on Bluebell Hill on the eve of her wedding on the very day and hour you met her and she's been trying to get to her wedding ever since! (Bennett Collection).

FURTHER READING

Beardsley, Richard K., and Rosalie Hankey. "The Vanishing Hitchhiker." *California Folklore Quarterly* 1 (1942): 303–335.

———. "A History of the Vanishing Hitchhiker." *California Folklore Quarterly* 2 (1943): 13–25.

Bennett, Gillian. "Alas, Poor Ghost!": *Traditions of Belief in Story and Discourse*. Logan, UT: University of Utah Press, 2005. See pp. 159–166.

Goss, Michael. *The Evidence for Phantom Hitch-Hikers: An Objective Survey of the Phantom Hitch-Hiker Phenomenon in All Its Manifestations*. Wellingborough, UK: Aquarian Press in conjunction with ASSAP, the Association for the Scientific Study of Anomalous Phenomena, 1984.

Jones, Louis C. "Hitchhiking Ghosts in New York." *California Folklore Quarterly* 3 (1944): 284–291.

Musick, Ruth Ann. *Coffin Hollow and Other Ghost Tales*. Lexington, KY: University of Kentucky Press, 1977.

Tucker, Elizabeth. *Campus Legends: A Handbook*. Westport, CT: Greenwood Press, 2005. See pp. 68–69.

"The White Lady of Longnor." Extract from the *Buxton Advertiser* [Derbyshire, UK] (June 24, 1933), Reprinted in *Letters to Ambrose Merton* 22 (Summer 2000): 1–2.

See: The Devil at the Disco; The Vanishing Hitchhiker 1 (Introduction)

THE VANISHING HITCHHIKER 4: THE COAT ON THE GRAVE

This is probably the least common variant of the Vanishing Hitchhiker legend. It begins and ends like stories of the party-going ghost but has the same middle section as stories of the home-going ghost. So, in the "Coat on the Grave" variant the hitchhiker is picked up at or near a cemetery, and vanishes from the car while it is moving. Some token that indicates that the hitchhiker is a ghost is left for the driver to find. This may be a patch of seaweed on a car seat where the ghost of a drowned girl sat, or a coat or scarf the driver lent the girl and then discovers draped over a tombstone in the cemetery. In fact, more or less anything will do as long as it constitutes conclusive proof that the hitchhiker was really a ghost. Some versions of the well-known South African story of "The Uniondale Ghost," for example, tell how the hitchhiker was picked up by a motorcyclist, and how she disappeared from the pillion leaving behind the crash-helmet the driver had lent her (Schmidt 1990, 1). In one American version which was told by the writer's grandfather, the token is a turnip! (Eckerd 1982).

This variant has a more "traditional" feel than other versions of the Vanishing Hitchhiker legend. It seems that the ghost goes "walking" during the night and must return to her grave at cock-crow.

Example

I heard one about this young man—John Looker I think they said his name was— and he had been at an all-night party and he was driving home in the small hours. As he passed the cemetery he was stunned to see a young girl standing at the main gate, all by herself and dressed only in a sort of shift-type dress, sort of 60s style. He stopped to ask her if she wanted a ride and she said yes and got in the back. Introduced himself and asked her what she was called, she told him Sarah Adams. She was shivering so he asked her did she want to borrow his jacket. So he took his jacket off and gave it to her.

They had driven for a bit when he remembered that he hadn't asked her where she wanted to go. Turned round, and she wasn't there! Well, he thought that was really strange and creepy, but it was late and he was tired and he'd been drinking, so he just drove on thinking he must've imagined it. Got home, crashed out on his bed, thought nothing of it. Then in the morning he couldn't find his jacket anywhere. Then he remembered imagining he lent it to a strange girl.

Anyway, I can't remember why he thought of looking for it in the cemetery, but he did. And there it was—hanging on a statue of an angel on a grave. He looked at the writing on the grave, and it said "Sarah Adams, died 2nd November 1965. RIP." Weird, eh? (Bennett Collection).

FURTHER READING

Bennett, Gillian. "Alas, Poor Ghost!": *Traditions of Belief in Story and Discourse*. Logan, UT: University of Utah Press, 2005. See pp. 159–166.

———. "The Vanishing Hitchhiker at Fifty-Five." *Western Folklore* (1998): 1–19.

Brunvand, Jan Harold. *The Vanishing Hitchhiker: American Urban Legends and Their Meanings*. New York: Norton, 1981. See pp. 24–46.

Eckerd, W. L. (Dusty). "Who Put the Turnip on the Grave?" *Pennsylvania Folklife* 31 (1982): 115–116.

Goss, Michael. *The Evidence for Phantom Hitch-Hikers: An Objective Survey of the Phantom Hitch-Hiker Phenomenon in All Its Manifestations*. Wellingborough, UK: Aquarian Press in conjunction with ASSAP, the Association for the Scientific Study of Anomalous Phenomena, 1984.

See: The Vanishing Hitchhiker 1 (Introduction)

THE VANISHING HITCHHIKER 5: JESUS ON THE THRU'WAY

This story begins like the classic "Vanishing Hitchhiker" legend: the hitchhiker gets into the backseat of the car, speaks to the driver, and suddenly disappears. But this time, instead of giving directions or asking to be taken home, the hitchhiker issues a prophecy about the second coming or the end of the world, or announces that he is Jesus.

Folklorists first became aware of these stories in the second half of the 1970s. Later on, in the 1990s and into 2000, similar stories started appearing throughout the United States, and in places as far apart as New Zealand and Norway, about strange hitchhikers who announced that Jesus would appear as he had done in biblical times on the road to Emmaus. About the same time, there were reports from Ohio, Pennsylvania, California, Florida, Mississippi, and Tennessee about mysterious disappearing hitchhikers who told the driver that "Gabriel's lips are on the trumpet" (presumably the "last trump" at the end of the world). An article in *FOAFtale News* surveys these occurrences ("This May be the Last Issue of *FOAFtale News*").

Example 1 was collected in Arizona. Example 2 comes from Scandinavia.

Examples

1. Someone . . . was driving on a deserted road towards Holbrook on a cold rainy night. As she was driving, she saw a figure on the side of the road, soaking wet trying to thumb a ride. She felt sorry for the person, stopped the car, and a young man sat down in the front seat. After a long period of silence he said, "Jesus is coming again." She turned to look at him, and he was gone (Ed. 1979, 47).

2. A married couple was driving along a country road. They were going to a wedding. They saw a young man standing by the side of the road, hitchhiking. They stopped to pick him up . . . When they took a good look at him, they were a bit surprised. He was barefoot and had long hair and a beard. Usually they would not pick anybody up who looked like that. But he had a nice face, so they gave him a lift. . . .

   Then all of a sudden, after driving for about ten or fifteen minutes, the young man said,

   "Do you know Jesus?" . . .

   They got embarrassed by his question and did not know how to answer him.

   Finally the wife said,

   "Yes, we do."

"Well that's good," said the young man, "because, Jesus, that's me."

They shuddered and did not know what to say to that. Finally the wife turned round to look at the young man. But he was gone! ...

Later when they stopped at a gas station to fill up, they told the attendant about their experience because they felt a need to talk about it.

The man looked at them and said:

"You are the tenth family today who has told me about this" (Kvideland and Sehmsdorf 1988, 385–386).

FURTHER READING

Ed. [Keith Cunningham]. "The Vanishing Hitchhiker in Arizona—Almost." *Southwest Folklore* 3 (1979): 46–50.

Ellis, Bill. *Aliens, Ghosts, and Cults: Legends We Live.* Jackson, MI: University Press of Mississippi, 2003. See pp. 99–116.

Fish, Lydia M. "Jesus on the Thru'way: The Vanishing Hitchhiker Strikes Again." *Indiana Folklore* 9 (1976): 5–13.

Kvideland, Reimund, and Henning Sehmsdorf, eds. *Scandinavian Folk Belief and Legend.* Minneapolis, MI: University of Minnesota Press, 1988. See pp. 378–392.

"This May be the Last Issue of *FOAFtale News.*" *FOAFtale News* 33–34 (June 1994): 10–11.

See: The Vanishing Hitchhiker 1 (Introduction)

THE VANISHING HITCHHIKER 6: HITCHHIKING PROPHETS, SAINTS, AND ALIENS

Vanishing hitchhikers are very often ghosts, but a common type of story features another sort of non-human hitchhiker who asks for a ride and then mysteriously disappears. In legends collected in Hawaii from the 1930s to the 1970s, for example, the hitchhiker is identified as Pele, the volcano goddess of Hawaiian tradition (Luomala 1972). In our first example below the hitchhiker is supposed to be an alien, and in our second example the strange hitchhiker is identified as one of the Three Nephites of Mormon tradition.

Very often these otherworldly personages give help, or a warning, or make a prediction. In many versions collected in the 1940s, for example, the hitchhiker warns the driver not to go to the Chicago World's Fair because the Enchanted Island will sink into the lake. Similarly, when Mount St. Helens erupted in 1980 it was reported that a mysterious woman in white was begging a ride from travelers in the Seattle area, warning that the volcano was about to explode, and then disappearing from the vehicle (Simpson 1985). And during the 1950s, stories about Nephites warned members of the Mormon Church about coming food shortages.

As usual, there is nothing very new about stories like these. A friend told us of a story related by an old woman in Russia during World War II. It recounts how one night a truck driver was going along the main road when he saw a woman by the roadside. She was old and grey-haired. She held out her hand, so he stopped the truck and let her get up into the cab beside him. As they were traveling along, she said to him, "Look over there. That's the past." The truck driver looked to his left and saw a field of rye, very tall. Then she said, "Look over there. This is the future!" and the truck driver looked to the right and saw crosses and graves. Then the woman disappeared. The truck driver arrived at his destination and was told that war had been declared (Elizabeth A. Warner, personal communication).

Examples

1. In the early hours of August 27th 1972 an Argentinian mechanic named Eduardo Dedeu was returning to his home by car when he noticed a man thumbing a lift (in some versions of the tale Dedeu is approached whilst he is mending his car radio).

   The man was dressed in a long coat with the collar turned up, and a cap, making it difficult for Dedeu to see his face. Dedeu stopped his car and the man got in, but when he was asked his destination, the man, whose face Dedeu later described as "elongated," answered unintelligibly (other versions state that the noise of the radio prevented Dedeu from hearing what was said).

   Further attempts at conversation by Dedeu met with the same response and so they travelled in silence until reaching the 710 kilometre mark, when suddenly the car lights went out and Dedeu had to stop the car. As he stopped Dedeu noticed what he thought at first was an overturned bus in the road with a large blue light in the centre and two small lights in the side.

   As Dedeu got out of the car he was blinded by a sudden, intense flash of white light, and at the same moment felt intense heat which made him shelter behind the car door. All this took place in a matter of seconds and when he was able to look up Dedeu could see that the object in the road was now moving away to the left and was displaying a green light on the underside and white light in its windows.

Intending to leave the scene as quickly as possible Dedeu got back into the car to discover that the mysterious hitch-hiker had vanished! There was no sign of him and only the open door and broken door handle on the floor spoke of his passage. At that moment the car lights came back on, allowing Dedeu, who was by now considerably shaken, to drive to the next town where he reported his experience to the police. The police interviewed Dedeu for four hours in the presence of a doctor; his account was taken to be coherent and the doctor could find nothing medically wrong with him (Roberts 1987, 29).

2. (*In Mormon theology the Nephites were three of the ancient disciples of Christ who had been allowed to keep their earthly form until the Second Coming, and work among the Mormon congregation. Folklorist William Wilson studied 50 Nephite–Vanishing Hitchhiker stories from the Brigham Young University Archive and believes such stories have been popular since the 1930s [Wilson 1975]. To understand the Nephite story below you have to be aware that it is a religious duty for Mormons to trace their ancestors*).

While doing his genealogy a man came to a dead end. He searched every source he knew but could not find this link that would enable him to go on in the finding of his ancestors.

This fellow was working in northern Nevada and drove the desert roads every day to and from work. One morning he saw an old man hitchhiking on one of those desert roads. He stopped to pick him up and during the drive they talked of the Mormon Church and the young man mentioned his problem with his genealogy. Still out in the desert the hitchhiker asked to be let out just up the road. Before he got out of the car he offered a newspaper to the other man to read. When the man looked back the hitchhiker had vanished; there was no sign of him but the newspaper was on the seat. He was greatly surprised to see that it was from England and a very old newspaper at that. The paper was turned to the obituaries and a name caught the young man's eyes. It was the name of his last link before the dead end in his genealogy work. In this paper he found the names and information he needed to do more work on his genealogy.

Thinking about it later, he thought this must surely have been one of the three Nephites sent to help him (Ed. 1979, 47).

FURTHER READING

Ed. [Keith Cunningham]. "The Vanishing Hitchhiker in Arizona—Almost." *Southwest Folklore* 3 (1979): 46–50.

Ellis, Bill. *Aliens, Ghosts, and Cults: Legends We Live.* Jackson, MI: University Press of Mississippi, 2003. See pp. 99–116.

Luomala, Katharine. "Disintegration and Regeneration, the Hawaiian Phantom Hitchhiker Legend." *Fabula* 13 (1972): 20–59.

Roberts, Andy. "The Hitch Hiker from Space." *The Supernatural* 1.10 (1987): 28–30.

Simpson, Elizabeth. "Mount St. Helens and the Evolution of Folklore." *Northwest Folklore* 4.1 (1985): 43–47.

Wilson, William A. " 'The Vanishing Hitchhiker' Among the Mormons." *Indiana Folklore* 8 (1975): 79–97.

See: The Ghost in Search of Help for a Dying Man; The Vanishing Hitchhiker 1 (Introduction)

THE VANISHING HITCHHIKER 7: THE DOUBLE PROPHECY

This story, probably of nineteenth-century German origin and very popular during World War II, is a variation on legends about prophesying hitchhikers. It elaborates on the simple hitchhiker-as-prophet theme by having the mysterious hitchhiker make not one but two prophecies. The first one is about world affairs (often predicting the end of the war); the hitchhiker then says that the driver will know this is a true prophecy because at the end of his/her journey there will be a corpse in the car (Bonaparte 1947, 13–40).

A related wartime legend that was very widespread in France and the United Kingdom has the double prophecy motif without the mysterious disappearance. In these stories the driver comes across a gypsy woman and offers her a ride. As she gets out, she prophesies that he will have a corpse in the car by the end of the day. He laughs and asks her if she's got any other predictions. Yes, she says, Hitler will be dead in six months. The first story below follows this pattern and was published in a 1943 pamphlet designed to debunk current rumors in Britain. The second story was told in Poland in the 1980s.

Examples

1. A man was driving along in his car and gave a lift to a gypsy woman with a baby in her arms. When the gypsy got out she thanked him and made a prophecy that within 24 hours there would be a corpse in the car. The driver, being a bit skeptical, said facetiously: "Well, if there is, I hope it's Hitler's corpse." Then the gypsy is supposed to have said that Hitler would be dead in six months. The

story goes on that the motorist later passed the scene of an accident and was asked to drive an injured person to hospital. This he did, but the victim died before reaching the hospital. Thus the first part of the prophecy was fulfilled (Army Bureau of Current Affairs 1943).

2. A motorist picks up a woman dressed in black, who asks him to take her to a shrine to one of the many Black Madonnas in Catholicism. During the drive, she predicts a frightening future for the whole world, except for the people who remain under the protection of the Black Madonna. She asks him to promise that he will spread this message to all the people and, to cancel any doubt that she can tell him the future, predicts that within an hour will have a corpse in his car. After these words, she suddenly disappears from the speeding car. After two kilometers, the police stop him and ask him to take a critically injured person to the nearest hospital. On the way, the sick person dies (Ellis 2003, 107).

FURTHER READING

Army Bureau of Current Affairs. *Rumour* (January 16, 1943).

Bonaparte, Marie. *Myths of War*. London: Imago, 1947.

Ellis, Bill. *Aliens, Ghosts, and Cults: Legends We Live*. Jackson, MI: University Press of Mississippi, 2003.

See: The Vanishing Hitchhiker 1 (Introduction)

APPENDIX:
A PROVISIONAL LIST OF
URBAN LEGENDS IN FILM
AND LITERATURE

Urban legends have been included in films and literature in a variety of ways. For example, Stolen Body Parts legends have provided the complete plots for a number of films, short stories, and novels. The majority of legends, however, are used as subplots in works of fiction, or appear in conversations among the characters, sometimes with a purpose but at other times simply to entertain the audience. In this chapter we have identified a number of examples, which probably only represent the tip of a vast iceberg of such material. Consequently, if you come across any further examples, please let us know. We deliberately did not include a section on Urban Legends on Television simply because, even with today's technology, it is still comparatively difficult to locate and view old TV shows.

In each case the items have been listed under the titles we have used for the stories.

URBAN LEGENDS ON FILM

Films Using Multiple Legends
Urban Legend (1998)
Urban Legends: Final Cut (2000)
Urban Legends: Bloody Mary (2005)
Urbania (2000)
Urban Mythology (2000)

Films Using Single Legends

AIDS Aggressors
Via Appia (Germany 1992)

Alligators in the Sewer
Alligator (1980)
Candyman (1992)
Night Moves (1975)

Assailant in the Backseat
Mr Wrong (1985), also known as *Dark of the Night*
Nightmares (1983)

The Baby Roast
Candyman (1992)
No Deposit, No Return (1972), also known as *Hilary's Blues*
Preheat to 425° (2004)

The Baby Sitter and the Man Upstairs
Adventures in Babysitting (1987)
The Babysitter (1995)
The Call (2004)
Foster's Release (1971)
Lisa (1990)
The Sitter (1977)
When a Stranger Calls (1979)
When a Stranger Calls (2006)

Batman Frolics
The Indecent Woman (1991), also known as *De Onfatsoenlijke Vrouw* (1991)

The Blood Libel Legend
The Fixer (1968)

The Bosom Serpent
Alien (1979)
Aliens (1986)
Alien³ (1992)
Alien: Resurrection (1997)
Shivers (1975)
Star Trek II: The Wrath of Khan (1982)

The Boyfriend's Death
Dead Poets' Society (1989)
He Knows You're Alone (1980)
I Know What You Did Last Summer (1997)
Malcolm (1986)

Bunny Bounces Back
Dickie Roberts: Former Child Star (2003)

The Cadaver Relative
Burke and Hare (1972)

The Castrated Boy
Candyman (1992)

The Cat and the Salmon
Her Alibi (1989)

The "Death" of Paul McCartney
Sleepless in Seattle (1993)

The Death Car
Christine (1983)
Mr Wrong (1985), also known as *Dark of the Night*
Riding the Bullet (2004)

The Disappearing Room
Bunny Lake Is Missing (1965)
Dangerous Crossing (1953)
Flightplan (2005)
The Forgotten (2004)
The Lady Vanishes (1938)
The Lady Vanishes (1979)
The Midnight Warning (1932)
So Long at the Fair (1950)
Unheimliche Geschichten (1919)
Verwehte Spuren (1938), also known as *Like Sand in the Wind*

Death from Fear
Fraternity Row (1977)

Death Screams (1982), also known as *House of Death*

The Elephant That Sat on a Car
Bliss (1985)

The Doggie Lick
Campfire Tales (1997)

The Five Pound Note/The Unintentional Thief
Around the World in Eighty Days (2004)
Blue, Black and White (1987)
Boeuf Bourguignon (1988)
Clin d'Oeil (1992)
The Cookie Thief (1999)
Damned (1993)
The Lunch Date (1990)
The Prisoner of Second Avenue (1975)

The Hairy-Handed Hitchhiker
Panic (1979)

The Halloween Sadist
Candyman (1992)

The Hook
Buster and Billie (1974)
Campfire Tales (1991)
Campfire Tales (1997)
The Chromium Hook (2000)
The Hook-Armed Man (2000)
I Know What You Did Last Summer (1997)
Lovers Lane (1999)
Meatballs (1980)

Killer Clowns
Clownhouse (1989)
Killer Klowns from Outer Space (1988)

Left at the Roadside
The Likely Lads (1976)
With Six You Get Eggroll (1968)

The Man in the Middle
Weekend at Bernie's (1989)

"Mary Whales I Believe In You"
Candyman (1992)
Candyman: Day of the Dead (1999)
Candyman: Farewell to the Flesh (1995)

The Microwaved Pet
Gremlins (1984)
Medium Rare (1987)
The Wild Life (1984)

The Mouse in the Coke Bottle
Strange Brew (1983)

"Out of the Mouths of Babes..."
Le Clan des Siciliens (1969), also known as *The Sicilian Clan*

The Philanderer's Porsche
The First Wives' Club (1996)

Roaming Gnomes
Amélie (2001)

Serving the Dog
Rich and Strange (1931), also known as *East of Shanghai*
Theatre of Blood (1973)

The Severed Fingers
Mad Max (1979)

Sit!
Amos and Andrew (1993)
Police Academy 3: Back in Training (1986)
Private Benjamin (1980)

Smiley Gangs
The Krays (1990)

The Smuggler
Crocodile Dundee in Los Angeles (2001)

The Solid Cement Cadillac
California Dreaming (1979)
Mystic Pizza (1988)
Stolen: One Husband (1990)

The Spider in the Boil
Bliss (1985)

Stolen Body Parts
Allure (1999)
Blood Salvage (1990)
Butterfly Kiss (1995)
Coma (1978)
Dirty Pretty Things (2002)
The Donor (1995)
The Harvest (1992)
Intern Academy (2004)
Saw (2004)
Spare Parts (2003)
Traitement de Choc (1973), also known as *Shock Treatment*

The Stolen Corpse
National Lampoon's Vacation (1983)
The Wrong Box (1966)

Stuck on You
Hot Resorts (1985)

The Superglue Revenge
Reservoir Dogs (1992)

The Suppressed Product
The Formula (1980)
The Man in the White Suit (1951)
The Naked Gun 2 $^{1/2}$: The Smell of Fear (1991)

The Surpriser Surprised
The Date (1997)

They Are Not Dead
Elvis is Alive! I Swear I Saw Him Eating Ding Dongs Outside the Piggly Wiggly's (1998)
Triggermen (2002)

Urban Cannibals and Human Sausage Factories
L'Auberge Rouge (1951), also known as *The Red Inn*
Eating Raoul (1982)
Eat the Rich (1987)
Fried Green Tomatoes at the Whistle Stop Cafe (1991)

De Gronne Slagtere [*The Green Butchers*] (2003)
Hannibal (2001)
Motel Hell (1980)
Soylent Green (1973)
Lo Strangolatore di Vienna (1971), also known as *The Mad Butcher of Vienna*
Sweeney Todd: The Demon Barber of Fleet Street (1936)
The Undertaker and His Pals (1966)

The Vanishing Hitchhiker

Mystery Train (1989)
Pee-Wee's Big Adventure (1985)
Return to Glennascaul: A Story That Is Told in Dublin (1951)
Mr. Wrong (1985), also known as *Dark of the Night*

White Slavers

Burn Up! (1991)
Caged Women II (1996)
Fighting the White Slave Traffic (1929)
The Harem (1985)
The Inside of the White Slave Traffic (1913)
Invitation to Ruin (1968)
Knock Out Bondage #9 (2004)
Knocked Out, Tied Up 1 (1995)
Spartan (2004)
Traffic in Souls (1913)

URBAN LEGENDS IN LITERATURE

AIDS Aggressors

Defoe, Daniel (ed. Anthony Burgess and Christopher Bristow). *A Journal of the Plague Year: Being Observations or Memorials of the Most Remarkable Occurrences, as Well Public as Private, Which Happened in London During the Last-Great Visitation in 1665. Written by a Citizen Who Continued All the While in London. Never Made Public Before.* London: Nutt, 1722; Harmondsworth, UK: Penguin Books, 1986, 117.

Kauffman, Reginald Wright. *Daughters of Ishmael.* 14th ed. London: T. Werner Laurie, 1925, p. 217.

Klawans, Harold L. *Legacy: Toscanini's Fumble and Other Tales of Clinical Neurology.* Chicago: Contemporary Books, 1988, pp. 113–128.

Maupassant, Guy de. "Bed No. 29." [1884]. In *The Complete Short Stories.* . . . Garden City, NY: Hanover House, 1955, pp. 570–577.

Alligators in the Sewers
Campbell, Robert. *Hip-Deep in Alligators.* New York: New American Library, 1987.

Didion, Joan. "Sentimental Journeys." In *After Henry.* New York: Simon and Schuster, 1992, p. 288.

Lippman, Peter. *The Great Escape or The Sewer Story.* New York: Golden Press, 1973; Racine, WI: Western Publishing Co., 1973.

Pynchon, Thomas. *V.* London: Vintage, 1995.

Sharp, Alan. *Night Moves.* London: Corgi, 1975, p. 65.

Waring, Richard. *Alberto the Dancing Alligator.* Illus. Holly Swain. Cambridge, MA: Candlewick, 2002.

The Assailant in the Back Seat
Howard, Elizabeth Jane. *Mr. Wrong: A Collection of Short Stories.* Harmondsworth: Penguin, 1979, pp. 9–45.

The Babysitter and the Man Upstairs
Bowen, Gail. *The Wandering Soul Murders.* Toronto: McClelland and Stewart, 1992, p. 45.

Coover, Robert. "The Babysitter." In *Pricksongs and Descants.* New York: Penguin, 1969, pp. 206–239.

Stine, R. L. *The Baby-Sitter.* New York: Scholastic, 1989.

———. *The Baby-Sitter II.* New York: Scholastic, 1991.

——— *The Baby-Sitter III.* New York: Scholastic, 1993.

Batman Frolics
King, Stephen. *Gerald's Game.* New York: Viking, 1992.

Reidy, Sue. "Alexandra and the Lion." In *The Penguin Book of Contemporary New Zealand Short Stories.* Ed. Susan Davis and Russell Haley. Auckland: Penguin, 1989, p. 184.

The Blood Libel Legend
Chaucer, Geoffrey. "The Prioress's Tale." In *The Canterbury Tales by Geoffrey Chaucer.* Ed. N. F. Blake. London: Edward Arnold, 1980, pp. 427–480.

Malamud, Bernard. *The Fixer.* New York: Farrar, Straus and Giroux, 1966.

The Bosom Serpent
Anobile, Richard J. *Star Trek II: The Wrath of Khan.* Photostory. New York: Pocket Books, 1982.

Calisher, Hortense. "Heartburn." *New American Mercury* 72 (1951): 30–39. Included in the author's *In the Absence of Angels*. Boston, MA: Houghton Mifflin, 1951 and *Collected Stories*. New York: Arbor House, 1975. Reprinted in J. K. Cross, ed. *Best Horror Stories*. London: Faber and Faber, 1957; John Hollander, ed. *American Short Stories Since 1945*. New York: Harper Perennial Paperback, 1968; Irving Howe, ed. *Fiction as Experience*. New York: Harcourt Brace Jovanovich, 1978; and A. Ryan, ed. *Haunting Women*. New York: Avon, 1988.

Cather, Willa. *O, Pioneers!* Boston: Houghton Mifflin, 1913; New York: New American Library Signet Classic, 1989, Chapter 2.

Crispin, A. C. *Alien: Resurrection*. New York: Warner Books, 1997.

Dahl, Roald. *My Uncle Oswald*. New York: Alfred A. Knopf, 1980, Chapter 8, p. 90.

Foster, Alan Dean. *Alien*. New York: Warner Books, 1979.

———. *Aliens*. New York: Warner Books, 1986.

———. *Alien* [3]. New York: Warner Books, 1992.

———. *The Complete Alien Omnibus*. New York: Warner Books, 1993.

Hawthorne, Nathaniel. "Egotism; or the Bosom Serpent." *United States Magazine and Democratic Review* 12 (March 1843): 255–261. Included in *Mosses from an Old Manse*, Boston, 1846. Reprinted in Riverside Edition of Hawthorne's Works, Boston, MA: Houghton Mifflin, 1883.

Linklater, Eric. *Juan in America*. London: Jonathan Cape, 1931, p. 406.

McIntyre, Vonda N. *Star Trek II: The Wrath of Khan. A Novel*. New York: Pocket Books, 1982.

Walker, Marjorie. "The Summer of the Serpent." *Carleton Miscellany* 11 (1971): 31–47.

The Boyfriend's Death

Bowen, Gail. *The Wandering Soul Murders*. Toronto: McClelland and Stewart, 1992, p. 45.

Bunny Bounces Back

Gorog, Judith. "An Absolutely True Bunny Story." In *On Meeting Witches at Wells*. New York: Philomel, 1991, pp. 99–101.

The Cadaver Arm

Baroja, Pío. *The Tree of Knowledge* [Trans. Aubrey F. G. Bell]. New York: Howard Fertig, 1974, Chapter 6, pp. 28–37.

Kerr, M. E. *Dinky Hocker Shoots Smack!* New York: Harper and Row, 1972, Chapter 14, p. 160.

The Castrated Boy

Barker, Clive. "The Forbidden." In *In the Flesh*. New York: Pocket Books/Simon and Schuster, 1986, pp. 110–111.

Reading, Peter. "Going On." In *Book I: Ukelele Music and Book II: Going On*. London: Secker and Warburg, 1985, p. 66.

The Cat in the Package

D'Amato, Barbara. "Stop, Thief!" In *Sisters in Crime 4*. Ed. Marilyn Wallace. New York: Berkley Books, 1991, pp. 341–352.

Maloney, Russell. "What's Wrong With the American Theatre." In *It's Still Maloney, or Ten Years in the Big City*. New York: Dial Press, 1945, p. 44. Reprinted in *The American Imagination at Work: Tall Tales and Folk Tales*. Ed. Ben C. Clough, New York: Alfred A. Knopf, 1947, p. 693; *Sidewalks of America: Folklore, Legends, Sagas, Traditions, Customs, Songs, Stories and Sayings of City Folk*. Ed. B. A. Botkin, Indianapolis, IN: Bobbs-Merrill, 1954, p. 693.

Rutt, Diane. "Who Let the Cat Out of the Bag in Austin, Texas." *The Texan Woman* 1.3 (1974): 14. Reprinted in *The Folktale Cat*. Ed. Frank de Caro, Little Rock, AR: August House, 1992, pp. 130–131.

Sayers, Dorothy L. "The Fantastic Horror of the Cat in the Bag." In *Lord Peter Views the Body*. London: Victor Gollancz, 1979, pp. 63–78.

Yevtushenko, Yevgeny. *Wild Berries*. New York: William Morrow and Co., 1984, Chapter 12, pp. 170–172.

The Choking Doberman

Boyer, Rick. *The Penny Ferry*. Boston: Houghton Mifflin, 1984, Chapters 2 and 3.

Gorog, Judith. "Juno." In *On Meeting Witches at Wells*. New York: Philomel, 1991, pp. 30–33.

Wolitzer, Hilma. *In Palomar Arms*. New York: Farrar, Straus and Giroux, 1983, Chapter 3, pp. 26–27.

The Colander Lie-Detector

London, Jack. "Master of Mystery." In *Children of the Forest*. London: Mills and Boon, 1902, pp. 96–120.

MacDonald, Peter V. *From The Cop Shop: Hilarious Tales from our Men and Women of the Badge*. Toronto: Stoddart, 1996, p. 179.

The Corpse in the Cask

B. L. W. "The Tun of Red Wine: An Incident that Occurred at a Town in Spain During the Peninsular War." *Burton's Gentleman's Magazine*. 2 (May 1838): 341–343.

Dahl, Roald. "Lucky Break: How I Became a Writer." In *The Wonderful Story of Henry Sugar and Six More*. New York: Alfred A. Knopf, 1977, pp. 201–202.

———. *My Uncle Oswald*. New York: Alfred A. Knopf, 1980, Chapter 8, pp. 93–94.

Poe, Edgar Allan, "Thou Art The Man." *Godey's Lady's Book* 29 (November 1844): 219–224.

Walpole, Horace. "The Peach in Brandy: A Milesian Tale." In *Hieroglyphic Tales*. Strawberry-Hill, T. Kirgate, 1785, 25–31.

The Death Car

Cohen, Daniel. "The Death Car." In *Railway Ghosts and Highway Horrors*. New York: Scholastic Inc., 1991, pp. 89–95.

Howard, Elizabeth Jane. *Mr. Wrong: A Collection of Short Stories*. Harmondsworth: Penguin, 1979, pp. 9–45.

King, Stephen. *Christine*. New York: Viking Press, 1983. Paperback: New York: Signet Book, New American Library, 1983.

———. *From A Buick 8*. New York: Scribner, 2002, pp. 26, 59, 101, 279, 295, 297, 313, 315.

———. "Riding the Bullet." In *Everything's Eventual*. New York: Scribner, 2002, pp. 422–423.

The Devil at the Disco

Theroux, Peter. "Aliens in Arabia." In *Sandstorms: Days and Night in Arabia*. New York: Norton, 1990, pp. 16–17.

The Disappearing Room

Belloc-Lowndes, Mrs. [Marie Adelaide]. *The End of Her Honeymoon*. New York: Charles Scribner's Sons, 1913; London: Methuen, 1914; London: Wright and Brown, [1936]; facsimile reprinted of the Scribner's text, New York: Arno Press, 1976.

Hemingway, Ernest. "Red and Black Laughter." In *The Torrents of Spring: A Romantic Novel in Honor of the Passing of a Great Race*. [1933]. London: Jonathan Cape, 1964, Part 5, pp. 49–52, 155–156.

Piper, Evelyn. *Bunny Lake Is Missing*. New York: Harper and Brothers, 1957; London: Secker and Warburg, 1957.

Rising, Lawrence. *She Who Was Helena Cass*. New York: George Doran, 1920.

Straus, Ralph. "The Room on the Fourth Floor." In *The Fireside Book of Suspense*. Ed. Alfred Hitchcock. New York: Simon and Schuster, 1947, pp. 96–105.

"Surely You're Joking, Mr. Feynman!" In *Adventures of a Curious Character. Autobiographical Anecdotes by the Physicist Richard Feynman, as Told to Ralph Leighton, Collected Over a Period of Seven Years*. New York: Norton, 1985. Paperback: New York: Bantam Books, 1986, pp. 9–10.

Thompson, Sir Basil. "The Vanishing of Mrs. Fraser." In *Mr. Pepper Investigator*. London: J. Castle, 1925. Reprinted in *Great Short Stories of Detection, Mystery and Horror*. Ed. Dorothy L. Sayers, 2nd. Series. London: Victor Gollancz, 1931, pp. 415–429; *The Second Omnibus of Crime: The World's Great Crime Stories*. Ed. Dorothy L. Sayers, New York: Blue Ribbon Books, 1932, pp. 297–310.

Thorne, Anthony. *So Long at the Fair*. New York: Random House, 1947.

van de Wetering, Janwillem. *The Mind-Murders*. Boston: Houghton Mifflin Company, 1981. New York: Pocket Books, 1983, pp. 144–147.

White, Ethel Lina. "Signature." In *The Wheel Spins*. New York: Harper and Brothers, 1936, Chapter 26.

Woollcott, Alexander. "The Vanishing Lady." In *While Rome Burns*. New York: Viking, 1934. Reprinted in *The American Imagination at Work: Tall Tales and Folk Tales*. Ed. Ben C. Clough, New York: Alfred A. Knopf, 1947, pp. 695–696; *The Portable Woollcott*. New York: Viking, 1949; *Invitation to Short Stories*. Eds. H. L. Willis and W. R. McGillivray, Toronto: Macmillan, 1958, pp. 78–85; *The Vanishing Lady and Other Stories*. New York: Macmillan, 1964, pp. 9–15.

The Double Theft

Shah, Idries. "The Sheep and the Purse." In *The Way of the Sufi*. London: Jonathan Cape, 1968, pp. 214–215.

The Elephant that Sat on a Car

Carey, Peter. *Bliss*. New York: Harper and Row, 1986, pp. 68–72.

Carey, Peter, and Ray Lawrence. *Bliss: The Film*. London: Faber and Faber, 1986, pp. 62–67.

———. *Bliss: The Screenplay*. St Lucia, Queensland: University of Queensland Press, 1986, pp. 62–67.

Francis, Dick. *Smokescreen*. London: Michael Joseph, 1972; London: Pan Books, 1974, pp. 85–86.

Merrill, Jean, and Ronni Solbert. *The Elephant Who Liked to Smash Small Cars*. New York: Pantheon Books, 1967.

van de Wetering, Janwillem. *The Corpse on the Dyke*. Boston, MA: Houghton Mifflin, 1976, pp. 150–152.

The Exploding Toilet

Atwood, Margaret. *Bodily Harm*. Toronto: McClelland and Stewart, 1981, pp. 266.

The Failed Suicide

Smith, Sir Sydney. *Mostly Murder*. London: Harrap, 1959, pp. 261–281; American edition, New York: David McKay, 1960. Reissued, with new foreword, New York: Dorset Press, 1973; New York: White Lion Publishers, 1973. Reprinted London: Harrap 1973, 1986.

The Five Pound Note/The Unintentional Thief

Adams, Douglas. *So Long, and Thanks for All the Fish*. New York: Harmony Books, 1984, pp. 107–111.

Bryant, Louise. *Six Months in Russia*. New York: Arno Press, 1970, pp. 269–270.

Trollope, Thomas Adolphus. "A Moonlight Visit to the Coliseum" (c. 1877). Quoted in Charles C. Bombaugh, *Facts and Fancies for the Curious from the Harvest-Fields of Literature*. Philadelphia, PA: J. B. Lippincott, 1905, pp. 419–420.

Framed

Elgart, J. M. "Framed Up." In *Over Sixteen*. New York: Elgart Publishing, 1951, p. 161.

The Hairy-Handed Hitchhiker

Woollcott, Alexander. "Story-Teller's Holiday." "Shouts and Murmurs" column. *The New Yorker* (April 15, 1933): 26.

The Halloween Party

Cerf, Bennett. *Laugh Day. A New Treasury of Over 1000 Humorous Stories and Anecdotes*. New York: Doubleday, 1965, pp. 183–184.

The Halloween Sadist

Atwood, Margaret. *Cat's Eye*. Toronto: McClelland-Bantam, 1989, p. 409.

Bowen, Gail. *A Colder Kind of Death. A Joanne Kilbourn Mystery*. Toronto: McClelland and Stewart, 1994, p. 13.

The Hook

Barker, Clive. "The Forbidden." In *In the Flesh*. New York: Pocket Books/Simon and Schuster, 1986, pp. 89–147.

Carlson, Ron. "The Chromium Hook." *Harper's Magazine* (October 1995): 63–70.

Clark, Matt. *Hook Man Speaks*. New York: Berkley Books, 2001.

Coulthard, Ron. "Hooked." *Cold Mountain Review* (1985): 44.

Grafton, Sue. *H is for Homicide*. New York: Fawcett Crest, 1991, Chapter 19, p. 241.

Kerr, M. E. *Dinky Hocker Shoots Smack!* New York: Harper and Row, 1972, Chapter 11, pp. 133–134. Paperback: New York: Dell, 1972, Chapter 11, pp. 130–131.

King, Stephen. "Tales of the Hook." In *Danse Macabre*. New York: Everest House, 1981, pp. 32–34.

Phillips, Jayne Anne. "Blind Girls." In *Black Ticket*. New York: Dell Publishing, 1979, pp. 27–30.

Kentucky Fried Rat

Garland, Alex. *The Beach*. New York: Riverhead Books, 1977, pp. 57–58.

The Loaded Dog

Crump, Barry. "Harry Again." In *A Good Keen Man*. Wellington: A. H. and A. W. Reed, 1960, p. 115.

Harris, Rolf, Mark Leigh, and Mike Lepine. *True Animal Tales*. London: Century, 1996, pp. 65–66.

Lawson, Henry. "The Loaded Dog." In *Henry Lawson's Best Stories*. Chosen by Cecil Mann. Sydney: Angus and Robertson, 1966, pp. 9–15.

London, Jack. "Moon-Face." In *The Call of the Wild, White Fang, and Other Stories*. Ed. Earle Labor and Robert C. Leitz, III. New York: Oxford University Press, 1990, pp. 309–314.

The Man in the Middle

Clough, Ben C., ed. "The Middle Man." In *The American Imagination at Work: Tall Tales and Folk Tales*. New York: Alfred A. Knopf, 1947, pp. 355–356. Reprinted in *Sidewalks of America: Folklore, Legends, Sagas, Traditions, Customs, Songs, Stories and Sayings of City Folk*. Ed. B. A. Botkin, Indianapolis, IN: Bobbs-Merrill, 1954, p. 521.

Robin, Ralph. "Open Ears." *The Magazine of Fantasy and Science Fiction*. 5.2 (August 1953): 77–82.

Woollcott, Alexander. "The Man in the Middle." "Shouts and Murmurs" column. *The New Yorker* (February 22, 1930): 38.

———. "Miscellany." "Shouts and Murmurs" column. *The New Yorker* (March 15, 1930): 34. Reprinted in *The American Imagination at Work: Tall Tales and Folk Tales*. Ed. Ben C. Clough, New York: Alfred A. Knopf, 1947, p. 356.

"Mary Whales I Believe in You"

Barker, Clive. *Candyman: Farewell to the Flesh. The Riveting Screenplay from the Chilling Motion Picture*. London: Polygram Film Productions, 1995.

Solwitz, Sharon. *Bloody Mary*. Louisville, KY: Sarabande Books, 2003.

The Mexican Pet

Lee, Mrs. R. "Rats." In *Anecdotes of the Habits and Instincts of Animals*. London: Griffiths Farren Okeden and Welsh, 1891, pp. 216–217.

The Microwaved Pet

Gipe, George. *Gremlins*. New York: Avon Books, 1984, p. 177.

The Murdered Son

Camus, Albert. *Le Malentendu*. In *Caligula and Cross Purpose* [Le Malentendu] [Trans. Stuart Gilbert]. Harmondsworth, UK: Penguin, 1965, pp. 99–156.

Warren, Robert Penn. "The Ballad of Billie Potts" [1944]. In *Robert Penn Warren: Selected Poems 1923–1975*. New York: Random House, 1976, pp. 271–284.

Woollcott, Alexander. "Folk-Lore." "Shouts and Murmurs" column. *The New Yorker* (December 12, 1931): 36.

The Nude Bachelor

Galbraith, John Kenneth. "December 16—Cambridge." In *The Ambassador's Journal: A Personal Account of the Kennedy Years*. Boston, MA: Houghton Mifflin, 1969, p. 5.

Ilf, Ilya, and Yevgenii Petrov. "Conversations with a Naked Engineer." In *The Twelve Chairs* [1928] (Trans. John Richardson). New York: Vintage Books, Random House, 1961, Chapter 25.

van de Wetering, Janwillem. *Tumbleweed*. Boston, MA: Houghton Mifflin Company, 1976, pp. 165–166.

The Nude Housewife

Beatty, Jerome, Jr. "Funny Stories." *Esquire* (November 1970): 44, 46, 48, 50.

Nemerov, Howard. "Poetics." In *Trying Conclusions: New and Selected Poems 1961–1991*. Chicago: University of Chicago Press, 1991, pp. 109–110.

O'Neill, Eugene. *The Iceman Cometh*. London: Jonathan Cape, 1947, pp. 131–133, etc.

Philanderer's Porsche:

Engel, Howard. *The Suicide Murders: A Benny Cooperman Mystery*. Toronto: Clarke, Irwin and Co., 1980; first published in the United States by St. Martin's Press, 1984; Paperback: Harmondsworth: Penguin, 1985, Chapter 9.

Goldsmith, Olivia. "The Wives Getting Even." In *The First Wives Club*. New York: Simon and Schuster, 1992. Book Three, Chapter 2, pp. 346–360; and Chapter 8, pp. 418–419; New York: Pocket Books, 1993. Book Three, Chapter 2, pp. 367–383, and Chapter 8, p. 448.

Parr, Jack, with John Reddy. "Stories in Their Anecdotage." In *My Saber Is Bent*. New York: Simon and Schuster, 1961, Chapter 16, pp. 142–143.

Van Gieson, Judith. *The Lies That Bind*. New York: Harper Collins, 1993, p. 101.

Roaming Gnomes

Radley, Sheila. *Fate Worse Than Death*. New York: Charles Scribner's Sons, 1986, p. 10.

The Roommate's Death

Arlen, Michael. "The Gentleman from America." In *May Fair*. New York: George H. Doran, 1925, pp. 224–250. Reprinted in *The Omnibus of Crime*. Ed. Dorothy L. Sayers, New York: Payson and Clarke, 1929; *The Haunted Omnibus*. Ed. Andrew

Laing, New York: Farrer Strauss, 1937; *Great Ghost Stories of the World*. Ed. Andrew Laing, Garden City, NY: Blue Ribbon Books, 1941; *Great Tales of Terror and the Supernatural*. Eds. Herbert A. Wise and Phyllis Fraser, New York: The Modern Library, 1944, pp. 212–230.

Serving the Dog
Collins, Dale. *Rich and Strange*. London: George G. Harrap, 1930, Chapters 21 and 22.
Thackeray, William Makepeace. *The History of Pendennis*. Vol. 1. London: Bradbury and Evans, 1849, Chapter 20, pp. 193–194.

The Smuggler
Elkin, Benjamin. *Gillespie and the Guards*. New York: Viking, 1956.

Solid Cement Cadillac
Beatty, Jerome, Jr. "Funny Stories." *Esquire* (November 1970): 44, 46, 48, 50.
Burke, James Lee. *Dixie City Jam*. New York: Hyperion, 1994, Chapter 20, pp. 228–229.
Parr, Jack, with John Reddy. "Stories in Their Anecdotage." In *My Saber is Bent*. New York: Simon and Schuster, 1961, Chapter 16, pp. 138–139.

The Spider Boil
Greig, Francis. *The Bite and Other Apocryphal Tales*. London: Jonathan Cape, 1981. Published in the United States as *Heads You Lose and Other Apocryphal Tales*, New York: Crown, 1982. [Contains literary versions of an additional twenty urban legends.]

Stolen Body Parts
Baer, Will Christopher. *Kiss Me, Judas*. New York: Viking, 1998.
Cook, Robin. *Coma*. Boston, MA: Little Brown, c. 1977.
Jasion, Patrice. *Unholy Harvest*. Philadelphia, PA: Xlibris Corporation, 1999.
Kaufelt, David A. *Spare Parts*. New York: Warner Books, 1978.
Paine, Tom. "Scar Vegas." In *Scar Vegas and Other Stories*. New York: Harcourt, 2000, pp. 40–58.
Pearson, Ridley. *The Angel Maker*. New York: Delacorte, 1993, p. 10.
Robinson, Frank M. *The Donor*. New York: Tom Doherty Associates, 2004.

The Stolen Corpse
Brain, Russell. *Tea With Walter De La Mare*. London: Faber and Faber, 1957, p. 70.
Burgess, Anthony. *The Piano Players*. London: Hutchinson, 1986, Chapter Twelve and a Half, p. 191.
Peyrefitte, Roger. *Diplomatic Conclusions* [La Fin des Ambassades] [Trans. Edward Hyams]. London: Thames and Hudson, 1954, Part 2, Chapter 1, p. 88.

Robbins, Tom. *Another Roadside Attraction*. New York: Doubleday and Company, 1971. Paperback: New York: Ballantine Books, 1972, pp. 292–293.

Stevenson, Robert Louis, and Lloyd Osbourne. *The Wrong Box*. London: Longmans, Green and Co., 1889.

The Suppressed Product

Appleton, Victor. *Tom Swift and His Talking Pictures or The Greatest Invention on Record*. New York: Grosset and Dunlap, 1928, Chapters 21 and 22, pp. 179–193.

Bradbury, Ray. "The Flying Machine." In *The Golden Apples of the Sun*. [1953]. London: Rupert Hart-Davis, 1970, Chapter 7.

Davidson, Lionel. *The Sun Chemist*. New York: Alfred A. Knopp, 1976.

Heinlein, Robert A. "Life-Line." [1939]. In *The Past Through Tomorrow*. New York: G. P. Putnam's Sons, 1967, pp. 15–29.

Kerouac, Jack. *On the Road*. [1957]. Harmondsworth, UK: Penguin, 1983, Part 2, Chapter 7, pp. 141–142.

King, Stephen. *The Tommyknockers*. New York: G. P. Putnam's Sons, 1987, Chapter 10 (Parts 8 and 9), pp. 355–362.

Orwell, George. *The Road to Wigan Pier*. London: Victor Gollancz, 1937; Harmondsworth, UK: Penguin Books, 1981, p. 181.

Robin, Ralph. "Open Ears." *The Magazine of Fantasy and Science Fiction*. 5.2 (August 1953): 77–82.

Wyndham, John. "Heaven Scent." In *Gooseflesh and Laughter*. New York: Ballantine Books, 1956, pp. 65–66.

The Surpriser Surprised

Ayckbourn, Alan. *A Small Family Business*. London: Faber and Faber, 1987, Act 1: 5–6.

Jack, Donald. *That's Me in the Middle. The Journals of Bartholomew Bandy, Vol. Two*. Toronto: Doubleday, 1973, p. 235.

McCullers, Carson. *The Heart is a Lonely Hunter*. Boston, MA: Houghton Mifflin, 1940. Paperback: Harmondsworth, UK: Penguin Books, 1961, p. 208.

Nicholson, Geoff. *The Food Chain*. Woodstock, NY: Overlook, 1992, Chapter 11, pp. 153–168.

The Theater Tickets

Elgart, J. M., ed. "Sincerely Yours." *Furthermore Over Sexteen*. Vol. 4. New York: Grayson Publishing, 1955, p. 110.

Klein, Dave. *Blind Side*. New York: Charter, 1980, Chapter 16, pp. 189–199.

Paar, Jack, with John Reddy. "Stories in Their Anecdotage." In *My Saber Is Bent*. New York: Simon and Schuster, 1961, Chapter 16, pp. 140–141.

They Are Not Dead

Brewer-Giorgio, Gail. *Orion*. Atlanta, GA: Legend Books, Inc., 1979.

———. *Orion*. New York: Tudor Publishing, 1989.

Morrow, Cousin Bruce, and Laura Baudo. *Cousin Brucie! My Life in Rock 'N' Roll Radio*. Intro. Neil Sedaka. New York: Beech Tree, 1987, pp. 204–206.

Shea, Robert, and Robert Anton Wilson. *The Illuminatus Trilogy*. New York: Dell, 1975.

Thieves Get Their Just Deserts

Hardy, David. *What a Mistake!*. Secaucus, NJ: Castle, 1987, p. 109.

Trueman, Stuart. "Artful Dodger on the Border." In *Tall Tales and True Tales from Down East*. Toronto: McClelland and Stewart, 1979, pp. 38–45.

Twain, Mark. [Samuel Langhorne Clemens]. *Adventures of Huckleberry Finn* [1885]. New York: Norton, 1977, pp. 212–214.

Urban Cannibals and Human Sausage Factories

Bond, Christopher Godfrey. *Sweeney Todd: The Demon Barber of Fleet Street*. London: Samuel French [1974].

De Charmoy, Cozette. *The True Life of Sweeney Todd: A Collage Novel*. London: Gaberbocchus Press, 1973. Reprinted New York: Da Capo Press, 1977.

Dickens, Charles. *The Pickwick Papers* [1836]. Ed. James Kingsley Oxford: Clarendon Press, 1986, Chapter 31, pp. 464–465.

———. "The Guest." *The Holly Tree Inn. Being the Extra Christmas Number of Household Words* 12 (Christmas 1855): 1–9. Reprinted in Charles Dickens. *Christmas Stories*. London: Oxford University Press, 1956, p. 104.

Flagg, Fannie. *Fried Green Tomatoes at the Whistle Stop Cafe*. New York: McGraw-Hill, 1987, pp. 365–367.

Harris, Thomas. *Hannibal*. London: William Heineman, 1999, pp. 468–475.

Hazleton, Frederick. *Sweeney Todd: The Demon Barber of Fleet Street*. London: W. H. Allen, 1980.

Shakespeare, William. *Titus Andronicus* [1594]. Act 5, Scenes 2 and 3.

Sondheim, Stephen. *Sweeney Todd the Demon Barber of Fleet Street: A Musical Thriller*. New York: Dodd, Mead and Co., 1979.

The Vanishing Hitchhiker

Brien, Jean. "The Girl in the Rose-Colored Shawl." In *The Unseen: Scary Stories, selected by Janet Lunn*. Toronto: Lester, 1994, pp. 26–28.

Butler, Robert Olen. "A Ghost Story." In *A Good Scent from a Strange Mountain*. New York: Henry Holt and Co., 1992, pp. 111–123.

Carmer, Carl. "The Lavender Evening Dress." In *Dark Trees to the Wind: A Cycle of York State Years*. New York: William Sloane Associates, 1949. Reprinted in *Folklore in*

American Literature. Eds. John T. Flanagan and Arthur Palmer Hudson, Evanston, IL: Row, Peterson, 1958, pp. 99–101. Also in *The Life Treasury of American Folklore*. New York: Time-Life, 1961, pp. 252–56.

Cerf, Bennett. "The Current Crop of Ghost Stories." In *Famous Ghost Stories*. New York: Vintage Books, 1944, pp. 360–361.

Cohen, Daniel. "[Phantom Hitchhiker]." In *Phone Call from a Ghost: Strange Tales from Modern America*. New York: Pocket Books, 1988, pp. 105–106.

———. "The Most Famous Ghost." In *Railway Ghosts and Highway Horrors*. New York: Scholastic Inc., 1991, pp. 12–24.

———. "The Phantom Hitchhiker." In *The Phantom Hitchhiker and Other Ghost Mysteries*. New York: Kingfisher, 1995, pp. 60–64.

Gregory, Nan. "No-Post." In *Next Teller: A Book of Canadian Storytelling, collected by Dan Yashinski*. Charlottetown, PEI, Canada: Ragweed Press, 1994, pp. 197–200.

Howard, Elizabeth Jane. *Mr. Wrong: A Collection of Short Stories*. Harmondsworth, UK: Penguin, 1979, pp. 9–45.

Irving, Washington. "The German Student." In *Tales of a Traveller. . . .* London: John Murray, 1824. Reprinted in Charles Neider, ed. *The Complete Tales of Washington Irving*. Garden City, NY: Doubleday and Co., 1975, pp. 223–227.

Justice, Jennifer. "The Vanishing Hitchhiker." In *The Ghost & I: Scary Stories for Participatory Telling*. Cambridge, MA: Yellow Moon Press, 1992, pp. 105–111.

Leach, Maria. "The Ghostly Hitchhiker." In *The Thing at the Foot of the Bed*. New York: Philomel Books, 1959, pp. 71–72, 120.

Wood, Charles Lindley, second Viscount Halifax. "The Ghostly Passenger." In *Further Stories from Lord Halifax's Ghost Book*. London: Geoffrey Bles, 1937, pp. 27–28.

Woollcott, Alexander. "Thankfully Received." "Shouts and Murmurs." column. *The New Yorker* (November 14, 1931): 34.

Young, Richard, and Judy Dockrey Young. *Ghost Stories from the American Southwest*. Little Rock, AR: August House, 1991, pp. 33–34, 138–139.

White Slavers

Kauffman, Reginald White. *The House of Bondage*. New York: Moffat, Yard, 1911.

Robin, Ralph. "Open Ears." *The Magazine of Fantasy and Science Fiction*. 5.2 (August 1953): 77–82.

The Will

Donleavy, J. P. *The Lady Who Liked Clean Rest Rooms: The Chronicle of One of the Strangest Stories Ever to be Rumoured about Around New York*. New York and West Stockbridge: Thornwillow Press, 1995; New York: St. Martin's Press, 1997.

FURTHER READING AND ONLINE RESOURCES

T he purpose of this chapter is to make available a range of material that provides further background to the stories we have included, and also to furnish the means to further explore the world of the urban legend.

These resources have been grouped under the following headings:

Reference Works
Further Reading
General Collections
Journals, Magazines, and Newsletters
Online Resources

In the Case of Reference Works, Further Reading, and General Collections, we have only included readily accessible books in the English language. In all three areas many hundreds of other relevant articles exist. Rather than itemize them individually, you will find that the books we have listed, along with the Online Resources, will guide you to this larger body of material.

REFERENCE WORKS

Bennett, Gillian and Paul Smith. *Contemporary Legend: A Folklore Bibliography*. New York: Garland, 1993.

———. *Contemporary Legend: A Reader*. New York: Garland, 1996.

Brunvand, Jan Harold. *Encyclopedia of Urban Legends*. Santa Barbara, CA: ABC-CLIO, 2001.

de Vos, Gail. *Tales, Rumors, and Gossip: Exploring Contemporary Folk Literature in Grades 7-12*. Westport, CT: Libraries Unlimited, 1996.

FURTHER READING

This section contains both case studies of specific urban legends and studies of some of the more common themes found in the legends.

Bennett, Gillian. *Bodies: Sex, Violence, Disease, and Death in Contemporary Legend.* Jackson: University Press of Mississippi, 2005.

Bennett, Gillian, and Paul Smith, eds. *Monsters with Iron Teeth: Perspectives on Contemporary Legend III*. Sheffield: Sheffield Academic Press for the International Society for Contemporary Legend Research in association with CECTAL, 1988.

———, eds. *The Questing Beast: Perspectives on Contemporary Legend IV*. Sheffield: Sheffield Academic Press for the International Society for Contemporary Legend Research in association with CECTAL, 1989.

———, eds. *A Nest of Vipers: Perspectives on Contemporary Legend V*. Sheffield: Sheffield Academic Press for the International Society for Contemporary Legend Research in association with CECTAL, 1990.

Bennett, Gillian, Paul Smith, and J. D. A. Widdowson, eds. *Perspectives on Contemporary Legend Volume II*. Sheffield: Sheffield Academic Press for the Centre for English Cultural Tradition and Language, 1987.

Best, Joel. *Threatened Children: Rhetoric and Concern about Child-Victims*. Chicago: University of Chicago Press, 1990.

Bonaparte, Marie (Trans. John Rodker). *Myths of War*. London: Imago Publishing, 1947.

Bondeson, Jan. *A Cabinet of Medical Curiosities*. Ithaca, NY: Cornell University Press, 1997.

Brewer-Giorgio, Gail. *Is Elvis Alive?* New York: Tudor Publishing, 1988.

Campion-Vincent, Véronique. *Organ Theft Legends*. (Trans. Jacqueline Simpson) Jackson, MI: University Press of Mississippi, 2005.

Clarke, Jerome. *Unnatural Phenomena*. Santa Barbara, CA: ABC-CLIO, 2005.

Denisoff, R. Serge, and George Plasketes. *True Believers: The Elvis Contagion*. New Brunswick: Transaction Publishers, 1995.

Donovan, Pamela. *No Way of Knowing: Crime, Urban Legends and the Internet*. New York: Routledge, 2004.

Drimmer, Frederick. *Body Snatchers, Stiffs and Other Ghoulish Delights*. New York: Carol Publishing Group, 1992.

Dundes, Alan, ed. *The Blood Libel Legend: A Casebook in Anti-Semitic Folklore.* Madison, WI: University of Wisconsin Press, 1991.

Dundes, Alan. *Bloody Mary in the Mirror: Essays in Psychoanalytic Folkloristics.* Jackson, MI: University Press of Mississippi, 2002.

Ellis, Bill. *Aliens, Ghosts and Cults: Legends We Live.* Jackson, MI: University Press of Mississippi, 2003.

Enders, Jody. *Death by Drama and Other Medieval Urban Legends.* Chicago: University of Chicago Press, 2002.

Fine, Gary Alan. *Manufacturing Tales: Sex and Money in Contemporary Legends.* Publications of the American Folklore Society, New Series. Knoxville, KY: University of Tennessee Press, 1992.

Fine, Gary Alan, and Patricia A. Turner. *Whispers on the Color Line: Rumor and Race in America.* Berkeley, CA: University of California Press, 2001.

Fine, Gary Alan, Véronique Campion-Vincent, and Chip Heath, eds. *Rumor Mills: The Social Impact of Rumor and Legend.* New Brunswick, NJ: Aldine Transaction, 2005.

Fox, Mike, and Steve Smith. *Rolls-Royce, The Complete Works: The Best 599 Stories about the World's Best Car.* London: Faber and Faber, 1984.

Goldstein, Diane E. *Once Upon a Virus: AIDS Legends and Vernacular Risk Perception.* Logan, UT: Utah State University Press, 2004.

Goss, Michael. *The Evidence for Phantom Hitchhikers: An Objective Survey of the Phantom Hitch-Hiker Phenomenon in All its Manifestations.* Wellingborough, UK: The Aquarian Press/Association for the Scientific Study of Anomalous Phenomena, 1984.

Jacobson, David J. *The Affairs of Dame Rumor.* New York: Rinehart and Company, 1948.

Jennings, Karla. *The Devouring Fungus: Tales of the Computer Age.* New York: Norton, 1990.

Kahn, E. J. *The Big Drink: The Story of Coca-Cola.* New York: Random House, 1950.

Kapferer, Jean-Noel. *Rumors: Uses, Interpretations, and Images.* New Brunswick, NJ: Transaction Publishers, 1990.

Kimmel, Allan J. *Rumors and Rumor Control: A Manager's Guide to Understanding and Combating Rumors.* Mahwah, NJ: Lawrence Erlbaum Associates, 2003.

Koenig, Fredrick. *Rumor in the Marketplace: The Social Psychology of Commercial Hearsay.* Dover, MA: Auburn House, 1985.

Marcus, Greil. *Dead Elvis: A Chronicle of a Cultural Obsession.* New York: Doubleday, 1991.

McKale, Donald M. *Hitler: The Survival Myth.* New York: Stein and Day, 1981.

Morin, Edgar, with Bernard Paillard, Evelyne Burguière, Claude Capulier, Suzanne de Lusignan, and Julia Vérone [Trans. Peter Green]. *Rumour in Orleans.* London: Anthony Blond, 1971.

Reeve, Andru J. *Turn Me On, Dead Man: The Beatles and the "Paul-Is-Dead" Hoax.* Bloomington, IN: Author House, 2004.

Relfe, Mary Stewart. *The New Money System.* Montgomery, AL: Ministries, 1982.

Richardson, James T., Joel Best, and David G. Bromley, eds. *The Satanism Scare.* New York: Aldine de Gruyter, 1991.

Sapolsky, Harvey M., ed. *Consuming Fears: The Politics of Product Risks.* New York: Basic, 1986.

Schechter, Harold. *The Bosom Serpent: Folklore and Popular Art.* Iowa City, IA: University of Iowa Press, 1988 [2nd ed., New York: Peter Lang, 2001].

Sharp, Robert M. *The Lore and Legends of Wall Street.* Homewood, IL: Dow Jones-Irwin, 1989.

Shergold, Marion, with Pamela Cockerill. *Craig Shergold. A Mother's Story.* Toronto: Bantam, 1993.

Smith, Paul, ed. *Perspectives on Contemporary Legend: Proceedings of the Conference on Contemporary Legend, Sheffield, July 1982.* Sheffield: CECTAL, 1984.

Thompson, Kenneth. *Moral Panics.* London: Routledge, 1998.

Tucker, Elizabeth. *Campus Legends: A Handbook.* Westport, CT: Greenwood, 2005.

Turner, Patricia A. *I Heard It Through the Grapevine: Rumor in African-American Culture.* Berkeley, CA: University of California Press, 1993.

Victor, Jeffrey S. *Satanic Panic: The Creation of a Contemporary Legend.* Chicago: Open Court, 1993.

Whatley, Mariamme H., and Elissa R. Henken. *Did You Hear About the Girl Who . . . ? Contemporary Legends, Folklore, and Human Sexuality.* New York: New York University Press, 2000.

GENERAL COLLECTIONS

Apps, Roy. *The Vanishing Hitch-hiker: Modern Myths of the Macabre.* Illus. David Wyatt. London: Corgi, 1998.

Bishop, Amanda. *The Gucci Kangaroo and Other Australian Urban Legends.* Hornsby, New South Wales: The Australasian Publishing Company, 1988.

Brown, Yorick, and Mike Flynn. *The Best Book of Urban Legends Ever!* London: Carlton Books, 1999. Reprinted as *Urban Myths.* London: Carlton Books, 2003, and *The 500 Best Urban Legends Ever!* New York: ibooks, 2003.

Brunvand, Jan Harold. *The Vanishing Hitchhiker: American Urban Legends and Their Meanings.* New York: Norton, 1981.

———. *The Choking Doberman and Other "New" Urban Legends.* New York: Norton, 1984.

———. *The Mexican Pet: More "New" Urban Legends and Some Old Favorites.* New York: Norton, 1986.

———. *Curses! Broiled Again! The Hottest Urban Legends Going.* New York: Norton, 1989.

———. *The Baby Train and Other Lusty Urban Legends.* New York: Norton, 1993.

———. *Too Good To Be True: The Colossal Book of Urban Legends.* New York: Norton, 1999.

———. *The Truth Never Stands in the Way of a Good Story.* Urbana, IL: University of Illinois Press, 2000.

———. *Be Afraid. Be Very Afraid: The Book of Scary Urban Legends.* New York: Norton, 2004.

Busby, Cylin. *The Chicken-Fried Rat: Tales Too Gross to be True.* New York: Harper Trophy, 1998.

Clark, Matt. *Hook Man Speaks.* New York: Berkley Books, 2001.

Cohen, Daniel. *The Headless Roommate and Other Gruesome Tales.* New York: M. Evans, 1980.

———. *Southern Fried Rat and Other Gruesome Tales.* New York: M. Evans, 1983.

———. *The Beheaded Freshman and Other Nasty Rumors.* New York: Avon, 1993.

Craughwell, Thomas J. *Alligators in the Sewers and 222 Other Urban Legends.* New York: Black Dog and Leventhal, 1999.

———. *The Baby on the Car Roof and 222 Other Urban Legends.* New York: Black Dog and Leventhal, 2000.

———. *The Cat in the Dryer and 222 Other Urban Legends.* New York: Black Dog and Leventhal, 2002.

———. *Urban Legends: 666 Absolutely True Stories That Happened to a Friend . . . of a Friend . . . of a Friend.* New York: Black Dog and Leventhal, 2005.

Dale, Rodney. *The Tumour in the Whale.* London: Duckworth, 1978.

———. *It's True, It Happened to a Friend: A Collection of Urban Legends.* London: Duckworth, 1984.

———. *The Wordsworth Book of Urban Legends.* Ware, Herts: Wordsworth Editions, 2005.

Daly-Weir, Catherine. *The Exploding Toilet: Tales Too Funny to be True.* New York: Harper Trophy, 1998.

Dickson, Paul, and Joseph C. Goulden. *There Are Alligators in our Sewers and Other American Credos.* New York: Delacorte Press, 1983.

———. *Myth-Informed: Legends, Credos, and Wrongheaded "Facts" we all Believe.* New York: Perigee Books, 1993.

Fiery, Ann. *The Completely and Totally True Book of Urban Legends.* Philadelphia, PA: Running Press, 2001.

Fleming, Robert Loren, and Robert F. Boyd, Jr. *The Big Book of Urban Legends: Adapted from the Works of Jan Harold Brunvand.* New York: Paradox Press, 1994. [Contains an introduction and commentaries by Brunvand.]

Genge, N. E. *Urban Legends: The As-Complete-As-One-Could-Be Guide to Modern Myths.* New York: Three Rivers Press, 2000.

Gilson, Kristin. *Tales Too Scary to Be True: The Baby-sitter's Nightmare.* Intro. Jan Harold Brunvand. New York: HarperTrophy, 1998.

Goldstuck, Arthur. *The Rabbit in the Thorn Tree: Modern Myths and Urban Legends of South Africa.* Harmondsworth, UK: Penguin, 1990.

———. *The Leopard in the Luggage: Urban Legends from Southern Africa.* Harmondsworth, UK: Penguin, 1993.

———. *Ink in the Porridge: Urban Legends of the South African Elections.* Harmondsworth, UK: Penguin, 1994.

———. *The Aardvark and The Caravan.* Harmondsworth, UK: Penguin, 1999.

Harding, Nick. *Urban Legends.* Harpenden: Pocket Essentials, 2005.

Healey, Phil, and Rick Glanvill. *Urban Myths.* London: Virgin, 1992.

———. *The Return of Urban Myths.* London: Virgin, 1993.

———. *Urban Myths Unplugged.* London: Virgin, 1994.

———. *Gruesome Urban Myths.* Bucks: Ginn and Company, 1995.

———. *Now! That's What I Call Urban Myths.* London: Virgin, 1996.

———. *Stranger than Fiction: Urban Myths.* Penguin Readers Level 3. Edinburgh Gate, Harlow, UK: Pearson Education, 1998.

Hennigan, Brian. *Brian Hennigan's Scottish Urban Myths.* Edinburgh: Black and White Publishing, 2002.

Holt, David, and Bill Mooney. *Spiders in the Hairdo: Modern Urban Legends.* Little Rock: August House, 1999. [Also an Audio Cassette.]

———. *The Exploding Toilet: Modern Urban Legends.* Little Rock, AR: August House, 2004.

Morgan, Hal, and Kerry Tucker. *Rumor!* New York: Penguin, 1984.

———. *More Rumor!* New York: Penguin Books, 1987.

Pollock, Robert. *Good Luck, Mr Gorsky: Exploring Urban Myths.* Birkenhead, Auckland: Reed Books, 1999.

Poundstone, William. *Big Secrets: The Uncensored Truth About All Sorts of Stuff You Are Never Supposed to Know.* New York: Quill, 1983.

———. *Bigger Secrets: More Than 125 Things They Prayed You'd Never Find Out.* Boston, MA: Houghton Mifflin, 1986.

———. *Biggest Secrets: More Uncensored Truth About All Sorts of Stuff You Are Never Supposed to Know.* New York: Quill, 1993.

Presley, Paul. *101 Urban Legends.* UK: Dennis Publishing, 1996.

Reeve, Robin. *The Book of Urban Legends.* London: Michael O'Mara Books, 2002.

Robshaw, Brandon, and Rochelle Scholar. *Urban Myths*. London: Hodder and Stoughton and the Basic Skill Agency, 2003.

Romper, Richard. *Urban Legends: The Truth Behind All Those Deliciously Entertaining Myths That Are Absolutely, Positively, 100% Not True!* Franklin Lakes, NJ: New Page, 1999.

———. *Hollywood Urban Legends: The Truth Behind all Those Delightfully Persistent Myths of Film, Music and Television*. Franklin Lakes, NJ: New Page Books, 2001.

Schwartz, Alvin. *Scary Stories to Tell in the Dark*. New York: Harper and Row, 1981.

———. *More Scary Stories to Tell in the Dark*. New York: J. B. Lippincott, 1984.

———. *Scary Stories 3: More Tales to Chill Your Bones*. New York: Harper Collins, 1991.

Scott, Bill. *Pelicans and Chihuahuas and Other Urban Legends*. St. Lucia, Queensland: University of Queensland Press, 1996.

Seal, Graham. *Great Australian Urban Myths: Granny on the Roofrack and Other Tales of Modern Horror*. Sydney: Angus and Robertson, 1995.

———. *Great Australian Urban Myths*. Revised ed. *The Cane Toad High*. Sydney: Harper Collins, 2001.

Segaloff, Nat. *The Everything: Tall Tales, Legends, & Outrageous Lies Book*. Holbrook, MA: Adams Media Corporation, 2001.

Sherman, Dale. *Urban Legends of Rock & Roll (You Never Can Tell)*. Burlington, Ontario: Collector's Guide Publishing, 2002.

Smith, Paul S. *The Book of Nasty Legends*. London: Routledge and Kegan Paul, 1983.

———. *The Book of Nastier Legends*. London: Routledge and Kegan Paul, 1986.

Tamarkin, Bob. *Rumor Has It: A Curio of Lies, Hoaxes and Hearsay*. New York: Prentice Hall, 1993.

Toropov, Brandon. *The Complete Idiot's Guide to Urban Legends*. Indianapolis, IN: Alpha, 2001.

Townsend, John. *Mysterious Urban Myths*. Chicago: Raintree, 2004.

Wiebe, Karl. *This Is Not a Hoax: Urban Legends on the Internet*. Baltimore, MD: Publish America, 2003.

Young, Richard, and Judy Dockrey Young. *The Scary Story Reader*. Little Rock, AR: August House, 1993.

Zimmerman, Keith, and Kent Zimmerman, with Jamie Hyneman, Adam Savage, and Peter Rees. *Mythbusters: The Explosive Truth Behind 30 of the Most Perplexing Urban Legends of All Time*. New York: Simon Spotlight Entertainment, 2005.

JOURNALS, MAGAZINES, AND NEWSLETTERS

Contemporary Legend: The Journal of the International Society for Contemporary Legend Research. 1 (1991): ongoing.

Dear Mr Thoms: A Folklore Miscellany Published by The British Folk Studies Forum. 1 (November 1986) to 36 (November 1994).

FOAFtale News: The Newsletter of the International Society for Contemporary Legend Research. 1 (September 1985) ongoing. Issues 36 (January 1995) onward are available online at http://users.aber.ac.uk/mikstaff.

Fortean Times: Journal of Strange Phenomena. 1 (Fall/Winter 1976): ongoing. <http://www.forteantimes.com>

Letters to Ambrose Merton: A Quarterly Folklore Miscellany. 1 (February 1995) to 28 (Summer 2002).

The Skeptical Inquirer: The Magazine for Science and Reason. 1 (1976): onward. <http://www.csicop.org/si/index>

ONLINE RESOURCES

The Online Resources section lists only sites that have proved, to a greater or lesser extent, to have an element of stability and so are not likely to disappear overnight. They all have a proven track record and offer useful information on the topic.

Urban Legends Reference Pages: http://www.snopes.com/

The AFU & Urban Legends Archive: http://tafkac.org/

David Emery's Urban Legends and Folklore: http://urbanlegends.about.com/

Urban Legends and Modern Myths: http://www.warphead.com/urbanlegends/

Warphead. Urban Legends: http://www.warphead.com/modules/news/

Hoaxes and Urban Legends. How to Hoax-Proof Yourself: http://www.walthowe.com/navnet/legends/legends.html

The Spirit of La Llorona: http://www.lallorona.com/

Centers for Disease Control and Prevention. Health Related Hoaxes and Rumors: http://www.cdc.gov/doc.do/id/0900f3ec80226b9c

US Department of Energy. Computer Incident Advisory Capability: http://hoaxbusters.ciac.org/

Symantec Security Response. Hoax Page: http://www.symantec.com/avcenter/hoax.html

Folklore. The Urban Legend Site: http://maxpages.com/folklore

Urban Legends and Modern Myths: http://members.tripod.com/~dasasc/legends.html

Myths, Legends, Folklore, & Faery Tales: http://members.tripod.com/~SaraAnnette/lore/index.html

Urban Legends: http://pages.nyu.edu/~gap200/firstpage.html

TAPS. The Atlantic Paranormal Society.com: http://www.the-atlantic-paranormal-society.com/urbanlegends.html

Urban Legends: http://www.angelfire.com/zine/TheHaunt/urbanlegends.html

Urban Legends and Myths: http://www.geocities.com/SunsetStrip/Pavilion/4128/ UrbanLegends.html

The Urban Legend Combat Kit: http://www.netsquirrel.com/combatkit/

Urban Legends. Unsolved Mysteries: http://www.unsolvedmysteries.com/default.asp? action=cat21

Urban Legends and Hoaxes Resource Center: http://www.scambusters.org/legends. html; http://www.scambusters.org/otherhoaxes[1-16].html

Protect Yourself from Internet Scams—Subscribe to Internet ScamBusters: http:// www.scambusters.org/

Truth or Fiction Email Reality Check. Verify Rumors: http://www.truthorfiction.com/

Ship of Fools Webguide. Urban Myths and the Paranormal: http://ship-of-fools.com/ Web/topics/myths.html

Net47. Urban Myths and Legends: http://www.delta-9.com/net47/myth/

Castle of Spirits. Urban Legends and Classic Ghost Stories: http://www.castleof spirits.com/classic.html

Urban Legends and Modern Folklore: http://www.geocities.com/area51/7416/

Comics Should Be Good. Comic Book Urban Legends Revealed History: http://good-comics.blogspot.com/2005/06/comic-book-urban-legends-revealed.html

Google Groups: alt.folklore.urban: http://groups.google.com/group/alt.folklore.urban

Committee for the Scientific Investigation of Claims of the Paranormal: http://www. csicop.org/

URBAN LEGEND TITLE INDEX

INDEX TO URBAN LEGENDS ON FILM

INDEX TO URBAN LEGENDS
IN LITERATURE

SUBJECT INDEX

About the Authors

GILLIAN BENNETT is an independent scholar and the author of numerous works on ghost stories and urban legends. She has edited several works with Paul Smith and is also the author of *"Alas, Poor Ghost!": Traditions of Belief in Story and Discourse* (1999) and *Bodies: Sex, Violence, Disease, and Death in Contemporary Legend* (2005).

PAUL SMITH is Professor of Folklore at Memorial University of Newfoundland. His work encompasses contemporary legend, traditional drama, and folklore and popular literature. With Gillian Bennett, he has edited numerous works, including *Contemporary Legend: A Folklore Bibliography* (1993) and *Contemporary Legend: A Reader* (1996).